实用进出口函电写作

Practical Letter and Email Writing for Import and Export

胡茵芃　孟庆升　编著

南开大学出版社

天　津

图书在版编目(CIP)数据

实用进出口函电写作:英文 /胡茵芃,孟庆升编著.
—天津:南开大学出版社,2013.7
ISBN 978-7-310-04208-1

Ⅰ.①实… Ⅱ.①胡…②孟… Ⅲ.①进出口贸易—
英语—电报信函—写作 Ⅳ.①H315

中国版本图书馆 CIP 数据核字(2013)第 123709 号

南开大学出版社出版发行

出版人:孙克强

地址:天津市南开区卫津路 94 号 邮政编码:300071
营销部电话:(022)23508339 23500755
营销部传真:(022)23508542 邮购部电话:(022)23502200

*

河北昌黎太阳红彩色印刷有限责任公司印刷

全国各地新华书店经销

*

2013 年 7 月第 1 版 2013 年 7 月第 1 次印刷
260×185 毫米 16 开本 27.75 印张 710 千字

定价:54.00 元

如遇图书印装质量问题,请与本社营销部联系调换,电话:(022)23507125

前　言

随着我国经济的迅速发展、对外交流合作的深化，以及国际贸易活动的网络化，我国对外贸易的结构、规模和方式等发生了重大变化，从而对外贸从业人员提出了更高的专业要求。为了更好地顺应国际贸易发展的新形势，我们结合外贸行业的特点编写了《实用进出口函电写作》一书。本书旨在提高学习者在外贸背景下英语语言的实际运用能力，增进对国际贸易的常规、外贸函电常用语句及实务写作的了解，培养符合国际贸易规范的外贸函电写作能力。

本书包括 14 个教学单元。其中第 1 单元系统地介绍了外贸函电写作的基本知识；第 2 至 14 单元则遵循外贸常规流程，依次介绍了信用查询、建立贸易关系、询盘、推销信、报盘、还盘、订购、包装、付款、保险、装运、索赔和理赔、代理等内容。

本书每个单元包括三个部分：

1. **背景知识介绍**：针对国际贸易业务各个环节用英语进行了深入浅出的讲解，使学习者了解国际贸易的常规流程和业务知识。

2. **常用语句**：对各类外贸信函写作步骤进行了归纳总结，为学习者提供了实践写作的各类提纲。在各写作步骤常用语句部分，本书提炼了函电中出现频率较高的表达方式，并且进行了分类，形成一个语料库，方便学习者选择使用。

3. **电子邮件范例**：本书的范例以国际贸易中常用的电子邮件为载体，讲解外贸函电的写作技巧和特点。这些范例均源于编者长期的教学实践和研究成果，或选自真实的国内外贸易公司的业务往来函电，或选自原版的英语商务书籍及有影响力的企业网站，不仅反映了当今国际贸易沟通内容和形式的变化，而且极具代表性和实用性。每则范例都附有详细的注释，并且对常用术语进行了讲解，有利于学习者深入掌握外贸函电的写作技巧和方法。

为增强本书的实用性，附录部分选用了 SWIFT 信用证、销售合同、海运提单样本、外贸函电常用词汇缩写等内容。学习者可根据学习和实践的需要，参考使用。

本书还配有练习册，通过设计新颖、编排合理且与实践联系紧密的阶梯性练习，帮助学习者巩固外贸函电的写作技巧和方法，掌握制作与审核相关单据的要求。此外，练习还增强了填制合同、审查信用证和撰写改证函等技能的训练。

本书既可供高等院校商务英语、国际经济与贸易及其他相关专业的师生使用，也可供业已从事和有志于从事外贸工作的人员学习使用。

由于编者水平有限，书中疏漏之处在所难免，希望专家、同仁与读者多提宝贵意见。

编　者
2013 年 3 月

Contents

Unit 1　Introduction to Letter and Email Writing

信函和电子邮件写作概述

背 景 知 识

1. The Components of a Business Letter (商务信函的组成部分)

(1) Letterhead	**Dunbar & Co. Ltd.** 55 Castle Street, Glasgow, Scotland, DF8 56S, UK Tel: (44-131) 6233700　Fax: (44-131) 6233701
(2) Reference	Your ref: 65887 Our ref: GJI566
(3) Date	1 March, 2012
(4) Inside Name and Address	Tianjin Everbright Trading Co. Ltd. 98 Hongqi Rd. Tianjin 30000 China
(5) Attention Line	Attn: Purchasing Manager
(6) Salutation	Dear Sirs,
(7) Subject Line	Re: Electric Stoves
(8) Body	We are glad to receive your letter of February 26, informing us of your interest in our electric stoves. We have been manufacturing quality electric stoves since 1974 and enjoying increasing market shares in many countries. We are enclosing you a new sample book of electric stoves we have recently produced. You will earn a special discount of 2% provided we receive your order before the end of this month. We are looking forward to receiving your order at an early date.
(9) Complimentary Close	Yours faithfully,

(10) Signature	H. Woods & Co. Ltd. **David Creith** David Creith Regional Manager
(11) Enclosure	Enclosure: a sample book
(12) CC	CC: Cecilia Humphries, Marketing Manager
(13) Postscript	P.S. Looking forward to your visit at the Trade Fair on 25 April in London.

(1) Letterhead or Heading (信头)

Letterhead includes the sender's name, postal address, telephone number, fax number, email address, website and logo of the sender's company, if any.

Usually letterhead is printed in the up-center or at the top left margin of a letter paper. For example:

Systems A/S Corporation

Borups Alle 177, P. O. Box 80, DK-2000Frederiksber, Copenhagen, Denmark

Tel: +45 38183449

Fax: +45 38183448

Website: www.systems.com

Email: info@mslang.com

When a letter runs more than one page long, the second page, i.e. continuation sheet, should use the letter paper of the same quality as the first page. The heading on the second page is necessary for quick identification, including the page number, the name of the receiver, and the date of the letter. For example:

Mrs. Alice Rawsthorn   -2-   July 4, 20_ _

---

or

Mrs. Alice Rawsthorn, July 4, 20_ _, Page 2

---

or

Timmy Imp. & Exp. Corporation

Page 2

July 4, 20_ _

---

(2) Reference (编号)

In business communication, when a company writes to another, each will give a reference. The reference may be a file number, departmental code or the initials (all in capitalized letters) of the signer followed by that (normally in lower case letters) of the typist of the letter. If the sender uses a reference number in the previous letter, the writer should quote this number after the notation "Your ref:" in the reply letter. If the writer's letter has a file number to refer to, it is written after "Our ref:" to avoid confusion. The reference number is usually positioned two lines below the letterhead. For example:

Your ref: DF/0901

Our ref: JB/GS (or JB:GS, JB/gs, JB:gs)

(3) Date (日期)

The date should always be typed in full and not abbreviated (e.g. December for Dec.) and the –th, -st, -nd and-rd that follow the date can be omitted (e.g. 5 May for 5th May, June 1 for June 1st).

Avoid typing dates in figures, e.g. 10/2/2012, since it is likely to cause confusion. British form follows the order of date, month and year while the American practice is to write in the order of month, day and year. So 10/2/2012 could be taken as either October 2, 2012 or February 10, 2012.

The date is placed two lines below the reference, either on the righthand side or on the lefthand side, depending on the layout of the letter.

(4) Inside Name and Address (封内名称和地址)

This is the receiver's name and address. It appears exactly the same way as on the envelope and its order should be from the smaller place to the larger one such as:

(1) Name of the person addressed

(2) Title/position of the person addressed

(3) Name of organization

(4) Street number and name

(5) City, State and postal code

(6) Country of destination

The inside name and address is usually typed at the left margin about two lines below the date.

Look at the following examples.

To a company: (致某公司)	To a job title: (致公司中某职位)	To a specific person: (致公司某人)
Fashion Clothing plc. 77 Eastern Road Chiswick London 89S 5FE UK	Director of Production Fashion Clothing plc. 77 Eastern Road Chiswick London 89S 5FE UK	Mr. Robert Keats Director of Production Fashion Clothing plc. 77 Eastern Road Chiswick London 89S 5FE UK

(5) Attention Line (经办人、收阅人)

Attention line is used when the sender of a letter wishes to direct the letter to a specific person, a job title or a department of the receiver's company. This will speed up the sorting process within a company. It is generally put two lines below the inside name and address. For example:

Fashion Clothing plc.
77 Easten Road
Chiswick
London 89S 5FE
UK

Attention: Mr. Robert Keats

Other forms of attention line can be adopted as follows:

Attn: Marketing Manager
ATTENTION: PURCHASE MANAGER
For the attention of Mr. Johnson Blair

(6) Salutation (称呼)

Salutation is the complimentary greeting with which the receiver opens his letter. Its form depends on the sender's relationship with the receiver. Salutation is usually typed two lines below the inside address or the attention line. Look at the table below.

Formal salutation (to a single person with name known)	Formal salutation (to a single person with name unknown)	Informal salutation (to a single person with name known)	Formal salutation (to more than one receiver or a company)
Dear Mr. /Ms. /Miss/ Mrs. + surname,	Dear Sir, Dear Madam, Dear Sir or Madam, Dear Production Manager,	Dear Tom, Dear Shakira,	Dear Sirs, Gentlemen: Dear Customers, Dear Friends, Dear Readers, Dear Subscribers,

(7) Subject Line (主题栏、事由栏)

Subject line is actually the general idea of a letter. It calls the receiver's attention to the topic of the letter. It is inserted between the salutation and the body of the letter, starting with the word "Subject:" or "Re:" and sometimes underlined. For example:

Dear Mr. Green,

Re: Claim No. DG392 for 50 Cases of Tea Sets

We have just received...

The following examples are other styles for the subject line:

Subject: Chinese Pure Silk Products
Our Order No. 487

URGING PROMPT SHIPMENT

(8) Body (正文)

This is the main part of a letter. It expresses the sender's ideas, opinions, purposes and wishes. The body of a business letter typically has three paragraphs: introductory paragraph, one or more body paragraphs and concluding paragraph. If there has been previous correspondence, the reply letter will refer to it in the first paragraph. The sender's plans, hopes and expectations will be expressed in the last paragraph. The body of a letter is positioned two lines below the salutation, or below the subject line, if any.

When writing, pay attention to the following:

(1) Your letter should be simple, clear, courteous, grammatically correct and to the point.

(2) Keep each paragraph addressing one topic.

(3) Keep your letter in an attractive and pleasing appearance by accurate typing and artistic displaying.

(9) Complimentary Close (结尾敬语)

Complimentary close is merely a polite way of ending a letter. It keeps up with the salutation. The first letter of the first word of the complimentary close is capitalized, followed by a comma, and placed two lines below the body of the letter. The most commonly used sets of salutation and complimentary close are:

Salutation	Complimentary Close
Dear Sirs,	Yours faithfully, Yours very faithfully, Faithfully yours,
Gentlemen:	Yours truly, Truly yours, Very truly yours,
Dear Mr. Henry,	Yours sincerely, Sincerely yours, Very sincerely yours,
Dear Melisa,	Best wishes, With kind regards, Yours, Best regards,

(10) Signature (签名)

A complete signature part consists of the name of the signer's company, the signer's handwritten signature, type-written signature and job title or position. Since hand-written signatures are sometimes illegible, the name of the signer is usually typed below the signature, and followed by his job title or position. Never sign a letter with a rubber stamp. The signature is to type immediately below the complimentary close. For example:

Yours faithfully,
THE NATIONAL TRANSPORT CO.

Kate Tylor

Kate Tylor
Manager

(11) Enclosure (附件)

If catalogs, price lists, samples, documents, etc. are sent together with a letter, the sender should add the enclosure notation such as "Enclosure:", "Enc." or "Encl." at least two lines below the signature at the left margin. For example:

Encls. Commercial Invoice (3 copies)

Insurance Policy

Enclosure: 1 sample

Enc. (3)

Enclosure: as stated

(12) CC (抄送)

When the writer wants to send the copies of the letter to others, type "cc" or "CC" two lines below the signature or enclosure at the left margin. For example:

C.C. Mr. George Blair, Sales Manager

c.c. Jia Hua Aluminum Trading Company

(13) Postscript (附言、再启)

If the sender wishes to add something he forget to mention or for emphasis, he may add his postscript (often shortened into "P.S.") two lines below the carbon copy notation, for example:

P.S. The latest price list will be airmailed to you tomorrow.

*ps. Through the month of December we are having a storewide liquidation sale on **ALL** our products. So call or email me today for a copy of our most up-to-date price list.*

But the postscript part should be avoided in a business letter.

2. Layouts of Letter Writing

Usually there are three styles of business letters. They are the indented style, the block style and the modified block style.

2.1 Indented Style (缩进式)

In the indented style the letterhead is typed in the up-middle part. The date is placed on the right margin of the paper, so are the complimentary close and the signature block. Each line of the inside name and address is indented 2-3 spaces. The first line of each paragraph is indented 2-8 spaces. For example:

Prima International Co., Ltd.

17 Fuxing Road, Futian District, Shenzhen 518048, Guangdong, China

Tel: 86-21-755-82919889   Fax: 86-21-755-82919888

Website: www.primaintl.com
Email: info@primaintl.com

Your ref: MG/879
Our ref: S124

July 2, 20_ _

Hans Dizard
Purchasing Manager
Bradley Trading Inc.
221 Norman Bay Road,
Norman Bay, NSW 2252,
USA

Dear Mr. Dizard,

Re: Your Order No. 2052

We have received your Order No. 2052 in duplicate dated June 28, 2007.

In reply, we regret to say that the said order cannot be filled at this time due to the delay on the part of the bankruptcy of our major supplier. This means that we have to find another supplier who could fulfill all the outstanding contracts we have to complete. As you will appreciate, this will take some time.

We are confident that we should be able to arrange to get our materials and deliver consignments to our customers by the middle of next month.

We regret for the unfortunate situation over which we had no control and apologize for the inconvenience.

If you would like to discuss this matter further, please feel free to contact us.

Yours very sincerely,

Prima International Co., Ltd.

Guangjun Zhang

Guangjun Zhang
Export Manager

2.2 Block Style (齐头式)

In the block style, every part of a letter is typed from the left margin. It is convenient to be typed and commonly used. For example:

H. Woods & Co. Ltd.
Nesson House, Newell Street
Birmingham B15 3EL, UK
Tel: (44-121) 4560000   Fax: (44-121) 4560001

Your ref: 05485
Our ref: IP21

1 March, 2001

L. M. Jiang
Purchasing Manager
Shanghai Sun Technology Trading Co. Ltd.
72 Zhongshan Rd.
Shanghai 200001
China

Dear Mr. Jiang,

Re: Electric Stoves

We are glad to receive your letter of February 23, informing us of your interest in our electric stoves.

We have been manufacturing quality electric stoves since 1974 and enjoying increasing market shares in many countries. We are enclosing you a new sample book of electric stoves we have recently produced. You will earn a special discount of 2% provided we receive your order before the end of this month.

We are looking forward to receiving your order at an early date.

Yours sincerely,
H. Woods & Co. Ltd.

Larry Crane

Larry Crane
Regional Manager

Enclosure: a sample book

2.3 Modified Block Style (改良齐头式)

In the modified block style, the first line of each paragraph in the body of the letter is typed 4-6 spaces indented. The inside name and address are typed at the left margin while the date, complimentary close and signature are typed at the right corner of the letter paper. This is a traditional style. For example:

The Nile Trading Co. Ltd.

161 Pyramid Street, Alexandria, Egypt
Tel: (20-3) 4900000   Fax: (20-3) 4900001

Your ref: MG/879
Our ref: AA/jh

11th May, 2001

China Motorbike Co. Ltd
34 Fazhan Street
Jinan, Shandong
P. R. C.

Attention: Export Manager

Dear Sirs,

Subject: Motorbikes

We are interested in importing a range of motorbikes and would be grateful if you would send us a copy of your latest catalogue, your price list and export terms. Could you also let us know the name of your import agent in Egypt?

We look forward to hearing from you.

Yours faithfully,
The Nile Trading Co. Ltd.

Abdul Aziz

Abdul Aziz
Import Coordinator

C.C. Mr. John Mullen

3. The Layout of Envelope

In the upper left corner of a business envelope is normally printed the return address, that is, the address of the sender. The receiver's name and address should be typed about middle part of the envelope. The postmark or stamps should be placed in the up righthand corner. The bottom lefthand corner is for post notations such as "Confidential", "Printed Matter", "Sample", "Via Air-mail", "Sample of No Value", "Urgent" or "Photo Enclosed", etc. See a sample below:

The Magellan Group. Inc.
3111 Charles St., Apt, 1A
Baltimore, MD 21218
U. S. A.

> Fujian Provincial Cereals, Oils & Foodstuffs
> Imp. & Exp. Corporation
> 8/F Foreign Trade Building, 35 Hubin Rd., Xiamen, 361004
> Fujian, China
>
> Registered

4. Principles of Letter Writing

Generally speaking, business letter writing follows the rules of 7Cs, that is, correctness, courtesy, consideration, completeness, concreteness, conciseness, and clarity.

4.1 Correctness (准确)

Correctness means not only correct grammar, punctuation and spelling, but also giving factual information, accurate figures and exact terms in writing business letters. Compare the following sentences:

Our competitors' prices are 2%-3% lower than us.

Our competitors' prices are 2%-3% lower than ours.

It is the lowest price available to you.

It is the lowest price that we can offer you now.

4.2 Courtesy (礼貌)

Courtesy means to show tactfully in business letters the honest friendship, thoughtful appreciation, sincere politeness, considerate understanding and heartfelt respect. Modal auxiliaries such as "will", "would", "can", "could", "may", "might" are often used to express questions, requirements or suggestions in a more polite way. Such expressions are useful: "Would you please...", "Would you kindly ...", "We would appreciate ...". Look at the following examples:

We should appreciate it if you would let us know what discount you may grant us if we place an order for 20,000 sets.

We are glad to confirm your order of May 23 for 30,000 pieces of Plastic Toys.

Would you please effect shipment no later than September 23?

Courtesy becomes more important in business letters that convey bad news or messages. As such letters may do harm to the receiver's benefit and may therefore not be accepted by the receiver, writing skills for courtesy becomes more crucial, which may include:

(1) Using neutral words instead of negative ones.

It is important to avoid words with strong negative meanings like "refuse", "unpleasant" or "carelessly", etc. which are offensive and are likely to make people feel upset or even offensive. Compare the following two sentences:

Your order will be delayed for two weeks.

Your order will be shipped in two weeks.

(2) Using passive voice

The use of passive voice can leave the writer uninvolved in the unfavorable news conveyed in the business letter. It also obscures the actor, which helps eliminate partly (and sometimes completely) the responsibility of the actor for the bad news. Compare the following sentences:

You have put us into inconvenience by your delay in delivery.

We have been put into inconvenience by the delay in delivery.

(3)　Using hedges

Hedges can make the expressions more flexible so as to improve and maintain the relationship between the sender and the receiver. Some hedges like "sort of", "kind of", "somewhat", "to some extent" limit the negative effect of the bad news and soften the tone of the expression. Other hedges such as "I'm afraid", "I'm sorry", "I'm sorry to inform you that", "It is said" and "according to the contract" are used to express the writer's hesitation or speculation. Compare the following sentences:

We can't deliver all the goods in one lot.

We regret to inform you that we can't delivery all the goods in one lot.

We cannot accept the price you offered.

I'm afraid we cannot accept the price you offered.

4.3 Consideration (体谅)

Consideration means trying to put yourself in the receiver's place, to give consideration to his or her wishes, demands, interests and difficulties.

In a positive business letter, lay stress on the use of pronoun "you" to express the sender's concern towards the receiver. More use of "you" can highlight the benefit to the receiver from the sender. Compare the following sentences:

We are pleased to inform you that if you could supply goods of this type and quality required, we may place regular order for large quantity.

You will be pleased to know that you will obtain our regular orders for large quantities if you could supply goods of this type and quality required.

In a negative business letter, avoid using the pronoun "you" but use the third personal pronoun and passive voice in order to ease the tension. Compare the following sentences:

You didn't reply our letter on time.

We did not receive the reply on time.

4.4 Completeness (完整)

Completeness means all the necessary information is conveyed in business letters and all the composing parts are included. It is necessary for the sender to plan his writing and make an outline beforehand and then write the letter accordingly. Before sending the letter, it is also essential to check the completeness of the letter's structure and contents.

4.5 Concreteness (具体)

Concreteness means what is said in the letter should be specific, definite rather than vague, abstract and general, for vague or general information can cause ambiguity or even disputes. Compare the following sentences:

I refer to your recent communication.
I refer to your letter of June 7.

We confirm our order dispatched yesterday.
We confirm our order of May 3.

We have opened the L/C.
We have opened an irrevocable Letter of Credit No. 548 for the amount of USD 40,000 covering our Order No. 132 with the Bank of China, Tianjin Branch.

4.6 Conciseness (简洁)

Conciseness means that complete message is expressed in a way that is briefest but does not sacrifice clarity or courtesy. A good business letter should be precise and to the point. Generally speaking, simple words, phrases and short sentences are more efficient than clauses. Try to compare the following examples:

enclosed herewith
enclosed

at this time
now

due to the fact that
because

We wish to acknowledge receipt of your letter.
We appreciate your letter.

Please be advised that we have received your L/C.
We have received your L/C.

4.7 Clarity (清楚)

Clarity means that you express yourself clearly and logically in the simplest language, for plain, simple words are more easily understood and logical arrangement of the information is easy to follow. When writing, avoid ambiguous word what has more than one meaning in the same context and avoid jargon which refers to the abbreviations or special words that are difficult for the receiver to understand. Look at the following sentences:

One of our CSOs will contact you later.
One of our Customer Service Officers will contact you within 24 hours.

5. Layout of Email Writing

(1) Date and time of sending an email	Date: Sat, 20 Nov 2012 11:04:30
(2) Sender's email address	From: sharon0408@ sz-je.com
(3) Recipient's email address	To: robinson_grant@gmail.com
(4) Carbon copy	Cc: shakirahuan@ sz-je.com
(5) Blind carbon copy	Bcc: kathyjuan@ sz-je.com
(6) Subject	Subject: Re: Request for the information about your new products
(7) Salutation	Dear Mr. Grant,
(8) Body	Thank you for your inquiry about our new products. The attached file is our latest catalog. If you need further information, please feel free to contact us. We are looking forward to hearing from you.
(9) Complimentary close	Yours sincerely,
(10) Sender's full name	Sharon Huang
(11) Sender's job title and department	Sales rep, Overseas Sales Division
(12) Sender's company name	Joylemarry Electronic Co., Ltd.
(13) Postal address of the company	5th Floor, Block B, Puhua Technology Park, Industrial Park Road, Tongsheng Community, Dalang Street, Baoan Dist., Shenzhen, Guangdong, China
(14) Contact information of the company	Tel: 0755-33582693 Fax: 0755-33581878-820 Email: sharon0408@ sz-je.com Web: http://www.sz-je.com/
(15) Statement	The information in this email and any attachments is confidential and intended only for the use of the individual(s) to whom it is addressed. If you are not a named addressee or otherwise an intended recipient, you are requested to immediately notify the sender and to delete this email and all attachments from your system.

(1) Date and time of sending an email (发邮件时间)

The date and time of sending an email is shown automatically by the email server.

(2) Sender's email address (发件人邮箱地址)

The sender's email address is also given automatically by the email server.

(3) Recipient's email address (收件人邮箱地址)

The recipient's email address can be selected from the address book, or automatically generated by clicking the button "Reply".

(4) Carbon copy (抄送)

If the email is intended to be sent to other people for their information, enter their email addresses in the "CC" box.

(5) Blind carbon copy (密送)

If the email is intended to be sent to other people for their information while their email addresses are not to be displayed in the main recipient's email, enter their email addresses in the "BCC" box.

(6) Subject (主题)

The recipient will evaluate the importance of the email received according to the subject. Therefore the subject should be concise, clear and to the point. Some abbreviations are suggested. For example:

RE: "回复" (I am replying to your questions.)

URGENT: "紧急" (This message has high priority.)

FYI: "仅提供信息，无需回复" (For your information only, no reply required.)

In addition, it is also preferred to use the business document's number or the product's model as the subject. For example:

BC-DL988 Induction Cooker

Order No. GF0909

Sales Contract No. 12989

Invoice 2546

Above all, avoid leaving the subject box a complete blank.

The commonly used email subjects are summarized as follows.

咨询类	
咨询	Inquiry
有关 LBP2900 打印机的咨询	Inquiry for LBP2900 printer
索要资料	Information request
疑问	Question
简单的问题	Quick question
有关贵方新产品的问题	Question about your new products
请求类	
请求	Request/REQ
索要相关信息	Request for information
索要产品目录	Request for product catalog
请求许可	Request for permission
约定	Appointment
通知、信息类	
通知	Announcement/Notice
邮箱地址	My email address
更改邮箱地址	Change of email address

更改地址	Change of our address
迁移	We are moving
变更营业时间	Change in business hours
休假	Vacation
调动	Relocation
信息	Information
回信类	
贵方电子邮件	Your email
贵方传真	Your fax
贵方 3 月 10 的来信	Your letter of March 10
贵方委托事宜	Your request
报价	
报价	Quotation/Price quote
JK340 型笔记本电脑报价单	Quotation for JK340 laptop computer
订货类	
订货	Order
紧急订货	Rush order
JK340 型笔记本电脑订货事宜	Order for JK340 laptop computer
订货编号 2245	Order No. 2245
更改订货编号 2245	Change in our order No. 2245
取消订货编号 2245	Cancellation of our order No. 2245
发票类	
发票	Invoice
有关第 2341 号发票的支付事宜	Your payment for invoice No. 2341
发货类	
装运时间	Shipping schedule/Shipping date
第 2784 号订单的发货事宜	Shipment for your order No. 2784
出差类	
2 月访问贵公司事宜	My visit in Feb.
去芝加哥出差事宜	My trip to Chicago
8 月 7 日的安排	My schedule on August 7
行程表	Itinerary
确认类	
您在中国期间的安排	Arrangements for your stay in China
预约确认	Confirmation of reservation
批准	Approval
抱怨、索赔类	
有缺陷的商品	Defective goods

发错的商品	Wrong product
第 4650 号发票的出错事宜	Error in invoice No. 4650
延迟出货	Delayed shipment
致谢类	
感谢	Thank you
感谢您的协助	Thank you for your help
感谢您的材料	Thank you for the data/information
感谢您的邮件	Thank you for your email
祝贺类	
祝贺！	Congratulations!
恭喜您升职	Congratulations on your promotion!
道歉类	
道歉	Apology
有关缺陷产品的致歉	Apology for the defective products
抱歉	Sorry
问候类	
你好	Hello
你怎么样	How are you?
其他	
紧急	Urgent
重要	Important
报告	Report
邀请	Invitation
附件	Attachment

(7) Salutation (称呼)

Normally we use "Dear Mr. (Mrs.) + surname".

If the relationship between the sender and the receiver is close, use "Dear + name".

If the recipient's name is unknown, use "Dear Sir/Madam".

(8) Body (正文)

The language can be formal or informal based on the recipient and the contents of the email. Besides, when abbreviations are used, make sure that they are properly understood by the recipient.

The frequently used email abbreviations are given as follows.

ASAP = as soon as possible	尽快
BBL = be back later	回头见
BFN = bye for now	再见
BRB = be right back	马上回来
BTW = by the way	顺便问一下
B/W = between	……之间

CU/CUL = see you/see you later	再见
Div. = division	分部
Dept. = department	部分
FAQ = frequently asked questions	常问的问题
FYI = for your information	供您参考
FTF = face to face	面对面
HAND = have a nice day	祝愉快
Info = information	信息
LTNS = long time no see	好久没见
pls = please	请
REQ = request	请求
Re = regarding	关于……事宜
Sect. = Section	科
TYIA = thank you in advance	先行致谢
thru = through	通过
WRT = with respect to	关于
w/ = with	和……
w/o = without	没有……

(9) Complimentary close (结尾敬语)

If the recipient's name is not known, use "Yours faithfully,".

If the recipient's name is known, use "Yours sincerely," or "Sincerely," to show the formal relations.

If the recipient's name is known, use "Best Regards," or "Regards," to show the informal and close relations.

(10)-(14) Signature (署名)

The signature function of the email server can be taken advantage of.

The signature block usually contains the sender's full name, job title, department, company name, company's address, telephone number, fax number, email address, website, etc.

(15) Statement (声明)

Sometimes confidential information is included in the email or the enclosure. To be safe, it is advised to add a statement to the end of the email, which requests the not-intended or not-named recipient to delete this email.

The statement in the example is translated as below:

"本邮件及附件中的信息属机密内容，只允许收件人接收。如果你与收件人姓名不符或并非应收取该邮件的人，请迅速与发件人联系并将本邮件及附件从系统中删除。"

电子邮件常用语句

● Attachment

- I am attaching a text file to this message.
  我在该信息后附上一个文本文件。
- Attached is our latest catalog you requested.
  附件是您要求的我公司最新的产品目录。
- I am attaching files in two kinds of format.
  给您附上两种格式的文档。
- This is a Microsoft Word file.
  这是微软的 Word 文件。
- I can not open the attached file.
  我无法打开附件。
- I cannot open the attached photo file.
  我无法打开附件中的图像文档。
- Please tell me how to open the attachment.
  请告知打开附件的方法。
- Do I need particular software to open the attachment?
  打开附件时需要特殊的软件吗？
- I don't have Adobe Flash Player.
  我没有 Adobe Flash Player 软件。
- Could you send a file in text format?
  请用文本格式发给我，好吗？
- Please send a pdf file.
  请用 pdf 格式发过来。
- The file is unreadable.
  无法读取文件。
- I cannot read the attachment on my computer.
  我的电脑无法读取附件。
- I can't read Korean characters on my computer.
  我的电脑不识别韩语。
- I use Windows 7.
  我使用 Windows 7 操作系统。
- The software this file was made with is not installed in my computer.
  我的电脑里没有安装生成该文档的软件。

● Forwarding Emails

- I am forwarding the email from our client.

现转发来自我们客户的电子邮件。

- Could you forward this email to the proper person in charge of sales?
  您能否把该电子邮件转发给负责销售的人员？

- Your email has been forwarded to our customer service department.
  我们已将您的电子邮件转发给我公司的客户服务部。

● 　 Compressing and Decompressing

- The attached file is compressed.
  附件为压缩文件。

- Please expand the file.
  请将文件解压。

- Please decompress the attachment after downloading.
  请在下载后将附件解压。

● 　 Problems with Sending and Receiving Emails

- The email I sent you came back.
  我发给您的电子邮件被退回来了。

- I cannot send any message.
  我无法给您发出任何信息。

- There might have been an error during transmission.
  收信时好像发生了什么问题。

- You sent the email to the wrong address.
  您把电子邮件发到了错误的邮箱地址。

- My computer was broken down.
  我的电脑坏了。

- Our server was down.
  我们的服务器停止运转了。

● 　 Others

- Do you have Microsoft Excel?
  您有微软的 Excel 软件吗？

- What browser software do you use?
  您使用哪种浏览软件？

- Please click on the "Open from Applications" in the box menu.
  请点击菜单中的"从应用程序打开"。

- You can download the software from the Internet.
  您可以从网上下载需要的软件。

- Please delete the file I sent you yesterday.
  请将我昨天发去的文档删除。

- I hope the attached data is helpful.
  我希望附件数据能帮到您。

- Welcome to our website!
  欢迎登录我们的网站！

- Our website was moved to http://www.aaa.com.
  我们的网站地址变更为 http://www.aaa.com。

- Please refer to the following URL for further details of our new services.
  有关新服务的详细内容请参照以下 URL。

- Please click the following link for information about our new product.
  有关新产品的信息请点击以下链接。

- If you don't know the product name, search by the product type to the left of the web page.
  如果您不知道产品名称，请从网页左边的商品类型开始检索。

- If you would like to have a catalog of the model AA, please contact us at the following address.
  如需要 AA 型产品目录，请按下述地址与我们联系。

- We will give a reduction of 5% to order online.
  在线购买的话，我们将给予 5%的优惠。

- You can buy all of our products from our online store.
  您可以在网店购买我公司的所有产品。

- Now through September 10, get free delivery on orders over US$300 from ABC online store.
  至 9 月 10 日止，在 ABC 网店订货 300 美元以上免运费。

- We will send you the order confirmation by email within 24 hours. Please review your order details and save the email.
  我们会在 24 小时内给您发送确认订单的电子邮件。请您再次查看订单的详细内容并保存该电子邮件。

- The order confirmation email contains your customer number and your order number.
  订单确认邮件中记载有您的客户编号及订单号。

- If you have additional questions, please visit our customer support website.
  如有更多疑问，请浏览我公司客户支持网页。

- For questions related to the following products, contact us at carlson@abc.com.
  有关以下产品的疑问，请联系 carlson@abc.com。

- For more information, call us at 86-22-38572211, or email us at info@abc.com.
  如需更多信息，请电话联系 86-22-38572211 或发送电子邮件至 info@abc.com。

- If you have questions before your purchase, please feel free to contact us anytime by email.
  如您在购买之前有疑问，请随时发送电子邮件联系我们。

- If your question is about our consulting service, please use the link below.
  如果您的问题是关于咨询服务方面的，请使用以下链接。

电子邮件范例

1. An Email for Establishing Business Relations

Background: Goodman 先生于 9 月 18 日向金狮电动玩具公司发去电子邮件，希望建立贸易关系。次日金狮公司业务经理叶国林回复电子邮件，表示同意。

From: Daniel Ye <danielye24@goldenliontoys.com.cn>

Date: Monday, September 19, 2009, 9:35 AM

To: goodmanmail@yahoo.com

Subject: Re: Establishing Business Relations

Dear Mr. Goodman,

We are pleased to receive your email message dated September 18.

We are very interested in your suggestion of establishing business relations with us, for this just coincides with our desire.

We have been one of the leading exporters of Electronic Toys in our country and enjoyed a high reputation in the European markets.

In order to promote the development of our business and relationship, we are attaching our catalogs covering the items we are dealing in at present for your reference. If you find any items are of interest to you, please let us know immediately.

We appreciate your prompt reply.

Yours sincerely,

Daniel Ye

Daniel Ye

Business Manager

Golden Lion Electronic Toys Co., Ltd.

47 Fukang Road, Tianjin, China

Tel.: 86-22-24357788

Fax: 86-22-24358789

Email: danielye24@goldenliontoys.com.cn

Website: http://www.goldenliontoys.com.cn

Notes
1. This just coincides with our desire.   这一点与我方愿望不谋而合。
2. for your reference   供你方参考
3. catalog   n. 产品目录
4. cover   vt. 包括，涵盖
5. item   n. 产品，项目，条款
6. deal in   经营，从事
    Our company is dealing in the import of electronic calculators in Australia.   我公司在澳大利亚从事计算器的进口业务。

2. An Email for Reply to an Inquiry

Background: Bill Cade 先生于 9 月 16 日向卓越电气产品公司发去电子邮件，对 26－7010 型号的石油工具询价。当日卓越公司的总经理 Stephen Yang 回复电子邮件，提供替代品，并将邮件抄送给出口部经理 Sam Smith。

From: Stephen Yang<stephen_yang@superelectricalpro.com>

Date: Thursday, September 16, 2009, 2:31 PM

To: Bill Cade <cade188@online.sh.cn>

CC: Sam Smith <sammanager@superelectricalpro.com>

Subject: Your Inquiry for Our Oil Tool

Dear Mr. Cade,

Thank you for your email message dated September 16 in which you inquire for our Oil Tool Model 26-7010. We appreciate your interest but we can no longer supply it as the production has been discontinued. We are sure about our new product Model 26-7020 is an excellent replacement.

The quality and performance are much improved and are enjoying very good sales. We will arrange to send you a catalog and price list to you at once. If you are interested, we can send samples later.

Thank you again for your inquiry and hope to receive your reply soon.

Yours sincerely,

Stephen Yang

****

Stephen Yang

Managing Director
Super Electrical Products Co.
4 Peace Avenue, Shekou, Shenzhen, China
Tel.: 86-755-26884512
Fax: 86-755-26884510
Email: stephen_yang@ superelectricalpro.com
Website: http://www.superelectricalpro.com

Notes

1. inquire for sth   对某产品询价
2. replacement   n. 替代品，代用品，也可以用 substitute
3. performance   n. 性能，特性
   The new machines have presented excellent anti-shock performance.   新机器展现出优良的防震性能。
4. enjoy good sales   畅销，大量销售
5. arrange   vt. 安排，准备，计划
   You can ask my secretary to arrange a time and place for our next meeting.   你可以和我的秘书定好我们下次会议的时间和地点。
   I've arranged to see her tonight.   我已安排今晚同她见面。
   arrange for sb/sth to do sth   安排、准备某人/某事以做某事，注意介词用 for。如：
   I've arranged for a car to pick them up at the station.   我已安排了一辆汽车去车站接他们。
   He's arranged for me to attend the meeting.   他已安排我去参加会议。
6. price list   价目表，价格表

3. An Email for Apologies for Shipping a Wrong Order

Background: Pelton 皮革有限公司的 Tom Benson 先生向 Martin Pearl 先生因错运货物而致歉，并提出解决方法。

From: Tom Benson<bensonbusiness@pelton.com>
Date: Wednesday, May 6, 2009, 9:17 AM
To: martinpearl@jsingh.com
Subject: Apology for Shipment of Wrongly-delivered Order

Dear Mr. Pearl,

Thank you for email message of 5 May regarding your Order No. 784.

We are sorry to learn that there was a mix-up in your order. We are now sending the consignment to you by airfreight. It should reach you within a week.

The necessary documents will be sent without delay by mail.

Please hold the wrongly-delivered goods.

We offer our sincere apologies for the delay. If you have any further requirements, please contact us immediately.

Yours sincerely,
Tom Benson

================================

Tom Benson
Service Manager
Pelton Leather Co., Ltd.
6 Grange Road, Exeter, Devon, UK
Tel.: 90983
Fax: 64908
Email: bensonbusiness@pelton.com
Website: http://www.pelton.com

Notes

1. regarding   prep. 关于，类似的还有 as regards, in regard to, with regard to
   Regarding the balance, we will advise you of the position in a few days.   关于剩余数量的情况，我方将于日内告知。
2. mix-up   n. 混淆
3. reach you   抵达贵处。注意 reach 是个及物动词，后面要有宾语，而 arrive 是不及物动词，后面常接介词 in 或 at。试比较：
   We believe that the goods will reach you in good condition.   我方相信货物会完好地抵达贵处。
   We believe that the goods will arrive (in your place 或 at your end) in good condition.
4. document   n. 单据，在外贸业务中，常指各种装运单据，也可指各种商业票据
5. without delay   立即，也可以用 without further delay, with the least possible delay 等
6. hold   vt. 保留，保存
7. wrongly-delivered goods   错发的货物
8. offer/make an apology to sb for sth   因为某事向某人致歉
   They have to make an apology to customers for the rude behavior of their salesman.   他们不得不为销售人员粗鲁的行为而向顾客致歉。

Unit 2　Credit Inquiry
信用查询

背 景 知 识

1. The Importance of Credit (Status) Inquiry

In international trade, it is necessary that the seller and the buyer have some knowledge of the counter party's credit information. To inquire about credit status becomes more important if they have no business relations before. This can help avoid risks, especially when a large sum of money is involved. Requesting such information is called "credit inquiry".

As an importer, he can supply his foreign exporter with his reference, such as his own bank, golden customer, important supplier, agent or governmental institutes, so as to show his strong financial standing and good reputation. As an exporter, he had better make credit inquiries through various channels (see 2. Channels of Making Credit Inquiry) to ensure that he is dealing with a reliable importer.

2. Channels of Making Credit Inquiry

There are many channels of making credit inquiries. One can obtain credit information through the following channels:

➢ a bank reference (the most commonly used way and considered objective and reliable but much simpler, lacking deeper understanding)

➢ the companies that have business relations with the company under investigation (the company will, of course, select those who will speak favorably of it. Therefore, you should take reports from these references with care.)

➢ inquiry agencies (popular nowadays and usually providing a satisfactory Business Credit Report that may contain detailed information covering over 20 sections of content, including Important Events, Summary, Finance, Credit Record, Operations, Industrial Comparison, Risk Analysis, Credit Rating, etc.)

➢ business directories (providing some basic information)

➢ Chinese Commercial Counselor's Offices in foreign countries

➢ foreign Commercial Counselor's Offices in China

➢ chambers of commerce (this kind of trade reference is more detailed but subjective)

No matter which channel is used, make sure all these letters, faxes or emails, coming and going, should be treated as strictly confidential.

信用查询信函写作步骤

1. The name of the company to be inquired about and its address and the relationship
2. What you need to know about the company
3. Your assurance of keeping the reply as confidential and your thanks

信用查询常用语句

1. The name of the company to be inquired about and its address and the relationship

- We have received an application for credit from ABC Company who gives your name as a reference.

  我们收到 ABC 公司的一份赊购申请书。它将贵公司推荐给我们作为其信用证明人。

- The subject company has referred us to your Bank for detailed information about its credit standing and business capacity.

  标题项下的公司介绍我方向贵行了解该公司信用状况及业务能力的详情。

- The subject company is now offering to represent us in the sale of our products, and has referred us to your bank for detailed information about...

  标题项下的公司有意向代理我们的产品，并指定贵行来提供关于该公司……的详细情况。

- The under-mentioned firm has recently asked if they could represent us in the marketing of our products in the United States as our sole agent.

  有一家商行最近与我公司联系，询问能否成为我公司产品在美国销售的独家代理。

- We are on the point of executing a considerable order from J. A. Husman Co., P.O. Box386, Karachi.

  我们正准备执行位于卡拉奇、邮政信箱为 386 号的胡斯曼公司签署的一份大宗订单。

2. What you need to know about the company

- Could you provide us with the requisite financial information so that we can open your new account immediately? Please include a recent financial statement, the name of your bank and references, together with any other relevant credit details.

  烦请提供相关的财务资料，以便尽快开立新账户。有关资料应包括最近的财务报告书、开户银行名称、证明文件以及其他详细的信用资料。

- As this is their first order on documents against payment terms and we have no information about this firm, we are desirous to know their credit standing with the help of your company.

由于是第一次按照付款交单方式与该公司交易，而且我方对该公司不了解，所以向贵公司询问该公司的信用状况。

- We shall appreciate your giving us such information including their financial standing, the extent of their business and their reputation for meeting the obligations.

  如有可能请介绍下列情况：该公司的经济实力、业务范围及履约能力。

- We shall highly appreciate it if you will give us your frank opinion on these matters regarding the company.

  如能给予关于该公司的这些情况的坦率意见，我方将不胜感激。

- We would like to know their general financial reliability. In particular, their trade with us will involve a standing credit of US$400,000. We would be pleased if you would let us know whether this credit is justified in view of their record in meeting payment dates.

  我们想知道他们的大概财务可信度，特别是该公司与我公司的交易涉及 40 万美元的信用额度。从该公司付款情况记录看，这个信用额度是否合适？

3. Your assurance of keeping the reply as confidential and your thanks

- Any information you may provide for us will be treated in absolute confidence and without responsibility from your esteemed Bank.

  贵方提供的任何资料都将严格保密，贵行对此不负任何责任。

- We assure you that any information you may give us will be treated in strict confidence and we shall be glad to reciprocate the favor at any time.

  贵公司提供的任何情况我们都将绝对保密，希望日后能为贵公司提供同样的服务。

- We thank you for your courtesy.

  感谢贵方的好意。

- Thank you for your help in this matter.

  感谢贵方对此事的协助。

- We shall be much grateful if you can give us any information at an early date.

  如蒙早日提供材料，我方将十分感激。

回复信用查询常用语句

Favorable Reply

- This company has extensive dealings with countries all over the world. We should consider it quite reliable for such an engagement as you mentioned.

  该公司有着极其广泛的国际贸易。有关贵方与该公司订约一事，我们认为它是可以信赖的。

- In answer to your inquiry, we give you the following information you asked for: The company you mentioned is an old-established one who has been enjoying high reputation. They have now a sound business standing with an excellent business turnover.

  兹答复贵方询问，贵方提及的公司是一家老字号且享有很高的声誉。公司经营状况良好且业绩出色。

- The company has supplied our firm with qualified goods for over 30 years. They have always provided complete satisfaction with in-time delivery, moderate prices and superior quality.

  该公司为我公司提供了 30 多年的优质产品。他们一直提供送货及时、价格合理、质量过硬的优质服务。

- We cooperated with this firm very well. It is always punctually meeting its commitments.

  我方与该公司合作十分愉快。它总能按时履约。

- We inform you that our business relations with the firm have been most satisfactory.

  到目前为止，我公司与该公司的业务来往都很令人满意。

- We have finished three transactions with this firm during the past two years. Each contract was less than USD10,000. Their payments have been timely. It has a good reputation within the trade.

  我方在过去两年间与该公司完成了三笔低于 1 万美元的交易。他们能及时付款，在业界享有良好声誉。

Unfavorable Reply

- The firm makes payments quite irregularly. And more than one occasion, we have had to press for them.

  该公司付款很不规律。我们曾不止一次地催款。

- In recent years the company has experienced a serious difficulty in finance and delayed in executing their normal payment. We would suggest you to pay more attention to the business with them.

  近年来该公司经历了严重的财务危机，一直拖欠付款。建议贵方与该公司交易时多加注意。

- Recently the company referred to seems to be getting into troubles because of overtrading.

  近年来该公司由于过度交易而陷入危机。

- We should believe the company to be trustworthy and reliable, though we are bound to say that they have not always settled their accounts with us on time.

  虽然该公司值得信赖，但我方有义务说明该公司不能总是按时付款。

- Recently they appear to have over-traded and owing to bad management, things are not so well as before. As that being the case, we should recommend a policy of caution.

  最近由于过度贸易和经营不善，该公司的经营状况大不如前。因此，我方建议对该公司持谨慎态度。

Confidential Statement

- The foregoing information is given in confidence and for your private use only.

  上述资料应保密且只能供贵方参考。

- However, this is just our personal view and we assume no responsibility to your further business with them. We wish you to make further information.

  然而此乃个人意见，故对今后贵公司与该公司的交易概不负责。希望贵方再做查询。

- This is our personal opinion and we assume no responsibility in your proposed business negotiations. We hope the above is satisfactory and will help you in making a decision.

这只是我们的个人观点，对您提到的贸易磋商不承担责任。我们希望这个答复让贵方满意，并能够帮助贵方做出决定。

- Please note that this information is furnished without any responsibility on our part and should be held strictly confidential.

  请注意此信息我方不承担任何责任且应严格保密。

- It is a condition of this letter that the name of this Bank will not be disclosed in the event of our report being passed on to your clients.

  本函有一个条件，即在把我方的报告转告贵方的客户时，请勿泄露我行的名称。

写作范例

1. A Letter for Credit Inquiry to a Trade Reference

Background: 美国的 Marshall Jones 有限公司欲与新加坡 Chan 贸易公司进行贸易往来，并提供 Galax Inc. 公司总经理 John Bradley 先生作为其信用证明人。Chan 贸易公司的陈经理向 John Bradley 进行信用查询。

Chan Trading Ltd.

8 Orchard Road, Kaki Bukit District, Singapore, 415938

Tel: 68484218

Fax: 68444218

Website: www.chanthsy.com

Email: tradechan@chanthsy.com

July 23, 20__

Mr. John Bradley

Galax Inc.

422 Madison Avenue, 31st Floor

New York, NY 10022-7001

United States

Dear Mr. Bradley,

Your name has been given to us as a credit reference by Marshall Jones & Co. Ltd. in your city, who wants to start business with us and gives us a purchase order for USD25,000 worth of merchandise.

We should be grateful if you could let us have your opinion on their reputation and financial standing. Essential facts would include how long the owner, Marshall Jones, has had an account with you and whether he has any outstanding debts.

Any information given to us will be surely treated in strict confidence. What's more, we are willing to provide you with the same service when necessary. I have enclosed a postage paid envelope for your convenience.

Thanks a lot for your attention to this matter. We are looking forward to your early reply.

Yours sincerely,
Chan Trading Ltd.

T. S. Chan

T. S. Chan
Managing Director

Notes

1. credit reference   信用证明人，信用参考
   I have the names of people we do business with abroad for credit references.   我这里有和我们做过生意的外国客户的名录，以供查询我们的信誉。

2. worth of sth   值……（金额）的量
   ten pounds' worth of petrol   十英镑的汽油
   US$2,500 worth of order   2500 美元的订单

3. merchandise   n. 货物，商品，常用作集合名词，泛指商品，不特指某一商品，前面不可加不定冠词，也没有复数形式。如：
   quality merchandise   高级商品
   This class of merchandise is usually sold on D/A terms.   此类商品通常按承兑交单出售。
   其他常见的"货物，商品"的表达还有：
   commodity   n. 可数名词，是较正式用词，通常指较大范围的商品，尤指国际贸易中的商品，如：
   the commodities market   商品市场
   Trading in commodities was brisk.   商品交易很兴旺。
   goods   n. 统指货物，永远是复数形式，不能直接与数词连用，只能用量词词组，如 fifty tons of goods
   article   n. 常指一种商品，而不指一类商品，同一种商品而有不同规格，如编货号，常用此词，并缩写为 Art.，如：
   Art. No. 101   第 101 号商品
   item   n. 原意为"项目"，但在商务中常用来代表前面所说的货物，如：
   Thank you for your inquiry for our canned fruits, but we regret to advise that this item is not available at present.   谢谢你们对我们罐头水果的询盘，但很抱歉，眼下没有存货。
   material   n. 一般指作原料用的商品，如：
   It is our hope to purchase a shipment quantity of this material.   我们希望购买数量够一次装

运的这种货物。

cargo n. 通常指船舶、飞机或其他交通工具运载的货物，复数形式 cargoes（英），cargos（美）

4. one's opinion on sth   对……提出某人的意见

He was asked to give his honest opinion on the present economic situation.   已请他对当前的经济形势直言不讳地发表意见。

Thank you for your frank opinion on the reputation regarding that company.   感谢贵方对该公司的声誉所提供的坦率意见。

5. have an account with sb   与某人有业务往来

account   n. 账户，户头

have an account at/with that bank   在那家银行有账户

Will you pay cash or shall I charge it to your account?   您愿意付现金还是记入您的账户里？

on account   预付，赊购，赊账

I'll give you £20 on account.   我先付你 20 英镑。

The firm used to buying spare parts on account.   该商行过去常常赊购零件。

6. outstanding   adj. 未偿付的，未完成的

outstanding debts   未偿清的债务

an outstanding issue   悬而未决的问题

7. confidence   n. 信心，秘密

have confidence in…   对……信得过，对……有信心

I am sorry I don't have confidence in that financial institute.   很抱歉，我对那家金融机构信不过。

in (strict) confidence   （严格）保密

Your information will be treated strictly in confidence.   贵方提供的信息将严格保密。

confident   adj. 有信心的

be confident of/in…   对……有信心，确信

We are confident of persuading our customer to place a trial order.   我方有把握说服客户试订。

We are confident that we shall be able to give you big orders if you would cooperate with us on delivery, price and quality.   我方确信，如果贵方在交货、价格和质量方面和我方全力合作，我方将向贵方大量订购。

We feel confident that we can push the sale of your products in this market.   我方确信能在此市场推销你方产品。

confidential   adj. 绝密的，保密的

confidential information   机密情报

Any information you may give us will be treated as strictly confidential.   贵方提供的任何资料都将严格保密。

8. a postage paid envelope   邮资已付的信封

9. for one's convenience   为了方便

10. courtesy   n. 好意，协助

2. Favorable Reply to a Credit Inquiry from a Company

Background: Galax Inc.公司总经理 John Bradley 先生回复 Chan 贸易公司的陈经理，对美国的 Marshall Jones 有限公司给予了有利的信用证明。

Galax Inc.

422 Madison Avenue, 31st Floor, New York, NY 10022-7001

Tel: 212-756-3300   Fax: 212-751-0497

Website: www.galax.firstmanhattan.com

~~~~~~

July 30, 20_ _

Mr. T. S. Chan

Chan Trading Ltd.

8 Orchard Road

Kaki Bukit District, 415938

Singapore

Dear Mr. Chan,

We have received your letter of September 5, in which you ask us to give you information about the credit standing of the company referred to in your letter.

We welcome this opportunity to assure you of our complete confidence in the said company. The company was established in 1994. Its registered capital was USD160,000. They are general importers and exporters, commission agents and manufacturers' representatives. Their main imports from Singapore are household electric appliances, office furniture, digital cameras and textiles. It has carried on business in this city for many years and held in the highest esteem, both for his business ability and for his reliability in meeting obligation.

We have been doing business with it for over six years. He has always settled his accounts promptly on the set date. On the whole its reputation is good and sound.

Mr. Marshall Jones, the president, is considered to have rich experience in this line. We believe that business transactions with this firm will prove to be satisfactory.

We hope the information will be helpful to you and we understand that this reply is without responsibility on our part and you will treat it as confidential.

Yours sincerely,

Galax Inc.

John Bradley

John Bradley

General Manager

Notes

1. the said company　该公司

   类似的表达有 the company concerned, the company in question, the company referred to, the company you inquired about, the company mentioned

2. registered capital　注册资金

3. esteem　n. 尊重，尊敬

   She is held in high/great/low esteem by those who know her well.　熟悉她的人都极为/非常/不太尊重她。

4. settle an account with sb　向某人付款，结账

5. on the set date　在规定日期

6. sound　adj. 正直的，诚实的

3.　An Email Credit Inquiry to a Bank Reference

Background: 澳大利亚悉尼市的 Thomas Wilson 有限公司向中国莎丽装饰品公司赊购总值为 50000 美元的货物。由于双方是第一次开展贸易，所以 Thomas Wilson 有限公司提供太平洋银行作为公司的信用证明。中国莎丽装饰品公司的销售经理陈先生发电子邮件向该银行进行查询。

From: chkt3421@sallyornaments.com

To: infodept@pacificbank.com

Date: Wednesday, March 23, 20＿＿, 10:24 am

Subject: Credit Inquiry

C.C.: lily_liu23@sallyornaments.com

Dear Ms. Collins,

We have received an order of USD50,000 from Thomas Wilson Co., Ltd., 56 Clark Street, Sydney, and they have provided your bank as the bank reference.

Before we grant credit of this amount we should be grateful for any information you can give us about their financial standing, the extent of their business, and their reputation for meeting obligations.

We promise that any information provided by you will be kept strictly confidential. Since the above-mentioned company expects an early decision from us, we would be extra grateful for an early comment.

We are looking forward to hearing from you.

Yours sincerely,
Richard Chen
Sales Manager

Notes

1. they have provided your as the bank reference   他们提及贵行为证明人
2. grant credit   允许赊购

4.   Favorable Reply to a Credit Inquiry from a Bank

Background: 太平洋银行信息咨询部经理 Mary Collins 发电子邮件回复中国莎丽装饰品公司的销售经理陈先生，对澳大利亚悉尼市的 Thomas Wilson 有限公司给予了有利的信用证明。

From: infodept@pacificbank.com
To: chkt3421@sallyornaments.com
Date: Friday, March 25, 20_ _, 11:29 am
Subject: Re: Credit Inquiry

Dear Mr. Chen,

The company you inquired about in your letter of March 23, 20_ _, has been maintaining an account with us for the past twenty years, during which they have never failed to meet their obligation. Their balance sheets of recent years attached will show you that their import business in ornaments has been managed and operated under a satisfactory condition.

We believe that business transactions with this firm will prove satisfactory.

Please note that this information is furnished without any responsibility on our part and should be held strictly confidential.

Yours sincerely,
Mary Collins
Manager of Information Dept.

****

Notes

1. maintaining an account with us　与我方保持账目往来
2. fail to do sth　未能做某事
   They failed to get the goods ready for shipment on time.　他们未能按时将货物备妥待运。
3. balance sheet　资产负债表，表示企业在一定日期（通常为各会计期末）的财务状况（即资产、负债和业主权益的状况）的主要会计报表，可让所有阅读者于最短时间了解企业经营状况。
4. under a satisfactory condition　在令人满意的情况下
   be in good/bad/excellent condition　处于好的/坏的/极佳的状况
5. furnish vt. 为……提供家具，提供
   furnish an office　用家具布置办公室
   a furnished apartment　带家具的公寓
   furnish…with…　为……提供……
   We hope we have furnished you with all the information you required in your email.　希望我方为贵方提供了电子邮件中索要的所有资料。
   The Seller is expected to furnish the Buyer with all the necessary documents to evidence the existence of the accident.　卖方应向买方提供一切必要文件以证明事故存在。

5. Unfavorable Reply to a Credit Inquiry from a Credit Inquiry Agency

Background: 中国辽宁玩具有限公司的赵经理向 Elite 征信所发电子邮件，希望能调查韩国 Laam 进出口公司的信用情况。该征信所电子邮件回复，对韩国 Laam 进出口公司给予了不利的信用证明。

From: bernard990@eliteinquiries.com
To: zhttchina@fhtoys.com
Date: Monday, April 28, 20＿＿, 13:15 pm
Subject: Re: Credit Inquiry

Dear Mr. Zhao,

Upon receipt of your email of March 23, we made inquiries concerning the company you mentioned and have obtained the following information.

About a year ago an action was brought against the firm by one of its suppliers for recovery of the sums due though payment was recovered in full.

Our inquiries reveal nothing to suggest that the firm be not straightforward. It seems to us that the firm's difficulties were due to bad management and, in particular, overtrading.

Consequently, most of the firm's suppliers either give only very short credit for limited sums or make deliveries on a cash basis.

It would therefore, appear inadvisable to enter into transactions of large amount with this company.

We are pleased to have been of service to you in the matter but ask you to ensure that the information we have given you is treated as strictly confidential.

Yours sincerely,
Bernard Higgins
Manager

Notes

1. concerning   prep. 关于，相当于 regarding, respecting，如：
   information concerning the earthquake   有关地震的消息
2. recovery   n. 偿还
3. Our inquiries reveal nothing to suggest that the firm be not straightforward.   我们的调查并不能表明该公司不够诚信。
4. give only very short credit for limited sums   给予非常有限的短期信用额

Unit 3　Establishing Business Relations

建立贸易关系

1. The Sources of Obtaining Information about Potential Trade Partners

Establishing business relations actually means to choose and determine the trade partner. This is the first step for a company to start its business because transaction can be made only after the business relations have been built. It is vital for a company to seek new customers as well as to hold old ones, especially for a company that wishes to expand its market and enlarge its business scope and turnover. But by what sources can a company obtain the necessary information about a new market and a new customer? The following channels are frequently used to secure the necessary information of its potential trade partner.

(1) banks

(2) advertisements in newspapers, periodicals, magazines, from broadcast, TV and through Internet

(3) introduction from his business connections

(4) introduction from his subsidiaries or branches, agents abroad

(5) Chamber of Commerce both at home and abroad

(6) Commercial Counselor's Office in Embassy

(7) attendance at various kinds of trading fairs and exhibitions both at home and abroad

(8) self-introductions or inquiries received from the merchants abroad.

2. Letters about Requesting to Establish Business Relations

When writing a letter to establish business relations, the writer usually informs the receiver of the following:

(1) source of information (one of the ways above), i.e. where or from whom the writer obtains the receiver's name and address

(2) intention of writing this letter, e.g. to establish business relations with the receiver

(3) self-introduction of the writer's company, generally including two parts: introduction to the business scope and its main products to buy or sell and reference as to his company's financial position and integrity

(4)   indication of having sent the enclosed catalog, samples or price list if the writer is an exporter or indication of making requests for these materials if the writer is an importer

(5)   expectation of cooperation and an early reply from the receiver.

Make sure that the letter is cordial and warm, stressing the writer's sincere desire of cooperating with the receiver and of entering into a favorable trade connection, since the first impression matters a lot.

建立贸易关系写作步骤

1.   Source of information

2.   Intention of the letter

3.   Self-introduction (business scope, finances and credit standing)

4.   Enclosure or request

5.   Hope of receiving an early reply

建立贸易关系常用语句

1.   Source of information

- We have learned/heard from… that…
  我方从……获悉……

- We have read your advertisement in the……
  我方在……上看到了贵方的广告。

- We have obtained your name and address from *The Journal of Commerce*.
  我方从《商业日报》获悉贵方的名称和地址。

- Your name and address has been given to us by…
  通过……，我方得知了贵方的名称和地址。

- We learn your company from the Internet that you are one of the leading manufacturers in this line.
  我方从网上了解到贵公司是这一行业的主要生产商之一。

- We are given to understand that you are potential buyers of Chinese…, which comes within the frame of our business activities.
  我方得知贵方是中国……（产品）的潜在购买商，而该产品属于我方的经营范围。

- Your name and address has been recommended to us by…, with whom we have done business for many years.
  与我方有多年贸易往来的……向我方推荐了贵方的名称和地址。

- We note with pleasure from our Commercial Counselor in… that you are interested in establishing business relations with us on the supply of ...

从我方在……（地点）的商务参赞处得知了贵方因……供应事宜欲与我方建立贸易关系。

2. Intention of the letter

- We write to you now with a view to building up business relations with your firm.

  兹具函以期与贵公司建立贸易关系。

- We express our desire to establish business relations with your firm.

  我们表达和贵公司建立业务关系的愿望。

- We see that your firm specializes in Light Industrial Goods, and we shall be glad to enter into business relations with you.

  我们看到你们经营轻工产品，很高兴与贵公司建立业务关系。

- As this item falls within the scope of our business activities, we shall be pleased to enter into business relations with you.

  由于该产品属于我方的经营范围，我方十分高兴与贵方建立贸易关系。

- We approach you today in the hope of establishing business relations with you.

  今与贵方联系，希望能与贵方建立贸易关系。

- We shall be pleased to enter into direct business relations with you on the basis of equality, mutual benefit and exchanging needed goods.

  希望能在平等、互利、互通有无的基础上与贵方建立直接的贸易关系。

- Being closely connected with reliable wholesalers here, we shall be able to do considerable import business with you.

  我方与此地可靠批发商有密切联系，希望能与贵方做可观的进口业务。

3. Self-introduction (business scope, finances and credit standing)

- Our company deals in/trades in/handles/is in the line of/specializes in the import and export of ...

  我公司经营……的进出口业务。

- We are one of the largest/leading/major exporters/importers of... in our county/in this region and have been in this line for many years.

  我方是我国/本地……（产品）的最大/主要的出口商/进口商之一，且从事该行业已有多年。

- It is a pleasure for us to introduce ourselves to you as a commission agent for... We have been in this post for over 5 years now.

  我方有幸自荐，我方是……（产品）的代理商，从事该行业已有五年多了。

- We are a state-operated corporation and in a position to accept orders against customers' samples specifying design, specification and packing requirements.

  我们是一家国有企业，能够根据客户提供的样品花样、规格和包装要求供货。

- This is to introduce the Pacific Corporation as exporters of light industrial products having business relations with more than 80 countries in the world.

  现介绍太平洋公司，它是轻工产品的出口商，与世界上 80 多个国家都有商务联系。

- ... is within/falls within/lies within/comes within/comes under our business scope.

……（产品）属于我方的经营范围。

- We refer you to The Bank of Switzerland if you wish to make any inquiries on our credit standing.

  如果对我方信用状况有任何疑问， 请向瑞士银行查询。

- Our bankers are ... They can provide you information about our business and finances.

  我方的银行是……。他们可以向贵方提供有关我方的业务和财务状况。

- For/As to/Regarding/As regards/With regard to/In regard to our credit standing, please refer to... /we are permitted to mention..., as a reference.

  关于我方信用状况，请向……查询/我方已征得……的同意，将其作为我方的查询之处。

4. Enclosure or request

- We enclose a copy of our latest... covering the details of all the items available/suppliable/provided for export at present, and hope some of them will be of interest to you.

  我方随函附寄最新的包括目前可供出口的所有产品详情的……并且希望贵方会对一些产品感兴趣。

- We attach a copy of... for your reference and hope that you would contact us if any item is interesting to you.

  我方附件发送了一份……以供贵方参考，并且期望若贵方对任何产品感兴趣与我方联系。

- We airmailed a brochure/price list/illustrated catalog/sample/sample book to acquaint you with our products/business lines now available for export.

  我方向贵方航寄了产品手册/价格表/带插图的产品目录/样品/样本，以便贵方熟悉我方目前可供出口的产品。

- We are enclosing our latest illustrated catalog together with the price list.

  随价目表附寄我方最新的图解产品目录。

- We will be pleased to have your catalog and samples.

  我方将很高兴收到贵方的产品目录和样品。

- We would appreciate receiving details regarding your commodities.

  如收到贵方产品的详情，我方将不胜感激。

5. Hope of receiving an early reply

- We are looking forward to your favorable and prompt reply.

  期盼贵方有利及尽早的回复。

- We appreciate your immediate reply.

  贵方尽早回复，我方将十分感激。

- We look forward to providing you with high quality products and superior customer service.

  期盼给贵方提供优质产品及卓越的服务。

- If you are interested in any of our products, please contact us with your requirements.

  如果贵方对任何产品感兴趣，请就你方需求与我方联系。

- We sincerely hope we could cooperate with you soon.

  衷心希望不久能与贵方合作。

- Looking forward to hearing from you soon.

  期盼早复。

写 作 范 例

1. A Letter from a Manufacturer to an Importer

Background: 中国飞扬包具生产企业出口部的 Bill Chen 给加拿大 Modern 背包贸易公司的 Howard Binks 去函，希望双方能建立贸易关系。

Feiyang Bag Products Co. Ltd.

219 Xinhua Rd., Yanling County, Xuchang

Henan, 461200, China

Tel: 86-374-2281459

Fax: 86-374-2281657

Website: www.feiyangbags.com

****

6 August, 20＿＿

Mr. Howard Binks

Modern Backpacks Trading Co.

78 Riverside Avenue

Vancouver

Canada

Dear Mr. Binks,

We have obtained your name and address from a commercial website: www.alibaba.com. We understand that you are one of the major importers of backpacks in Canada and we are now writing you for the establishment of business relations.

We take this opportunity to introduce ourselves as a manufacturer dealing in backpacks with various designs. Our products are of high quality and good design with very high reputation. In our over seven years' export experience, we have supplied our clients with a wide range of durable backpacks at very competitive prices. We believe that we will have a promising future if we cooperate with each other.

In order to acquaint you with our business lines, we are enclosing a copy of our latest catalog regarding the details of all the items available for export at present for your reference, and hope some of these items will be of interest to you. Quotations and samples will be sent to you upon receipt of your specific inquiries.

We are looking forward to your favorable reply.

Yours sincerely,

Bill Chen

Bill Chen

Export Department

Encl. one copy of catalog

Notes

1. manufacturer　n. 制造商，生产商，厂商

   manufacture　n. & v. 制造（品），制造业

   manufactured goods/articles/products　人工制品/制成品/工业产品

   Chinese manufactures = Chinese makes　中国制品

   silk manufactures　丝制品

   textile manufacture　纺织业

   of Chinese/home/foreign manufacture　中国/本国/外国制造

2. establishment of business relations　建立贸易关系

   "建立"还可以说 set up, enter into, build up

   "贸易关系"也可以说 trade relations, trade connections, business relationship

3. deal in　经营

   类似的表达有 handle, trade in, specialize in, be in the line of

   Our company is in the line of the import and export of chemical products.　我公司经营化工产品的进出口业务。

4. durable　adj. 结实的，耐用的

5. at competitive prices　以有竞争力的价格

   competitive power/strength/edge　竞争力

   If your price is competitive, we will place an order with you.　如果贵方价格具有竞争力，我方将向贵方下订单。

6. acquaint sb with sth　使某人熟悉、了解某事

   In order to acquaint you with our products, we airmailed you two samples this morning.　为使贵方熟悉我方产品，我方于今晨航寄样品两份。

   The illustrated catalog and samples are of great help to acquaint us with your latest products.

带插图的目录和样品对我们熟悉贵方最新的产品大有帮助。

7. enclose　v. 随函附寄

We enclose a copy of our latest price list.　我方随函附寄最新的价目表一份。

上面的例句也可以说：

We send you under cover a copy of our latest price list.

under cover　随函附寄

enclosed　adj. 随函附寄的（the enclosed 可用以指随函附寄的东西）

enclosure　n. 附件（缩写为 Enc.或 Encl.）

8. latest catalog　最新的产品目录

9. regarding　prep. 关于

类似的表达还有 as regards, with regard to, in regard to

Regarding the terms of payment, we require confirmed and irrevocable Letter of Credit.　关于支付条件，我方要求保兑的、不可撤销的信用证。

10. available for export　可供出口的

The Item No. 25 is not available.　第 25 号货物缺货。

We will ship the goods by the first available steamer next month.　货物将由下月第一条便船装运。

11. for your reference　供贵方参考

还可以用 for your information, for your consideration, for your scrutiny, for your perusal, for your inspection

12. inquiry　n. 询盘，询价

inquiry for　对某商品询价

At the moment, there are only small inquiries for such goods.　目前对这类商品只有小数量的询盘。

We have an inquiry for 5,000 pairs of silk socks.　我方现有 5 千双丝袜的询价单一份。

询价单也可以说 inquiry note/sheet，如：

We enclose our Inquiry Note No. A34.　随函附寄我方第 A34 号询价单。

make an inquiry for sth　对……询价

They made a fax inquiry for 200 metric tons of polished rice yesterday.　昨天他们发来传真，对 200 公吨精白米询价。

inquire　v. 询购，询价，询问

inquire for sth　询购某物

The goods you inquire for are out of stock.　所询之货已脱销。

Thank you for your email inquiring for tea sets.　感谢询购茶具的电子邮件。

inquire about　打听某事

They have inquired about the possibility of the sale of their products.　他们曾打听过有无可能销售他们的产品。

I want to inquire about the quantity you require for next quarter.　我想打听一下贵方下季度所需要的数量。

inquire into　调查，了解

It's our duty to inquire into this matter.　我方将负责调查此事。

The whole matter has to be inquired into.　整个事情必须查清。

13. quotation　n. 报价

quotation list/table/sheet/form　报价单/报价表/价目表

14. upon receipt of　一经收到

15. favorable　adj. 有利的，优惠的

favorable reply　有利回复，佳音

favorable price　优惠的价格

2.　An Email From an Importer to an Exporter

Background: 南京洁而净科技有限公司海外业务部的 James Zhao 给澳大利亚 Dawood 贸易公司的 Johnson Field 发电子邮件，希望双方能建立贸易关系并进口感应式干手器。

From: jameszhao804@hotmail.com

To: johnsonfield@yahoo.com

Date: Monday, 6 June, 20＿＿, 9:23 AM

Subject: Request to Establish Business Relations

Dear Mr. Field,

Your name and address is given to us by the Commercial Counselor's Office of Australian Embassy in China, who has informed us that you are one of the leading exporters of Sensor Hand Dryers extensively to Asia. As this item falls within the frame of our business activities, we are contacting you in the hope of entering into direct business connections with you.

We are one of the leading importers of Hand Dryers in China and have imported the products for about 10 years. We are very well connected with the major dealers in this line and have built a sound reputation in this market. Our market survey indicates that there is always a ready market in China for the products, provided they are high in quality and reasonable in prices. Therefore we feel confident that by our joint efforts, it is hopeful to enlarge our business scope and realize mutual benefit.

In order to have a better understanding of your company and products, we shall appreciate it if you would send us your illustrated brochure and latest price list together with other necessary information.

For more information about us, please visit our website: www.jieerjing.com.cn. As to our finances and credit standing, please refer to the Bank of China, Nanjing Branch.

We are looking forward to your favorable and early reply with keen interest.

Yours sincerely,

James Zhao

****

James Zhao

Overseas Business Department

Nanjing Jie Er Jing Technology Co. Ltd.

12 North Taoyuan Road, Gaochun Economic Development Zone

Nanjing, 210007, Jiangsu

Tel: 86-25-84635488

Fax: 86-25-84486554

Email: jameszhao804@hotmail.com

Website: www. jieerjing.com.cn

Notes

1. commercial counselor   商务参赞

   Commercial Counselor's Office   商务参赞处

2. embassy   n. 大使馆

   the American Embassy in China   美驻华大使馆

   ambassador   n. 大使

3. inform   vt. 通知，告知，后面必须有宾语

   inform sb of sth   通知某人某事，类似用法的动词还有 notify, advise

   Please inform us of your trade terms and send us your samples.   请告知我方贵方的交易条件并寄送样品。

   Please inform us of the market conditions at your end.   请告知你方市场情况。

   We wish to inform you that we are in the market for chemicals.   兹告知贵方我方欲购化工产品。

   He was kept informed of the fluctuation of the prices.   他不断得到物价波动的消息。

4. leading   adj. 主要的，大的

5. fall within   属于

   类似的表达有 be within, lie within, come within, come under

6. business scope/lines/sphere/activities/frame   经营范围

7. contact   vt. 与……接洽，与……联系（注意该动词在使用时不能再与介词 with 搭配。approach 也是这种用法，但 approach 可用被动语态），如：

   We'll contact you again as soon as any fresh supply comes in.   一旦有新货源上市，我们立即再与你方联系。

   Please don't hesitate to approach us again.   请立即与我方再次联系。

   We have been approached by several buyers for the supply of walnuts.   已有好几家买主与我

方联系核桃供应事宜。

8. in the hope of 希望，以期，为了，还可以用 with a view to，后面都接名词或动名词，如：
   Will you please let us know your business terms and forward your samples in the hope of getting into business in the near future? 请寄来样品并告知交易条件，以期在不久的将来进行交易。
   With a view to supporting your sales, we have specially prepared some samples of our new products. 为了支持你们的销售，我们专门准备了新产品的样品。

9. be very well connected with… 与……联系甚广，与……有密切联系

10. dealer n. 商人，经销商
    exclusive dealer 独家经销商
    deal n. & v. 贸易，成交，经营
    make/do a deal with… 与……做交易
    deal on credit 凭信用交易，赊账买卖

11. there is a ready market for… 对……有潜在的需求，也可以将 market 换成 demand

12. enlarge business scope 扩大经营范围
    expand market 扩大市场
    extend our interests 扩大双方的经营

13. have a better understanding of 更好地了解……

14. appreciate vt. 感激，感谢
    常用结构有：
    后接名词：We highly appreciate your close cooperation. 感谢贵方密切配合。
    后接动名词：We shall appreciate your giving this matter your serious consideration. 若贵方对此事给予认真考虑，我方将不胜感激。
    后接从句：We shall appreciate it very much if you could send us a sample book by air immediately. 如能立即航寄样本一份，我方将十分感激。

15. illustrated adj. 带有插图的

16. brochure n. 产品手册

17. finances n.（常用复数）财务状况

18. standing n. 情况，状况
    credit standing 信用状况
    financial standing 财务状况

19. refer 作为动词，常见的意思及用法有：
    (1) 谈及，提到（与 to 搭配）
    We refer to our fax dated May 20. 兹谈及我方 5 月 20 日传真。
    Referring to your inquiry of May 12, we very much regret that we have no supply in stock. 关于贵方 5 月 12 日询盘，非常抱歉我们手头无现货。
    (2) 参照，参阅（与 to 搭配）
    Please refer to our email of July 2. 请参阅我们 7 月 2 日的电子邮件。
    We referred to our records and found that the said commission had already been paid. 我们查阅了我方记录，查明该笔佣金已付。

(3) 提交，交付（与 to 搭配）

We have referred this matter to our factory in Dalian.　我们已将此事提交我们在大连的厂家处理。

(4) 指示，接洽（与 to 搭配）

We have referred them to you for their requirements.　我们已请他们向你们洽购所需货物。

Your Commercial Counselor's Office has referred us to you for establishing business relations with your corporation.　贵国商务处让我们与您联系有关与贵公司建立业务关系事宜。

reference　n. 谈到，关于

with reference to, in reference to, reference is made to 常置于句首，表示"关于"，如：

With reference to our usual payment terms, we can do otherwise than L/C at sight.　关于通常的支付条件，我们除即期信用证外也接受其他做法。

In reference to the quality of the new product, no complaint can be made.　新产品的质量无可挑剔。

Reference is made to your inquiry of March 2.　兹关于贵方 3 月 2 日的询盘。

3. A Positive Reply to an Email of Building Business Relations

Background: 澳大利亚 Dawood 贸易公司的 Johnson Field 发电子邮件回复南京洁而净科技有限公司海外业务部的 James Zhao，同意双方建立贸易关系并提供有关公司和商品信息的资料。

From: johnsonfield@yahoo.com

To: jameszhao804@hotmail.com

Date: Tuesday, 7 June, 20＿＿, 9:15 AM

Subject: Glad to Establish Business Relations

Dear Mr. Zhao,

Thank you for your email message dated 6 June, from which we have learned that you are interested in our company and in the market for our products. We are glad to establish business relations with you.

We are the leading exporters dealing in various washroom accessories for private and business customers, for example, hand dryers, soap dispensers, paper towel dispensers, liquid soap, paper towel, etc. which enjoy great popularity in the world market. We provide the best quality products at very reasonable price. We pride ourselves with the 100% satisfactory warranty. If you are not happy with our product, you can exchange or ask for refund within 14 days of purchase with no questions asked (For details, please refer to the Warranty Condition webpage of our website: www. dawoodwashroom.com). We provide up to 5 years extended warranty on all our hand dryers.

As requested, we are airmailing our illustrated brochure and latest price list covering the main items available for export at present for your information. We are sure that our products will comply with your requirements.

To learn more about us, please go to our website: www.dawoodwashroom.com.

We are expecting a considerable volume of business between us.

Best regards,
Johnson Field

****
Johnson Field
Export Manager
Dawood Trading Ltd.
38 Golden Street, Glen Waverley, Victoria, 3150, Australia
Tel: 61-3-95116878
Fax: 61-3-95116007
Email: johnsonfield@yahoo.com
Website: www.dawoodwashroom.com

Notes

1. be in the market for   欲购买
    One of our clients is in the market for Chinese Black Tea.   我方一客户欲购买中国红茶。
2. washroom accessory   浴室配套设施
3. soap dispenser   给皂机
    paper towel dispenser   自动型纸巾桶
    liquid soap   洗手液
4. enjoy great popularity   享有盛誉
    类似的表达有：
    The goods are most popular in our market.
    The goods have commanded a good market.
    The goods are selling fast.
    The goods enjoy fast sales.
    The goods are universally acknowledged.
    "畅销品"可以说 ready seller, quick seller, quick-selling product
5. warranty   n. 保修期
    The machine is still under warranty.   这台机器仍在保修期内。
6. exchange   v. 换货
7. refund   n. 退款
    claim/pay/obtain a refund   要求/支付/获得退款
    refund   vt. 退还，偿付

refund a deposit　退还押金

Postage costs will be refunded to you.　邮费将退还给你。

8.　be happy with sth　对某物感到满意

We are pleased to know that you are happy with our after-sales service.　我们很高兴得知您对我们的售后服务感到满意。

9.　as requested　按照贵方要求，也可以说 at your request

10.　comply with　满足

名词形式是 in compliance with　满足，依照，按照

in compliance/agreement/accordance/conformity with　与……一致

In compliance with your request, we are sending you by air a catalog together with a range of pamphlets for your reference.　按要求，我们航寄目录一本，并随附小册子一套，供你方参考。

11.　a considerable volume of business　大笔交易

英语中表示"业务，交易"的词比较多，常用的有 business, transaction, deal 等。其中 business 是不可数名词，而 transaction 和 deal 是可数名词。因此，"两笔交易"的表达是 2 transactions 或 2 deals 或 2 items of business。现将 business，deal，transaction 的用法总结如下。

business　n. 商业，贸易，业务，交易，买卖（都是不可数名词），如：

We have done business with them for many years.　我们与他们已做了多年生意。

What's your line of business?　你们经营什么业务？

They have concluded substantial business with that company.　他们已与该公司达成大量交易。

另外，business 还有"工商企业，公司，商行（可数名词）"之意，如：

He owns a small electric appliance repair business.　他拥有一个小型电器修理行。

There are many businesses engaged in the line of furniture.　许多企业从事家具行业。

deal　v. & n. 交易（可数名词），如：

Through mutual efforts, we have closed several big deals with them.　由于共同努力，我们已与他们达成几笔大交易。

deal in　经营，意思与 trade in, handle 一样，如：

This business deals in the export of plastic toys.　这家企业经营塑料玩具的出口业务。

deal with　与……打交道，与……做生意，处理……，如：

We have been dealing with your branch in Paris in the past few years.　这几年我们一直与你方在巴黎的分公司做生意。

Please deal with the order carefully.　请认真处理该订单。

transaction　n. 处理，交易（可数名词），如：

For large transactions, we prefer payment by sight L/C.　对于大笔交易，我方建议用即期信用证支付。

We hope you will tell us the name of your bank before the conclusion of the first transaction between us.　在达成第一笔交易前，请告知贵方银行名称。

4. A Negative Reply to an Email of Establishing Business Relations

Background: 新西兰 Ardrich 有限公司的业务经理 Sullivan Smith 发电子邮件回复温岭迅达电器有限公司出口部的 Marco Xia，婉拒了对方建立贸易关系的请求并表明了原因。

From: sullivan_ardrich@ardrich.com.nz
To: marcoxia_xunda@xundaelectron.com
Date: Thursday, 2 July, 20__, 10:15 AM
Subject: Re: Request to Establish Trade Relations

Dear Mr. Xia,

Thank you for your email of July 1, expressing your interest in our products and desire of entering into trade relations with us.

But much to our regret, we are unable to meet your requirement to establish relations for the moment. We are currently represented by another company as our exclusive agent in your region and in accordance with terms and conditions of Exclusive Agency Agreement we are prohibited from distributing our products by other companies.

Obviously, this is not an appropriate time to cooperate with your company. But we promise to keep your email and will get in touch with you as soon as the agreement expires.

We express our regret again and sincerely hope that we may have the chance to cooperate and establish a long-term and mutual benefit trade relation in the near future.

Best regards,

Yours sincerely,
Sullivan Smith

****

Sullivan Smith
Business Manager
Ardrich Limited
8 Hannigan Drive, Auckland, 1072, New Zealand
Tel: 64-9-5702584
Fax: 64-9-5702544
Email: sullivan_ardrich@ardrich.com.nz
Website: www. ardrich.com.nz

Notes

1. much to our regret 使我方十分遗憾的是

2. We are currently represented by another company as our exclusive agent. 我方当前由另一家公司做我方的独家代理。

   agent n. 代理商

   commission/multiple agent 佣金代理商，一般代理商（在同一地区和期限内委托人可以同时委派几个代理人代表委托人行事。代理人不享有独家专营权。佣金代理完成授权范围内的事务后按协议规定的办法向委托人计收佣金）

   exclusive/sole agent 独家代理商（在指定地区和期限内单独代表委托人行事，从事代理协议中规定的有关业务的代理人。委托人在该地区内不得委托其他代理人）

3. terms and conditions 交易条款，交易条件

4. exclusive agency agreement 独家代理协议

5. expire vi. 期满，终止

   When does your equipment lease expire? 你们的设备租赁何时到期？

   expiration n. 终止，期满，满期

   The two parties decided not to cooperate at the expiration of the agreement. 协议期满后双方决定不再合作。

5. An Email Requesting to Resume the Business Relations

Background: 英国 Greenham Industrial 公司的出口部经理 Gerry Brown 在查看过去几年间的账目时，发现公司的客户之一 Metal Containers Company 已经很久没订购过产品了，所以 Gerry Brown 给该公司的采购部经理发电子邮件，希望能与过去有贸易往来的 Metal Containers Company 恢复贸易关系。

From: gerrybrown-export@greenham.com

To: importdept@metalcontainers.com

Date: Monday, 28 August, 20_ _, 03:30 PM

Subject: A Request of Resuming Trade Relations

Dear Purchasing Manager,

When taking a retrospective glance of our accounts for the past years, we find that we have not received any order from your corporation for quite a long time.

Assuming that you are still in the market for the products that we export, we would be very pleased if you could inform us of your current needs and whether you will place an order.

Our products have been greatly improved both in technology and packaging. We are sending you by airmail the new samples and quotations. If our products still meet your requirements, we hope to resume our trade relations. If you need any further information, please feel free to contact me at 89445651.

Thank you for your attention and expect your early and favorable reply.

Yours sincerely,
Gerry Brown

****

Gerry Brown
Export Manager
Greenham Industrial Company
54 Butik Street, Birmingham, England
Tel: 89445651
Fax: 89445678
Email: gerrybrown-export@greenham.com
Website: www.greenham.com

Notes

1. resume   v. 再开始，重新取得
   They resumed the production of nylon products after an interval of two years. 在停产两年后，这家公司又重新开始生产尼龙产品。
2. take a retrospective glance   回顾
   retrospective   adj. 回顾的
3. assuming (that)…   假设，假如
   Assuming it fails to settle its payment on the set date, we would be put in a very awkward situation.   假设这家公司不能在规定日期前付清货款，那么我们将陷入十分尴尬的境地。

Unit 4　Inquiry

询　盘

An inquiry is a request for transaction particulars on certain goods or service. It is usually made by importers in international trade. If it is a first inquiry from an importer, the writing structure is similar to the one of establishing business relations, in which one asks for such things as catalog, price list or quotation sheet and sample. An inquiry letter helps the importer have a general idea about information of the goods the importer is interested in.

Later on if the importer receives a positive reply from the exporter and finds the prices and samples satisfactory for purchase, he may send out another inquiry to the exporter to get more and detailed information about trade terms concerning the appointed goods before making a purchase decision, such as price, terms of payment, delivery date, discount, minimum order quantity, etc. In this case, the importer is actually asking for a quotation or an offer. Through comparing these quotations or offers, the importer chooses the most competitive one to make a deal.

询盘写作步骤

1. Your interests in the specific products
2. Inquiry for detailed information about trade terms
3. Hope of cooperation and an early reply

询盘常用语句

1.　Your interests in the specific products

● We are the leading dealer in art and craft items in this district where Chinese art and craft items are particularly popular. There is a steady demand here for high-class goods of this type, especially in brighter colors.

我方是本地区主要的工艺品经销商。中国工艺品在此地十分畅销而且对这类高档商品有稳定的需求，特别是色彩鲜艳的。

- We have recently received many inquiries from our retailing shops for the said items. We are sure there would be brisk demands on our side.

  最近我方收到了许多零售店发来的对该商品的询价。我方相信该商品在我方市场能畅销。

- In the June 13 issue of the *Korea Trade Bulletin*, you advertise pens, pencils, etc. We are in the pen and pencil business, and are always looking for additional sources of supply as well as completed units of other manufacturers that we can sell.

  从 6 月 13 日《韩国贸易公报》上看到贵公司有关钢笔和铅笔等的广告。我公司专营钢笔及铅笔生意，经常寻找制造厂及其所能出售的货品。

- We are much interested in your water bottle No. 6 shown on page 2 of your July catalog, and would like to have a sample bottle, preferably with "ABC Company" insignia printed on both sides of it.

  我们对贵方 7 月产品目录第 2 页上所登的第 6 号水杯很感兴趣，希望惠寄一只水杯样品，最好在水杯两面都印上"ABC 公司"标志。

- As we are interested in buying bamboo floor from the principal manufacturers at the most competitive prices, we have decided to approach you.

  我们有意从生产竹地板的主要厂商那里以最具竞争力的价格购买竹地板，因此我们决定与你们联系。

- Your Energy Saving Lamps Type No. UVS23 are of great interest to us.

  我方对贵方第 UVS23 号节能灯很感兴趣。

2. Inquiry for detailed information about trade terms

- We are in the market for … and shall be glad to receive your best possible quotation, indicating origin, detailed specifications, packing, and quantity available for the said goods.

  我方欲购……（商品）。希望收到贵方对该商品的报价，包括原产地、具体规格、包装、可供的数量。

- Would you please quote us your lowest prices for the goods listed below, inclusive of our 2% commission?

  请向我方报下列商品的最低价，包括我方 2%的佣金。

- If you can promise delivery before April, your products should find a ready sale in this market.

  如果贵方能在四月前交货，贵方产品将会在我方市场畅销。

- Enclosed please find samples of our cotton socks. If you are able to supply us with 5,000 dozen, we would be pleased to have you quote the favorable price CIF Macao.

  随函附寄我方棉袜样品。如你方能供货 5000 打，请报最优惠的澳门成本加运保费价。

- Would you please let us know what discount you give for large quantities?

  请告知大量购买的折扣是多少。

- Please send us your best offer by fax indicating packing, specifications, quantity available, and earliest time of delivery.

请传真报最优惠盘，包括包装、规格、可供数量及最早交货期。

- If you can supply goods of the type and quality required, please make us a firm offer and quote your lowest prices.

  如果贵方能提供该型号的指定质量的产品，请向我方报实盘及最低价。

- We would be pleased if you could quote us a price for Printed Shirting on the basis of FOB Manila.

  如能报印花衬布的马尼拉离岸价，我方将十分高兴。

3. Hope of cooperation and an early reply

- We would like to place considerably large orders with you if the prices you quote are very competitive.

  若贵方报价极具竞争力，我方将大量订购。

- We can assure you of our repeat orders in future if both the price and the quality are found acceptable.

  如果价格和质量可以接受的话，我方保证会长期订购。

- If your prices are in line, we trust substantial business can be concluded.

  若贵方价格可行，相信双方可以达成大笔交易。

- We hope this will be a good start for long and mutually profitable business relations.

  我方希望这将是双方长期互利贸易关系的良好开端。

- We trust you will give this inquiry your immediate attention and let us have your reply at an early date.

  相信贵方会立即处理我方询盘并及早回复。

- We await your information with great interest.

  期盼贵方的资料。

写 作 范 例

1. A First Inquiry for Handbags

Background: 英国 The Merton Shop 进口部经理 Sandra Jones 在中国进出口商品交易会上对中国广州市的 M & S 皮革制品有限公司生产的各种高级皮革手提包很感兴趣，于是向该公司发去首次询盘。

The Merton Shop

9 Green Street

Manchester, EC1A 1BB

England

Tel: 44-152-1256878

Fax: 44-152-5487966

---

http://www.merton.com

Email: businessdept@merton.com

****

May 12, 20_ _

Iven Guo

Marketing Vice-President

M & S Leather Products Co. Ltd.

Zhenxing Industrial Zone

Shiling Town

Guangzhou, 510850

Guangdong

China

Dear Ms. Guo,

I have seen your products at China Import and Export Fair in April this year and am particularly interested in your high-fashion handbags in a variety of leathers.

We operate a quality retail business and are well connected with major dealers in the line of leather products in our region. Although our sales volume is not large, we obtain high prices for our goods.

Would you please send me a copy of your handbag catalog with details of your prices and payment terms? I would find it helpful if you could also supply samples of the various sample skins of which the handbags are made.

I look forward to hearing from you soon.

Yours sincerely,

Sandra Jones

Director of Import Dept.

Notes

1. China Import and Export Fair   中国进出口商品交易会，俗称广交会（Canton Fair），创办于 1957 年春季，每年春秋两季在广州举办，迄今已有五十余年历史，是中国目前历史最长、层次最高、规模最大、商品种类最全、到会客商最多、成交效果最好的综合性国际贸易盛会。自 2007 年 4 月第 101 届起，广交会更名为"中国进出口商品交易会"。

2. leather   n. 皮革

   leather shoes/gloves/belts   皮鞋/皮手套/皮带

3. operate vt. 经营，管理

They operate three factories and a huge warehouse.   他们管着三家工厂和一个大仓库。

operation n. 公司，（常用作复数）业务活动

a huge multinational electronics operation   一家大规模的跨国电子公司

be involved in building/banking/business operations   经营建筑业/银行业/商业

4. quality retail business   高档零售业

5. sales volume   销量，也可以说 volume of sales，如：

Our goal is to increase turnover to small and new customers, while still keeping the volume of sales to the large buyers.   我们的目标就是在保持对大客户的销量的同时，增加对中小客户的销量。

6. payment terms   付款方式，支付条件

7. sample skins   皮革样本

2. A Positive Reply to the First Inquiry

Background: 中国广州市的 M & S 皮革制品有限公司的营销副总裁回复英国 The Merton Shop 进口部经理 Sandra Jones 发来的首次询盘，并表示希望早日收到对方的订单。

M & S Leather Products Co., Ltd.

Zhenxing Industrial Zone, Shiling Town

Guangzhou, 510850, Guangdong, China

Tel: 86-20-22679984

Fax: 86-20-84698779

http://www.ms-leather.com

****

May 17, 20_ _

Ms. Sandra Jones

Director of Import Dept.

The Merton Shop

9 Green Street

Manchester, EC1A 1BB

England

Dear Ms. Jones,

Your inquiry of May 12 is receiving our attention. I am pleased to hear that you are interested in our products.

I am sending you a copy of our latest catalog under separate cover, together with samples of some of the skins we regularly use in manufacturing our products.

I regret to say that we cannot send you the full range of samples. You can be assured, however, that such skins as crocodile and sheep leather, though not included, are of the same high quality.

Mr. Alex Lin, our European Sales Manager, will be in the UK next week and will be pleased to call on you. He is authorized to discuss the terms of an order with you or to negotiate a contract. He will have with him a wide range of our products. When you see them, I think that you will agree that only the best quality materials are used, and that the high standard of workmanship will appeal to the most discriminating buyer.

We also manufacture a variety of leather belts and gloves in which you may be interested. They are fully illustrated in our catalog and are of the same high quality as our handbags. Mr. Lin will be able to show you examples when he calls.

I look forward to receiving an order from you soon.

Yours sincerely,
Iven Guo
Marketing Vice-President

Notes

1. receive one's attention   得到某人的重视、办理

   attention   n. 办理，处理

   Your inquiry of April 2 has been passed on to us for our attention.   贵方 4 月 2 日的询盘已转交我方处理。

   We believe our request will receive your immediate attention.   相信我方的请求会得到贵方及时的处理。

2. under separate cover   另函

   under cover   随函附寄

3. full range of   全套，也可以说 full set of

4. assure   vt. 使……确信，向……保证，主要有以下四种用法：

   assure sb of sth

   We assure you of our prompt delivery. 我们向贵方保证可以立即交货。

   assure sb that…

   We assure you that we shall do our best to expedite shipment. 请相信我们会尽快装运。

   be/rest assured of sth

   Please be assured of our large order. 请确信我方会大量订购。

   be/rest assured that…

   You may rest assured that we will contact you as soon as fresh supply becomes available. 请相信一俟我方有新的供货，我方即与贵方联系。

而拼写与 assure 类似的 ensure 的用法和 guarantee 相近：

ensure sb sth   保证某人获得某物

If you ensure us payment, we will forward them the shipment on D/P basis.   如果你们担保付款，我们将按照付款交单方式把这批货发运给他们。

ensure sb against sth   保证某人避免某事

His insurance ensured him against money loss in case of fire.   他投了保，以保证遭到火灾时不受经济损失。

ensure that…   保证……，确保……

They ensure that the goods will be packed in strong export cases.   他们保证货物要用坚固、适合出口货物的箱子包装。

5. crocodile and sheep leather   鳄鱼皮和绵羊皮

6. call on sb   拜访某人

    call at a place   拜访某地

    call at your office   拜访贵公司

7. be authorized to do sth   被授权做某事

    The board is also authorized to declare stock dividends.   董事会也有权决定股票分红。

    We are authorized to send your shipment by air express.   我方被授权以航空特快发运你方货物。

8. negotiate a contract   洽谈合同

9. workmanship   n. （工匠的）工艺，技术，也可以用 craftsmanship

10. appeal to   吸引

    appeal to the most selective buyer   吸引最挑剔的买主

11. discriminating   adj. 有鉴赏力的，有识别力的，敏锐的

12. illustrate   vt. 为某物做插图或图表

    illustrate a book   给书做插图

    a well-illustrated catalog   有精美插图的产品目录

3. An Inquiry for Baby Underwear

Background: 澳大利亚悉尼市的 Binton 贸易公司总经理 Henry Coacher 给中国天悦童装制造公司出口部经理 Tony Hu 发来电子邮件，对第 764 号儿童内衣进行询价。

From: henrycoacher12@yahoo.com

To: tonyhubusiness@tianyue.en.alibaba.com

Sent: Monday, December 11, 20_ _, 14:12 pm

Subject: Inquiry for Baby Underwear Model No. 764

Dear Mr. Hu,

We are glad to note from your email of December 12 that, as a manufacturer of Baby Apparel, you are also desirous of establishing direct business relations with us.

In order to acquaint ourselves with the quality and craftsmanship of your supplies, we have browsed your website: www.tianyue.com and studied your on-line products available for export. At present, we have great interest in Baby Underwear Model No. 764 suitable for 1-3 months' babies. We shall be pleased to receive from you by email all necessary information about the trade terms regarding the said goods, especially hoping you to quote us your lowest price, CIF Sydney, inclusive of our 3% commission, stating the earliest date of shipment and the term of packing as well as the discount if we order 3,000 pieces.

If your product quality can be satisfactory and your price and discount can compare favorably with those of other suppliers, we feel confident of placing a large order with you and we believe there is a promising future and long cooperation between us.

We are glad to receive your early reply.

Yours sincerely,
Henry Coacher
General Manager

Notes

1. baby apparel   童装
2. be desirous of sth/doing sth   渴望某事/做某事
   We are desirous of restoring relations between us.   我方渴望恢复双方的关系。
   desire   v. 渴望，盼望
   We desire to establish business relations with you.   我方渴望与贵方建立贸易关系。
3. supplies   n. 产品，货物，商品，也可以用 offers, offering
4. quote   vt. 报价
   用法是 quote sb a price for sth   向某人报某物的价格，如：
   Please quote us your lowest price for digital cameras.   请向我方报数码相机的最低价。
   其中，sb，a price，sth 都可以分别省略，即
   quote sb a price   向某人报价，如：
   Please quote us your lowest price.   请向我方报最低价。
   quote sb for sth   向某人报某产品的价，如：
   Please quote us for digital cameras.   请向我方报数码相机的价格。
   quote a price for sth   报某产品的价，如：
   Please quote your lowest price for digital cameras.   请报数码相机的最低价。
   quote for sth   报某产品的价，如：
   Please quote for digital cameras.   请报数码相机的价格。
7.　CIF (… named port of destination) = Cost, Insurance and Freight，成本加运费、保险费的缩写，后加目的港名称。按 CIF 术语成交，虽然由卖方安排货物运输和办理货运保险，

但卖方并不承担保证把货送到约定目的港的义务，因为 CIF 是属于装运交货的术语，而不是目的港交货的术语。另外两个常用价格术语为：FOB (… named port of shipment) 船上交货（指定装运港），习惯上称为装运港船上交货，俗称离岸价；CFR (… named port of destination)，成本加运费价。

8. commission　n. 佣金

inclusive of our 3% commission　包括我方 3%的佣金

draw/receive a commission of 5% on each sale　在每笔生意中抽取 5%的佣金

All prices are net without commission.　所有的价格都是不含佣金的净价。

commission agent　佣金商，代理商

佣金＝含佣价 X 佣金率

佣金＝含佣价－净价

佣金通常以英文字母 C 表示，比如每公吨 1000 美元 CFR 西雅图包含佣金 2%，可写成：每公吨 1000 美元 CFRC2 西雅图。其中的"C2"即表示佣金率为 2%。

9. date of shipment　装运期，还可以说 time of shipment, shipment time (date)

delivery date　交货期，还可以用 time (date) of delivery, delivery time

10. discount　n. 折扣

at 25% discount　打 75 折

discount of 30%　打 7 折

A 3% discount is already substantial.　3%的折扣已经不少了。

allow/give/make/grant sb …% discount　给予某人……%的折扣

They give 10% discount for cash payment.　如现金付款他们给予 10%的折扣。

cash discount　现金折扣，是企业为鼓励对方及时付款而给出的现金优惠。如果现金折扣表示为：2/10，1/20，N/30，则表示如果在 10 天内付款，则可以有 2%的现金折扣，如果在 20 天之内付款，则有 1%的现金折扣，如果在 30 天之内付款，则没有现金折扣。

11. compare favorably with　与……相比优惠

12. place an order with sb for sth　向某人订购某物

If your quotation is in line with the market, we intend to place an order with you for 5,000 sets. 如果贵方报价符合市价，我方欲向贵方订购五千台。

place a large order　大量订购

4.　A Positive Reply to the Inquiry for Baby Underwear with Quantity Discount

Background: 中国天悦童装制造公司出口部经理 Tony Hu 回复澳大利亚悉尼市的 Binton 贸易公司总经理 Henry Coacher 对第 764 号儿童内衣的询盘。为了吸引大客户、大订单，Tony Hu 表示 Binton 公司如能大量订购，可给予优惠。

From: tonyhubusiness@tianyue.en.alibaba.com

To: henrycoacher12@yahoo.com

Sent: Monday, December 11, 20＿＿, 16:22 pm

Subject: Re: Inquiry for Baby Underwear Model No. 764

Dear Mr. Coacher,

We are pleased to receive your email inquiry dated December 11, and thank you very much for your interest in our Baby Underwear Model No. 764 suitable for 1-3 months' babies.

In accordance with the instruction given in your inquiry, we attach our illustrated catalog, quotation CIF Sydney, inclusive of your 3% commission, our earliest date of shipment and the term of packing, from which you can see that our price is very competitive compared with those of other suppliers, and the quality as well as the style also has the competitive edge.

Thanks to our ample stocks, immediate dispatch is guaranteed. What's more, for a total purchase of no less than 4,000 pieces, we would grant 10% discount, and for a total purchase larger than 6,000 pieces, we would like to offer 20% special terms.

We look forward to receiving your order.

Yours sincerely,
Tony Hu
Export Manager

Notes

1. ample　adj. 丰富的，充足的
   ample stock　库存充裕
2. a total purchase　总订购量

5.　An Inquiry for Digital Photo Frames

Background: 在美国芝加哥举办的消费类电子产品展中，中国奥明电子产品进出口公司大中华区业务经理 Fred Johns 对美国 Dantex 有限公司的新型电子产品——电子相框很感兴趣，向该公司销售部发来电子邮件，对第 PX2331 号产品进行询价。

From: fjohns2pu@aomingelectro.com
To: marketingdept@dantex.com
Sent: Thursday, June 23, 20＿＿, 15:12 pm
Subject: Inquiry for Digital Photo Frames Model No. PX2331

Dear Sirs,

We were impressed by the selection of Digital Photo Frames that were displayed on your stand at the Consumer Electronics Exhibition that was held in Chicago last month. We find Model No. PX2331 is of particular interest to us.

We are a large chain of retailers in line of consumer electronics and looking for a manufacturer who could supply us with the subject products for the teenage market.

As we usually place very large orders，we would expect a quantity discount in addition to a 20% trade discount off net list prices，and our terms of payment are normally 30 days draft, documents against payment.

If these conditions interest you, you may receive orders for over 1,000 pieces at one time. Please give us your usual business terms concerning these goods.

We hope to hear from you soon.

Yours faithfully，
Fred Johns
China Trade Manager

Notes

1. the selection of sth   供选购的某物
   a shop with a huge selection of paperbacks   有大量平装书可供选购的书店
2. stand   n. 展位，摊位
3. consumer electronics   消费类电子产品，如电视机、影碟机、摄像机、组合音响、电话、个人电脑、家庭办公设备、家用电子保健设备、汽车电子产品、数码相机、手机
4. trade discount   商业折扣，同行折扣，批发折扣
   商业折扣是指企业根据市场供需情况，或针对不同的顾客，在商品标价上给予的扣除。商业折扣是企业最常用的促销方式之一。企业为了扩大销售、占领市场，对于批发商往往给予商业折扣，采用销量越多、价格越低的促销策略。
5. 30 days draft   30 天期的汇票，见票后 30 天付款的汇票
6. documents against payment   付款交单，分为两种：即期付款交单（D/P at sight）是指买方应凭卖方开具的即期跟单汇票，于见票时立即付款，付款后交单；远期付款交单（D/P after sight）是指买方对卖方开具的见票后××天付款的跟单汇票，于提示时应即予承兑，并应于汇票到期日即付款，付款后交单。

6. A Negative Reply to the Inquiry for Digital Photo Frames

Background: 美国 Dantex 有限公司销售部经理 Marco Grassi 回复中国奥明电子产品进出口公司大中华区业务经理 Fred Johns 对第 PX2331 号电子相框的询盘。由于该产品已经脱销，为赢得商机，Marco Grassi 劝说对方改订替代品。

From: marketingdept@dantex.com
To: fjohns2pu@aomingelectro.com
Sent: Thursday, June 23, 20＿＿, 16:10 pm

Subject: Re: Inquiry for Digital Photo Frames Model No. PX2331

Dear Mr. Johns,

Referring to your email of June 23, in which you inquire about our Digital Photo Frames Model No. PX2331. We appreciate your interest but we regret that we are unable to supply it for the moment.

The reason is that the product you demand has been out of stock due to its superior quality and reasonable price as well as its powerful functions. However, we are confident that another new Model No. PX2379 is a perfect replacement, whose quality and specification are greatly improved and are also enjoying best sales. We are sure that you will find a ready sale for this excellent product.

We have sent you the price list, illustrated catalog in the attachment.

We look forward to your favorable reply and long-term business cooperation with you.

Yours sincerely,
Marco Grassi
Sales & Marketing Manager

Notes

1. out of stock　脱销，无存货
2. replacement　n. 替代品，替换物
3. specification　n. 规格，尺寸

Unit 5　Sales Promotion
推　销　信

背景知识

1. "AIDA" Formula

Sales promotion plays an important part in the sales process. Some of the functions include identifying new prospects, responding to inquiries, following up on sales calls, acknowledging an order, problem solving and getting repeat business. The winning sales promotion can succeed by following the AIDA formula, which stands for "Attention, Interest, Desire and Action."

1.1 Inviting Buyers' Attention

First, the sales promotion must get the buyers' attention with an effective lead paragraph that goes straight to the point or offers an element of intrigue. There are two common approaches that work well.

(1) Open with an intriguing question or statement that grabs the buyers' attention and compels him or her to read on. Here are some examples:

Is there a power to complete multiple projects on time and on budget? (For Project Management Software)

I'm writing to you about your husband. (For insurance if the husband dies.)

(2) Open with a list of 5 or 6 benefits, with the biggest benefit put at first and others followed in an order of declining importance. Here's the template:

> *How would you like to...*
>> *Biggest benefit*
>> *2nd biggest benefit*
>> *3rd biggest benefit*
>> *and so on . . .*

1.2 Arousing Buyers' Interest

Hook the reader's interest. This is usually a clear statement of the buyers' problems, needs or wants. What's new? What's in it for the buyer? Bear in mind that the buyer isn't interested in the seller or seller's products. They are interested in what the seller can do for them. Here is an example:

For enterprises with sales of more than $1 billion, a best-in-class IT Asset Management program could yield $7 million savings annually, based on an IT budget of $50 to $60 million.

1.3 Creating Buyers' Desire

The sales promotion should create a desire, the desire to eliminate or minimize the potential for future loss or the desire to gain something (prestige, more time, more profits, etc.). Provide a compelling reason to buy from the seller instead of the seller's competitors. It's a unique advantage customers get only if they buy from the seller.

Another importance is trust. Make buyers trust the seller by providing field tests or studies of the seller's product, the long business history the seller's company has been for, the fame the seller's brand enjoys, the seller's guarantee, favorable comments from current customers and from those on the seller's client list.

1.4 Leading to Buyers' Action

Last but most important, the sales promotion must have a call to action. The seller must ask the buyers to do the action that the seller wants, whether it is to buy or to click on a website. Explain how to do it and make it so easy for them to do so (as many payment methods as possible). For Example:

*Don't delay. Take advantage of this **Special Price Offer**. Call **NOW** to place your order or complete the coupon below and send your order by email, fax or postal mail **TODAY**!*

2. The Use of P.S. at the end of the Sales Promotion

Sometimes, it is of help to use a P.S. (postscript) in sales promotion and restate the seller's most power benefit and sales offer in it. Most people will read a P.S. first before reading the sales promotion, so it is important to make P.S. have a very strong sales message and a call to action.

3. The Writing Style of the Sales Promotion

Use a friendly conversational style when writing a sales promotion letter. Do not try to use large words or try to impress the prospects with good command of the English language. Instead, write a sales promotion letter as if the seller were talking to his best friend.

推销信写作步骤

1. Inviting Buyers' Attention
2. Arousing Buyers' Interest
3. Creating Buyers' Desire
4. Leading to Buyers' Action

推销信常用语句

1. Inviting Buyers' Attention

- Thank you for your time on my email and I'm dropping in to try to find the opportunity for us to work together.

  感谢您阅读我的电子邮件。拜访贵方是想寻求双方合作的机会。

- For half a century, ABC Company has been a leading manufacturer of office equipment in North Europe.

  半个世纪以来 ABC 公司都是北欧地区办公设备制造商的领先者。

- I am an independent financial "lifestyle" coach. In this position my responsibility is to give you the best financial and life planning advice possible so you make the best financial choices based on your life goals.

  我是一名独立的金融理财师。我的职责是给您提供最佳的理财和生活规划建议，以便您能根据自己的生活目标，做出最佳的理财选择。

- If you have been thinking about selling your commercial property, or you have been considering investing in additional commercial properties, we want the opportunity to talk with you.

  如果您一直在考虑卖掉自己的商业财产，或考虑投资另一份商业财产，请与我们联系。

- How would you like to receive (the first benefit) and (the second benefit)? Read on! This might be the most important letter you ever receive.

  您如何才能得到（好处一）和（好处二）？请继续读下去。这可能是您收到过的最重要的信了。

- Do not buy this product elsewhere unless it has these features:

  除非这种产品有这些优点，否则不要在它处购买该产品。

- Can your typist turn out 500 perfect copies an hour?

  您公司的打字员能每小时打 500 份准确无误的文件吗？

- Sure, others will try to sell you a product of lesser quality, but can they offer you: …?

  当然其他卖家将会销售质次的产品，但他们能够给您提供……吗？

2. Arousing Buyers' Interest

- Sound too good to be true? I thought so when I first learned about…

  听起来太棒了而不像是真的？当我第一次听说……时，也是这么想的。

- I know this sounds outrageous. I'd be skeptical too.

  我知道这个听起来太不可思议了。我也很怀疑。

- Yes, that's fact! All this will be done within 8 minutes.

  是的，这是真的！所有的一切都会在 8 分钟内完成。

- Do these results sound unbelievable? I thought so too, but then…

  这些结果听起来令人难以置信？我一开始也这么认为，但是然后……

- But the more I learned about…, the more I knew that I should give it a try. Here's why you should too…

  但是我了解……越多，我就越认为该试一试。这些是您也应该试一试的理由……

- No one can match this offer.

  此产品独一无二。

- You'll get over ten times your money's worth in value! Guaranteed!

  保证您能获得十倍之多的超值享受！

- Extraordinary savings (quality, add-on products, longevity, warranty, etc.)!

  超值的节省（品质、附件、使用寿命及保修等）！

- We offer you unbelievable quality for only one-tenth the usual price.

  我们的产品质量优异但价格只是同类产品的十分之一。

- You may ask how we can possibly do all this. Here's how…

  您可能会问我们是如何做到所有这些的。原因是……

3. Creating Buyers' Desire

- Buy completely at our own risk…

  您购买，我们承担……的风险。

- You pay nothing unless you are totally satisfied.

  使用满意后再付钱。

- There is no risk with our complete satisfaction, money-back guarantee!

  我们保证让您完全满意，否则退款，您没有任何风险。

- No questions asked. Simply return the product within 30 days and we'll refund your money in full.

  不提任何问题。只要在购买之日起 30 天内退货，我们将全额退款。

- Remember, you keep the free bonus. Even if you decide to take advantage of our No Risk, Total Satisfaction, Money-back Guarantee, the bonus are yours to keep—our gift to you for simply trying our…

  记着，您可以留着这份赠品。即使您决定利用我们的零风险、完全满意及退款保证，这份赠品仍是您的——这是我们给您的小礼物，以便您能试用我们……

- Besides the remarkable cost-effectiveness, to choose ABC, you will also enjoy:

  A complete range of series products to select from;

  Up-to-date technical upgrades and updates;

  24 hours post-sales service support from our strong tech-support team.

  除了可以显著地降低成本，选择 ABC，您将同时得到：

  可供选择的全套系列产品；

  最新的技术更新；

  我们强大的技术支持团队带来的 24 小时售后服务支持。

- For an old customer like you, we are willing to allow a 15% commission on each machine, plus a special discount of 5% on all orders received before the end of next month.

  对于您这样的老客户，我们愿意每一台机器给 15%佣金。此外，对于在下月底前收到的订单，我们还给予 5%的特别折扣。

- Although costs have been rising steadily since last month, we have not yet raised our prices, but may have to do so when present stocks run out.

  尽管从上月起成本已经不断上涨，但是我们还没有提价，但不排除库存清空后有调价的可能。

- But you don't have to take my word for it. Here's what our satisfied customers are saying.

  但是您可以不相信我所说的。以下是我们客户所说的。

4. Leading to Buyers' Action

- So, why not give my service a try? I know you will be very pleased with how I will help you, and if for any reason you are not pleased, you have lost nothing.

  所以，为什么不试试我的服务？我的服务肯定能让您满意。而且即便您不满意，您也不会有任何损失。

- If you have any question or want more information, please feel free to contact me.

  如果您有任何疑问或需要详情，请与我联系。

- For more information, or to schedule a time for us to meet, please call me at (123) 456-7890 or email me at…. I look forward to meeting with you.

  欲得到更多的信息，或安排时间与我见面，请给我打电话（123）456－7890，或给我发电子邮件……。期待与您见面。

- If you want to experience the same outstanding results as our other clients, please call us today for a free, no-obligation consultation.

  如果您想体验其他客户得到的卓越服务，请今天就给我们打电话，我们将免费提供无约束力的报价。

- Just give me a call at 89845155 for more detailed information.

  如您需要更详尽的信息，请拨打 89845155 进行咨询。

- For a free quote, please call us today at 800-600-568 or visit us online at www.furniture.com. Our website has many pictures of the office furniture we have in stock. Our website also shows our current specials.

  如果想免费查询有关价格的信息，您可以拨打电话 800-600-568 或者访问我们的网站 www.furniture.com。我们的网站上有产品的图样和当前的促销产品。

- Order today and I'll send you… — a $50 value! But remember, I am offering this free bonus for a limited time… so order now!

  今天就订购，我将寄送给您价值 50 美元的……！但请记住，我只在……有限的时间里给您该赠品。所以现在就订购吧！

- For more information please go to our website at www.abc-textile.com.

  如您需要更多信息，请访问我们的网站 www.abc-textile.com。

- We await your order with great interest.

  我们期盼您的订单。

写作范例

1.　A Sales Promotion for the Announcement of Catalog Price Reductions

Background: James Laver 经理给客户 Bonnie Tyler 小姐发去电子邮件，告知产品目录中某些产品开始促销，希望对方及早订购。

From: laver_james@ghhs.com

To: tylerhers34@hotmail.com

Date: Tuesday, July 12, 20__, 11: 32 am

Subject: Catalog Price Reductions

Dear Miss Bonnie Tyler,

This is my favorite kind of email. How many emails have I had to write over the years advising you of a price increase? Why, you ask, am I so happy? Read on!

This is to advise you that, for a limited period of time, we are reducing prices on certain items in our catalog.

Take a moment to review the attached catalog. I have circled in red ink the items that are temporarily reduced. What an opportunity!

Please take advantage of these prices. If you wish to order large quantities, give me a call and we will try to work out mutually acceptable terms and conditions.

In any event, get your order in, as these prices are only in effect until 30 July, 20__.

I do enjoy writing this type of email. Thank you in advance for your order.

Yours very sincerely,

James Laver

Manager

Notes

1.　mutually　adv. 互相地，共同地

2.　in any event　无论如何，还可以说 in any case, at any rate, at all events

3.　be in effect　有效

2. A Sales Promotion for Providing Services to Save 75% - 80% on Office Systems Furniture

Background: Shine 办公室装修设计公司的市场营销部经理 Jane Manton 向新客户 Pat Duggan 先生介绍公司的服务内容，并建议对方查询公司网站，以获得更多信息。

From: mantoncom1995@shineofficeinteriors.com
To: dugganfhs231@sdu.com
Date: Monday, November 23, 20_ _, 9: 48 am
Subject: Services to Save 75%-80% on Office Systems Furniture

Dear Mr. Duggan,

Shine Office Interiors wants to help your business save up to 80% on office systems furniture. We specialize in refurnished and secondhand name-brand workstations including Haworth, Herman Miller and Steelcase. Why pay full price for new workstations when you can get beautiful professional-quality secondhand and refurnished systems furniture at up to 80% off?

As a full service dealer we have products and services to help you design, furnish and install workstations, reception areas and conference rooms. We are networked with wholesalers and distributors throughout the U.S. to offer you an extensive range of products to meet all of your needs and at a price that is guaranteed to fit your budget. And, we will personally deliver and install your office furniture for you so your project is done correctly, on-time and on-budget.

For a free quotation, please call us today at 1-800-000-0000 or visit us online at www. shineofficeinteriors.com. Our website has many pictures of the office furniture we have in stock. Our website also shows our current specials. If you want an amazing deal, check out our website.

We also buy used workstations and office furniture. If you have office furniture you want to sell, we would love the opportunity to bid on it. We work with dealers throughout the United States and Canada who will offer you top dollar for your used office furniture. For more information, please call us at 1-800-000-0000.

Warmest Wishes,

Yours very sincerely,
Jane Manton
Marketing Manager

P.S. Through the month of December we are having a storewide liquidation sale on **ALL** office furniture so we can make room for our 20_ _ inventory. This is your opportunity to actually steal furniture from us. Call or email me today for a copy of our most up-to-date inventory and price list.

Notes

1. refurnished   adj. 翻新的，重新设计的
2. name-brand   adj. 名牌的，知名品牌的
3. workstation   n. 办公设备
4. distributor   n. 经销商
5. budget   n. 经费，预算
6. special   n. 特价商品
7. bid on/for sth   对某物出价
   She bid US$500 for the painting.   她出 500 美元买这幅画。
8. storewide liquidation sale   全店清仓甩卖
9. inventory   n. 库存，存货

3. An Email Requesting for a Demonstration

Background: 方正电脑公司的业务经理 James Qiao 向一名老客户发去电子邮件，推销一款激光打印机，并希望预约，以演示机器的性能。

From: jamesqiao@foundercomputer.com
To: dickenshappy@alibaba.com
Date: Thursday, December 2, 20＿＿, 10: 45 am
Subject: Demonstration of Founder Laser Printer

Dear Mr. Dickens,

As a Founder Personal Computer user, you have learned how rich a range of functions it performs.

Now we can offer you a high-speed laser printer that gives your work the appearance of expensive typeset copy. Letters, manuals, instructions, catalogs, price lists—all can be printed directly by the Founder PC, and one can save on such printing jobs.

Would you kindly give me thirty minutes to show you the versatility of this new printer to do the work you need done? I will call you at the beginning of next week to set up a mutually convenient appointment.

Sincerely yours,
James Qiao
Business Director

Notes

1. manual   n. 使用手册，用户指南
2. instruction   n. 使用说明书

3. versatility   n. 多功能性

4. A Sales Promotion for Women's Wallets and Key Cases

Background: Dunhill 公司的推销部经理 Andrea Coates 给多位顾客发去信函，推销公司的产品，并随函附寄皮革样品。

Dear Madam,

Have you ever felt anything quite as soft and quite as strong?

Believe it or not, this enclosed sample of the leather used in our new Dunhill women's wallets and key cases will offer you such a feeling.

Give a touch to the sample and you will find that the leather our manufacturer is going to use is just as soft as a piece of cloud. But top quality leather is only one feature of the new Dunhill; style is another, which won this year's National Fashion Award for its gentleness and elegance. Wherever you go with it, you may be sure that your Dunhill wallet and key case will draw attention (perhaps even envy) from your lunch or dinner partners.

In addition, the Dunhill wallet has plenty of room for currency, photos, credit cards, and it even has a secret compartment for haven-knows-what. As for the key case, it is slim, smart and easily accommodates eight keys. For your information, both the wallets and key cases are designed in a variety of colors available in camel, white, navy blue, brown and black.

As a result of the recognition, it is not surprising that this fashion line of our wallets and key cases are being sold by all the top department stores in our country and have also been accepted by many dealers from European markets.

Complete the order form and return it right now. We trust that your trial order may convince you that this 85-dollar wallet and key case set is of excellent value. You will receive a bottle of foam cream (leather clean) as a gift if you let us have your preference by sending the complete order form before August 25.

Yours faithfully,
Andrea Coates
Promotional Manger
Dunhill Leather Products Co., Ltd.

Notes

1. key case   钥匙套

2.   compartment   n. 隔断

3.   haven-knows-what   秘密

4.   smart   adj. 可爱的

5.   accommodate   vt. 容纳

The CD-ROMs will accommodate the works of all English poets from 600 to 1900.   这些光盘能存下从公元 600 年到 1900 年所有英国诗人的作品。

6.   navy blue   海蓝

7.   foam clean (leather clean)   皮革清洗剂

5.   A Sales Promotion Email for a Voice Recorder

Background: Newsmy 数码产品经销商 Jane Manton 向一名老客户发去电子邮件，推销一款录音笔，并表示可以预约上门演示。

From: janesales@newsmydigital.com

To: robertswork@macmachine.com

Date: Wednesday, October 15, 20＿＿, 11: 00 am

Subject: An Amazing Product for You—Newsmy Voice Recorder!

Dear Mr. Roberts,

Have you ever thought how much time your typist wastes in taking down your words? It can be as much as a forth of the time he spends on working. Why not record your words—on our Newsmy—and save this time for other jobs he can be doing while speaking is in progress?

You will be surprised how little it costs. For fifty-two weeks in the year your Newsmy works hard for you, without lunch breaks or holidays. You can't even give it too much to do. And all for less than an average month's salary for a secretary! It will take your dictation at any time, and anywhere—after office hours, at home, or even while you are traveling. It does away with mis-transcriptions in short-hand and can even do away all together with typewriting since Newsmy can play the recorded messages.

The Newsmy is efficient, dependable, time-saving and economical. It is backed by our international reputation for reliability, is in regular use in thousands of offices all over the world. It gives superb reproduction quality—every syllable as clear as a bell. It is unbelievably easy to use. You just insert a pre-loaded memory card, press a button, and your Newsmy is ready to record dictation, instructions, reviews, telephone conversations or whatever you will say. Nothing could be simpler or more efficient. Our unique after-sales service contract ensures lasting operation at the peak of efficiency.

Some of your business partners are sure to be using Newsmy. Ask them about it before you place an order; or fill in the attached card if you prefer, and we will arrange for our sales representative for your area, to give you a call and a demonstration. Just state a day and time.

With best regards.

Jane Manton
Sales Director

Notes

1. in progress   正在进行中

   The construction of that new state highway is now in progress.   那条新的州高速公路的建设现在正在进行中。

   Improvement work in progress, please come to visit us again later!   网页改善工程进行中，请日后再来浏览。谢谢!

2. dictation   n. 口授，听写，口述内容

   The new secretary takes dictation very well.   那位新秘书善于记录口授。

   The letter was by Mr. Moy's dictation.   信是莫埃先生口授的。

3. do away with   取消，去掉，废除

   The long-range goal for us must be to do away with all high-cost and low-efficient product range.   我们的远期目标必须是取消高成本低效率的产品系列。

   They decided to do away with the rule.   他们决定取消这一规定。

4. transcription   n.（根据录音或笔记整理的）笔录本，文字本

5. short-hand   速记

   She's taking the letter at her boss' dictation in short-hand.   她正在用速记方法记录老板的口述信件。

   For the administrative assistant to an executive, short-hand and typing skills will be required.   高级管理人员的行政助理需要速记和打字技能。

6. back   v. 支持，赞助

   Their investment plan was backed by the government.   他们的投资计划得到了政府支持。

7. superb reproduction quality   一流的放音效果

8. as clear as a bell   十分清楚的

   The tool manual is as clear as a bell.   这份工具手册十分清楚，容易看懂。

9. memory card   记忆卡

10. We will arrange for our sales representative for your area, to give you a call and a demonstration.   负责该地区的销售代表会给您致电并上门提供样品演示。

Unit 6　Offer

报　盘

1.　Definition of an Offer

Making an offer is a very important step in the international business. An offer is a proposal to supply goods on stipulated terms made by offerer (seller) to offeree (buyer) in order to enter a contract. It is often a reply to an inquiry, but it is also made even if no inquiries are received from abroad. In the latter case, sellers may make offers or quotations voluntarily according to the existing supply and market situations of the commodity. An offer includes trading terms put forward by offerers to offerees, on which the offerers are willing to conclude business with the offerees. These terms mainly include name of commodity, brand, specifications, quantity, price, packing, payment and shipment, etc.

2.　Types of Offers

There are two kinds of offers. One is firm offer, and the other is non-firm offer.

A firm offer is a definite expression that the offerer is ready to close, within the stipulated time, business with the offeree on the terms and conditions put forward. It is irrevocable and unchangeable. The offerer can not cancel, change, or revise the terms and conditions as he pleases. Once the offer is accepted by the offeree without any reverse, the business is done. Therefore, when making firm offers, the offerer should first state clearly that it is not a non-firm but firm offer. Then, he should highlight the date of validity which is subject to the time (the offerer's time zone) of receiving the offeree's reply, not to the time of sending out the acceptance.

A non-firm offer is a non-undertaking expression of the offerer who is not bound by the terms and conditions listed. The content of a non-firm offer is not so completed as that of a firm offer. It has no term of validity, but often with the remark:

This offer is subject to our final confirmation. (此报盘以我方最后确认为准。)

This offer is subject to prior sale. (此报盘有权先售。)

This offer is subject to being unsold. (此报盘以货物未售出为准。)

This offer is on approval. (此报盘买方看货后再订。)

报盘写作步骤

1. Expressing Thanks for the Inquiry and the Validity if the Offer is Firm
2. Stating the Business Terms and Conditions
3. Hoping to Receive an Order

报盘常用语句

1. Expressing Thanks for the Inquiry and the Validity if the Offer is Firm

Quotation

● In accordance with the request of your Mr. Smith at Guangzhou Fair, we are honored to send you samples and a price list for our products.

根据贵公司史密斯先生在广交会上的要求，我们很荣幸在此给您寄上一些有关我方产品的样品和报价单。

● We understand that there is a good demand for soybeans in your market, and take this opportunity of attaching our quotation for your consideration.

我方了解到贵方市场对黄豆的需求强劲。我方借此良机附上我方报价单，供您参考。

● We thank you for your Inquiry List No. 303 and enclose our Quotation Sheet No. 104 for the captioned goods.

感谢贵方第 303 号询价单。兹随函附寄第 104 号标题项下商品的报价单。

● We thank you for your inquiry of January 5 and are sending you, under separate cover, a sample of leather shoes together with our price sheet.

谢谢贵方 1 月 5 日的询盘，另函寄上我方的价格单和皮鞋样品。

● We have learned that there is a good demand for walnut meat in your market, and take this opportunity of enclosing our Quotation Sheet No. 345 for your consideration.

我方获悉贵方市场对核桃仁的需求很大，现随函附寄第 345 号报价表供参考。

Non-firm Offer

● We welcome your inquiry of July 11 and thank you for your interest in our products. In reply, we are glad to making you, without engagement/obligation, the following offer:

感谢贵方 7 月 11 日的询价及对我方产品感兴趣。兹回复询价，我方报虚盘如下：

● We wish to state that our quotations are subject to alteration without notice and to our confirmation at the time of placing your orders.

我方报价如有变更，恕不另行通知。贵方订购时，以我方确认为准。

● As requested, we are offering you the following subject to our final confirmation.

根据贵方的要求，现我方就如下货物向贵方报价，以我方最后确认为准。

- The supply is limited and no further notice will be given for any change in price at any time.
  供货有限，我方报价会随时变动而不另行通知。

- The offer is made without engagement and all orders will be subject to our written acceptance.
  此报盘无约束力，所有订货将以我方书面接受为准。

- All prices in the price lists are subject to our confirmation.
  报价单中所有的价格以我方最后确认为准。

Firm Offer & Validity

- In reply to your inquiry of… we are giving/making/sending you an offer as follows, subject to your reply here/reaching us by 5 p.m., our time/Beijing time, Tuesday, August 2.
  兹回复贵方 X 月 X 日的询价，我方报盘如下，以北京时间 8 月 2 日周二下午 5 点前收到贵方答复为有效。

- Provided we receive your order by May 15, we make you a firm offer for delivery by the end of June at the prices quoted.
  若在 5 月 15 日前收到贵方订单，我方将按报价发 6 月底前交货的实盘。

- We are enclosing a proposal on the equipment we discussed, along with the specification sheet. The prices offered are good for 20 days from today unless otherwise specified.
  随函附寄商讨的设备的报价及规格表。除非另有规定，报价自今日起 20 天内有效。

- This offer will remain firm until the end of the month, beyond which date the terms and prices should be discussed anew.
  实盘有效期至本月底，此日期之后的条款及价格需重新商讨。

- This offer will remain/be effective/valid/firm/open/available/good until…
  该报盘有效期至……

- This offer is open for a week from…
  该报盘自……起一周内有效。

- The offer is good only for acceptance reaching us before the end of this month.
  此报盘以贵方在本月底之前接受并送达我方为有效。

- This offer must be withdrawn if not accepted within five days.
  如 5 日内不接受，则该盘撤销。

- At your request, we now keep this firm offer open for a further ten days from May 13.
  应要求，此实盘有效期自 5 月 13 日起再延长 10 天。

2. Stating the Business Terms and Conditions

Commodity

- All items for which we have quoted are made of very best quality leather and can be supplied in a range of designs and colors wide enough to meet your clients' requirement.
  所报商品均用优质皮革制成且有多种设计及颜色，相信可以满足贵方客户的要求。

- As you know, all kinds of patterns are made of cashmere, which are very beautiful and colorful.
  贵方已了解，所有的款式均由羊绒制成，设计美观且颜色鲜艳。

Price

- We offer these goods at a very special price of US$50 per piece.

  兹以每件 50 美元的优惠价格报价。

- We would like to help you to reach a decision by offering you a special reduction of 20% on all the products in our catalog.

  本公司愿将目录中所有产品提供两成的优惠折扣给予贵方，以助于您达成订购的决定。

- We are making you an offer for 500 dozen Men's Shirts at USD 80.00 per dozen CIFC5 San Francisco for shipment in May.

  我方现向你方报 500 打男式衬衫，每打 80 美元 CIF 旧金山价，包括 5% 的佣金，5 月装运。

- According to the price in the international market and our production cost, the price of 50 tons of aluminum sheets is US$800 per metric ton CIF Rotterdam.

  根据国际市场行情和我们的生产成本，这 50 吨铝板的价格是：鹿特丹成本加运保费价每公吨 800 美元。

- Please note that all our prices are quoted on CIF basis. This is our general practice which, we trust, will be acceptable to you.

  请注意我方所有报价均为 CIF 价。这也是我方的惯例，相信贵方可以接受。

- All quotations, except firm offers, are subject to the Seller's final confirmation. Unless otherwise stated or agreed upon, all prices are net without any discount.

  除了实盘，所有报价均由卖方最后确认为准。除非另有规定或达成一致，所有价格均为不含佣金的净价。

- The prices quoted are closely calculated and considerably moderate. Since these articles are best-selling in European markets thanks to their superior quality, considerable business has been done with other customers at these prices.

  我方报价是经过精确计算而且相当合适的。由于产品质量优异，在欧洲市场上十分畅销，我们已按此价与其他客户达成可观的交易。

- The prices are subject to change at the end of the month because there is every indication that the cost of materials is rising.

  价格月底会有变动，因为原材料的成本可能上涨。

- The price we quoted is accurately calculated, but in order to encourage business, we are prepared to allow you a discount of 4%.

  此报价经过仔细计算，但为了促进交易，我方打算给予 4% 的折扣。

Payment

- Our terms are cash on delivery.

  我方的付款方式是货到付款。

- Payment is to be made by confirmed, irrevocable L/C payable by draft at sight to be opened 30 days before the time of shipment.

  付款方式为装船期前 30 天开立的保兑的、不可撤销的凭即期汇票支付的信用证。

- We accept terms of payment by D/P at 30 days' sight.

  我方接受见票 30 天后付款交单。

- Payment: 30% T/T + 70% T/T against the copy of B/L
  支付：30%前 T/T（作定金），70%后 T/T，见提单副本付款
- Payment: 30% T/T + 70% irrevocable L/C at sight
  支付：电汇 30%为定金，其余 70%用不可撤销即期信用证
- Payment: 50% T/T +50% T/T against the copies of documents
  支付：50%前 T/T，50%后 T/T，见单据副本付款
- Deposit is 30% of total value; the balance should be paid before shipment.
  预付 30%，余款交货前付清。

Shipment & Delivery

- Shipment is to be made/effected in May.
  5 月装运。
- The goods will be shipped in August/September, 2011.
  货物将在 2011 年 8 月或 9 月装运。
- Shipment is to be made within one month upon receipt of relevant L/C.
  收到相关信用证后一个月内装运。
- We will deliver the goods within 30 days after receipt of your L/C but specific time is to be fixed upon receipt of your official order.
  我们将在收到你方信用证后 30 天内装运，但具体的时间要在收到你方的正式订单后再定。
- Shipment is to be made in three equal monthly installments beginning from August.
  货物从 8 月开始按月分三批等量装运。

Packing

- Packing charges are included in the price, and we can make delivery whenever you wish.
  此价已含包装费，可按贵方要求随时交货。
- The goods are packed in bales or in wooden cases at seller's option.
  货物由卖方决定装入捆包或木箱内。
- The goods are to be packed in boxes of one piece each, twenty boxes to a carton.
  货物用盒子装，每盒装一件，20 盒装一纸箱。
- The goods are to be packed in polybags of 2 kg, 20 polybags to a carton.
  货物用塑料袋装，每袋装 2 千克，20 袋装一纸箱。
- The goods are packed in strong wooden crates.
  货物装入结实的木板条箱。

Insurance

- Insurance is to be covered by the seller for 110% of the invoice value against All Risks and War Risk.
  卖方按照发票金额 110%投保一切险和战争险。
- Insurance is to be effected by the Buyer.
  保险由买方办理。

3. Hoping to Receive an Order

● We are sure that these goods will meet your requirements, and we look forward to your early order.

相信货物能满足贵方要求，期盼早日收到贵方订单。

● If you find our proposal acceptable, please confirm by return. We look forward to the pleasure of serving you.

若贵方接受我方报价，请回执确认。期待为您服务。

● We think we have covered every point of your inquiry. If not, please do not hesitate to email us again. It will be a pleasure to give you an immediate reply.

相信我方已全面回复贵方的询价。如有疑问，请发电子邮件。我方很乐意立即回复。

● We are allowing special terms to customers who place order before the end of this month.

在月底前订购将有优惠。

● We trust the above offer will be of interest to you and await your orders.

相信贵方会对上述订单感兴趣，期待您的订单。

● We trust you will find our quotation satisfactory and look forward to receiving your order.

相信贵方会对我方报价满意，期盼收到贵方的订单。

● We would advise you to place an order immediately as there is every indication that a great advance will shortly take place.

建议贵方立即订购，因为所有迹象都显示，价格即将急速上涨。

● In view of the heavy demand for this line and our quantity is limited, we advise you to order at once.

由于该产品系列的需求旺盛，且我方的数量有限，建议贵方早日订购。

写 作 范 例

1. A Non-firm Offer for Woolen Mixed Embroidered Scarf

Background: 尼泊尔加德满都市某纺织品公司销售经理 Amogh Dhakhwa 回复中国天津某贸易公司对羊毛混纺手绣围巾的询盘，报虚盘。

From: amogh_dhakhwa@alibaba.com
To: wangvictor@alibaba.com
Date: Wednesday, August 23, 20__, 11: 44 am
Subject: Re: Inquiry for Woolen Mixed Embroidered Scarf No. 55

Dear Mr. Wang,

We thank you for your inquiry of August 21 and are pleased to inform you that the item listed in your inquiry is in stock. We are glad to send you our offer for the goods you required as follows:

Commodity: "Reeta" Brand Woolen Mixed Embroidered Scarf No. 55

Place of Origin: Nepal

Material: 70% wool and 30% acrylics

Size: available in various customized sizes

Weight: 2lbs

Color: yellow, brown, green, red assortment

Supply Ability: 1,000 pcs per day

Minimum Order Quantity: 10,000 pcs

Price: US$ 35.00 per piece CIF Xingang

Delivery: 4 weeks after receipt of L/C

Payment: 70% by irrevocable, confirmed Letter of Credit payable by draft at sight opened through the Bank of China, Tianjin Branch, and D/P based on 30% payment in advance

Packing: PVC bag

Discount: on orders for 1,500 pieces or more, we allow a special discount of 4%.

The offer is subject to our final confirmation as the prevailing price in the international market is fluctuating.

The item is of high quality and has enjoyed a good reputation in the North America area. We have got many repeat orders from our customers in Canada and U.S. Of course, the price offered is also very competitive. You may be assured that our products will be also marketable in your area.

By the way, please inform us when you will come to Kathmandu, so that we can arrange the accommodation and timetable for your visit to our factory.

We are looking forward to receiving your order.

Yours sincerely,

Amogh Dhakhwa

Sales Manager

Notes

1. 动词 quote 与 offer 的区别

   (1) 从内容多少上来看，前者往往只含商品、价格、数量，而后者指报盘，除价格外，还包括品名、规格、数量、包装、装运、付款方式等。

   (2) 从约束力大小来看，offer 较固定，卖方价格报出后，一般不能轻易变动，而 quote 则不同，卖方报价后，不受约束，可根据情况略加调整。

   (3) 从用法结构来看：

   quote sb a price for sth   向某人报某产品的……价

offer (sb) (sth)　（向某人）（发某产品的）报盘

make sb an offer (a price) (for sth)　（向某人）（发某产品……价的）报盘

如：请向我方报 5000 辆男式自行车纽约成本加运保费最低价。

Please quote us the lowest price, CIF New York, for 5,000 Men's Bicycles.

Please offer us 5,000 Men's Bicycles (on) CIF New York (basis).

Please make us an offer CIF New York for 5,000 Men's Bicycles.

offer sb　向某人报盘

We will offer you upon receipt of your inquiry. 一俟收到贵方的询盘，我方即（向贵方）报盘。

offer sth　对某物报盘

We can offer walnuts at much lower prices. 我方能以低得多的价格发核桃的报盘。

2. be in stock　有货，有库存

   be out of stock　无货

   supply (the goods) from stock　供现货

   be in short supply　缺货

3. quotation　n. 报价

   send/give/make sb a quotation for sth　向某人报某物的价

   You may rest assured that we have sent you our most favorable quotation for the radio sets.　请确信我方已向贵方报收音机的最优惠价。

4. woolen mixed embroidered scarf　混纺手绣围巾

5. place of origin　原产地

6. acrylics　n. 晴纶，学名为丙烯酸树脂

7. customized　adj.（按照客户的意思）订制的，改制的

   customized dressing　高级订制礼服

   customized T-shirt　改制的 T 恤

8. lb.是重量单位 pound 的缩写，复数是 lbs.

9. assortment　n. 花色，种类

10. pc.是 piece 的缩写，pieces 的缩写是 pcs.

11. by irrevocable, confirmed Letter of Credit payable by draft at sight opened through the Bank of China, Tianjin Branch　由中国银行天津分行开立的不可撤销的、保兑的、凭即期汇票支付的信用证

    Letter of Credit　信用证，常缩写为 L/C

    即期信用证　a sight L/C，或 an L/C at sight

    即期信用证又可以称为凭即期汇票支付的信用证　an L/C payable by (payable against, available by) draft at sight

    远期信用证　a usance (time, term) L/C

    见票后 30 天议付的信用证　an L/C available by draft at 30 days after sight，或 30 days L/C

    irrevocable letter of credit　不可撤销信用证

    按《跟单信用证统一惯例》（第 600 号出版物）第 3 条 C 款的规定："信用证是不可撤销的，即使信用证中对此未作指示也是如此。"如遇要撤销或修改，在受益人向通知修改

的银行表示接受该修改之前，原信用证的条款对受益人依然有效。

12. D/P，全称是 Documents against Payment，付款交单

付款交单是经济贸易交易中付款方式的一种。指出口方在委托银行收款时，指示银行只有在付款人（进口方）付清货款时，才能向其交出货运单据，即交单以付款为条件，称为付款交单。按付款时间的不同，又可分为即期付款交单（Documents against Payment at sight，简称 D/P at sight）和远期付款交单（Documents against Payment after sight，简称 D/P after sight）。

13. PVC bag　塑料袋

14. subject to　以……为条件（为准）

subject to our final confirmation　以我方最后确认为准

subject to our written acceptance　以我方书面接受为准

subject to sample approval　以样品得到确认为条件

subject to prior sale　以先售出为准

subject to goods being unsold　以商品未售出为准

subject to first available steamer　以装第一艘轮船为准

subject to your reply reaching here before...　以你方答复在……之前到达我方为准

2.　A Non-firm Offer for Arts and Crafts

Background: 中国手工艺品公司营销经理 Peter Qian 回复美国某贸易公司对手工艺品的询盘，报虚盘并将交易条件置于附件中。在电子邮件的正文中对折扣问题给予解释。

From: peterqianmarketing@craftgallery.com

To: cornelltrading@sher.trading.com

Date: Monday, September 23, 20＿＿, 9:54 am

Subject: Re: Inquiry for Arts and Crafts

Attachment: catalog and price list

Dear Ms. Cornell,

We acknowledge with thanks receipt of your email of May 16, from which we were pleased to learn of your interest in our arts and crafts items. As requested, we are now attaching a copy of our catalog and current price list for the captioned goods. Also attached are details of our conditions of sale and terms of payment.

Regarding a special discount you asked for, we agree to grant you a discount of 3% so as to enable you to push the sale of our products, provided that the purchase exceeds an annual total of £3,500.00. We think it would be reasonable that no special allowance could be given on annual total purchase below £3,500.00.

As the prices of raw materials are rising and the market is recovering, there is a strong demand for our goods and we trust that our quotation will be acceptable to you and we await with keen interest your trial order.

> Yours sincerely,
>
> Peter Qian
>
> Marketing Manager

Notes

1. arts and crafts　手工艺品
2. acknowledge receipt of　告知收到，……收悉
    acknowledgement　n. 收到
    We have for acknowledgement your fax of July 23.　贵方 7 月 23 日的传真收悉。
3. as requested　应贵方要求
    还可以说 at your request, according to your requirement, in compliance with your requirement
4. the captioned goods　标题项下的货物，这里指 Arts and Crafts，类似的表达有 the subject goods, the goods/article mentioned in the subject line
5. provided　conj. 假如，如果
    Provided that you grant us 5% commission, we are ready to place a large order with you in the near future.　如果贵方给予我方 5% 的佣金，我方将不久向贵方大量订购。
6. exceed　vt. 超过
    China's gross domestic product (GDP) is expected to exceed 15 trillion yuan (US$1.85 trillion) in 2005.　2005 年中国国内生产总值将超过 1.85 万亿美元。
    A tolerance not to exceed 5% less than the amount of the credit is allowed.　允许支取的金额有 5% 的减幅。
7. with keen/great interest　怀着极大的兴趣，殷切地
8. trial order　试订

3. A Firm Offer for Bedding Sets and Request for a Bid for Jacquard Cushions

Background: 加拿大 Rostar 纺织品贸易公司出口部经理 Andrew Gray 向中国宁夏 Greenland 床上用品有限公司经理 Grant Bao 报 300 套床品套件的实盘，并要求对方对提花靠垫递价。

From: graysuccess@rostartextile.com

To: grantbao353@greenland.bedding.com

Date: Friday, January 17, 20 _ _, 10:56 am

Subject: Firm Offer for Bedding Sets and Request for a Bid for Jacquard Cushions

Dear Mr. Bao,

This is to confirm your email of 16 January, asking us to make you a firm offer for Bedding Sets CFR China port.

We emailed you this morning offering you 300 sets of Bedding Sets at US$ 53.00 per set, CFR China port, for shipment during February/March 20 _ _. This offer is firm, subject to the receipt of your reply before 10 February, 20 _ _.

Please note that we have offered our most favorable price and are unable to entertain any counter offer.

With regard to jacquard cushions, we advise you that the few lots we have at present are under offer elsewhere. If, however, you were to make us a suitable bid, there is a possibility of our supplying them. As you know, at present, there is a heavy demand for these commodities and this has resulted in increased prices. You may, however, take advantage of the strengthening market if you send an immediate reply.

Yours sincerely,
Andrew Gray
Export Manager

Notes

1. bedding set　床品套件
2. jacquard cushion　提花靠垫
3. entertain　vt. 接受，愿意考虑
    He refused to entertain our proposal.　他拒不考虑我们的提议。
4. counter offer　还盘
5. the few lots we have at present are under offer elsewhere　我们目前仅有的少数几笔货已转向别处报盘
6. bid　n.（买方）递盘，递价，投标
    递盘又叫买方发盘，可以视作买方提出的报盘。此种情况常见于当卖方的货物畅销，或者卖方不知道行情，对买方是否愿意购买没有把握时，卖方经常要求买方先报盘。
    make a bid of £50 for a painting　为一幅画出价 50 英镑
    Please make a bid for 30 Electric Scooters.　请为 30 辆电动车出价。
7. There is a heavy demand for...　对……有大量的需求。
    a growing demand　不断增长的需求
    a large/great demand　大量的需求
    a latent/potential/possible/prospective demand　潜在的需求
8. increased price　价格上涨
    类似的表达有：
    Your price is a bit high.　你方价格有点高。
    Your price is too high.　你方价格太高。
    Your price is rather stiff.　你方价格相当高。
    Your price is excessive.　你方价格过高。
    Your price is prohibitive.　你方价格令人望而却步。
    Your price is out of the line with the market level.　你方价格与市价不符。
    Your price is unreasonable/unworkable/impracticable/infeasible/unrealistic.　你方价格不合理/不可行/行不通/不切实际/不现实。

9. the strengthening market 上涨的行市

4. A Firm Offer for Nylon Sports Sweaters

Background: 中国某制衣厂业务经理 J. P. Howell 回复美国某服装进出口公司的询盘，对尼龙运动衫报实盘，并敦促对方尽早下订单。

From: jphowellmail@baleno.garment.com
To: charlesstronglove@yahoo.com
Sent: Tuesday, December 2, 20＿＿, 14: 47 pm
Subject: Firm Offer for Nylon Sports Sweaters

Dear Mr. Strong,

We wish to thank you for your inquiry of November 11, asking us to make you a firm offer for 18,000 dozen of the captioned goods.

In compliance with your request, we are offering for your consideration:

Commodity: Nylon Sports Sweaters in different color/pattern assortments.
Size: Large (L), Medium (M), Small (S)
Packing: Each sweater is wrapped in a polybag and 8 dozen packed in a standard export cardboard
        carton.
Price: CIFC5 San Francisco per dozen in US$
        L: 192.24
        M: 168.12
        S: 144.00
Shipment: 6,000 dozen each size per month, beginning from January, 2010
Payment: by confirmed, irrevocable L/C payable by draft at sight to be opened 30 days before the
        time of shipment

This offer is firm, subject to your reply reaching us by 5 pm, Beijing time, December 15.

There is little likelihood of the goods remaining unsold once this particular offer has lapsed. We have made a good selection of samples suited to your country, and sent them to you today by parcel post. Their fine quality, attractive designs and the reasonable prices will convince you that these goods are of good value.

We are expecting to receive your order with us.

Yours very sincerely,

| J. P. Howell |
| Operational Manager |

Notes

1. nylon sports sweater 尼龙运动衫
2. dozen n. 打
   该词与数词连用时，复数不加"s"，如：
   a dozen 一打
   6,000 dozen tea sets 6000 打茶具
   hundred, thousand, million 等词的用法与 dozen 类似
3. standard export cardboard carton 标准出口硬纸板箱
4. CIFC5 = Cost, Insurance and Freight, including a commission of 5% 成本加运保费价，含 5%的佣金
5. to be opened 30 days before the time of shipment 装船期前 30 天开立的
6. lapse vi.（权利、任期、期限等）终止，失效
7. parcel post 包裹
8. be of good value 物有所值

5. A Firm Offer for Refrigerators

Background: 埃及亚瑟电器行向中国永昌家用电器进出口公司发来电子邮件，希望对三种规格的海尔牌电冰箱发实盘。永昌公司区域经理 Maria Sanchez 用电子邮件回复亚瑟电器行的询盘。

From: mariasanchezjob@ychappliance.com
To: karimhanen@alibaba.com
Sent: Thursday, February 11, 2010, 15:16 pm
Subject: Firm Offer for Haier Refrigerators

Dear Mr. Hanen,

Your fax of February 10 asking us to offer you Haier refrigerators has received our immediate attention. We are pleased to know that you are interested in our products.

In reply to your inquiry, we take pleasure in making you an offer as follows, provided your reply reaches us within 7 days from today:

Specification	Quantity (set)	Price (US$)
BYD212	1,000	410.00
BYD175	1,000	380.00
BYD219	500	395.00

The price is on the basis of CIF Safaga.

Packing: at buyer's option

Shipment: total quantity to be delivered by 3 equal monthly shipments, March through May, 2010

Payment: 100% by irrevocable, revolving letter of credit

We have sent you by airmail two copies of illustrated catalogs of various models as per your request.

Because our stock on hand has been quite low owing to heavy commitment, we hope you may place early order with us.

Yours sincerely,

Maria Sanchez

Regional Manager

Notes

1. 名词 offer 后常接介词 for，但当买方提及卖方的报盘时，也可接 of。如：

    Please make us an offer CIF London for 20 metric tons of Brown Cashmere.   请向我方发 20 公吨棕色山羊绒伦敦到岸价的报盘。

    We confirm your offer of 2,000 kilos of Black Tea.   贵方 2000 千克红茶的报盘收悉。

2. receive our immediate attention   得到我方的立即关注/处理/重视

3. in reply to   兹答复

4. take pleasure in/of doing sth，或 take pleasure to do sth   很高兴做某事

5. at one's option   由某人来决定

6. total quantity to be delivered by 3 equal monthly shipments   全部货物分三个月三次平均装运

7. 100% by irrevocable, revolving letter of credit   全部由不可撤销的循环信用证来支付

    revolving letter of credit   循环信用证，是指信用证被受益人全部或部分使用后，又恢复到原金额，再被受益人继续使用，直至用完规定的使用次数或累计总金额为止的信用证。主要是用于长期或较长期内分批交货的供货合同，一般在等量分批均匀交货情况下使用。使用这种信用证，买方可节省开证押金和逐单开证的手续及费用。

8. as per   按照，根据

    We handle a wide range of light industrial products as per the list enclosed.   我们经营多种轻工业品，详见附表。

    As per your request, we have marked the cases with gross, tare and net weights.   我们已按贵方要求在箱上注明毛重、皮重及净重。

9. stock on hand   当前的库存

10. heavy commitment   大量承约

6. A Firm Offer for Cotton Towels

Background: 英国 Belle View Textiles 有限公司市场部经理 Andrea Coates 回复香港 Peace Spinning 贸易公司的采购部经理 Danis Zhang 4 月 20 日发来的询价。根据买方要求的尺寸和图案设计，对棉质毛巾报有效期为 7 天的实盘。

From: andreamarket@belleviewtextiles.com
To: danisforever@peacespinningtrading.com
Sent: Tuesday, April 20, 20_ _, 14:26 pm
Subject: Re: Inquiry for Cotton Towels

Dear Mr. Zhang,

We receive with thanks your inquiry of April 20, and are pleased to make you the following offer regarding our cotton towels in size and pattern you require:

Quantity: 6,000 sets of cotton towels
Unit price: US$8.00 per set, including 3% quantity discount
Terms of payment: irrevocable L/C at sight
Delivery: FOB Hamburg, shipment to be made before June 1

We must stress that this offer is firm for 7 days only, due to the high demand in our market.

Our towels, made of natural cotton, have appealed to customers in many countries because of its comfort, softness and attractive design. We believe they can satisfy your customers too, either as a gift or for personal use.

We hope to receive your order at an early date.

Yours sincerely,
Andrea Coates
Marketing Manager

Notes

1. pattern   n. 图案，花样，设计
   Our client doesn't like the pattern on the fabric.   我们的客户不喜欢那块布料上的图案。
2. natural cotton   天然棉花
3. appeal to   吸引，喜欢
   Bright colors appeal to the customers at our end.   鲜艳的颜色吸引我方市场的客户。

Unit 7   Counter Offer

还　盘

A counter offer is an offer made by one of the two parties in response to a previous offer during negotiations for a final contract. Usually an exporter makes an offer that needs to be agreed by the importer. When the importer finds that the quality of the goods is fine, price is reasonable and the terms and conditions in the offer are acceptable through his careful study of the offer and the current market situation, he may probably place an order promptly. However, if the importer disagrees with the offer, he may decline the offer, or most probably, make a counter offer, requiring some changes of the terms and conditions and putting forward his own proposal or conditions. Thus, the importer makes a counter offer.

Upon receipt of the counter offer, the seller may weight the advantages and disadvantages and decide to accept or decline it according to the concrete situation. He may also put forward some new alteration opinion. This is regarded also as a counter offer.

The whole process is somewhat like bargaining on a free market. In foreign trade, we call it negotiations on trade terms and conditions. Thus through times of negotiations, agreement is reached upon, contract signed and business done.

When writing a counter offer, the exporter or the importer should clearly state his objections to certain terms and conditions offered and convince the other part of his position. Therefore, he should give proper reasons to support his objections and then state his own proposals most explicitly so as to avoid unnecessary ambiguity or misunderstanding.

还盘写作步骤

1. Thanks for the Offer
2. Being Unable to Accept and Giving Reasons
3. Making Concrete Suggestions or Amendments
4. Hoping to Receive Favorable Reply

$$\boxed{\text{还盘常用语句}}$$

1.   Thanks for the Offer

- We thank you for your offer by fax of September 3 for 5,000 pieces of the captioned goods at ￡9.50 per piece CIF Hamburg.

  感谢贵方 9 月 3 日传真发来的标题项下商品五千件 CIF 汉堡每件 9.5 英镑的报盘。

- We are glad to inform you that we have received your offer for the captioned goods on July 13.

  我方很高兴地告知贵方，我方已于 7 月 13 日收到贵方标题项下产品的报盘。

- We thank you for your Quotation Sheet No. 134 for your NVR54 Medical Apparatus and Instruments, and we have given it very careful consideration.

  感谢贵方第 134 号型号为 NVR54 的医疗器械的报价单，我方进行了仔细研究。

- We refer to your offer by email dated May 2 for 2,000 metric tons of Steel Sheet.

  兹关于贵方 5 月 2 日电子邮件发来的对两千公吨钢板的报盘。

2.   Being Unable to Accept and Giving Reasons

Price (in Buyer's sense)

- We immediately contacted our customers and they showed great interest in the quality and designs of your products. However, they said that your price is 10% higher than the average.

  我们立即与我们的客户联系，他们对你们产品的质量和设计很感兴趣。但是，他们认为你们的价格比平均价高 10%。

- We can obtain a price of ￡24.00 per set from a local firm, which is ￡2.00 per set lower than your price.

  我方可从当地工厂得到每套 24 英镑的报价，这比贵方价格低 2 英镑。

- We find your quality as well as delivery date satisfactory. We find your price is not up to the present market level/is out of the line with the prevailing market.

  我方对贵方的质量和交货期感到满意。但价格与当前市场行情不符。

- Information indicates that some kinds of the said articles made in other countries have been sold here at a level about 5% lower than that of yours. We do not deny that the quality of your products is slightly better, but the difference in price should, in no case, be so big.

  信息显示，在此地销售的其他国家制造的上述种类的商品其价格比贵方的低 5%。我方无法否认贵方产品的质量稍好，但价差绝不应该如此之大。

- In reply, we regret to inform you that our clients find your price much too high/on the high side.

  兹回复，我们很遗憾地告知我们的客户认为贵方的价格太高/偏高。

- We don't deny we are interested in your products, as you know. However, we find that we can obtain from another firm a price of 5% lower than that of yours.

  正如贵方了解的，我们确实对贵方产品感兴趣。但是我方可以从另一家商号处购得该产品，且价格比贵方低 5%。

- We feel that your quotation is not proper because the price for such material is on the decline at present.

  我们认为你方价格不合适，因为该种材料的价格正在下跌。

- As the prices of raw materials have dropped considerably and the retail prices of your motor bikes here have fallen by 10%, to accept present prices would mean a heavy loss to us, not to speak of profit.

  由于原材料价格已大幅度降低，而贵方摩托车在此地价格也下降了10%，因此接受贵方目前的报价对我们来说意味着巨大损失，更不用说有利润了。

Price (in Seller's sense)

- I'm afraid we can't reduce our price to the level you have indicated. To be frank with you, your counter offer can barely cover our production cost.

  恐怕很难将价格降到贵方要求的水平。坦率地说，贵方还盘几乎不够我方的生产成本。

- We are not in a position to entertain business at your price, since it is far below our cost.

  我方无法按贵方价格成交，因为该价格远远低于产品的成本价。

- We feel it regrettable that you find our price on the high side. As stated in our previous email, our goods are well received in many countries because of their fine quality and reasonable price. All our prices have been carefully calculated and cut to the limit, at which we have done large business with other buyers in different countries.

  很遗憾贵方认为我方的报价过高。我方上封电子邮件里提到，由于精致的品质和合理的价格，我方产品在很多国家广受欢迎。我们所有的报价都是经过认真计算，并降到了最低，以此价格我们与不同国家的买主做出很多大宗交易。

- Your counter offer is too low and groundless; therefore it cannot serve as a basis for further negotiation with our manufacturers.

  你方还盘太低且无根据，故不能作为与我方生产厂家继续磋商的依据。

- We have cut our price to the limit. We regret, therefore, being unable to comply with your request for further reduction.

  我方已将价格降到极限，因此很抱歉无法满足贵方进一步降价的要求。

- We very regret to say that there is no possibility of our cutting down of the price to the extent you indicated i.e. 3%. As you know, materials have risen substantially in the meantime. In these days, we have received a crowd of inquiries from buyers in other directions and expect to close business at something near our level.

  非常抱歉我方无法将价格降至贵方所说的程度，即3%。贵方应该有所了解，原材料价格巨幅上涨。这些天，我方从它处收到买方的许多询盘并欲按我方报价成交。

Delivery

- Delivery before March is a firm condition of this order, and we reserve the right to refuse goods delivered after that time.

  三月份前交货是该订单的必要条件。如延迟交货，我方保留拒绝接受货物的权利。

- As the time of delivery indicated is not too far and in the line with the requirement of the endusers, we are instructed to accept your quotation on condition that you guarantee shipment of the whole lot, once for all, before September 1.

由于贵方交货期较近，符合我方客户要求，我们可接受贵方报盘，但贵方必须保证 9 月 1 日前一次性全部交货。

- Since the goods are in urgent need, would you please agree to our proposal that the time of delivery should be shifted from "the end of July" to "the beginning of July"?

由于急需该货，请贵方同意我方的建议，将交货期从"七月底"改为"七月初"。

Payment

- Under the present circumstances, this question is particularly taxing owing to the tight money condition and unprecedentedly high bank interest.

目前，由于银根紧而且银行的利率空前高，这个问题确实使我方感到十分棘手。

- To be frank, D/A is impossible because we would take a considerable risk. Perhaps after more business together, we would agree to D/P terms.

说实话，承兑交单不可行，因为我们承担的风险太大。也许以后彼此生意做多了，我们可以同意付款交单方式。

- When we open a letter of credit with a bank, we have to pay a sum of deposit, which would increase the cost of our import and tie up our funds.

我们在银行开立信用证时，要支付一笔押金，这样会增加我们进口的成本且积压我们的资金。

3.   Making Concrete Suggestions or Amendments

Buyer's Suggestions

- We would like to place our orders with you if you could bring down your prices at least by 15%. Otherwise, we can do nothing but turn elsewhere to cover our demands.

如果贵方能至少降低 15%，我们愿向贵方下订单。否则，我们只得从别处购买。

- A further slight price reduction of 3% will ensure you a substantial increase of the turnover as a whole, and so is your profit.

如价格能再稍微下调 3%，那么贵方的营业总额定可大幅度增加，利润也一样。

- You could benefit from higher sale with a little concession, say a 2% reduction.

只要贵方稍做让步，降价 2%，则可以从大量销售中获益。

- Our clients told us if you can reduce your price to ￡8.55 per piece, they will increase by 1,000 pieces. So there is a good chance of concluding a bigger transaction with them if you can meet their requirement.

我们的客户告诉我们如果你们能将价格降至每件 8.55 英镑，他们将增加一千件。所以若能满足他们的要求，这将是与他们达成大笔交易的好机会。

- We would request you to give us an 8% commission instead of 5% and to accept the minimum order of 500 dozen.

请给予我方 8%的佣金而不是 5%，并请接受 500 打的最低定购量。

- The minimum quantity required is 500 kg. But we would accept up to a maximum of 800 kg, if the quality is high.

贵方要求起订量虽然是 500 千克，但如果质量优良，我方将需求 800 千克。

- However, we would give our suggestion of an alteration of your payment terms. In view of our long business relations and our amicable cooperation prospects, we suggest you accept either cash against documents on arrival of the goods or drawing on us at 60 days' sight.

  然而我方建议贵方改变付款方式。鉴于我们长期的业务关系及友好的合作前景，故建议贵方接受货到后凭单付款或向我方开出见票后 60 天付款的汇票。

- To be on the safe side, we only accept payment by confirmed, irrevocable L/C against shipping documents for our exports at present.

  为了安全起见，我们现在只接受保兑的、不可撤销的信用证凭装船单据付款。

- As we are in urgent need of these products, we require September shipment.

  由于急需这些产品，我方要求 9 月装船。

- The materials supplied must be absolutely waterproof and we place our order subject to this guarantee.

  供应的材料必须防水，只有贵方保证这一点，我方才下订单。

Seller's Suggestions

- To step up the trade, we counter offer as follows, subject to your reply here by…

  为了促进贸易，我方还盘如下，以……前收到贵方回复为有效。

- It is our policy not to discount our standard prices. However, we are willing to make an exception in this case as an introduction for our products.

  对标准价格不打折是我方的规矩。但作为对我方产品的一种推广，我方愿意破例一次。

- If you raise your counter offer by 3%, it will stand a better chance of being considered.

  要是贵方还价再提高 3%，还可以有机会再考虑一下。

- In order to encourage your business with us, we are prepared to meet you half way by making further reduction of 5% in our original quotation.

  为促进我们双方的贸易往来，我方愿意折中一下，在我方原报价基础上再降价 5%。

- In order to help you develop business, we are prepared to allow you a special discount of 3% on an order amounting to 6,000 sets or over.

  为促进贵方业务发展，我们准备对 6000 套以上的订单给予 3%折扣的特别优惠。

- We would be willing to discuss a volume discount if your order volume is doubled.

  如果贵方的订货量能翻一番，我方将乐于与贵方讨论批量订货的折扣问题。

- We may consider allowing you a 3% commission on condition that your minimum quantity for the first order reaches 300 dozen.

  我们可以考虑给予贵方 3%的佣金折扣，但前提是贵方的首次订单量达到 300 打。

- We are anxious to do what we can to help you establish new business, and are prepared to allow you a special discount of 8%, if payment is made within 20 days.

  我方愿尽一切所能帮助贵方开展新的业务，所以如果贵方能在 20 天内付款，我方准备给予贵方 8%的优惠折扣。

4. Hoping to Receive Favorable Reply

- As the market is of keen competition, we recommend your immediate acceptance.

  由于市场竞争激烈，建议贵方立即接受。

- It is in view of our long-standing relationsip that we make you such a counter offer. As the market is declining, we hope you will consider our counter offer most favorably and email us acceptance as soon as possible.

  考虑到我们长久的合作关系，我们如此还盘。由于市场需求不断下滑，希望贵方能认真考虑我方还盘，尽快回复。

- We hope you will take advantage of this opportunity so that you will benefit from the expanding market.

  希望贵方能抓住这次机会，以便从不断扩大的市场中获益。

- We appreciate your priority to the above request and an early favorable reply.

  贵方对上述请求优先考虑及早日有利的回复，我方将不胜感激。

- We await your favorable reply with great interest.

  期盼收到贵方有利回复。

- We hope you would accept this price and place your order at an early date.

  希望贵方接受此价格并早日订购。

写作范例

1. A Counter Offer from Buyer on Price of Wool

Background: 中国某羊毛物资进出口公司总经理 Katharine Andrews 对新西兰某羊毛工业公司第 231 号 100 吨羊毛的报盘还盘，认为其价格偏高，建议对方降价 5%并在 20__年 9 月底交货。如能同意，则可能增加订购数量至 150~180 吨。

From: katharineandrews@usgh.com

To: blissfarwer@teesl.com

Date: Wednesday, July 21, 20__, 15:44 pm

Subject: Re: Offer No. 231 for 100 Tons of Wool

Dear Mr. Bliss,

We have carefully tested the samples of your wool sent to us on July 20. We are pleased to inform you that the samples have impressed us favorably.

However, we feel that the prices you quoted are a little too high. To accept the prices you quote would also leave us with only a small profit on our sales since this is an area in which the principal demand is for articles in the medium price range.

We like the quality of your goods and also the way in which you have handled our inquiry and would welcome the opportunity to do business with you. If you can reduce your prices by 5% or so and make delivery by the end of September, 20_ _, we may be able to place an order for 150-180 tons. If you cannot do so, then we have to regretfully decline your offer.

It must be understood that we have the right to return any goods that do not tally with the samples submitted. Payment terms as usual.

We are awaiting your prompt reply.

Yours sincerely,
Katharine Andrews
Managing Director

Notes

1. leave sb with sth   给某人留下某物
    After paying for our equipment, we are still left with quite an amount of cash.   支付了设备款后，我们还剩下不少现金。
2. principal   adj. 主要的
    the principal members of the company   公司的高级官员
    principal food   主食
    principal points   要点
    principal office   总部，总社
    The principal aim of the policy is to increase the sales volume in this area.   该政策的主要目的是提高这一地区的销售量。
    The low salary is her principal reason for leaving the job.   工资太低是她辞去工作的最重要的原因。
    n. 校长，本金，委托人
    the principal of a college   大学校长
    repay principal and interest   付还本金和利息
    I must consult my principals before agreeing to your proposal.   我得同委托人商量后才能接受你的建议。
3. in the medium price range   中等价位的，中档的
4. make delivery   交货
    take delivery   提货
5. decline   vt. 谢绝，下降
    decline an invitation   谢绝邀请
    decline to place a repeat order   谢绝下续订订单
    The price of 14 inches TV set declined from 400 to 320 yuan each. 14 英寸的电视机每台从

400 元降到 320 元。

6. It must be understood that...   应该……

7. tally with   符合，与……一致，还可以用 conform to

Your quotation doesn't tally with the current market level.   你们的报价与当前行情不符。

2. A Counter Offer from Buyer on Reduction of Minimum Quantity

Background: 澳大利亚某布业有限公司销售主管 D. Brand 对中国某纺织品公司的第 154 号 3 种颜色防辐射布料的报盘还盘，建议对方将起订量由每种颜色一万米降至七千米。

From: brand_reflection@pg.business.com

To: bushabc@sohu.com

Date: Tuesday, April 7, 20_ _, 9:56 am

Subject: Re: Offer No. 154

Dear Mr. Bush,

We thank you for your fax of April 6 offering us Anti-radiation Fabric in pink, brown and green.

We have given our careful consideration to your offer. However, we regret to inform you that the minimum of 10,000 meters per color is too big for this market.

In case you can reduce the minimum to 7,000 meters per color, there is a possibility of placing orders with you, because a considerable quantity of this material is required on this market for manufacturing various kinds of functional garments such as Anti-radiation Maternity Dress.

We hope you will reconsider our suggestion. If later on you can see any chance to do better, please let us know.

Yours sincerely,

D. Brand

Sales Executive

Notes

1. minimum quantity   最低起订量

2. There is a possibility of doing sth.   有可能做某事。

   类似的结构还有 There is a good chance of doing sth，如：

   There is a good chance of finalizing an order with them if the present price can be lowered to meet their requirement.   如果能降低价格以满足他们的要求，这将是得到他们订单的一个好机会。

3. a considerable quantity of   相当数量的，数量可观的

We can offer you a considerable quantity of first-grade walnut meat from stock at present.   我方目前可现货供应相当数量的一级核桃仁。

3. A Counter Offer from Buyer on Prices for Leather Gloves

Background: 中国某皮具有限公司采购部经理 Brenda Stanton 向新加坡某皮具制品公司两千双皮手套的报盘还盘，认为其 CIF 上海每双 25 美元的报价太高，并与印度制造的产品价格做比较，建议对方降价至每双 20 美元。

From: brendastantonlls@yahoo.com

To: delia_lawrence@leatherprod.stey.com

Sent: Friday, August 23, 20＿＿, 14:58 pm

Subject: Re: Offer for 2,000 Pairs of Leather Gloves

Dear Ms. Lawrence,

We are pleased to receive your offer of August 23 for 2,000 pairs of leather gloves at US$ 25.00 per pair CIF Shanghai and samples you very kindly sent us.

In reply, we appreciate the good quality of the goods and think the time of shipment acceptable, but we very much regret to state that our end-users here find your price too high and out of line with the prevailing market level. Information indicates that some parcels of Indian makes have been sold in our area at the level of a much lower price.

Such being the case, it is impossible for us to persuade our end-users to accept your price, as articles of similar quality is easily obtainable at a much lower figure. If you are prepared to reduce your limit to, say US$ 20.00 per pair CIF Shanghai, we might come to terms. If you could, we might be able to order 4,000 pairs.

It is in view of our long-standing business relationship that we make you such a counter offer. As the market is declining, we hope you will consider our counter offer and fax us your acceptance as soon as possible.

Yours sincerely,

Brenda Stanton

Purchasing Manager

Notes

1. regret   v. 抱歉，惋惜，引为遗憾

   We regret we are unable to do as requested.   我很抱歉我们不能够按照你的要求去做。

   We regret to say that we cannot accept your price.   很遗憾地说，我们不能接受你方的价格。

We very much regret our inability to accept your price.   我们对不能接受你方的价格感到非常遗憾。

We regret being unable to meet your request.   很遗憾我们不能按照你的要求去做。

2. information indicates = indications show   有迹象表明，有时也用 for your information，多置于句首

3. parcel   n. 一批货

4. make   n. 牌号，型号，制造式样（多指工业产品）

   I like digital cameras of Japanese make.   我喜欢日本造的数码照相机。

   He almost knows all the makes of American cars.   他几乎知道所有美国汽车的牌子。

5. end-user   n. 用户，也可以说 client, customer

6. prevailing market level   当前的市价，prevailing 也可以换做 current, present, ruling

7. such being the case   既然如此，事实既然是这样，也可以说 this/that being the case

8. come to terms   达成交易。

4.   A Counter Offer from Seller on Price and Payment Terms

Background: 中国某厨具用品有限公司出口销售部经理李建昌对比利时某贸易公司关于价格和支付条件的还盘做出答复，并向对方发出有效期为四天、付款方式为即期信用证的实盘。

From: lijianchang2004@alibaba.com

To: kevinhassid90@fhs.orfs.com

Date: Monday, March 18, 20＿＿, 9:58 am

Subject: A Firm Offer for Whistling Kettle, Tea Set, Server Set and Tableware

Dear Mr. Hassid,

Thank you very much for the email of March 17. We are glad to learn that you are willing to push the sale of our goods in your area.

However, we are sorry to tell you that we can not comply with your counter offer. The prices we offered are most competitive if you take the quality and the excellent packing into consideration. But in order to develop our market in your area and long-term cooperation between us, we have decided to give you an exceptional offer as follows:

Commodity	Article No.	Packing	Cartons per 20' FCL	CIFC5 Antwerp in USD
Whistling Kettle	S6320	6 sets/ctn	300	17.31 per set
4-piece Tea Set	S5130	6 sets/ctn	300	21.31 per set
Server Set	S9420-7	1 set/ctn	365	57.03 per set
Tableware	S8310	10 sets/ctn	365	7.97 per set

We would like to call you attention that this offer is valid only for four days.

As to the terms of payment, we only accept sight L/C for the moment. If only after several satisfying business, we can take D/P and other flexible ways of payment into consideration.

For the market is firm with an upward tendency, we advise you to accept our prices without any delay.

We are looking forward to receiving your order.

Yours sincerely,

J. C. Lee

Export Sales Manager

Notes

1. counter offer v. & n. 还盘

   该词作为动词可拼写为 counter offer, counteroffer；而作为名词时为 counter offer, counteroffer, counter-offer

   The price you counteroffered is not in line with the prevailing market. 你方还盘价与市价不符。

   We are sorry to tell you that we can not accept your counter-offer. 歉告，我方不能接受贵方还盘。

2. long-term/longstanding cooperation 长期合作

3. Article No. 货号

   常见的货号编法有：

   国际码：如 693 0939 20021 6，其中 693 代表中国，0939 代表厂家，20021 是产品编号，6 是修正码，是通过前面的数字计算出来的。

   企业内部码：编码的方式依照企业内部的规则，只要内部明白即可。

4. 20' FCL = 20 Feet Full Container Load 一个 20 英尺整柜

   集装箱有 20 英尺和 40 英尺之分，国际上以长度为 20 英尺的集装箱为国际计量单位，也称国际标准箱单位，通常用来表示船舶装载集装箱的能力，也是集装箱港口吞吐量的重要统计和换算单位。而集装箱又叫柜，所以 20 英尺集装箱又可以叫做 20 尺小柜。40' FCL 就是大柜。以上都是指整柜（Full Container Load, FCL）。拼柜或拼箱叫 LCL（Less than Container Load, LCL），也分 20'和 40'两种。

5. CIFC5 = CIFC5% 到岸价含 5%的佣金

6. whistling kettle 鸣音水壶

7. tea set 茶具

8. server set 餐具（多用以指刀叉、汤匙之类）

   tableware 餐具（多用以指盘、杯、碟、碗之类）

9. ctn.是纸箱（carton）的缩写

10. call one's attention   提醒某人注意，还可以把 call 换成 arouse, draw, attract, invite 等

11. D/P (Documents against Payment)   付款交单，托收付款方式的一种，另一种叫 D/A (Documents against Acceptance)，承兑交单。与付款交单（D/P）相比，承兑交单是在进口商未付款之前，即可取得货运单据，凭以提取货物，因此可以视为出口商为进口商提供了资金融通上的便利，但出口商的风险增加了，一旦进口商到期不付款，出口商便可能钱货两空。

12. firm with an upward tendency   坚挺且有上涨的趋势

13. without any delay   立即

5. A Counter Offer from Seller on Commission

Background: 中国龙胜水晶工艺品公司拒绝了进口商提高佣金的要求，但鉴于双方长期的贸易合作，愿意资助进口商两万美元，用于广告和促销宣传活动。

From: timjia_business@longshengcrystal.com

To: mariaglassware@freetrading.com

Date: Monday, September 3, 20＿＿, 15:10 am

Subject: A Credit of US$20,000 to You!

Dear Mrs Stevenson,

Thank you very much for your email of September 3, and we are very pleased to know you are willing to introduce our products in your market and increase your advertising. However, in the email you also request we increase the commission on any new lines you handle.

We are confident that the competitive prices, peerless design and excellent quality of our goods will surely ensure increasing sales. As for the request for the increased commission, we find it difficult to allow any further discount, because the price we offer is the bottom price.

However, considering our long-term business cooperation, we would like to contribute a credit of US$20,000 for advertising and sales campaign on our products. We suppose this may be a satisfying alternative and a more practical way to meet your requirement.

We look forward to your early reply and your order.

Yours sincerely,

Tim Jia

Sales Manager

Notes

1. peerless   adj. 无与伦比的，出类拔萃的
2. bottom price   最低价，也可以说 rock bottom price

   This is our bottom price. We can't make any further concession.   这是我们的最低价了。我们不能再让了。

3. contribute   v. 出（钱、力、主意等），捐助，捐献，贡献

   Each party in the joint venture shall contribute at least US$3,000 to the fund.   合资企业的每一方都应至少向基金会捐款 3000 美元。

4. credit   n. （给某人的）一笔钱
5. sales campaign   促销活动
6. alternative   n. 可能性中的选择

   We have no alternative but to cancel the order.   我们别无选择，只能取消订单。

6. A Counter Offer from Seller on Price

Background: 浙江天华高档杯具有限公司销售主管 Julia Tian 拒绝了进口商 7%折扣的要求，并表示所报价格是经过仔细计算，且与许多客户在此价位达成了大宗交易，如不能接受此报价，希望将来还能继续合作。

From: juliatian@sohu.com
To: nigelfreedom89@jbfroyal.com
Date: Wednesday, June 8, 20＿＿, 10: 10 am
Subject: Re: Requesting a 7% Allowance

Dear Mr Teal,

In reply to your email of June 8 requesting a 7% allowance, we regret that it is impossible for us to accept your counter offer, even to meet you halfway.

Your email stated that you can get vacuum flasks of the same quality at much lower prices, but we are sure that our products are far superior in quality to any others of the same price level. Actually the prices we quoted are closely calculated. Thanks to the high quality, considerable business has been done with many customers in other markets at these prices. You will be convinced of our reasonable quotation through a fair comparison of quality between our products and similar products from other sources. Therefore, considering the quality of the goods offered, we do not feel our prices are excessive at all but keep our original offer.

If you still do not accept our offer, we hope we will cooperate in other business in the future. We assure you that we always do our utmost to the customers' satisfaction.

Yours sincerely,
Julia Tian
Sales Supervisor

Notes

1. allowance   n. 折扣，津贴，补贴

2. meet you halfway   折中，各让一半，各退一步

   In order to conclude the transaction, let's meet each other halfway.   为了达成交易，我们各让一半。

3. vaccum flask   保温水瓶

4. superior to   比……更好，比……更优秀

   In every case, competitive products are superior to monopoly ones.   总而言之，互相竞争的产品要优于垄断性的产品。

   Organic food is superior to regular food in many ways.   有机食品在很多方面都优于普通食品。

5. considerable   adj. 大量的，可观的

   A considerable number of people object to the government's attitude to the tariff.   相当多的人反对政府对待关税问题的态度。

6. be convinced of   坚信，确信

   Through years of dealing with you, we're convinced of your commercial integrity.   通过多年和你们打交道，我们确信你们的商业信誉可靠。

7. from other sources   从其他货源处，从它处，也可以说 from other channels

8. excessive   adj. 过量的，过多的

   The amounts they borrowed were too excessive to pay back before the deadline.   他们的借款过多了，以至于在最后期限前无法还清。

7. A Counter Offer from Buyer on Trade Discount and Earlier Delivery

Background: 韩国某礼品商贸有限公司贸易主管 Thomas Fox 对中国星美礼品公司一千打圣诞贺卡的报盘还盘，虽然对其 FOB 青岛每打 2 美元的价格感到满意，但请求对方给予 8%的贸易折扣以便推销商品，并希望将交货期由 12 月 1 日提前至 11 月 15 日以赶上销售季节。如能同意，客户将订购一千打。

From: thomasfox@yahoo.com

To: sunhongsmile@sina.com

Date: Thursday, October 9, 20＿＿, 9: 47 am

Subject: Re: Offer for 1,000 Dozen Christmas Cards

Dear Miss Sun,

We refer to your offer of October 8 for 1,000 dozen Christmas Cards at USD 2.00 per dozen FOB Qingdao, on usual terms.

We agree to your price and intend to place a large order, but should like to know if you are prepared to grant us a trade discount of 8% on your quoted price that would help us to introduce your goods to our customers.

Moreover, our customers can't accept the shipment of December 1. As they must have the goods on display in time for the Christmas season, the cards should be dispatched by November 15 at the latest. Since they urgently need the goods, our customers request us to email you to shift your delivery time from "December 1" to "on or before November 15". In that event, they would be able to place an order for 1,000 dozen, or they will get the goods from other sources. All other terms are acceptable.

We hope you will understand our position. In order to step up your business, please accept these unharsh conditions.

Please contact us as soon as possible.

Yours sincerely,
Thomas Fox
Trade Executive

Notes

1. urgently need   急需，类似结构还有 badly need, in urgent need of, badly in need of
2. shift   vt. 替换，转移，改变，这里也可以说 advance
3. step up the business   促进交易，还可以用 promote, develop, encourage 等
4. unharsh   adj. 不苛刻的，不严厉的

8. Reply to the Buyer's Counter Offer on Trade Discount and Earlier Delivery

Background: 中国星美礼品公司销售经理孙红对韩国某礼品商贸有限公司贸易主管 Thomas Fox 10 月 9 日发出的还盘回复，表示对价值超过两千美元的订单给予 5%的折扣，并同意将交货期提前至 11 月 15 日。

From: sunhongsmile@sina.com
To: thomasfox@yahoo.com
Date: Thursday, October 9, 20＿＿, 16: 30 pm
Subject: Re: Re: Offer for 1,000 Dozen Christmas Cards

Dear Mr. Fox,

We received your email of October 9, offering to purchase our Christmas Cards at an 8% discount and with a delivery before November 15.

In fact, the price we offered is entirely in line with the market and has been accepted by many other customers. However, with a view to helping you promote our cards in your area and obtain a large order from you, we do not consider our offer as strict limits. To our mutual benefits, we are prepared to offer you a special discount of 5% for an order exceeding USD 2,000.

As for the time of delivery, we can meet your requirement and advance your delivery from December 1 to November 15.

Thank you again for your interest in our products. We are looking forward to your large order and trust our mutual efforts will lead to prosperous business.

Yours sincerely,
H. Sun
Promotional Manager

Notes

1. in line with the market　与市场行情相符
2. an order exceeding USD 2,000　价值超过 2000 美元的订单
3. meet your requirement　满足贵方要求

   We are prepared to cut by 5% of our price to meet your requirement.　我方准备满足贵方要求，降价 5%。

Unit 8　Order

订　单

1.　Definition of an Order

An order can be an acceptance of an offer or sent voluntarily by a buyer. According to the general practice, once the buyer sends out the order and then the seller confirms the acceptance, the business is done. Both parties, the buyer and the seller, should bear conscientiously the responsibilities respectively; otherwise the opposite side reserves the right to make complaints and claims.

2. Important Components in an Order or an Order Form

An order should include:

(1)　Name of commodity, item number, specifications such as size, type and color

(2)　Quantity or weight

(3)　Price, including unit price and amount

(4)　Package

(5)　Date and method of shipment

(6)　Terms of payment

(7)　Insurance

For the sake of convenience, many firms have printed order forms of their own with the necessary particulars on them. This may help avoid negligence and errors. When placing orders, just fill in and send them out as an enclosure with the letters.

3. Seller's Accepting and Confirming an Order

When a seller receives a buyer's order, he usually acknowledges the receipt of the order first. There are some printed routine acknowledgements. If the seller accepts the order, he will send his confirmation of the order to the buyer.

In most cases, the seller would send a sales confirmation in duplicate to the buyer to be countersigned with one copy to be returned for file. And after receiving the seller's confirmation, the buyer opens a letter of credit, whereas the seller gets the goods ready for shipment after he receives the letter of credit.

订购写作步骤

1. Thanks for the Offer and Placing an Order
2. Stating the Trade Terms and Conditions of the Goods Ordered
3. Hoping the Seller to Accept

订购常用语句

1. Thanks for the Offer and Placing an Order

● We thank you for your Offer No. 465 of October 16 for Black Tea. We find both quality and prices satisfactory and are pleased to place an order with you for the following.

感谢贵方 10 月 16 日第 465 号红茶的报盘。我方对产品的质量和价格满意并十分高兴订购下列产品。

● We feel completely satisfied with the quality and prices and are pleased to give you an order for the following items on the understanding that they will be supplied from current stock at the prices named.

我方对质量和价格感到满意并订购下列产品，要求按指定价格以现货供应。

● Your samples of … received favorable comment from our customers, and we are glad to enclose our order for …

贵方……的样品得到我们客户的良好反映。现高兴地附上……订单。

● This is a trial order. Please send us 35 sets only so that we may tap the market. If successful, we will place larger orders with you in the near future.

这是试销订单，请先发来 35 台，以便开发市场。若畅销，随后必有较大数量的订单。

● We have, with many thanks, received your illustrated catalog and price list recently. Now we are sending you an Order No. 234 for 100 sets of your classical furniture.

近期收到了贵方附有插图的产品目录和价目表，非常感谢。现报我方订购贵方 100 套古典家具的第 234 号订单。

● As informed in our fax of April 12, we are intending to place a repeat order for your electromagnetic stoves.

我方 4 月 12 日传真通知贵方，有意再次订购贵方电磁炉。

● Apart from our order placed with you for men's shirts on November 1, we would like to order an additional 200 pieces of men's shirts.

我方希望再追加订购 200 件曾在 11 月 1 日向贵公司订购的男士衬衫。

● We confirm having purchased from you 7,000 tons of cement on the following terms and conditions.

我们确认已向贵方按下列条件购买七千吨水泥。

2.　Stating the Trade Terms and Conditions of the Goods Ordered

● Please supply in assorted colors: preferably 6 dozen each of red, yellow, green, blue and brown.

请按下列颜色搭配供货,最好红、黄、绿、蓝、棕各 6 打。

● The quality of the order must be exactly the same as that of your sample. Any goods inferior to the sample shall be rejected.

所订货物品质须与贵方样品完全相同。我们拒收一切质量低于样品的货物。

● If you can accept USD 2.75, send us a proforma invoice and we will open a letter of credit for 1,000 sets. The quality of the merchandise must be as high as that of your sample.

如能接受 2.75 美元的价格,请寄形式发票来。我们当即开立 1000 套的信用证。商品质量须与你们的样品一样好。

● We have decided to accept your quotation of US$ 3.50 per set CIF Guangzhou.

我们决定按每台 CIF 广州 3.5 美元的价格接受贵方的报盘。

● As for payment of this order, we will open irrevocable letter of credit in your favor right away through … Bank, to cover the total CIF value of the order.

至于这批订单的付款方式,我方将立即通过……银行开立以你方为受益人的不可撤销信用证,以支付 CIF 订单总值。

● The Order No. 842 must be stated on all the invoices and correspondence. Final shipping instructions will follow.

所有的发票和函件都必须指明是第 842 号订单。随后再寄最后的装运指示。

● Packing: Each cashmere sweater to be packed in a polybag, each dozen into a tin-lined carton, 10 dozen to a wooden case.

包装:每件羊绒衫装入一个塑料袋内,每一打装入一衬锡的纸箱内,每 10 打装入一木箱内。

● Shipping marks: on the outer packing, please mark wording "Fragile", "Handle with Care" and "Keep Away from Fire".

唛头:应在外包装上注明"易碎品"、"小心轻放"、"远离火"等标识。

● Other terms as per your offer.

其他条款参见贵方报盘。

● As we are in urgent need of the goods, we find it necessary to stress the importance of making punctual shipment within the validity of the L/C.

我们急需该货,认为有必要强调一下在信用证的有效期内按时交货至关重要。

● Our order is placed on condition that they are dispatched by 10 November at the latest.

我们下订单的条件是货物最迟在 11 月 10 日前发运。

3.　Hoping the Seller to Accept

● Please kindly confirm your acceptance of our order as soon as possible. As soon as you confirm the order, we will send the relative irrevocable L/C without delay so that you can arrange delivery upon receipt of our L/C.

请立即确认接受我方的订单。一旦贵方确认上述订单，我方将立即寄送相关的不可撤销信用证，以便贵方办理发货事宜。

- We shall greatly appreciate your confirmation of our order by return.
  如果贵方能立即确认接受我方的订单，我方将不胜感激。
- We appreciate your prompt shipment as the goods are urgently needed.
  货急用，请即装。
- We await your advice of shipment, or the earliest time you propose to ship by return of email.
  期盼贵方用电子邮件回复我方装运通知或告知我方贵方认为的最早的装运期。
- We trust you will give this order your immediate attention.
  相信贵方会给予我方订单及时的关注。
- Please arrange immediate shipment of this repeat order.
  请立即安排装运该续订订单。
- We trust that the current business is only the beginning of a series of transactions in the future.
  我们相信这笔交易只是未来一系列交易的先导。
- We sincerely hope that this trial order may lead to more important transactions.
  相信这次试订购将会增加我们日后更多更重要的贸易往来。
- This transaction, though small in amount, marks the beginning of our formal business relationship.
  这笔交易金额虽小，却标志着我们双方正式业务关系的开始。
- It is our hope that this order is the first step in the establishment of a long and happy business relationship.
  希望此订单是我们建立长期愉快的业务关系的第一步。

确认订单写作步骤

1. Thanks for the Order and Confirming it
2. Making Guarantee or Requirement

确认订单常用语句

1.   Thanks for the Order and Confirming it

- Thank you for your order of November 16 for computers. We are willing to confirm our acceptance as shown in the enclosed S/C No.1010.
  感谢贵方 11 月 16 日关于电脑的订单。正如随函附寄的第 1010 号销售确认书所示，我方很乐意确认接受贵方的订货。
- We accept your order for 2,000 sets of full-automatic washing machines and will arrange

shipment accordingly.

我方接受贵方 2000 台全自动洗衣机的订单，并将会安排相应的装运。

- We confirm your order for 3 M/Ts of walnut. We are working on your order and will keep you informed in time of progress.

  我方确认贵方三公吨核桃的订单。我方正在执行贵方订单并将随时告知进展情况。

- We have pleasure in confirming that we have accepted your order for solar water heaters with the specifications given in your letter.

  我方十分高兴地确认贵方来函中所要规格的太阳能热水器订单已被接受。

- In view of your urgent need of the goods and the good relations between our two parties, we have decided to accept your order in spite of the current tight supply position.

  鉴于你方急需该货且我们双方之间的良好关系，我方决定接受贵方订单，尽管目前供货很紧。

- As some items under your order are beyond our business scope, we can only accept your order partially. We hope this will not bring you inconvenience.

  由于你方订单项下的货物超出了我方经营范围，我方只能部分接受你方的订单。希望这样做不致给你方带来不便。

- Although your price is below our level, we accept, as an exception, your order with a view to initiating business with you.

  尽管贵方的价格低于我们的价格水平，我们还是破例接受你们的订单，以期达成与贵公司的首笔业务。

- Although the prevailing quotations are somewhat higher, we will accept your order on the same terms as before with a view to encouraging business.

  虽然现行价格都要高一些，可是为了鼓励贸易我们将按以往条件接受你方的订单。

2. Making Guarantee or Requirement

Guarantee

- We have confidence that you will be completely satisfied with our goods when you receive them.

  我方相信贵方收到货物后会感到很满意。

- We assure you of the punctual execution of your order.

  我们保证准时执行贵方订单。

- We assure you that the order will be handled with great care.

  我方保证将会慎重处理此订单。

- We are enclosing our Sales Confirmation No. 354 in duplicate of which please countersign and return one copy to us for our file.

  兹随函附寄我方第 354 号销售确认书一式两份，请会签后退回一份，以供存档。

- Our sales confirmation is being prepared and will be sent to you by express mail in two working days.

  我们正准备销售确认书，并会在未来两个工作日内以快递信件发送。

- We sincerely appreciate your confidence in our products and hope this is the first of many orders for years to come.

感谢贵方对我方产品的信任，希望此订单是未来众多订单的开始。

- We assure you that this order and further orders shall have our immediate attention.

  请确信我们会以非常重视的态度来处理贵方的本次订单和后续订单。

- Thank you again for this trial order, and we sincerely hope it will lead to further business.

  再次感谢贵方此次试购，我方真诚希望这将促使我们进一步交易。

Requirement

- We trust you will open the related L/C without delay.

  我方相信贵方会立即开立相关信用证。

- In order to carry out the order smoothly, you are requested to open the letter of credit in time. On our part, the goods will be shipped in good time to meet your requirement.

  为了顺利执行该订单，请贵方及时开立相关信用证。我方也会按要求按时发货。

写 作 范 例

1. An Order for Digital Video Cameras

Background: 中国广州某数码科技有限公司在得到美国某电子产品有限公司的报价后，对其价格和质量均感到满意，欲订购两种型号共五百台的数码摄像机，订单编号为 ET230，并希望对方尽早寄来对此订单的认收函。

From: anneyangrose@sleb.com

To: bensongentle@alibaba.en.com

Date: Tuesday, May 13, 20＿＿, 11: 23 am

Subject: Order No. ET230 for DCR-SR220E & DCR-SR85E Digital Video Cameras

Dear Mr. Benson,

We thank you for your quotation of May 10. We find both quality and prices satisfactory and are pleased to place an Order No. ET230 with you for the following:

Description	Quantity	Unit Price	Amount
DCR-SR220E	300 sets	US$ 800.00	US$ 240,000.00
DCR-SR85E	200 sets	US$ 630.00	US$ 126,000.00
		Total:	US$ 366,000.00

Total: SAY US DOLLARS THREE HUNDRED AND SIXTY SIX THOUSAND ONLY.

The above price is on CIF Guangzhou basis.

Packing: Each set is packed in a polybag, then in a cardboard carton lined with foam.

Payment: By irrevocable, documentary letter of credit payable by draft at sight

Delivery: As we need the goods urgently, please deliver within 40 days after receipt of the order.

Please send us your acknowledgement of this order at an early date. Upon receipt of your confirmation, we will arrange to apply for the establishment of L/C.

We trust that this initial order will lead to further dealings between our two companies.

Sincerely yours,

Anne Yang

Purchasing Manager

Notes

1. video camera (recorder)   摄像机

2. description n. 规格，货物描述，也可以用 specification

    在国际贸易中，商品规格有两种含义：一种是狭义的要求和条件，即指商品的大小、长短、宽窄、厚薄、粗细、轻重、面积、体积、容积等，也称为"尺寸规格"，用以表明某种商品应具有的外形条件，不涉及商品的品质和等级。另一种是广义的要求和条件，包括尺寸规格和品质条件（也称为技术条件或技术要求，如商品的外形、色泽、气味、滋味、结构、成分、性质或性能等）两方面的内容。在对外贸易业务中，采用广义的规格较多。

3. 金额的大写规则：英文中金额的大写由三个部分组成：SAY＋货币＋大写数字 (amounts in words) ＋ ONLY（相当于中文的"整"）。如：

    US\$ 1,146,725.00 (SAY US DOLLARS ONE MILLION ONE HUNDRED AND FORTY SIX THOUSAND SEVEN HUNDRED AND TWENTY FIVE ONLY)

    如果金额有小数，常见表达方法有三种：

    方法一：… AND CENTS … (cents in words) ONLY，如 USD 100.25 (SAY US DOLLARS ONE HUNDRED AND CENTS TWENTY FIVE ONLY)

    方法二：… AND POINT… (cents in words) ONLY，如 JPY 1,100.55 (SAY JAPANESE YEN ONE THOUSAND ONE HUNDRED AND POINT FIFTY FIVE ONLY)

    方法三：##/100 ONLY，如 EUD 13,658.85 (SAY EURO DOLLARS THIRTEEN THOUSAND SIX HUNDRED AND FIFTY EIGHT 85/100 ONLY)

4. irrevocable, documentary letter of credit payable by draft at sight 不可撤销的跟单即期信用证

    跟单信用证（Documentary Letter of Credit）是开证行凭跟单汇票或单纯凭单据付款的信用证。单据是指代表货物或证明货物已交运的运输单据，如提单、铁路运单、航空运单等，通常还包括发票、保险单等商业单据。国际贸易中一般使用跟单信用证。

5. acknowledgement of this order 订单的认收函

6. upon receipt of 一经收到，一俟收到

2. An Order for Instant Pearl Powder and Requesting for the Confirmation of the Order

Background: 中国上海华泰生物科技贸易开发公司在与马来西亚 Kaja 医药保健品公司经过几轮传真和电子邮件的磋商后，决定购买 Kaja 公司出品的三种规格的即食珍珠粉，并希望对方尽早确认第 YR－309 号订单，以便开立信用证。

From: wuchristina88@shhuataibio.com

To: hassanwan@mkaja.com

Date: Tuesday, April 3, 20＿＿, 14:25 pm

Subject: Order No. YR-309 for Instant Pearl Powder

Dear Mr. Hassan,

Further to our recent exchanges of faxes and emails, we would like to confirm the details of ordering the following goods:

Description: Instant Pearl Powder, Quality Standard Q/HZL 6-2005, of the following three
specifications (GM net weight):
A. 200　　　　　　B. 500　　　　　　C. 800

Quantity (Cans): A. 5,000　　　B. 4,000　　　C. 4,000

Packing: In standard export case:
A. 24 cans each　　　B. 24 cans each　　　C. 12 cans each

Unit Price: net per can CIF Shanghai in US$:
A. 4.20　　　　　B. 5.50　　　　　C. 8.60

Payment: 100% by irrevocable, confirmed letter of credit opened immediately through the Bank of
China, Shanghai Branch and drawn at sight

Delivery: May/June, 20＿＿

Shipping Marks: refer to our previous orders

Other terms as per your quotation.

Remarks: In addition to the ordinary shipping documents, please also submit Certificate of Origin
for the goods.

As usual, we will open the relevant L/C upon your confirmation of our order.

Once you confirm our order, we will send our Purchase Contract with our signature in duplicate.
Please countersign and return one copy for our file.

Thank you for your prompt services.

Yours sincerely,

Christina Wu
Import Manager

Notes

1. further to　继……之后
2. confirm　vt.
   (1) 确认，批准
   We confirmed having placed an order with you for 1,500 tons of soybeans.　我们确认已向你方订购 1500 吨大豆。
   The board of directors has confirmed his appointment as sales manager.　董事会已批准他为销售部经理。
   (2) 证实，肯定
   We now confirm our acceptance of your offer.　现证实已接受你方报盘。
   Latest developments confirm our prediction about the trend of the market.　最近的情况发展证实了我们对市场走向的预测。
   (3) 保兑
   Please advise the credit to the beneficiary and have it confirmed.　请向受益人通知信用证并予以保兑。
   confirmation　n. 确认，确认书
   Purchase Confirmation　购货确认书
   Sales Confirmation　售货确认书
   We are now making you the following offer subject to our final confirmation.　兹报盘如下，以我方最后确认为准。
   Please fax us your confirmation immediately.　请立即传真确认。
   Increase in inquiries is a confirmation of the rise in demand.　询盘的增多证实了需求的上升。
   confirmed　adj. 保兑的，如 confirmed letter of credit　保兑信用证
   confirming bank　保兑银行
   保兑信用证（Confirmed Letter of Credit）是指开证行开出的信用证，由另一银行保证对符合信用证条款规定的单据履行付款义务。对信用证加以保兑的银行为保兑银行（Confirming Bank）。保兑银行通常是由通知银行担任，会收取保证金和银行费用。
3. instant pearl powder　即食珍珠粉
4. Quality Standard Q/HZL 6-2005　质量标准 Q/HZL 6-2005（用来表明商品品质好坏的一种标准）
5. standard export case　标准出口箱
6. opened through the Bank of China　由中国银行开立
7. as per　按照，根据
   as per the enclosed documents　按照附寄的文件
   as per quotation list　根据价目表

8. remarks   n. 备注

9. shipping documents   装运单据

装运单据是指信用证要求的除汇票以外的所有单据（不限于运输单据）。在国际货物买卖中，装运单据具有十分重要的作用。它们是买方提取货物、办理报关手续、转售货物以及向承运人或保险公司请求赔偿所必不可少的文件。

10. submit   vt. 提交，呈交

The applicants when applying for inspection of export commodities shall submit foreign trade contracts.   申请出口商品检验的申请人需提交外贸合同。

11. Certificate of Origin   原产地证明书

Certificate of Quality   质量证明书

Certificate of Quantity   数量证明书

Certificate of Weight   重量证明书

以上证书都是常见的商品检验证书（Inspection Certificate），进出口商品经过商检机构进行检验或鉴定后，由该检验机构出具的书面证明被称为"商品检验证书"。商品检验证书起着公正证明的作用，是买卖双方交接货物、结算货款和处理索赔、理赔的主要依据，也是通关纳税、结算运费的有效凭证。

12. relevant L/C   相关信用证，也可用 relative, related, covering, concerned

3. An Attached Order for Clothing

Background: 美国纽约市的 Moda Fashion 公司经理向中国轻工业品进出口公司发来电子邮件，欲购四种产品，并将第 345 号订单通过附件发送。

From: wernersparks@nymoda.fashion.com
To: leejulie@bjlight.industry.com
Date: Friday, March 15, 20＿＿, 16: 47 pm
Subject: Order No. 345 for Four Items

Dear Ms Lee,

We have received with thanks your email of March 14 and all samples, which received favorable reaction from our customers, and we take pleasure in attaching our Order No. 345 for four items in assorted sizes, colors and designs.

We have decided to accept the 15% trade discount you offered and terms of payment, documents against payment. Would you please send the shipping documents and your sight draft to the City National Bank, 382 W 125th Street, New York, NY 10027?

If you do not have any of the listed items in stock, please do not send substitutes in their place.

As the goods are urgently required, we would appreciate delivery within the next six weeks.

We expect to find a good market for the goods and hope to place further and larger orders with you in the near future.

Yours sincerely,

Werner Sparks

Manager

THE MODA FASHION COMPANY
504 West Street

New York, 100027, U.S.

<u>ORDER FORM</u>

March 15, 20_ _

<u>Order No. 345</u>

CHINA NATIONAL LIGHT INDUSTRIAL

PRODUCTS IMP. & EXP. CORP.

Beijing, China

Please supply the following:

Commodity	Catalog No.	Qty	Unit Price (US$)	Amount (US$)
linen handkerchiefs: Red/Blue	45	500 doz. each	0.20	2,400.00
pigskin gloves: Black/Brown	65	2,000 pairs each	3.00	12,000.00
assorted orlon sport shirts	74	2,000 doz.	3.00	72,000.00
assorted cotton socks	30	5,000 pairs	0.40	2,000.00
			FOB Xingang	
			TOTAL	88,400.00

Remarks: 15% Trade Disc. Pymt. D/P Del. 6 weeks

for the Moda Fashion Company

Werner Sparks

Werner Sparks

Manager

<u>Notes</u>

1. receive favorable reaction   反映良好，深受好评
2. prompt delivery   立即交货
3. find a good market for   为……开辟良好的市场
4. place further and larger orders   长期且大量订购
5. linen handkerchief   亚麻手帕
6. pigskin gloves   猪皮手套
7. assorted orlon sport shirts   各种花色的奥纶运动衫
8. Disc. = Discount
9. Pymt. = Payment
10. Del. = Delivery

4. A Repeat Order for Fur Coat

Background: 加拿大Ricky高级服装有限公司业务经理Carl Borrow向中国杭州丽波丝绸服饰有限公司发来电子邮件，欲再次订购一千打相同颜色和款式的女式真丝睡衣，并希望货物能尽快装运。

From: carlbsho@rickyfashion.com
To: barrymorelas@hzlibo.silkgarments.com
Date: Wednesday, September 19, 20__, 13: 08 pm
Subject: Repeat Order for "Li Bo" Ladies' Silk Sleepwear

Dear Mr. Xiao,

On receipt of the shipment of "Li Bo" Ladies' Silk Sleepwear ex S. S. "HELSINKI", we are very pleased to inform you that we find the goods quite satisfactory.

As we have recently received many favorable comments for the said articles from our customers, we believe we can sell additional quantities in this market. We wish to book with you a repeat order for another 1,000 dozen of the same color and style.

If possible, please arrange for an early shipment of this repeat order, as we are badly in need of the goods.

We are pleased to have finalized business with you and expect that we can expand the trade between us in the future.

Yours sincerely,
Carl Borrow
Business Manager

Notes

1. repeat order   续订订单

   更多与 order 搭配的短语：

   order sheet/order form/order blank/order note   订单

   letter/mail order   信函订购

   verbal order   口头订购

   initial order   初次订单

   trial order   试销订单

   further order   更多的订单

   additional order   追加订单

   official/formal order   正式订单

   pressing order   紧急订单

   advance order   预订单

   regular order   长期订单

   fresh/new order   新的订单

   large order   大订单

   original order   原始订单

   split order   分批订单

   back order   逾期订单，未能按时交货订单，尚未交货订单

   sample order/order by sample   凭样订购，订购样品

   carry out/deal with/work on/attend to/effect/execute/fulfill/fill/handle an order   履行订单

   entertain an order   考虑订单

   dispatch an order   发货，寄出货品

   invite an order   请求订货

   confirm an order   确认订货

   duplicate an order   将订货增加一倍

2. Ladies' Silk Sleepwear   女式真丝睡衣

3. ex S. S. "HELSINKI" = shipped by the steamship "HELSINKI"   由 "HELSINKI" 轮装来

   S. S. 是 steamship 的缩写

   ex 和 per 的区别："由某轮装运"，从进口者角度来看，是 "装来"，用 "ex"；从出口者
   角度来看，是 "装走"，用 "per"。如：

   We have received the shipment of the fur coats ex S. S. "YANGZHOU".   我们已收到 "扬州"
   轮装来的皮大衣。

   We have shipped the fur coats per S. S. "YANGZHOU".   我们已把皮大衣装上 "扬州" 轮。

4. book with you a repeat order   向贵方续订……货物

   book an order with sb for sth = place an order = to order   向某人订购某商品

5.   A Confirmation of an Order for Bicycles

Background: 中国某自行车有限公司外销部经理 Dora Campbell 确认新西兰 Merida 自行车贸
易公司 Blair 先生发来的购买一千辆自行车的订单，并用附件寄送第 PB132 号销售确认书一

式两份，并保证会按时交货。

From: doracampbell@qweb.com
To: blairtony@merida.bicycle.com
Date: Wednesday, April 4, 20__, 15: 28 pm
Subject: Sales Confirmation No. PB132 for 1,000 Pieces of Ama Brand Bicycles

Dear Mr. Blair,

We thank you for your faxes of March 23 and April 3 informing us that you have accepted our offer of the subject goods.

Thanks to your cooperation in the negotiations on price, and terms and conditions, we have concluded a large transaction with you. In reply, we are very much pleased to confirm your order for 1,000 pieces of Ama Brand bicycles. Attached please find the relevant Sales Confirmation No. PB132 in duplicate. Please countersign and return one copy to us for our file.

We will try our best to arrange for the delivery in time as provided accordingly. Please open the relative L/C at an early date.

Hoping the goods will turn out to be your entire satisfaction and from now on we will enjoy business relations that are profitable to both of us.

Yours sincerely,
Dora Campbell
Export Sales Manager

Notes

1. Sales Confirmation 销售确认书
   销售确认书是买卖双方在通过交易磋商达成交易后，由卖方出具并寄给双方加以确认的列明达成交易条件的书面证明，是经买卖双方签署的确认书，是法律上有效的文件，对买卖双方具有同等的约束力。在国际贸易中常简写为 S/C。

2. terms and conditions 条款及条件，条款指大的方面，条件指具体方面。如有关支付，有用 L/C, D/P, D/A 的，这是条款。确定信用证付款方式后，进一步要求什么时候、通过什么样的银行开立等，这是条件。然而在商业书信中，区别不大，常连用。

3. conclude a transaction 成交，达成交易，其中 conclude 可以换成 strike, close, make; transaction 可以换成 deal, business, bargain

4. Attached please find... 附件是……

5. in duplicate 一式两份, 类似的表达有 in triplicate 一式三份, in quadruplicate 一式四份。一式四份及其以上也常用 in four copies, in five copies…或 in fourfold, in fivefold…

6. countersign vt. 会签，副署，连署

countersignature   n. 会签，副署，或 counter signature, counter-signature

会签是指买卖双方中的一方根据双方磋商的条件缮制货物买卖合同或确认书正本一式两份，一方签字后寄交给另一方。经对方查核无误并签字后，留存一份，另一份寄还，双方各执一份，作为合同订立的证据和履行合同的依据。

When the Sales Contract has been signed by the seller, it will be countersigned by the buyer. 销售合同经卖方签署后，须经买方会签。

Please return the duplicate completed with your countersignature.   请会签后退回一份。

7. for our file   供我方存档，也可用 for our record

8. arrange for the delivery   交货，常见的搭配为 effect shipment, make delivery, arrange delivery, arrange shipment

9. in time as provided   按照规定的时间

10. accordingly   adv. 相应地，按照要求，因此

    The contract stipulated that payment should be made by irrevocable letter of credit payable by sight draft, so you must act accordingly.   合同规定付款方式应为不可撤销的凭即期汇票支付的信用证，所以贵方必须照办。

11. You are requested to …   请贵方……

12. at an early date   尽早，类似的表达有 without delay, without further delay, with the least delay

13. turn out   证实，发觉是……

    We hope everything will turn out to be satisfactory in the end.   我们希望最终一切都令人满意。

6. A Confirmation of an Order and Informing the Delay in Delivery

Background: 印度某地毯企业总经理 Hans Black 确认中国某地毯贸易开发有限公司 Megan 女士发来的第 E304 号购买 1500 条地毯的订单。Hans Black 告知对方除了编号为 16－34A 号的商品需要五周才能装运外，其余商品三周内可装运，并询问对方是选择分开发货还是到齐发货。

From: hansblackjj@alibaba.en.com
To: meganbll@hotmail.com
Date: Thursday, September 15, 20＿＿, 17: 56 pm
Subject: Confirmation of Your Order No. E304

Dear Ms. Megan,

We are pleased to receive by email your Order No. E304 of September 14 for 1,500 pieces of carpets and are glad to understand that you are making great progress in pushing sales of our goods in your market.

All the items will be ready for shipment in three weeks with the exception of Catalog No. 16-34A which is hand made. The manufacturers are finding it impossible to comply with current demand for their stock is close to be exhausted but consecutive new orders are pouring in. Though the workers are speeding up the production, it will take 5 weeks to get them ready since the stock is now very low. Please indicate whether you would like to ship separately or wait for 5 weeks until all the items are ready.

We are sure you will appreciate the excellent craftsmanship and attractive pattern of our carpets.

We appreciate your cooperation and look forward to receiving your reply.

Yours very sincerely,

Hans Black

General Manager

Notes

1. comply with current demand　满足当前的需求，也常用 satisfy/meet one's requirement
2. The stock is close to be exhausted.　库存几近售罄。

   exhausted　adj. 售罄的，耗尽的，用光的

   Our stock of DB23 is exhausted and we have no idea when the material will be restocked.

   DB23 库存售罄，不知何时再能补进。
3. consecutive　adj. 连续不断的
4. pour in　涌入，到来

7. An Email for Offering Substitute

Background: 美国某电脑设备有限公司销售助理 Kevin Decker 感谢中国天津市恒华科技有限公司发来的购买计算机外围设备的订单，但遗憾地告知对方欲购买的 T342 型号产品停产，并表示可用新产品 E312 型代替。

From: kevindeckermor@alibaba.en.com

To: phillipszh@henghua.tech.com

Date: Monday, December 12, 20＿＿, 13:18 pm

Subject: Substitute for Model T342

Dear Mrs. Phillips,

Thank you for ordering more of our computer peripherals.

As you know, our policy is to continuously improve the quality and performance of our products. In recent years the demand for the modem you requested, Model T342, has fallen to such an extent that we have ceased to produce it.

In place of it, we can offer you our better model, E312. At the low price of only ￡11.50, new model is much cheaper but outperforms the old version by 3 times. The large and repeat orders we regularly receive from leading electronic products distributors is clear evidence of the popularity of this model.

We are sending you by parcel post a sample and a detailed technical data sheet for your reference, hoping that it is of interest to you.

With best regards.

Yours sincerely,
Kevin Decker
Marketing Assistant

Notes

1. substitute   n. 代用品，替代品
   基本用法是：
   We may offer/use A as a substitute for B.   我们可以用 A 代替 B。
   offer/use carton as a substitute for wooden case   用纸箱代替木箱
   We should like to take opportunity to offer you the following articles as a close substitute for your consideration.   我方借此机会向贵方提供下列产品作为替代品，供贵方参考。
   We leave it to your discretion to supply a suitable substitute, if you don't have what we want, but the price must not exceed US$ 0.35 per yard.   如无我方所需货物，可由你方选择合适的代用品，但价格不得超过每码 0.35 美元。
   We offer to sell ink refillable liquid chalk which is the ideal substitute of chalk.   我方提供可充墨水的液体粉笔作为粉笔的理想替代品。

2. computer peripheral   计算机外部设备、辅助设备，如与计算机连接工作的打印机、调制解调器或存储系统

3. modem   n. 调制解调器

4. the demand for…   对……的需求

5. to such an extent   到如此的程度
   to that extent   到那个程度
   to some extent   在某种程度
   to a great extent   在很大程度
   to a certain extent   在一定程度
   to the extent that (you indicated)…   到……（你说）的程度

6. cease   v. 停止
   The factory ceased production.   工厂停产。

7. in place of it   作为它的替代品

8. outperform   vt. 性能上超过

9. technical data sheet   技术说明书

Unit 9　Packing
包　装

1.　Functions of Packing

Appropriate packing can prevent or minimize the damage of the shipment and promote product sales. Its nature, cost and appearance deserve special care and attention. Suitable packing is of great importance in the following three aspects:

(1) The buyer is under certain conditions entitled to reject the goods if they are not packed in accordance with his instructions or with the provisions agreed upon.

(2) Packing should be designed to suit shipping requirements.

(3) Packing should conform to the regulations in the country of destination.

2.　Types of Packing

According to the function of packing, it can be divided into transport packing (usually known as outer packing) and sales packing (usually known as inner packing).

2.1　Transport Packing

Transport packing must be strong enough to protect the packed goods against such hazards as pilferage, rough handling, corrosion and crushing, etc. And it must also be as light and compact as possible to keep freight cost low.

2.2　Sales Packing

Sales packing is done mainly to push sales. Requirements for inner packing are increasingly high, with beautiful color, creative design and convenient handling as its chief concern. The design and the color should suit the customers' tastes. Nice packing helps find a market.

3.　Outer Packing Marks

Packing must be strikingly marked. Conventionally, outer packing marks mainly include transport marks, directive marks and warning marks. A transport mark consists of the name of the consignee or shipper, destination and packing number. Directive marks are eye-catching figures and concise instructions concerning manner of proper handling, storing, loading and unloading of the packed goods, e.g. "USE NO HOOKS", "HANDLE WITH CARE", "THIS SIDE UP". Warning marks are obvious symbols or words to warn people against the hidden danger or inflammables, explosives and poisonous products, eg. "CORROSIVES", "EXPLOSIVES", "ACID WITH CARE", "INFLAMMABLE", etc.

包装常用语句

Packing Requirements/Instructions

(1) Attractive Packing

- You can be assured that our design and color of packing would suit American taste.
  我们向您保证我们包装的设计和颜色会符合美国人口味的。

- In the packing of goods for comsumption, you must pay special attention to the characteristics of the people, their customs and traditions.
  包装消费品时，贵方必须特别注意该国人民的特点、习俗和传统。

- Our tablecloth is often presented as a gift, so it should be tastefully packed.
  我们常把台布作为礼物馈赠朋友，因此希望包装美观别致。

- A wrapping that catches the eyes will certainly help push the sales.
  吸引眼球的包装当然有利于推销。

- The quality of your product is quite nice and the packing should also impress buyers.
  贵方的产品质量不错，而包装也应该吸引顾客才好。

(2) Proper Packing

- We put great importance on proper packing and expect you to pack the above order properly.
  我们对包装很重视，希望贵方将上述订货妥善包装。

- Strong packing will ensure the goods against any possible damage during transit.
  结实的包装可以确保货物不会在运输途中受损。

- These goods won't be stowed away with the heavy cargo. Besides, we'll reinforce the cases with metal straps.
  这批货不会和笨重的货物堆放在一起，另外我方会用铁皮来加固箱子。

- Please take into account the boxes are likely to receive rough handling.
  请考虑到盒子可能会遭受野蛮装卸。

- The outer packing must be reinforced in order to minimize the extent of any possible damage to the goods.
  外包装必须加固，以便使货物万一遭到的损坏降到最低程度。

- Please ship the goods in strong export packing to ensure good condition on arrival.
  请将此货物用坚固的出口包装装运，以确保运达时货物完好无损。

- The packing of computers must be able to prevent dampness and rust and to stand shock and rough handling as well.
  计算机的包装必须能防潮、防锈，并能经受得住震动和野蛮搬运。

- Unless otherwise specified in the contract, the supplied goods shall be packed by export standard protective measures.

  除合同另有规定外，卖方供应的货物全部应按出口商品标准的保护方法进行包装。

- Such packing shall be strong enough and suitable for long distance ocean/air and inland transportation.

  该包装应为适合于长途海运或空运以及内陆运输的坚固包装。

- The machines must be well protected against dampness, moisture, rust and shock.

  机器必须仔细包装，以便防潮、防锈和防震。

- All export bicycles are wrapped in plastic-lined strong waterproof materials at the port and packed in pairs in light-weight crates.

  所有出口自行车在港口用内衬塑料、结实防水的材料包裹，每两辆装入一轻型的板条箱内。

- We use metal angles at each corner of the carton.

  每个箱角都用金属角加固。

- Each case is lined with foam plastics in order to protect the goods against press.

  箱子里垫有泡沫塑料以免货物受压。

- The goods are to be packed in strong export cases, securely strapped.

  货物应该用坚固的出口木箱包装，并且牢牢加箍。

(3) Ways of Packing

- How would you pack the shipment of computers we've ordered?

  我们订购的这批计算机贵方打算如何包装？

- We can pack the products according to your specification.

  我们可以按照贵方的规格进行包装。

- Containers are widely used in our shipment.

  我们装运时广泛采用集装箱。

- If you agree, we'll use wooden boxes for ourter packing.

  如果贵方同意，我方将采用木箱作为外包装。

- We suggest you have the outer packing changed, using wooden crates instead of cardboard boxes.

  我方建议贵方把外包装改一下，用板条箱代替硬纸箱。

- As for the packing of the products, please use our own brand name and also include a list of ingredients.

  至于商品包装，请用我公司的牌子，并加上成分说明。

- We use a polythene wrapper for each silk blouse.

  丝绸女衫的包装是每一件装一只聚乙烯袋子。

- The inner packing is plastic film and thus waterproof.

  内包装是塑料薄膜，因而可以防水。

- The gree peas can be supplied in bulk or in gunny bags.

  青豆可以散装，也可以用麻袋装。

- The cigars are packed 5 pieces to a small packet, 20 packets to a carton, and 144 artons to a cardboard container.

雪茄烟 5 支一包，20 包一条，144 条一纸箱。

- It is the usual practice here that 10 shirts are packed to a carton and 10 cartons to a strong seaworthy wooden case.

  按照我方这里的通常做法，每 10 件衬衫装一纸箱，每 10 纸箱装入一个适合于海运的结实木箱。

- The finished color TV sets shall be packed in cartons, 4 cartons to a wooden case suitable for long distance road transport.

  成品彩电将用纸箱包装，每 4 个纸箱装入一个适合于长途陆路运输的木箱内。

- Each bicycle is enclosed in a corrugated cardboard pack, and 5 are banded together and wrapped in sheet plastic.

  每辆自行车用瓦楞硬纸板箱包装，每 5 件捆扎在一起，并用塑料薄膜包裹。

- The piece goods are to be wrapped in kraft paper, then packed in wooden cases.

  布匹在装入木箱以前要用牛皮纸包好。

- The eggs are packed in cartons with beehives lined with shake-proof paper board.

  鸡蛋要用带蜂房孔、内衬防震纸板的纸箱包装。

- Each pill is put into a small box sealed with wax.

  每个丸药装入小盒后用蜡密封好。

- Please make the fruit jar airtight.

  请把果酱罐密封。

- The canned goods are to be packed in cartons with double straps.

  罐装货物在纸箱里，外面加两道箍。

- You'd better pack 2 or 3 designs in each box so that we can put them directly to the market for sale.

  装箱时最好每箱搭配上 2 个或 3 个花色品种，这样我方就可以直接投放市场销售了。

- In order to facilitate selling, it would be better to pack the goods with equally assorted colors.

  为了便于销售，最好将货物各种颜色平均搭配装箱。

- The fountain pen is placed in a satin-covered small box, lined with beautiful silk ribbon.

  金笔装在一个锦缎小盒里，再用一条漂亮的绸带系在外面。

Packing Charges

- Such shirts packed in cardboard cartons can save freight cost.

  使用硬纸箱包装这批衬衣可以节省运费。

- We would accept your offer if packing charges are included.

  如果包装费包括在内，我方愿意接受你方报价。

- We might as well provide you with special packing if you insist, but the additional cost will be borne by you.

  如果贵方坚持的话，我方可以提供特殊包装，但额外的费用应由贵方负担。

- We'll pack the goods in wooden cases instead of in cartons. But the extra packing charges will be for your account.

我方将把货物的包装由纸箱改为木箱，但额外的包装费用应由你方负担。

- If you insist, we can use wooden cases instead. But the charge for packing will be higher and shipment will have to be delayed.

  如果贵方坚持，我们可以改用木箱。但包装费用比较高，而且装运时间也得延期。

- If you require individual packing for the gloves, there will be a charge of US$300.

  如果你方要求手套按副包装，费用是 300 美元。

- Generally speaking, buyers bear the charges of packing.

  一般来说，买方承担包装费。

- Packing charge is about 3% of the total cost of the goods.

  包装费约为货物总值的 3%。

- Normally, packing charge is included in the contract price.

  商品的合同价一般包括包装费。

Labelling

- At least one label is attached to each packing case.

  每个包装箱上都拴上至少一个标签。

- Your Order No. 015 has almost been complete and we are eager to have your instruction regarding labelling to each package.

  贵方第 015 号订单货物已基本备妥，切盼收到关于包装标签的指示。

- We usually do the labelling ourselves as we are responsible for the brandlabels of our own products.

  标签通常由我方自己来贴，因为我方要对自己产品的牌子负责。

Shipping/Packing Marks

- On the outer packing, please mark wording, "Handle with Care".

  在外包装上请标记"小心轻放"字样。

- Every 100 dozen should be packed in a wooden case marked TM and numbered from No. 1 upward.

  每 100 打装入一标有"TM"的木箱内，编号从 1 开始。

- To be marked on each package with fadeless paint are the package number, gross weight, net weight, measurement and the wording "KEEP AWAY FROM MOISTURE", "HANDLE WITH CARE", etc.

  每只货箱上都要用不褪色油漆标明箱号、毛重、净重、尺寸以及"防潮"、"小心轻放"等字样。

- Kindly stencil our shipping marks in letters 4 inches high and give gross and net weight.

  请用 4 英寸大小的字母标示唛头，并注明毛重与净重。

- All boxes are to be marked as usual, but please number them consecutively from No.11.

  所有箱子都像往常一样标示唛头，但务请从 11 号开始顺序编号。

- On each package shall be stenciled conspicuously: port of destination, package number, gross and net weights, measurement and the shipping mark shown on the right side.

每件货物上都应醒目地标示目的港、件号、毛重及净重、尺寸，并在右侧标示唛头。

- We give you on the attached sheet with full details regarding packing and marking. These must be strictly observed.

  随函附寄包装及唛头细则一纸，请遵照办理。

- Please mark the cases as per the drawing given.

  请按所给图纸标记箱体。

Describing Weight

- We pack sugar in new gunny bags of 100 kg each.

  我们用新麻袋装糖，每袋 100 千克。

- The oil will be supplied in tins of 20 kilos net, two tins to a crate.

  油每桶净重 20 千克，每箱装两桶。

- Please do not omit mentioning the tare and gross weights in addition to the net.

  在净重之外请勿遗漏皮重和毛重。

- The gross weight for each case is around 45 kilos.

  每箱毛重约 45 千克。

- They will be packed 15 dozen to one carton, gross weight around 30 kilos a carton.

  该货每纸箱装 15 打，每箱毛重约 30 千克。

Packing Improvement

- We sincerely hope you can do something to improve the packing.

  我们衷心希望贵方能把包装改进一番。

- A large number of bed spreads we ordered from you last year were found stained when they reached us. I hope you will take measures to improve the packing.

  我们去年订购的那批床单运到时有不少被沾污，希望这次能采取措施改进一下。

- We have informed the factory to have the packing improved as you instructed.

  我们已通知厂家按照贵方要求改进包装。

- You'll note that our packing has been greatly improved.

  您会发现，我方的包装已有很大改进。

- We accept that the damage was not your fault but feel that we must modify our packing requirements to avoid future losses.

  我们理解此损坏非贵公司的过失，但感觉我们必须修改包装的方法，以避免同类事件的发生。

- I believe that our improved packing will satisfy the buyers at your end.

  我相信我方改进过的包装会使你方市场顾客满意。

- We are of the opinion that the packing improvement will push the sales a long way forward.

  我方认为改进包装将会大大促进销售。

包装常用短语

- packing charge   包装费
- packing instructions   包装要求，包装须知
- packing list   装箱单
- export packing   出口包装
- neutral packing   中性包装（出口商根据进口商授意使用的一种特别的商标，内外包装上都没有表示生产国、厂商或商品名称之类的任何标志）
- hanging packing   挂式包装
- unlabelled packing   无牌的包装
- nude packing   裸装
- consumer pack   零售包装
- gift-wrap   礼品包装
- bag (BG), sack (SK)   袋
- gunny bag   麻袋
- polyethylene bag, plastic bag   塑料袋
- zippered bag   拉链袋
- case, chest (CST)   箱
- box   盒
- wooden case (C)   木箱
- carton (CTN)   纸箱
- crate (CRT)   板条箱
- bale (B)   包
- bundle   捆
- tin, can   罐头
- basket   篮，篓，筐
- bottle (BOT)   瓶
- keg (KG)   小木桶
- iron drum (DUM)   铁桶
- cylinder   钢桶
- barrel (BRL)   琵琶桶
- waterproof paper   防水纸
- kraft paper   牛皮纸
- canvas   帆布
- fiber board   纤维板
- nylon strap   尼龙带
- adhesive tape   胶带

- stuffing material　填料
- nylon plastic　尼龙丝
- paper scrap　纸屑
- saw dust　木屑
- wax paper　蜡纸

写 作 范 例

1.　An Email from Importer Asking for the Packing Improvement

Background: 加拿大 APS 五金有限公司于 7 月 10 日收到中国北京欣华机电有限公司发来的 40 箱钢螺丝钉，但有 10 箱到货受损严重，因此对今后产品的包装提出了改进要求。

From: johnkentkk@aps.com.ca

To: matakchung@bjxinhua.com

Date: Tuesday, July 11, 20＿＿, 10:02 am

Subject: Packing Improvement for Steel Screws in Canada, U.S. and Mexico

Dear Mr. Ma,

On 10 July, we received your consignment of 40 cardboard cartons of steel screws you shipped to Ottawa.

We regret to inform you that of the 40 cartons, 10 were badly damaged and the contents had spilled, leading to some losses.

We accept that the damage was not your fault but feel that we must modify our packing requirements to avoid future losses.

The packing for Canada is to be in wooden cases of 120 kg net, each containing 10 kg x 12 packets. For U.S., we would like you to have the goods packed in double gunny bags of 60/70 kg each. As for the Mexican market, our buyers prefer 30-kilo cardboard cartons.

This will add further value to the products, which can provide for a wide range of tastes and selections. Kindly let us know whether these requirements could be met and whether they will lead to an increase in your prices.

We look forward to your early confirmation.

Yours sincerely,

John Kent

Import Coordinator

Notes

1. be badly damaged   受损严重
2. 常见的包装表示法如下：
    ● 从最内层包装到最外层包装：

    Sth is packed in a(n) …, … to a(n) …, … to a(n) …

    e.g. 钢笔 12 支装一盒，200 盒装一木箱。

    Pens are packed 12 pieces to a box, 200 boxes to a wooden case.

    ● 从最外层包装到最内层包装：

    A. Sth is packed in …(pl.), each containing … （适用于一层包装）

    e.g. 男式衬衫用纸箱包装，每箱装 50 打。

    Men's Shirts are packed in cartons, each containing 50 dozen.

    B. Sth is packed in …(pl.) of …(pl.), each containing … （适用于两层包装）

    e.g. 每双尼龙袜装一个塑料袋，12 双装一盒。

    Nylon socks are packed in boxes of 12 polybags, each polybag containing one pair.

    = Nylon socks are packed one pair in a polybag, 12 polybags to a box.

    C. Sth is packed in …(pl.) of …lbs/kilos/kgs net each. （适用于描述包装的重量）

    e.g. 橘子用板条箱装，每箱净重 50 千克。

    Oranges are packed in crates of 50 kilos net each.

3. The packing for Canada is to be in wooden cases of 120 kg net, each containing 10 kg ×12 packets. 发往加拿大的铁钉用木箱装，净重 120 千克，每箱内装重量各为 10 千克的 12 小袋铁钉。

4. For U. S., we would like you to have the goods packed in double gunny bag of 60/70 kilos each. 发往美国的铁钉用双层麻袋包装，每袋重 60 至 70 千克。

5. As for Mexican market, our buyers prefer 30-kilo cartons. 墨西哥市场上，客户喜欢装 30 千克的硬纸板箱。

6. This will add further value to the products, which can provide for a wide range of tastes and requirements.   这将会使产品增值，并能迎合更广泛的爱好和要求。

7. Kindly let us know…   敬请告知……

2. An Email from Exporter Informing Importer of the Packing

Background: 德国 Vanker 实业有限公司从中国深圳青维剪刀制造有限公司处购买了 2000 个不锈钢剪刀，到货完好且质量令人满意，欲再订购 CM902 型理发剪，于是询问此类产品的包装情况。青维公司在收到询问的电子邮件后，立即回复如下。

From: deboratian4587@szhqingwei.com

To: mortonbrookjr@vanker.com

Date: Wednesday, July 10, 20＿＿, 11: 13 am

Subject: Packing for Salon Hair Scissors Type CM902

Dear Mr. Brook,

We are pleased to learn from you that 2,000 pieces of Stainless Steel Scissors shipped to Hamburg on June 28 have arrived in perfect condition and you are completely satisfied with this consignment.

In reply to your email half an hour ago dated July 10 inquiring about the packing of Salon Hair Scissors Type CM902, we wish to state as below.

The goods are packed in boxes of one dozen each, 100 boxes to a carton. The dimensions are 17 cm high, 30 cm wide and 50 cm long with a volume of about 0.026 cubic meters. The gross weight is 23.5 kg, the net weight being 22.5 kg.

As to the shipping marks outside the carton, in addition to the gross, net and tare weights, your required wording "MADE IN CHINA" is also stenciled on the package. If you have any special preference in this respect, please let us know and we will meet you to the best of our ability.

Taking this opportunity, we would like to inform you that we used to pack our various scissors in wooden cases but after several trial shipments in carton packing, we found our cartons just as seaworthy as wooden cases. Besides, cartons are less expensive, lighter to carry and cost lower freight. So nowadays increasing clients are preferring carton packing to wooden case packing.

You may rest assured that we will give special care to the packing in order to avoid damage in transit. We trust that you will agree to our opinion and accept our carton packing.

Best wishes,

Yours sincerely,
Debora Tian
Export Sales Manager

Notes
1. arrive in perfect condition   到货状况完好
2. The goods are packed in boxes of one dozen each, 100 boxes to a carton.   货物用盒装,每盒装一打，100 盒装入一纸箱。
3. The dimensions are 17 cm high, 30 cm wide and 50 cm long with a volume of about 0.026 cubic meters.   包装尺寸为长 50 厘米、宽 30 厘米、高 17 厘米，体积大约 0.026 立方米。

4. The gross weight is 23.5 kg, the net weight being 22.5 kg.　净重 22.5 千克，毛重 23.5 千克。the net weight being 22.5 kg 是独立主格结构。其中分词 being 有自己的逻辑主语 net weight，而不是句子主语 gross weight。

5. the gross, net and tare weights　毛重、净重和皮重

6. If you have any special preference in this respect, please let us know and we will meet you to the best of our ability.　如果这方面还有什么特殊要求，请告知，我们定将全力满足。
to the best of our ability　竭尽全力

7. give special care to sth　特别注意某事

3.　An Email from Importer about Requirements on Shipment Packing

Background: 中国大连达菲服饰贸易有限公司于 2 月 11 日收到韩国 Betta 制衣厂发来的第 8098 号销售合同，经审阅后，发现包装条款表述得不够清楚。为避免日后产生麻烦，达菲公司的销售高级主管 James Xu 详细告知了韩方己方希望的货物运输包装，并将此内容在销售合同中做了脚注，会签后退回一份。

From: jamesxu-sales@dafeitrading.com

To: thomaskim_541@bettaclothing.com

Date: Thursday, February 11, 20__, 11:33 am

Subject: Requirements on Shipment Packing for Sales Contract No. 8098

Dear Mr. Thomas,

We are glad to receive your email dated February 11 attaching a Sales Contract No. 8098 in duplicate but wish to state that the packing clause in the contract is not clear enough. The relative clause reads as follows:

Packing: Seaworthy export packing, suitable for long distance Ocean transportation.

In order to avoid possible future trouble, we would like to make clear beforehand our packing requirements as follows.

The sweaters we ordered should be packed in polybag and 10 dozen to one carton, 10 cartons on a pallet, 10 pallets in FCL container.

On the outer packing please mark our initials TBP in a triangle, under which the port of destination and our order number should be stenciled. In addition, directive marks like "KEEP DRY", "KEEP AWAY FROM PRESSURE" should also be indicated.

We have made a footnote on the contract to that effect and are returning one copy of the contract, duly countersigned by us. We hope you will find it in order and pay special attention to the packing.

We look forward to receiving your shipping advice and thank you in advance.

Yours sincerely,
James Xu
Sales Executive

Notes

1. seaworthy　adj. 适合海运的，适航的
   Your packing must be strong, easy to handle and seaworthy.　包装必须牢固，易于搬运，且适合远洋运输。

2. beforehand　adv. 预先
   They proposed to make arrangement beforehand.　他们提议事先做好安排。
   Please inform us beforehand of the arrival of the goods at our end.　请提前告知我方货物抵达我处的时间。

3. pallet　n.（叉车搬运货物时用的）托盘，货盘
   The warehouse will hold more than 90,000 pallets storing 30 million Easter eggs.　那间仓库将用 9 万多个货盘装 3000 万只复活节彩蛋。
   CAPTAIN can help you solve the problem with specially designed industrial pallet system.　凯普逊公司专业设计生产的工业货架系统可以帮您解决这个难题。

4. FCL　整箱货，"Full Container Load" 的缩写
   We will allow you 1 % quantity free charge for FCL.　走整柜的话，我们会额外免费发整柜1%的数量。
   Freight to Asian ports in FCL is about US$30-35 cents/kg.　亚洲货运港口整箱是每千克30~35 美分。

5. outer packing　外包装
   It is at buyer's option whether the outer packing is in bales or in wooden cases.　外包装打包还是用木箱，由买方决定。

6. initials　n. 大写的首字母
   Sign your name and initials, i.e. your surname and the initial letters of your other names.　请签上您的姓及名字的首字母。
   What do those initials stand for?　那些大写的首字母代表什么？

7. stencil　v. 刷制
   stencil the shipping marks　刷唛头
   stencil conspicuously　清晰地刷制
   shipping marks　装运标志，唛头，运输标志，通常是由一个简单的几何图形和一些字母、数字及简单的文字组成，其作用在于使货物在装卸、运输、保管过程中容易被有关人员识别，以防错发错运。标准化的运输标志包括：
   ①收货人或买方名称的英文缩写字母或简称；
   ②参考号，如运单号、订单号或发票号；

③目的地名称；

④货物件数。

如：

ABCCO，收货人名称

SC9750，合同号码

LONDON，目的港

No.4-20，件号（顺序号和总件数）

8. directive marks　指示性标示，是一种操作注意标志，以图形和文字表达。如小心轻放（HANDLE WITH CARE）、由此起吊（LIFT HERE）、禁止翻滚（DO NOT ROLL）等。

9. footnote　n. 脚注

A footnote is made at the bottom of the page.　注脚列在书页下端。

The asterisk refers the reader to a footnote.　星号是让读者参看脚注。

10. to that effect　带有这（那）个意思

That is what he said, to that effect.　那便是他所说的话，大意是如此。

Its previous efforts to that effect had failed.　此前为达到此目标的一切努力均以失败告终。

11. find it in order　发现无误

12. shipping advice　装船通知

4.　An Email from Exporter Requesting the Change in Packing

Background: 中国一雨具出口商收到了来自新加坡某公司订购雨衣的订单。出口商对订单的包装条款进行了修改，并告知客户雨衣的新包装方式，及采用这种包装的诸多优点。

From: howardqiao_0805@tpwwares.com

To: martin_ghfee@matrixhome.com

Date: Wednesday, July 21, 20__, 10: 17 am

Subject: A Change in Packing Raincoats

Dear Mr. Martin,

Thank you for your order of June 21. We have pleasure in informing you that we can accept all the stipulated terms but the packing.

The packing mentioned in your order was of the old mode we adopted several years ago. Since then we have improved it with the result that our recent shipments have all turned out to be the full satisfaction to our customers.

Our raincoats are now packed each in a polybag and then in a carton, 10 dozen to a carton, with a gross weight around 30 kilograms. Each carton is lined with a polythene sheet and secured by overall metal strapping, thus preventing the contents from dampness and possible damage through rough handling.

We are of the opinion that since a polythene bag is used for each raincoat it is already for window display and looks attractive, which will certainly help the sales. Besides, the improved packing is light in weight and therefore easy to handle.

We state the above for your information and shall execute your order accordingly if we do not hear from you to the contrary before the end of this month.

Yours sincerely,
Howard Qiao
Export Manager

Notes
1.　mode　n. 模式
2.　with the result that　结果
3.　be lined with　内衬有
4.　polythene　聚乙烯
5.　secured by overall metal strapping　外面用金属条加固
6.　contents　箱内货物
7.　are of the opinion　认为
8.　window display　橱展
9.　to the contrary　相反的

5.　An Email from Importer about the New Packing

Background: 进口商收到出口商的电子邮件及发票，并得知所订购货物的包装发生了改变。进口商希望第一批如此包装的货物抵达后能使客户满意。

From: kpatel_heo@crowntextiles.com
To: pierre_31smso@regalclothing.com
Date: Wednesday, May 5, 20＿＿, 11: 13 am
Subject: About the New Packing

Dear Mr. Prost,

We have received your email of May 5 informing us that the goods ordered have been shipped per S.S. "Dongfeng" and thank you for your invoice No. 5668 in duplicate.

With regard to the packing for ready-made garments, you say that you have taken up the matter with the departments concerned and hold the opinion that packing in cartons will prevent skilful pilferage; such cartons are well protected against moisture; they are light and convenient to handle, etc. After discussing the matter with our clients, we find that your comments sound quite reasonable. However, we cannot be sure how things will prove to be until the first lot of the goods packed in such cartons arrives.

We think that if our clients are happy with the result of packing in cartons, you may continue using this packing in future. However, in case the result not being so, we are afraid that this will considerably affect the development of business between us.

You may be assured that in our mutual interest we shall do everything possible to give you our full cooperation.

As soon as the goods shipped by S.S. "Dongfeng" reach us, we shall not fail to communicate with you.

Yours sincerely,

K. Patel

Purchasing Manager

Notes

1. ready-made garments　成品服装
2. take up　提出，讨论如何处理
3. skilful pilferage　惯盗
4. considerably　adv. 极大地，相当地，非常地

6. An Email from Importer about Requirements on Sales Packing

Background: 中国浙江一家日化产品进口商认为出口商对其所订购的唇膏的包装描述过于模糊，因而告知出口商包装细节，包括包装材料、颜色和方式，并表示该包装方法经实践证明十分可行。

From: ivan_import012@siqicosmetics.com

To: margaretteddy@frw.com

Date: Friday, April 17, 20＿＿, 12:05 am

Subject: Requirements on Sales Packing for Our Order No. HD570

Dear Miss Wright,

We are pleased to receive your email of April 17 concerning the sales packing of the subject order.

After checking the order, we have to point out your packing suggestion is rather vague. To avoid disputes, we insist that the packing should be described in detail.

Here are our packing details for the lipstick packing: in order to make it ready for window display and look attractive, which will certainly help the sales, please pack each lipstick by skin card. The card is pink and printed with "Care for You" in blue, twenty cards in a color box, and ten boxes in a carton.

We have practiced this way of lipstick packing for years, and it has proved to be attractive and satisfactory to our customers.

We sincerely hope that you can follow our requirements of packing so as to avoid unforeseen trouble arising from faulty packing.

We look forward to your early reply.

Yours sincerely,
Ivan Li
Import Supervisor

Notes
1. sales packing   销售包装，内包装
2. dispute   n. 纠纷，争端，争议
    beyond dispute   无争论余地
    without dispute   毫无疑义，无争论余地
    in dispute   在争论中，尚未解决
3. skin card   贴体包装，多用于小件商品，如唇膏、牙膏等，常见的还有 slide card（插卡包装），blister card（泡壳包装）
4. The card is pink and printed with "Care for You" in blue.   请用粉色纸卡，并用蓝色字印上"Care for You"的字样。
5. color box   彩盒，即用卡纸和微细瓦楞纸板这两种材料制成的折叠纸盒和微细瓦楞纸盒，多用于中档包装，介于内包装和外包装之间。常见的还有白盒和邮购盒。
6. unforeseen   adj. 无法预料的，未预见的，偶然的，也可以用 unexpected
7. faulty packing   不当包装，错误包装

7. An Email from Importer about Requirements on Shipping Marks
Background: 进口商告知出口商信用证已经办理妥当，不日将抵达。并给出唛头样本，说明对唛头的要求。为免去每次发货时商讨唛头的麻烦，进口商表示若无特殊说明该唛头适合于每次包装。

From: brendan_japs@visioncorp.com
To: lovelyhans@balindustry.com
Date: Friday, April 17, 20_ _, 12:05 am

Subject: Requirements on Shipping Marks for Sales Contract No. 947

Dear Hans,

We are glad to inform you that we have sent by air the countersigned copy of contract No. 947 for 5,000 pieces of women's shirts. The L/C is on its way to you.

Please mark the outer packing with our initials FAE in a triangle, under which stencil the port of destination and S/C No. viz.

<u>FAE</u>

Tianjin
947

This is to apply to all orders unless otherwise specified.

Please email us as soon as shipment is effected.

Best wishes.

Brendan Zhao
General Manager

Notes
1. viz.　即，也就是，videlicet 的缩写，源自拉丁文，相当于 namely
2. unless otherwise specified　除非另有说明

Unit 10　Payment

付　款

1.　Definition and Types of International Trade Payment

International trade payment means the settlement of claims and debts or the transfer of money by certain method of transmission is carried out in international trade.

There are three major payment methods in international trade, including remittance, collection and letter of credit.

2.　Remittance

The payer (usually the buyer) remits a certain sum of money in accordance with the parties' agreement to the payee (usually the seller) through a bank. Payer may remit the sum in the following manner:

    a.　Mail Transfer (M/T)

    b.　Telegraphic Transfer (T/T)

    c.　Demand Draft (D/D)

This method of payment is often used for down payment, payment of commission and for sample, settlement of claim, etc.

3.　Collection

The exporter, as drawer of a draft (bill of exchange), hands the draft to his bank, the remitting bank, who in turn forwards it to the buyer through a collecting bank in the buyer's country. A draft (also called a bill) is a written order to a bank or a customer to pay someone on demand or at a fixed time in the future a certain sum of money. If shipping documents accompany the draft, the collection is called "documentary collection".

Documentary collection falls into two major categories: one is documents against payment (D/P); the other, documents against acceptance (D/A).

Documents against payment, as the term suggests, is that the collecting bank will only give the shipping documents representing the title to the goods on the condition that the buyer makes payment.

Where the paying arrangement is D/A, the collecting bank will only give the buyer the shipping documents after the buyer's acceptance of the bill drawn on him, i.e. the buyer signs his name on the bill promising to pay the sum when it matures. In return he gets what he needs, the shipping documents.

Under D/A, the seller gives up the title to the goods—shipping documents before he gets payment of the goods. Therefore, an exporter must think twice before he accepts such paying arrangement.

4.   L/C

A letter of credit (L/C) is a written instrument issued by the importer's bankers, authorizing the exporters to draw on them for a certain amount in accordance with the contract stipulations. Its advantage is that the L/C issued is the guarantee of the opening bank to pay in advance. It resolves the contradiction that both the importer and the exporter do not trust each other and avoids meeting any possible risks in doing business.

4.1 Opening an L/C

In international trade, there is seldom direct payment by the importer to the exporter. Payment is usually effected through a bank. When a sales contract is signed by the sellers and the buyers, the latter will instruct their bankers to open a letter of credit for the amount of the purchase and in favor of the export on the terms and conditions as stipulated in the contract.

4.2 Rushing the Establishment of an L/C

On execution of a contract, one of the necessary steps for the exporter is to urge the importer to establish L/C on time.

There are two different cases for rushing establishment of L/C. One is to remind, in advance, the importer of opening L/C in accordance with the time provided in the contract as the time of delivery is approaching and that the earlier establishment of L/C is beneficial to both parties. Another is to urge the importer to rush establishment of L/C if he has exceeded the time limit. Some measures the exporter can take would fix another time limit and give the importer a chance to make change, readjust the terms of price or quantity and ask the importer to open the L/C according to the readjustment, and even stop the business, cancel the contract, or lodge a claim.

4.3 Checking an L/C and Amending an L/C

Upon receipt of the letter of credit opened by the importer, the exporter should check it up item by item with great care according to the contract's stipulations. If there is any variance with the contract or error in the L/C, the exporter should contact the importer immediately for necessary amendments so as to guarantee the smooth execution of the contract.

On receiving the exporter's request for L/C amendment, the importer should instruct the relevant bank to amend the L/C accordingly and inform the exporter immediately. Only after another careful checking and finding it in order can the exporter arrange shipment and deliver the goods.

On the whole, it is waste of time and money and increases the expenses of the importer. When opening L/C, do it as accurately as possible so as to avoid the later amendment.

4.4 Extending an L/C

An exporter is sometimes unable to effect shipment of the goods on time because of some unexpected reasons. In this case, the exporter should ask the importer to extend through the bank the date of shipment or delivery to another date. Of course, the date of validity of the L/C should be extended accordingly at the same time. This is what is called extension of L/C.

The reasons for extension of L/C may be various. As for the exporter, lack of goods, any accident in manufacture, or inappropriate arrangement for transportation, may cause delay of shipment and delivery of goods. The importer himself is unable to open the L/C to the exporter with the time limit stipulated by the contract even if the exporter has already got the goods ready for shipment. Besides, natural disasters such as storm, typhoon, earthquake, flood or war, riot, strike may force the exporter to postpone his shipment and delivery of goods.

修改信用证写作步骤

1. Confirming the Receipt of the L/C
2. Pointing out the Discrepancies and Making the Suggestions
3. Hoping to Receive the Amendment to the L/C

修改信用证常用语句

1. Confirming the Receipt of the L/C
- We have received your L/C No. 452 for the amount of US$ 2,000 to cover your Order No. 678 for 200 cases of the goods.
  我方已收到贵方第 452 号，金额为 2000 美元，用以支付第 678 号订单项下的 200 箱货物的信用证。
- We have with many thanks received your captioned L/C.
  标题项下信用证收悉，非常感谢。

2. Pointing out the Discrepancies and Making the Suggestions
- On checking up the clauses/On examination of the clauses/On examining it carefully, we have regretfully found the following discrepancies in it:
  经仔细检查条款，我方很抱歉发现如下不符点：
- On perusal, we find that… Therefore, we are asking you to amend your L/C to read…
  经详阅，我方发现……。因此，请贵方将信用证改为……
- We find the stipulations in your L/C not in accordance with the contract.
  我方发现贵方信用证中的条款与合同不符。

- Please amend L/C No. 320 as follows:
    1) Amount to be increased up to US$...
    2) Validity to be extended to…
    3) The words "Transshipment Not Allowed" to be deleted.

  请按下述意见修改第 320 号信用证：

  （1）金额增至……美元。

  （2）有效期延至……

  （3）删掉"不许转船"字句。

- After we have checked the L/C carefully, we request you to make the following amendments:
    1) The quantity should be read: 1,000 M/Ts (5% more or less at Sellers' option).
    2) Partial shipments are allowed.

  我们在认真审核了信用证之后，请求你方做如下修改：

  （1）数量为：1000 公吨（允许 5%溢短装，由卖方决定）。

  （2）允许分运。

- We found your L/C No. 458 short-opened.

  我方发现贵方第 458 号信用证金额短缺。

- Your L/C No. 3345 being insufficient in amount, we have faxed for an increase.

  贵方第 3345 号信用证金额不足，我方已传真要求增加。

- Your L/C No. 456 is short of US$29.00

  贵方第 456 号信用证金额短少 29 美元。

- We find that the amount of your L/C is insufficient, because the premium for risk of leakage is not included. Please add the amount of the L/C to US$1,116,000.

  我方发现由于信用证金额未包括渗漏附加险费，因此信用证金额不足。敬请将信用证金额增至 1116000 美元。

- Please have the amount of your L/C No. 784 increased by HK$ 5,150.00.

  请将贵方第 784 号信用证金额增加 5150 港元。

- Please amend the amount of the L/C to read "2% more or less in quantity and amount".

  请修改信用证金额为"允许数量和金额有 2%的增减"。

- Please delete/cancel/get rid of/leave out/cross off the clause "by direct steamer" and insert/add the wording "Transshipment and partial shipment are allowed".

  请删掉"用直达轮装运"，并且加上"允许分运转船"。

- Please insert the clause "Transshipment at Hong Kong".

  请插入"在香港转船"的条款。

- On going over the terms and conditions, we find that the date of shipment is not extended as we have agreed.

  经查阅交易条款，我方发现未按我们同意过的将装运期延展。

- Your L/C stipulates 60 days sight, whereas our contract shows 30 days sight. So you are requested to make necessary amendment and advise us before March 20.

  你方信用证规定 60 天期，而我们合同是 30 天期。因此，请贵方做出必要的修改，并于 3 月 20 日前通知我方。

- Please amend L/C No. 877 to read "This L/C will expire on 22th June, 2009 in China."
  请将第 877 号信用证改为"该信用证将于 2009 年 6 月 22 日在中国到期。"
- Goods should be insured for 110% of the invoice value rather than 120%.
  货物应按发票金额的 110%投保，而不是 120%。
- Please reduce the quantity to 130 cases instead of 145 cases.
  请将数量减少至 130 箱，而不是 145 箱。

3. Hoping to Receive the Amendment to the L/C

- As the goods are now ready for shipment, you are requested to amend your L/C as soon as possible.
  由于货物已备妥待运，请贵方尽早改证。
- We appreciate your immediate attention to the amendment to the covering L/C.
  若尽早修改相关信用证，我方将十分感激。

开立信用证常用语句

- Thank you for your letter of August 16, urging us to open an L/C.
  谢谢贵方 8 月 16 日来函，催促我公司开立信用证。
- The L/C in your favor has already been opened and sent.
  以贵方为受益人的信用证已经开立并寄送给贵方。
- We have instructed our bank to open an irrevocable and confirmed L/C for the amount of US$17,000,000 in your favor.
  我们已经通知我公司银行开立以贵公司为受益人的、保兑的、不可撤销的信用证，金额为 17000000 美元。
- An irrevocable documentary L/C has been opened in your favor for the amount of RMB11,000,000 with Bank of China, valid until November 9.
  我公司已在中国银行开立了一张以贵方为受益人的、不可撤销的跟单信用证，金额为人民币 11000000 元，有效期截止到 11 月 9 日。
- We have today instructed our bank to open in your favor a confirmed, irrevocable letter of credit with partial shipment and transshipment allowed clause, available by draft at sight, against presenting the full set of shipping documents to the negotiating bank.
  我们今天已通知我方银行，开立以你方为抬头的、保兑的、不可撤销的、允许分运转船的信用证，凭即期汇票并提交全套装运单据向议付行议付。

催开信用证常用语句

- In reference to the 500 bottles of grape wine under our Sales Confirmation No. 0727, we wish to attract your attention to the fact that the date of shipment is approaching, but we haven't yet received your L/C up till now.

  关于第 0727 号销售确认书项下的 500 瓶葡萄酒，敬请贵方注意，货物装运日期临近，但我方迄今仍未收到相关信用证。

- The shipment time for your order is drawing near, but we have not yet received the L/C. Please open an L/C with dispatch in order that the shipment will be effected in time.

  贵公司订单的装运期已经临近，但我公司仍未收到相关信用证。请从速将信用证开到，以便我公司及时装运货物。

- We wish to remind you that/We wish to draw your attention to the fact that it was agreed that you would establish the required L/C upon receipt of our Sales Confirmation.

  我方提请贵方注意，双方同意一经收到我方的销售确认书即开立相关信用证。

- On the 20th of June we faxed you asking you to establish the L/C for the above mentioned order, and in your reply of 30th of June, you advised us that you would attend to this in a week or so. But up to now we have not had any information on this matter. Please check into it as soon as possible.

  6 月 20 日我方发传真给贵方，要求开立上述订单的信用证。在 6 月 30 日贵方的回复中，告知我方将在一周左右时间内办理。然而迄今为止，我方未得到任何消息，请尽快查询此事。

- Time is pressing, so we will appreciate your rushing the credit by fax.

  时间不多了，请贵方传真催开信用证。

- Please expedite/rush the L/C so that we can execute the order smoothly.

  请速开证，以便我方能顺利执行订单。

- As the goods have been ready, please rush the L/C covering S/C No. 452.

  由于货物已备妥，请速开第 452 号销售合同的信用证。

- We repeatedly requested you by faxes to expedite the opening of the relative L/C so that we might effect shipment for the above-mentioned order, but after the lapse of 3 months, we have not yet received the covering L/C.

  我方反复通过传真要求贵方迅速开立相关信用证，以便我方装运上述订单，然而 3 个月过去了，我方仍未收到相关信用证。

延展信用证常用语句

- As the earliest steamer sailing for your port is scheduled to leave Shanghai on or about January 3 next year, it is, therefore, impossible for us to effect shipment at the time you named.
  由于驶往贵港的最早的货轮预计在明年 1 月 3 日左右从上海启航，所以我方无法在你方指定时间内装运。
- This being the case, we have to ask you to extend the date of shipment to…, under advice to us by fax.
  既然如此，我方不得不要求贵方将装运期展至……，并传真告知。
- We are looking forward to receiving your extension of the above L/C, thus enabling us to effect shipment of the goods in question.
  我方期盼收到贵方对上述信用证的延展，以便我方能装运该货。
- We are faxing you today asking for a two-week extension of the L/C covering your Order No. 371 for 300 cases of frozen chicken.
  我方于今日传真要求延展用以支付第 371 号 300 箱冷冻鸡肉订单的信用证。
- Please have the validity of your L/C No. 326 extended until June 2 so that we may make delivery without fail.
  请延展第 326 号信用证有效期至 6 月 2 日以便我方交货无误。

付款常用短语及语句

- open/issue/establish an L/C　开立信用证
- urge (the establishment of) an L/C　催开信用证
- check the L/C　审证
- amend (or: amendment to L/C)　改证
- extend (or: extension of L/C)　展证
- withdraw/cancel/annul/revoke an L/C　撤销信用证
- L/C opener/applicant/accountee　信用证开证人
- L/C beneficiary　受益人
- sight L/C　即期信用证
- documentary L/C　跟单信用证
- standby L/C　备用信用证
- confirmed L/C　保兑信用证
- irrevocable L/C　不可撤销信用证
- transferable L/C　可转让信用证

- divisible L/C 可分割信用证
- revolving L/C 循环信用证
- opening/issuing bank 开证行
- informing/notifying/advising bank 通知行
- paying bank 付款行
- negotiating bank 议付行
- accepting bank 承兑行
- confirming bank 保兑行
- advance payment 预付款
- prompt/sight payment 立即支付，即期支付
- delayed/deferred/back/late/overdue payment 延期付款，逾期付款
- periodical/partial/progress payment = payment by installments 分期付款
- irregular payment 不定期付款
- payment in full 全部支付
- final payment 最后的付款
- outstanding/balance payment 余额付款
- cash payment 现金支付
- check payment 支票支付
- in default of payment 在未付款情况下

Discussing the Terms of Payment

- We wish to call your attention to the terms of payment since we have come to an agreement on all but the terms of payment.

  鉴于双方就其他相关事宜都已达成共识，我方来函商讨付款方式。

- According to our usual practice, our terms of payment are by irrevocable confirmed L/C by draft at sight.

  根据惯例，我方的付款方式是采用不可撤销的、保兑的、见票即付信用证。

- Our usual way of payment is by irrevocable and confirmed L/C by draft at sight for the amount of the contracted goods to be established in our favor.

  通常我方的付款方式是保兑的、不可撤销的、以我方为受益人的足额信用证，见票即付。

- As agreed, the terms of payment for the above orders are letter of credit at 60 days' sight or D/P sight draft.

  按照协定，上述订货的付款方式是见票 60 天的信用证，或付款交单的即期汇票。

- It will interest you to know that as a special sign of encouragement, we shall consider accepting payment by D/P during this sales pushing stage.

  贵方将有兴趣得知，作为特别的鼓励，我方将考虑在推销阶段接受付款交单的条件。

Changing Payment Method

(1) Requesting for Changing Payment Method

- Since we would like to save the expenses on opening an L/C, please consider the D/A payment method instead.

由于我公司想节省开立信用证的费用，所以请考虑以承兑交单方式付款。

- In spite of the terms of the contract, we would owe you a debt of gratitude if you could consider changing the payment method from D/P to D/A.

  虽然有合同条款规定，但如果贵方能考虑将支付方式从付款交单改为承兑交单，我方将不胜感激。

- Although the contract stipulates an L/C at sight as the payment method, please consider changing the method from an L/C at sight to a D/P at sight.

  尽管合同规定以即期付款信用证作为支付方式，但请考虑可否变为即期付款交单方式。

- We would be glad to place another order with you, provided that you will agree to a change in the terms of payment from T/T to D/A.

  如果贵公司同意将付款方式由电汇改为承兑交单，我公司愿向贵公司再订一批货。

- If you would kindly make easier payment terms, we are sure that such an accommodation would be conductive to encouraging business.

  如果贵方能放宽付款方式，我方相信贵方的通融一定会有助于促进贸易。

(2) Agreeing to the Change in Payment Method

- We are ready to accept your request for a change to the terms of payment.

  我公司接受贵公司更改付款方式的请求。

- We will agree to change the terms of payment from D/P to D/A.

  我公司同意将付款交单方式改为承兑交单方式。

- In compliance with your request, we exceptionally accept delivery against D/P at sight, but this should not be taken as a precedent.

  按照贵方要求，我方破例接受即期付款交单交货，但这种情况下不为例。

- As to payment, we are agreeable to draw on you at 30 days' sight, documents against acceptance.

  关于支付，我方同意向你方开出见票 30 天的承兑交单的汇票。

- We consent to reducing the down payment, payable on the signing of the contract, from fifteen percent to ten, provided that the contract price is increased by three percent.

  我方同意将签署合同时应预付的现款由 15%减少到 10%，但条件是合同价格增加 3%。

- In view of the amount of this transaction being very small, we are prepared to accept payment by D/P at sight for the value of the goods shipped.

  鉴于这桩交易的金额数目微小，我方打算接受凭即期的付款交单收取所运货物的款项。

(3) Declining the Change in Payment Method

- We regret we can't accept your request for changing the terms of payment from L/C to D/A.

  很抱歉，我方不能接受贵方将信用证付款方式改为承兑交单付款方式。

- We are afraid we must insist on L/C as the terms of payment instead of D/P.

  我公司仍然坚持用信用证付款方式，而非付款交单方式。

- We are afraid we still stick to T/T rather than D/D.

我公司仍然坚持用电汇付款方式，而不是即期汇票。

- We regret we cannot accept "Cash against Document on arrival of goods at destination".
  抱歉我方不能接受"货到目的地后凭单付款"的条件。

- Since we haven't known much about each other's credit status, we are afraid that we must insist on our usual practice of payment by L/C, the use of which will protect us with banks' involvement.
  鉴于目前双方都不太了解对方的资信情况，我方必须按照惯例坚持信用证支付，因为信用证的使用可以为我们得到银行的担保。

- As the total amount is so huge and the world monetary market is quite unstable at present, we cannot accept any mode of payment except the L/C.
  因为这次交易金额大，而且国际金融市场极其不稳定，所以我们除了接受信用证付款方式外，不接受其他的付款方式。

Delay in Payment

(1) Agreeing to the Delay in Payment

- We are fully aware of economic and market conditions at your end and understand the unpleasant situation you are confronted with. We are willing to accommodate your request.
  我方完全了解你方的经济和市场状况，并理解你方所面临的困境，愿意满足贵方的请求。

- We do sympathize with the difficult position you are facing now and are trying our best to find other ways to offer our help within the scope of our agreement.
  我方的确十分同情你方现在所面临的困难处境，并且正尽力设法在协议允许的范围内向你方提供帮助。

- Considering our long-period business relationship, we accept your request of extending the payment date.
  鉴于我们长期的合作关系，我公司接受贵公司延期支付的请求。

- Taking into consideration the embarrassing situation you are confronted with at present, we can accept the extension, but only until September 20 instead of October 5 you required.
  考虑到贵公司目前所处的困境，我们同意延期，但只能延到 9 月 20 日，而非贵公司要求的 10 月 5 日。

- To help you overcome the difficulties, we are happy to grant you an additional 30 days on all your payments as requested in your letter.
  为了帮助你方克服困难，按照你方来函要求，我们乐意将你方的付款期宽限 30 天。

- We have given every consideration to your request for a deferment of payment for an additional 20 days.
  我方仔细考虑了贵方延期 20 天付款的请求。

(2) Declining the Delay in Payment

- Much to our regret, we are not in a position to accommodate your request.
  很遗憾，我方无法满足您的要求。

- We are sorry we cannot agree to your request for extension of the payment date.

很抱歉我方不能同意贵方延长付款期限的要求。

- We urge you to arrange payment through your bank ASAP.

我方敦促贵方尽快通过银行安排付款。

- Unless the payment is made in accordance with the contract, we will have to cancel the contract and claim damages for your failure to honor the contract.

除非按照合同规定付款，否则我方将不得不取消合同，并因贵方没有履行合同而向贵方索赔。

- You are expected to make a continued effort to fulfill the agreement between us by making payments within stipulated time.

希望你方继续努力，履行我们之间的协议，在规定期限内付款。

Payment Reminder

- It is possible that the rush of business at this period of the year has caused you to overlook the payment of our account, US$75,000 which was due on May 30. We hope with this reminder, however, that you will find it convenient to send your check.

可能由于此间贵方业务过于繁忙，以致忽略承付 5 月 30 日应付款 75000 美元。希望贵方收到此催告信后，以最方便的方式，惠寄支票。

- It it now two weeks since we sent you our first invoice and we have not received your payment.

我公司的第一份发票已经寄出两周了，但仍未收到贵方的任何款项。

- The following items totaling US$12,000 are still open on your account. Please effect your payment within the next three days.

贵方的欠款总计为 12000 美元。请贵方在三日内把欠款付清。

- We must now insist that you send us your check for the amount. Unless we hear from you in five business days, we will take the unpleasant step of turning your account over to a collection agency.

目前我方坚持要求贵方立刻如数将款汇给我方。若在五个营业日内尚未收到贵方消息，我方将不得不采取措施把贵方欠款之事交由收款代理人办理。

- There must be some special reason for the delay in payment. Therefore, we would welcome an explanation along with your remittance.

一定有特殊原因致使贵方延期付款。因此，我方欢迎贵方来函解释，并随信附上汇款。

- Since the account is long overdue, we would very much appreciate your prompt processing of payment on your side.

由于该款逾期已久，我方将万分感谢贵方立即处理付款事宜。

- We received your payments of US$3,000 on July 2, and US$800 on July 9 respectively. This leaves a debit balance of US$500. We would like to remind you that in your leter of June 20 you promised to repay before the end of June.

我们分别在 7 月 2 日和 7 月 9 日收到 3000 美元和 800 美元两笔付款。这样还剩下欠款余额 500 美元。我们想提醒贵方，在 6 月 20 日来函中，贵方答应在 6 月底前付清欠款。

- We have tried several times to resolve the problem of your past due account, but the problem continues. Your account remains seriously overdue in the amount of US$5,000.

我们已数次试图解决您的逾期账目问题而未果。您 5000 美元的账目已严重逾期。

- In spite of your repeated promises to let us have a check, we are still without a settlement of your outstanding account, and therefore, unless the same is settled by the end of this month, we shall be compelled to hand over the matter to our solicitor.

  贵方虽多次答应付款结账，但迄今尚未结清。如在本月底前尚未拨款结清的话，我方只好委任我公司法律顾问处理。

Notification of Payment Made

- We have made remittance application to our bank and you should be able to receive the funds tomorrow.

  我们今天已经向银行提出汇款申请，贵公司应在明天收到汇款。

- We have taken immediate action to make the necessary arrangements and you should be able to confirm receipt of the funds in your account tomorrow.

  我方已采取紧急措施，贵方应在明天贵方的账户上收到汇款。

- We apologize for the delay in payment and we will make the payment within one day. Thank you for your patience.

  很抱歉我公司逾期付款。我方将在一日内付款。感谢贵公司的耐心等待。

- Our remittance was made this morning to your account with Bank of China, Beijing from Bank of Tianjin. The remittance number is 658941. Please ask your bank to recheck all incoming remittances.

  今日早上汇款已由天津银行汇往贵方在北京的中国银行账户，汇款号为 658941。请贵方与贵方银行重新核对汇入的款项。

- We have checked many times with our bank, which remitted the installment. According to the bank, the money was definitely credited to your account with Bank of Tianjin.

  我们已数次与我方汇款行核对过，银行确认已将款项汇入贵方在天津银行的账户上。

Notification of the Arrival of Payment

- We have received with thanks your remittance.

  我们已收到贵方汇款，十分感谢。

- Thank you for your letter dated yesterday, advising us of your remittance.

  感谢贵方昨日来函告知我方贵公司已汇款。

- We confirm receipt of RMB2,500,000 in our account with Bank of Tianjin.

  我方的天津银行账户已确认收到贵方人民币 2500000 的汇款。

写 作 范 例

1. A Request for the Delay in Payment and Reply (Positive & Negative)

Background: 进口商由于本国经济衰退，最近销售量急剧下降，因而向出口商发去电子邮件请求延期付款 20 天。

From: rahulagarwal@motherherbs.com

To: mintyan_hotel@yzkl.com

Sent: Wednesday, September 20, 20＿, 8: 50 am

Subject: A Request for Delay in Payment

Dear Ms. Yan,

You are no doubt aware of the recent sharp declines in sales in our market due to the recession here.

This decline has left us with huge inventories, the heavy burden on our finances.

Therefore, we are writing today to ask for your kind cooperation in dealing with this problem. We should be most obliged if you would grant us an additional 20 days on all payments.

Your usual prompt consideration of our request would help us a great deal at this difficult time.

Yours sincerely,

Rahul Agarwal

Marketing Executive Director

Notes

1. delay in payment　延期付款

    delay in delivery　延期交货

2. be aware of　意识到，了解，知晓

    Buyers must be aware of hazards associated with online auction sites.　购物者必须注意到在线拍卖网站上存在的危险。

3. recession　n. 经济衰退

    A rise in interest rates plunged the country deeper into recession.　利率的提高导致这个国家经济更加萧条。

    The recent recession was long and severe; many companies failed to weather the storm.　最近这次经济萧条时间长且严重，许多公司未能渡过难关。

4. inventory　n. 存货总值，存货清单

    We will need to call on our supplier to get more inventory.　我们必须请供应商送来更多存货。

    We need to get rid of our surplus inventory.　我们必须处理掉过剩的存货。

    The inventory showed that the store was overstocked.　清单显示商店存货过多。

    The store was closed for inventory all week.　那家商店因盘货暂停营业一星期。

5. burden　n. 负担，责任，义务

    The country is bearing the burden of an enormous external debt.　国家背负着巨额外债。

The administrative burden must be lifted from local government.　必须解除地方政府的行政负担。

6.　grant us an additional 20 days on all payments　对我们的支付款项多宽限 20 天

Positive Reply

From: mintyan_hotel@yzkl.com
To: rahulagarwal@motherherbs.com
Sent: Wednesday, September 21, 20＿＿, 10: 18 pm
Subject: Re: A Requesti for Delay in Payment

Dear Mr. Agarwal,

We have received your email of September 20, asking us to allow you a 20-day delay in payment.

Taking your situation and our long-period sound working relationship into consideration, we think it acceptable for you to prepare a further 20 days for payment for the goods. Luckily, we are now enjoying sufficient current funds and considering the unpleasant situation you are confronted with at present, we are willing to help you as far as possible.

We can allow you to send the total amount of our statement within 20 days. We hope this will help you out of the embarrassment and wish you to improve your sales more rapidly.

Very sincerely yours,
Mint Yan
Export Manager

Notes

1.　sound　adj. 友好的，完善的，健全的，合理的
Buy a policy only from an insurance company that is financially sound.　一定要从财务状况良好的保险公司购买保险。
2.　current funds　流动资金
The company has several overdue payments owing to the lack of current funds.　这家公司因为缺乏流动资金，已经有好几笔欠款了。
3.　be confronted with　遭遇
To the bank, managing risk is a problem they must be confronted with.　对于银行来说，如何管理风险是他们必须要面对的问题。
4.　statement　n. 账单，结算单
The company prepared a statement of its profits and losses.　该公司做了一份损益清单。

Negative Reply

From: mintyan_hotel@yzkl.com
To: rahulagarwal@motherherbs.com
Sent: Wednesday, September 21, 20__, 10: 18 pm
Subject: Re: A Request for Delay in Payment

Dear Mr. Agarwal,

Referring to your email of September 20, you mentioned that you were still not in a position to pay our invoice No. 910 of July 1 due to your company's financial crisis.

We express our sympathy for your situation. However, we have already been understanding enough to extend the date of payment twice. Please try to understand that we also have our obligations.

We must request you to arrange to make payment no later than September 30; otherwise we can only be forced to resort to legal actions.

Very sincerely yours,
Mint Yan
Export Manager

Notes

1. in a position to do sth　能够做某事
   We are in a position to accept a special order.　我们可以接受特殊订货。
   We are in a position to offer tea from stock.　我们现在可以报茶叶现货。
2. sympathy　n. 同情，怜悯
   We express our sympathy for your loss.　对你方的损失我方深表同情。
3. understanding　adj. 通情达理的，宽容的，能谅解的
   Try to be understanding.　请多谅解。
4. extend the date of payment　延期付款
   extend　v. 延期，延长，扩大
   They have extended the deadline by 24 hours.　他们已经将最后期限延长了 24 小时。
   This year they have introduced three new products to extend their range.　今年他们发布了 3 种新产品，以扩大产品范围。
5. obligation　n. 债务，负债
   He was relieved of the obligation to pay his debt.　他免除了支付债款的义务。
6. resort to　诉诸于，采取，动用

2. A Request for the Change in Payment Method and Reply (Positive & Negative)

Background: 进口商为了节省开立信用证所需的高额费用，劝说出口商将付款方式由即期信用证改为承兑交单，同时表明如果出口商同意其请求，则愿意再订一批货。

From: michael_marketing@frangrancenet.com

To: grace_fsl@hmsprayer.com

Sent: Monday, October 28, 20__, 14: 19 pm

Subject: A Request for the Change to Payment

Dear Ms. Chen,

Thank you for your Quotation No. 0825 of October 28.

We would be glad to place another order with you, on the basis that you kindly consent to a change in the terms of payment from L/C at sight to D/A, which will help us save a lot of expenses on opening the L/C. As we have a long-term and pleasant cooperation with you and we believe we have proved that we are reliable importers, please give our request your most serious consideration.

We look forward to your positive reply to our new arrangement of payment.

Yours sincerely,

Michael Nadboy

Marketing Director

Notes

1. consent to   同意

   The board of directors didn't consent to such an investment plan.   董事会没有同意这样的投资计划。

   We are sorry we are not in a position to consent to your request.   很抱歉我方无法同意您的请求。

2. reliable   adj. 可靠的，有信誉的

Positive Reply

From: grace_fsl@hmsprayer.com

To: michael_marketing@frangrancenet.com

Sent: Tuesday, October 29, 20__, 9:52am

Subject: Re: A Request for the Change to Payment

Dear Mr. Nadboy,

We are in receipt of your email of October 28, requesting a change in the terms of payment.

It has been our company policy to have L/Cs opened by all our overseas customers who wish to purchase our products. However, as you mentioned in your email, you have proved your reliability in the previous contracts. We thus consent to the change, but just for this time only. As to future transactions, we would prefer to discuss them with you on a deal-to-deal basis.

We hope that our reply is favorable to you.

Very sincerely yours,

Grace Chen

Sales Manager

Notes

1. for this time only   仅此一次，下不为例
2. on a deal-to-deal basis   一笔交易一笔交易地，在单笔交易基础上
3. be favorable to you   能使贵方满意

Negative Reply

From: grace_fsl@hmsprayer.com

To: michael_marketing@frangrancenet.com

Sent: Tuesday, October 29, 20_ _, 9:52am

Subject: Re: A Request for the Change to Payment

Dear Mr. Nadboy,

We are in receipt of your email of October 28, making a request for a change of the terms of payment from L/C to D/A, which may expose us to great risk.

While we have absolute confidence in your reliability, we regret that we still insist on our usual terms of payment by confirmed and irrevocable L/C. For the time being, we thus regret our inability to accept D/A terms in all transactions with our overseas customers.

We hope this will not affect our working relationship with you.

Very sincerely yours,

Grace Chen

Sales Manager

Notes

1. make a request for   请求

2. expose… to…   使遭受（危险或不快），使暴露

    The goods cannot be exposed to the sun and air.   这种货物不能接触阳光和空气。

3. have absolute confidence in   对……绝对有信心

4. regret our inability to do sth   很抱歉我方无法做某事

    We regret our inability to comply with your request for the moment.   很抱歉我方目前无法满足贵方的要求。

5. working relationship   合作关系，贸易关系，相当于 business relationship

3. A Request for Amending the Payment Terms and Positive Reply

Background: 美国某建材进出口公司与中国杭州法索尔瓷砖集团有限公司有过贸易往来，均采用即期信用证方式支付。在这笔交易中，美国方面希望修改付款方式为用电汇方式预付30%的货款，收到提单副本后再用电汇方式支付剩余70%的货款。

From: joycelee549@alibaba.com

To: gaozhl97mail@fsoceramic.com.cn

Date: Friday, February 21, 20＿＿, 14: 48 pm

Subject: Suggestion about New Arrangements of Payment

Dear Miss Gao,

We attach our Order No. 789. We have examined the specifications and price list for your range of ceramic tiles and now wish to place an order with you.

As we are in urgent need of new stock, we would be grateful if you would make up the order and ship it as soon as possible.

In the past we have traded with you on a sight credit basis. We would now like to propose a different arrangement. When you send us your confirmation of our order, we will remit 30% of the full amount by telegraphic transfer (T/T). And when the goods are ready for shipment and the freight space booked, you email us and we then pay the rest 70% upon receipt of your copy of B/L.

By doing so we can save the expense of opening a letter of credit. As we believe that this arrangement should make little difference to you, but should help our sales, we trust that you will agree to our request.

We look forward to receiving your confirmation of our order and your agreement to the new arrangements for payment.

Yours sincerely,

Joyce Lee
Business Manager

Notes

1. ceramic tile　瓷砖
2. make up the order　落实订单
3. on a sight credit basis　以即期信用证付款
4. remit the full amount by telegraphic transfer　电汇全额货款

   telegraphic transfer (T/T)　电汇

   电汇是汇款人将一定款项交存汇款银行，汇款银行通过电报（CABLE）、电传（TELEX）或环球银行间金融电讯网络（SWIFT）指示目的地的分行或代理行（汇入行）向收款人支付一定金额的一种汇款方式。电汇中的电报费用由汇款人承担，银行对电汇业务一般均当天处理，不占用邮递过程的汇款资金。

   前 T/T 指如果电汇方式预付货款，卖方收到货款后再发货。通常前 T/T 买方会付 30%的定金，等货生产完毕后再付余款，卖方收齐货款后发货。后 T/T 指通过电汇方式货到付款，买方收到货物后再付款。也有人把先预付部分定金（如 30%），收到卖方的提单确认件后付清余款称为后 T/T。在我国出口贸易中，最常用的是信用证，其次是 T/T，然后是即期 D/P。

   如果不采用单一的付款方式，则下面的付款方式对卖方来说比较适合：（1）30%T/T 定金 ＋ 70%即期、保兑的信用证；（2）即期、保兑的信用证 ＋ CIF 术语；（3）即期、保兑的信用证 ＋ FOB 术语；（4）30%T/T 定金 ＋ 70%提单传真件。

Positive Reply

Background: 中国杭州法索尔瓷砖集团有限公司认为美国某建材进出口公司所提出的理由合乎逻辑，因为法索尔公司不用承担风险，所以接受对方关于付款的建议，并以非常务实的态度提供本次提议所需的全部单据。

From: gaozhl97mail@fsoceramic.com.cn

To: joycelee549@alibaba.com

Date: Friday, February 21, 20＿＿, 16: 02 pm

Subject: Re: Suggestion about New Arrangements of Payment

Dear Mr. Lee,

Thank you for your email about two hours ago dated 21 February. We are pleased to acknowledge your Order No. 789 of the same date for ceramic tiles.

The modified terms of payment you propose are acceptable. A fax has been dispatched to you to confirm it.

All the items in your order can be supplied from stock and will be packed and ready for shipment immediately your remittance by telegraphic transfer is received.

The following documents will be airmailed to you immediately after shipment is made:
1. Bill of lading in duplicate
2. Invoice, CIF London, in triplicate
3. Insurance policy for 110% of invoice value
4. Guarantee of quality

We will, of course, notify you by email as soon as your order is shipped.

You can rely on us to give prompt attention to this and any future orders you may place with us.

Sincerely yours,
Z. L. Gao
General Manager

Notes
1. immediately your remittance by telegraphic transfer is received   一俟收到电汇款项
2. guarantee of quality   品质保证书

4. Informing the Exporter of the Establishment of L/C
Background: 美国某食品机械贸易公司进口部经理 Tim Smith 给中国天津某食品机械及包装有限公司发来电子邮件，告知用以支付 LQT 牌 FR78－098 型制冰机 160 台，总金额为 14720 美元的不可撤销的即期信用证已于 20_ _ 10 月 2 日通过美国的纽约银行开出。

From: timsmithsp@heow.machine.com
To: xiall0902@dks.tj.com
Date: Tuesday, October 2, 20_ _, 16: 25 pm
Subject: The L/C No. CN544 Has Been Opened through the Bank of New York!

Dear Mr. Xia,

We are glad to inform you that we have now opened an irrevocable Letter of Credit No. CN544 through our bank, the Bank of New York, on October 2, 20_ _, payable by draft at sight, for the amount of US$ 14,720.00 in your favor.

Details read as follows:
Unit Price: USD 92.00 CIF New York
Quantity: 160 sets

Total Amount: USD 14,720.00

Brand Name: LQT

Model: FR78-098

Latest shipment date: October 15, 20_ _

Expiry date: October 31, 20_ _

We hope you will get our L/C very soon.

This is our busy season. Please make sure that the shipment is effected within October, since punctual delivery is one of the important considerations in dealing with our market. We will place regular orders with your for more machines if your first shipment proves to be satisfactory.

We are awaiting your Shipping Advice.

Sincerely yours,

Tim Smith

Import Sales Manager

Notes

1. open an L/C　开立信用证，简称为开证，还可以说 establish, issue 等

   open an L/C with/through/by... bank　由……银行开立信用证

   信用证的主要内容：信用证虽然是国际贸易中的一种主要支付方式，但它并无统一的格式。不过其主要内容基本上是相同的，大体包括：（1）对信用证自身的说明：信用证的种类、性质、编号、金额、开证日期、有效期及到期地点、当事人的名称和地址、使用本信用证的权利可否转让等；（2）汇票的出票人、付款人、期限以及出票条款等；（3）货物的名称、品质、规格、数量、包装、运输标志、单价等；（4）对运输的要求：装运期限、装运港、目的港、运输方式、运费应否预付、可否分批装运和中途转运等；（5）对单据的要求：单据的种类、名称、内容和份数等；（6）特殊条款：根据进口国政治、经济、贸易情况的变化或每一笔具体业务的需要，可作出不同的规定；（7）开证行对受益人和汇票持有人保证付款的责任文句；（8）国外来证大多数均加注："除另有规定外，本证根据国际商会《跟单信用证统一惯例》即国际商会 600 号出版物（《ucp600》）办理。"（9）银行间电汇索偿条款（T/T reimbursement clause）。

2. for the amount of　金额为……

   for the amount of invoice/order value　金额为发票/订单总值

3. in one's favor = in favor of sb　以某人为抬头，以某人为受益人，对某人有利

   We open an irrevocable Letter of Credit No. 123 in favor of China National Metals and Minerals Import & Export Corporation, Beijing.　兹开立以中国五金矿产进出口公司为受益人的第 123 号不可撤销信用证。

   We have made arrangements with the Bank of Japan, Tokyo, to open a credit in your favor.

我方已安排东京日本银行开立了以你方为抬头的信用证。

The market situation is entirely in our favor.   市场情况完全对我方有利。

4. punctual delivery   按时交货

5. one of the important considerations in dealing with our market   与我方客户交易时的重要因素之一

6. shipping advice = shipping notice, advice of shipment, notice of shipment   装船通知

5. Urge the Establishment of an L/C and Reply

Background: 中国香港 Thaihood 国际有限公司与美国 Olyeem 电子产品贸易公司签订了销售确认书，确认向 Olyeem 公司销售 4000 副 MP3 墨镜，交货期为 5 月 15 日。但直到 4 月 20 日，Thaihood 公司仍未收到相关信用证，于是发电子邮件催促对方开证。Olyeem 公司收到催促函后，表示抱歉，并迅速通过花旗银行开立了第 5301 号总金额为 135 000 美元的信用证。

From: jialmail@thaihood.com
To: gray3232@olyeem.electronics.com
Sent: Wednesday, April 20, 20＿＿, 10: 11 am
Subject: Our Sales Confirmation No. V154

Dear Ms. Gray,

Concerning 4,000 pairs of MP3 Sunglasses under the subject Sales Confirmation, we wish to draw your attention to the fact that the date of delivery is approaching, but we still have not received your covering letter of credit up to the present.

Please do your utmost to expedite its establishment, so that we may execute the order within the prescribed time.

In order to avoid subsequent amendments, please see to it that the L/C stipulations are in exact accordance with the terms of the contract.

We look forward to receiving your favorable response at an early date.

Yours sincerely,
L. Jia
Managing Director

Notes

1. urge/rush the establishment of L/C   催证

2. under the subject Sales Confirmation   标题项下销售确认书中的，此处的介词"under" 指"在……项下的"、"在……中所提的"

3. we wish to draw your attention to the fact that...　我方希望贵方注意的是……
4. the covering/relevant/relative/related Letter of Credit　相关信用证
5. do one's utmost to do sth　尽力做某事
6. expedite　vt. 加快，促进，迅速处理
   expedite the shipment of the goods we ordered　加速装运我方的订货
7. within the prescribed time　在规定时间内
   prescribed　adj. 规定的，还可以用 stipulated, provided, stated
8. Please see to it that...　请务必做到……，类似的还有 Please make sure that...
9. stipulation　n. 条款，也可以说 term, provision, article, clause
10. in exact accordance/conformity with　与……完全一致

Reply

From: gray3232@olyeem.electronics.com
To: jialmail©thaihood.com.cn
Sent: Thursday, May 9, 20＿＿, 13: 20 pm
Subject: Re: Our Sales Confirmation No. V154

Dear Mr. Jia,

We have received your email dated April 20, urging us to establish the L/C for our Order No. KP23 for 4,000 pairs of MP3 Sunglasses.

We are very sorry for the delay in opening the L/C, which was due to an oversight of our staff. However, upon receipt of your email of April 20, we immediately, as requested, opened a Letter of Credit No. 5301 in your favor with the Citibank for the amount of US$135,000.00 to cover 4,000 pairs of MP3 Sunglasses. We trust the copy of the same is now in your hand, and you will receive the original copy in a day or two.

When receiving the above-mentioned L/C, you are kindly requested to execute immediate shipment, as per the Sales Confirmation No. V154. As soon as the goods are dispatched, please fax us details of the shipment, thus enabling us to arrange for the insurance here.

Please allow us to express again our regret for the inconvenience that has been caused to you. We await with keen interest your shipping advice.

Very sincerely yours,
Ronda Gray
Import Manager

Notes

1. oversight   n. 疏忽，忽略
2. the same   该短语常用来替代刚提及的事物，相当于 the above mentioned，以达到简洁的目的，此处指买方开出的信用证
3. in one's hand   在某人处，类似的还有 at one's end, in one's place
4. original copy   正本
5. You are kindly requested to do sth.   特请贵方做某事。
6. arrange for the insurance   办理保险

6. Amendment to an L/C to Allow Partial Shipment and Transshipment

Background: 中国某针织袜业有限公司在收到英国某纺织品进出口公司开来的第 2312 号金额为 150000 美元用以支付 16000 打弹力尼龙袜的信用证后，发现不允许分运转船。于是发电子邮件给出理由，请求改信用证为允许分运及转船。

From: huangmax_my23@kingsock.com
To: millersmile@shf.com
Date: Monday, September 19, 20＿ ＿, 10: 36 am
Subject: Your L/C No. 2312 for Stretch Nylon Socks

Dear Mr. Miller,

We are duly in receipt of your L/C No. 2312 issued by National Commercial Bank for the amount of US$150,000.00 covering 16,000 dozen Stretch Nylon Socks. On perusal, we find that transshipment and partial shipment are not allowed.

As direct steamers to your port are few and far between, it is almost impossible for us to book enough freight space for the whole lot each time. Therefore, we have to ship via Hong Kong more often than not. As to partial shipment, it would be to our mutual benefit if we could ship immediately whatever we have on hand instead of waiting for the whole lot to be completed. Such being the case, we are asking you to amend the L/C to read "Transshipment and Partial Shipment Allowed".

We shall appreciate it if you will modify promptly the covering L/C as requested, and inform us by email.

Yours sincerely,
Max Huang
Manager

Notes

1. amendment to an L/C　注意介词用 to

   改证可以说 amend/modify/adjust an L/C

2. partial shipment　分批装运，分运，也可以说 part shipment(s)或 partshipment(s)

   分批装运是指一笔交易的货物分若干批装运。

3. transshipment　转运，转船，也可以说 transhipment

   如果货物没有直达或一时无合适的船舶运输，则需要中途转船运输。按实际情况，买卖双方可以在合同中订明是否允许转船。若信用证未规定可否转船，按《跟单信用证统一惯例》规定，为允许转船。

   As there is no direct steamer to your port, please amend the L/C to allow/permit transshipment.
   由于没有驶往贵港的直达轮，请将信用证修改为允许转船。

4. stretch nylon sock　弹性尼龙袜

5. duly　adv. 如期地，按期地

   Your L/C No. 451 opened through the Bank of New South Wales has duly arrived.　贵方第451 号由新南威尔士银行开立的信用证已如期收到。

6. on perusal　经审阅，在细阅后

7. few and far between　稀少，也可以用 scarce

8. book freight/shipping space　预订舱位，订舱

   charter a ship/vessel　租船

   在货物交付和运输过程之中，如货物的数量较大，可以洽租整船甚至多船来装运，这就是"租船"。如果货物量不大，则可以租赁部分舱位来装运，这就是"订舱"。当卖方备妥货物，收到国外开来的信用证，并且经过审核无误后，能否做到船货衔接，按合同及信用证规定的时间及时将货物出运，主要决定于租船订舱这个环节。

9. via　prep. 经由

   The samples were sent via airmail.　样品已航寄。

10. more often than not　常常，也可以说 frequently

11. It would be to our mutual benefit if we could ship immediately whatever we have on hand instead of waiting for the whole lot to be completed.　如果能将我方现有货物立即装运，而不是等到整批货物备齐才装运，这将对我们双方都有利。

12. amend the L/C to read…　将信用证改为……，也可以用 amend the L/C reading…

    信用证常见不符点：信用证过期；信用证装运日期过期；受益人交单过期；运输单据不洁净；运输单据类别不可接受；没有"货物已装船"证明或注明"货装舱面"；运费由受益人承担，但运输单据上没有"运费付讫"字样；启运港、目的港或转运港与信用证的规定不符；汇票上面付款人的名称、地址等不符；汇票上面的出票日期不明；货物短装或超装；发票上面的货物描述与信用证不符；发票的抬头人的名称、地址等与信用证不符；保险金额不足，保险比例与信用证不符；保险单据的签发日期迟于运输单据的签发日期（不合理）；投保的险种与信用证不符；各种单据的类别与信用证不符；各种单据中的币别不一致；汇票、发票或保险单据金额的大小写不一致；汇票、运输单据和保险单据的背书错误或应有但没有背书；单据没有必要签字或有效印章；单据的份数与信用证不一致；各种单据上面的唛头不一致；各种单据上面的货物的数量和重量描述不一致。

7.   Amending the L/C Clauses of Amount, Shipment Time & Packing

Background: 中国某儿童用品有限公司在收到加拿大某玩具进出口公司开来的第 4523 号金额为 135000 美元用以支付 200 纸箱充气玩具的信用证后，经审核，发现该信用证金额不足，装运期及包装条款有误，于是发电子邮件要求修改这三处不符点。

From: yiqinghua@dankena.cn

To: maashamgn@gbinvista.com

Date: Friday, August 13, 20＿＿, 11: 48 am

Subject: Your L/C No. 4523 for Your Order No. 784

Dear Mr. Maas,

We confirm receipt of your L/C No. 4523 for the amount of US$135,000.00 in payment for your Order No. 784 covering 200 cartons of inflatable toys.

Among the clauses specified in your L/C, we find the following three points do not conform to the relative contract:

1)   When we checked the L/C with the relevant contract, we find that the amount of L/C is insufficient. The correct total value CIF Montreal of your order ought to be US$153,000.00 instead of US$135,000.00, the difference being US$18,000.00. Obviously it is a clerical mistake.

2)   Your L/C allows only half a month to effect shipment. But when we signed the contract, we have agreed that the delivery should be made within one month upon receipt of the L/C.

3)   As to packing, the contract stipulates that the goods should be packed in cartons and reinforced with nylon straps outside, but your L/C requires metal straps instead. We think we should arrange the packing as per the contract.

In view of the above, you are kindly requested to instruct your bank to increase the L/C amount by US$18,000.00, extend the shipment date and validity of the covering L/C to September 12 and September 27 respectively, as well as amend the term of packing.

Upon receipt of your amendment, we will make the necessary arrangements for shipment of the goods in question.

Yours sincerely,

Q. H. Yi

Sales Director

Notes

1. in payment for   用来支付，还可以用 for payment of, covering, to cover, for
2. conform to   与……相符，与……一致
3. total value of your order   贵方订单的总值
4. the difference being...   差额为……，也可以说 with a difference of...
5. the contract stipulates that...   合同规定……，也可以说 the contract states/provides that...
6. be reinforced/strengthened with nylon straps outside   外用尼龙带加固
7. extend the shipment date and validity of the covering L/C to September 12 and September 27 respectively   将相关信用证的装运期及有效期分别展至 9 月 12 日和 9 月 27 日
8. the goods in question   该货物，提及的货物，此处的 in question，意思是"该，所涉及的"，类似 the above mentioned, the said，如：

    The goods in question have been in good demand since the beginning of this year.   自今年初该货一直畅销。

8. Amendment to Five L/C Clauses

Background: 土耳其 DABENTI IC VE DIS TICARET LTD STI 在收到天津某有机食品贸易公司开来的第 A-903 号用以支付 260 公吨精炼葵花籽油的信用证后，经审核，发现该信用证存在 5 处不符点，于是发电子邮件要求改证。

From: yunuskulahcio@dabenti.com.tr
To: jinlaide@alibaba.com
Date: Thursday, October 2, 20_ _, 13: 54 pm
Subject: Your L/C No. A-903 for Our S/C No. 122

Dear Mr. Jin,

We are in receipt of your email of September 1, informing us of the establishment of your L/C No. A-903 issued by the Chartered Bank of Tianjin for our S/C No.122 covering 260 metric tons of Refined Sunflower Oil. The L/C in question has just come to hand. However, we regret to have found that there are certain clauses which do not conform to those of the contract. Hereby we list discrepancies for your attention:

1. The name of the beneficiary should read "DABENTI IC VE DIS TICARET LTD STI", instead of "DABEMT IC VE DIS TICARET LTD STI", the latter being the name of another corporation in Turkey.
2. Please insert the word "about" before the quantity and amount in your L/C as it is impossible for us to ship the goods in the exact quantity as contracted.
3. Commission is 3%, not 6%.
4. Shipment is to be made during October/November, instead of "on or before 30th October".
5. Goods should be insured for 110% of the invoice value, not 120%.

We suppose that the above mistakes are clerical and hope you will make the necessary amendments immediately by fax so that we can ship the goods in time.

We appreciate your prompt attention to the above.

Yours sincerely,
Yunus Kulahcio
Export Executive

Notes

1. Chartered Bank 渠打银行，标准渠打银行（Standard Chartered Bank）是一家总部位于英国伦敦市的英国银行。

2. the latter being the name of another corporation in Turkey 后者是土耳其另一家公司的名称 这是一种独立主格，由名词或代词加分词组成，作状语用。如：
    The L/C having been opened, we will effect shipment this month. 信用证已开出，我们这个月就发货。
    The contract already signed, both parties must abide by it. 合同已签署，双方必须遵守。

3. clerical mistake 笔误

4. as contracted 如合同所规定的

9. Extension of an L/C for the Goods are not Ready

Background: 天津科天贸易公司向美国 Ivy 生物化学制品公司出口 5 公吨鸡蛋黄，但由于供货商的耽误，无法按信用证规定四月底前装运，只能在 5 月 10 日左右装入从天津新港启航的"蓝海"号货轮，于是科天贸易公司发电子邮件给对方，请求延展信用证的装运期和有效期。

From: wanghw_1998@tjketian.com.cn

To: dodgemmsl@ivybiotech.com

Date: Thursday, April 28, 20＿＿, 9: 16 am

Subject: Your L/C No. 244 for 5 M/Ts of Egg Yolk

Dear Mr. Dodge,

We thank you for your L/C No. 244 covering your order for the subject goods.

Much to our regret, owing to some delay on the part of our suppliers, we are unable to get the goods ready for shipment before the end of this month. So we faxed you earlier today asking for an extension.

We expect the goods will be ready for shipment in the early May and we are arranging to ship them on S. S. "Blue Seas" scheduled to sail from Xingang on or about May 10.

We will make contact with the manufacturers to expedite delivery and trust you will extend by fax the time of shipment and the validity of the said L/C to May 15 and May 30 respectively, thus enabling us to effect shipment of the goods in question in time.

We send our sincere apologies for the delay and trust that you will give this urgent matter your prompt attention.

Yours sincerely,

H. W. Wang

Sales Manager

Notes

1.　extension of the L/C　展证
2.　on the part of our manufacturers　我方生产商方面的
3.　in the early May　五月上旬
　　in the middle of May = in the mid-May　五月中旬
　　in the late May　五月下旬
4.　be scheduled to sail from...　预计从……启航
5.　on or about　大约，也可以说 around

Unit 11   Insurance

保　险

1. Definition of Insurance

In international trade, the transportation of goods from the seller to the buyer is generally over a long distance by air, by land or by sea and has to go through the procedures of loading, unloading and storing. During this process it is quite possible that the goods encounter various kinds of risks, including losses. In order to protect the goods against possible risks, the buyer or seller before the transportation of the goods usually applies to an insurance company for insurance covering the goods in transit. What's more, the goods must be insured against these risks in accordance with the mode of transport used, the nature of the goods and the insurance terms stipulated in the contract.

2. Insurance Policy

An insurance policy is actually a contract, serving as evidence of the agreement between the insurer and the person taking out insurance. It forms part of the shipping documents. In return for payment of a premium paid by the insured, the insurer agrees to pay the insured a sum, if the event insured occurs. In the sales contract, insurance clause should be expressly stipulated, including insurer, insured, the criterion for the insurance clause, insured value and so on.

3. Classification of Insurance

Concerning means of transportation, there are four kinds of basic insurances: marine transportation insurance, land transportation insurance, air transportation insurance and parcel transportation insurance. Among them, marine insurance is the biggest item and the other three kinds of insurances just develop on its basis.

4. Marine Transportation Insurance
4.1 Insurance on FOB, CFR and CIF Basis

Who will effect insurance depends on the particular trade terms adopted. Usually under CIF terms, insurance is arranged by the exporter approaching an insurance company which has a department specializing in cargo insurance while under CFR, FOB terms the importer effects insurance, but he may ask the exporter to arrange insurance on his behalf.

4.2 Calculation of Insurance Amount

The amount insured must be at least the invoice value of the goods. The insurance amount is calculated as: cost of goods + amount of freight + insurance premium + a percentage of the total sum to represent a reasonable profit on sale of the goods.

Under a CIF contract, as per Ocean Marine Cargo Clauses of PICC (The People's Insurance Company of China) dated 1st January, 1981, it is common practice for the exporter to insure the goods for 10% above the invoice value, that is to say, 100% is for CIF invoice value and 10% is to cover a reasonable profit and some expenses. Sometimes, importers may request insurances to cover more than 110%. In such circumstances, the extra premium will be for buyer's account.

4.3 Types of Insurance Coverage with PICC

Insurance coverage varies in content. The People's Insurance Company of China provides three basic types: Free from Particular Average (F. P. A.), With Particular Average (W. P. A.) and All Risks. Nevertheless, the terms of insurance must clearly specify what insurance clauses are applicable, for China Insurance Clause (CIC) is different from the Institute Cargo Clauses (ICC). In this way, it will avoid any possible misunderstanding with regard to the responsibility of parties concerned.

保险常用短语及语句

- insurance agent/broker　保险代理人
- insurance amount　保险金额，保额
- insurance certificate　保险凭证
- insurance claim　保险索赔
- insurance company　保险公司
- insurance cover　保险
- insurance coverage　保险范围，险别
- insurance endorsement　保险批单
- insurance policy　保险单
- insurance premium　保险费，保费
- air transportation insurance　航空运输保险
- marine insurance　水险，海上保险，海运险
- ocean marine cargo insurance　海洋运输货物保险
- overland insurance　陆运保险
- overland transportation insurance　陆上运输保险
- parcel post insurance　邮包保险
- open policy　预约保险单，船名未确定保单，流动保单
- specific policy　单独保单，船名确定保单

- transferable policy   可转让的保单
- sum insured   保险金额
- policy-holder   保险客户
- termination of risk   保险责任终止
- insurance clause   保险条款
- insurance instruction   投保通知
- insurance conditions   保险条件
- risk insured, risk covered   承保险项

Requesting for Covering Insurance

- Please provide cover of £16,000 on WPA for this consignment, in transit from Shanghai to New York.
  请对这批从上海运往纽约的货物投保金额为 16000 英镑的水渍险。
- Please effect insurance on your side covering all risks and war risk.
  请在你处投保一切险和战争险。
- WPA coverage is too narrow for a shipment of this nature. Please extend the coverage to include TPND.
  对于这类货物投保水渍险是不够的。请再加上偷窃和提货不着险。
- Please insure against all risks as WPA is too narrow a coverage.
  请投保一切险，因为水渍险不够。
- So far as we know, there are risks of pilferage or damage to the goods during transshipment in Hong Kong, so please arrange insurance against the above risks.
  据我方所知，在香港转船期间有货物被盗或损坏的风险，请投保上述险别。
- Could you cover the Breakage of Packing Risk and Taint of Odor Risk for our consignment?
  贵公司能否为我公司的货物投保包装破裂险和串味险？
- We shall be grateful if you are to arrange the risk of rust for the steel we ordered from your company.
  如果贵方为我方从贵方订购的这批钢铁代办生锈险，我方将不胜感激。
- We shall be pleased to know whether you can take out the insurance of our perfume against the risk of breakage and the risk of pilferage.
  我方希望知道贵方可否为我方的香水投保破碎险和盗窃险。
- We shall be glad to hear whether you are prepared to issue an open policy for US$115,000 for our shipment.
  请告知我方货物可否开保险金额 115000 美元的预约保险单。

Reply to the Requesting for Insurance

- Our insurance coverage is for 110% of invoice value up to the port of destination only.
  我方按发票金额 110%投保，仅至目的港。
- Now that you require additional coverage, we have to ask you to bear the extra premium.
  既然你方要求额外的险别，我方只能要求你方承担额外的保费。

- War Risk is a special risk, for which an extra premium will have to be charged.

  海上货物运输战争险是一种特殊险，需要收取额外保险费。

- If you wish to secure protection against TPND, it can be easily done upon the payment of an additional premium.

  如果你方想通过偷窃和提货不着险使货物得到保障，只需要支付额外的保费即可办理。

- Please charge the additional premium for risk of leakage to the account of our company.

  敬请贵方将渗漏险所需的额外保险费记入我方账户。

- In the absence of definite instructions from our clients, we generally cover insurance against WPA and War Risk; if you desire to cover FPA, please let us know in advance.

  如果没有得到客户的明确指示，我们通常投保水渍险和战争险。如果贵方想投保平安险，请提前告知。

- The extent of insurance is stipulated in the basic policy form and in the various risk clauses.

  在基本保险单和各种险别条款中规定了保险范围。

- These kinds of risks suit your consignment.

  这些险别适合贵方的货物。

- The cover paid for will vary according to the type of goods and the circumstances.

  根据货物的种类和情况保险费会有变化。

- The rates quoted by us are very moderate. Of course, the premium varies with the range of insurance.

  我方所报的保险费率是十分合理的。当然，保险费随着保险范围而变。

写 作 范 例

1. An Email From Importer Asking Exporter to Cover Insurance on Behalf of Him & Exporter's Reply

Background: 英国 Universal 国际贸易公司从中国苏州东裕茶业有限公司按照 CFR 条件进口了 200 箱绿茶提取物和 300 箱紫砂茶具，希望东裕公司代为办理保险，并提出关于险别的要求。

From: rexparleymail@universal.industrial.com

To: niul_export@dongyu.tea.com

Date: Thursday, November 15, 20＿＿, 9: 51 am

Subject: Insurance on Our Order No. 101

Dear Mr. Niu,

We wish to refer you to our Order No. 101 for 200 cases of Green Tea Extract Powder and 300 cases of Zisha Tea Set, from which you will see that this order was placed on CFR basis.

As we now desire to have the consignment insured at your end, we shall be much pleased if you will kindly arrange to insure the same on our behalf. The main reason why we changed our mind is that we found the People's Insurance Company of China charges premium at lower rates.

We have to point out that the FPA coverage is not enough for the goods. For Green Tea Extract Powder, you should at least add Risk of Sweating and Risk of Odor. As to Zisha Tea Set, Risk of Clash and Breakage must be included. So we think it is better for you to cover All Risks at invoice value plus 10% with PICC.

We shall of course refund the premium to you upon receipt of your debit note or, if you like, you may draw on us at sight for the same.

We sincerely hope that our request will meet with your approval.

Yours sincerely,
Rex Parley
Importer Coordinator

Notes

1.   "投保，办理保险" 的表达：
     ● Sb + cover/arrange/effect/provide/take out insurance…
     说明保险情况时，insurance 后接介词的一般用法是：
     表示向保险公司投保时，接 with，如：insurance with the People's Insurance Company of China
     表示保额时，接 for，如：insurance for 110% of the invoice value
     表示所保的货物时，接 on 或 for，如：insurance on the 100 tons of wool
     表示投保的险别时，接 against，如：insurance against all risks
     表示保费或保险费率时，接 at，如：insurance at a slightly higher premium, insurance at the rate of 5%
     由卖方向中国人民保险公司按发票金额的 110% 对 100 公吨羊毛投保一切险。Sellers will cover insurance on 100 metric tons of wool for 110% of invoice value/for 10% above the invoice value/at the invoice value plus 10% against All Risks with PICC.
     ● insure, cover 的用法区别：
     insure (vt.)：后面可以加所保的货物、投保的险别，如：
     We want to insure <u>the goods</u> against all risks and war risk. 我们想将此货投保一切险和战争险。（所保的货物）
     The insurance company here insures <u>this risk</u> with a 5% franchise. 此间保险公司保这种险有 5% 的免赔限度。（投保的险别）
     insure (vi.)：It is necessary to insure against breakage. 投保破碎险是有必要的。

cover (vt.)：后面可以加所保的货物、投保的险别、insurance 和被保险人，如：

Please cover <u>the goods</u> against all risks. 请对此货投一切险。（所保的货物）

Please cover <u>all risks and war risk</u> for us. 请为我方投保一切险和战争险。（投保的险别）

The seller has covered <u>the insurance</u>. 卖方已经办理保险了。（insurance）

Please cover <u>us</u> against breakage. 请为我方投保破碎险。（被保险人）

● 用被动形式：Goods are covered/insured…

2. insurance coverage   险别，保险范围

PICC 制订的中国保险条款（China Insurance Clauses, CIC）中的海洋运输货物保险条款所包括的险别分基本险和附加险两种。

基本险有三种，分别为：平安险（Free from Particular Average, FPA）、水渍险（With Particular Average, WPA）、一切险（All Risks），这三种基本险的承保范围是逐渐递增的，即水渍险的承保责任范围除包括平安险的各项责任外，保险人还负责被保险货物由于恶劣气候、雷电、海啸、地震、洪水等自然灾害所造成的部分损失。一切险的承保责任范围除包括水渍险的各项承保责任外，保险人还负责被保险货物在运输途中由于一般附加险所致的全部或部分损失。

基本险承保责任起迄期限或称保险期限，采用国际保险业务中惯用的"仓至仓条款"（Warehouse to Warehouse，简称 W/W Clause）。

附加险是对基本险的补充和扩大，只能在投保某一种基本险的基础上才可加保。中国保险条款中的附加险有一般附加险（General Additional Risks）和特殊附加险（Special Additional Risks）之分。一般附加险只能在投保了主要险别即平安险、水渍险之后，再行加保，而不能单独投保。一般附加险都包括在一切险中，如投保人投保了一切险，就无须加保上述各项附加险。特殊附加险不包括在一切险的范围内，即使投保人投保了一切险，仍须与保险人特别约定，经保险人特别同意后，才能把特殊附加险的责任包括在承保范围之内。

一般附加险（General Additional Risks）：

偷窃和提货不着险（Theft, Pilferage and Non-delivery Risk, TPND）

淡水雨淋险（Fresh Water and Rain Damage Risk, FWRD）

渗漏险（Leakage Risk）

短量险（Shortage Risk）

混杂、玷污险（Intermixture and Contamination Risk）

碰损、破碎险（Clash and Breakage Risk）

串味险（Taint of Odor Risk）

受潮受热险（Sweat and Heating Risk）

钩损险（Hook Damage Risk）

包装破裂险（Breakage of Packing Risk）

锈损险（Rust Risk）

特殊附加险（Special Additional Risks）：

战争险（War Risk）

罢工、暴动、民变险（Strike, Riots and Civil Commotion, SRCC）

舱面险（On Deck Risk）

交货不到险（Failure to Deliver Risk）

出口货物到香港（包括九龙在内）或澳门存仓火险责任扩展条款（Fire Risk Extension Clause for Storage of Cargo at Destination Hong Kong including Kowloon, or Macau，简称 FREC）

进口关税险（Import Duty Risk）

货物拒收险（Rejection Risk）

黄曲霉素险（ Aflatoxin Risk）

3. We wish to refer you to…　兹关于……，请参见……，还可以用 We made reference to…

4. this order was placed on CFR basis　我们的订单是按照成本加运费订购的

按 FOB 或 CFR 条件成交的进口货物，由我进口企业自行办理保险。为简化投保手续和避免漏保，一般采用预约保险的做法，即被保险人（投保人）和保险人就保险标的物的范围、险别、责任、费率以及赔款处理等条款签订长期性的保险合同。投保人在获悉每批货物起运时，应将船名、开船日期及航线、货物品名及数量、保险金额等内容，书面定期通知保险公司。保险公司对属于预约保险合同范围内的商品，一经起运，即自动承担保险责任。而未与保险公司签订预约保险合同的进口企业，则采用逐笔投保的方式，在接到国外出口方的装船通知或发货通知后，应立即填写"装货通知"或投保单，注明有关保险标的物的内容、装运情况、保险金额和险别等，交保险公司，保险公司接受投保后签发保险单。两种情况下，投保的日期应不迟于货物装船的日期。

5. have the consignment insured at your end　在你地投保

consignment　n. 一批交付的货物，货物，委托装运的货物，有时与 shipment（船货）通用

a fresh consignment of bicycles　一批新到的自行车

The consignment has gone forward on s/s "East Wind".　这批货已由"东风"号轮装出。

Ten out of a consignment of thirty sewing machines shipped on s/s "Jinan" were damaged during transit.　由"济南"号轮装来的一批缝纫机，30 架中有 10 架已在运输途中损坏。

consignment　n. 寄售的货物，委托代销的产品，此时与 shipment 用法不同

As desired, we agree to ship our 500 pieces bicycles to you "on consignment".　按照贵方要求，我方同意以寄售方式装给你方 500 辆自行车。

You may sell the consignment merchandise at the prevailing market price less one percent.　你方可以按照比当前市价低 1%的价格销售寄售的货物。

at your end　在贵处，在你地，类似的表达有 in your place, on your side

6. insure the same on our behalf against All Risks at invoice value plus 10%　将上述货物按发票金额外加 10%代我方投保综合险

按照国际保险市场的习惯做法，出口货物的保险金额一般按 CIF 货价另加 10%计算，这增加的 10%叫保险加成，也就是买方进行这笔交易所付的费用和预期利润。保险金额计算的公式是：保险金额=CIF 货值×（1+加成率）。

投保人按约定方式缴纳保险费是保险合同生效的条件。保险费率（Premium Rate）是由保险公司根据一定时期、不同种类的货物的赔付率，按不同险别和目的地确定的。保险费则根据保险费率表按保险金计算，其计算公式是：保险费=保险金额×保险费率。

on one's behalf　代表某人

7. refund the premium to you   将保险费退还给你
   refund the deposit to you   将保证金退还给你

8. your debit note   你方的借记通知单，即将某笔款项借记到某人的账户（即从某人的账上提出）后给其发出的通知

9. draw on us at sight for the same   向我方开出金额为该批货物总值的即期汇票

10. meet with your approval   得到你方的同意

Reply

Background: 中国苏州东裕茶业有限公司同意代为办理保险，并要求对方用电汇方式支付相应的保险费。同时，告知货物将于下个月 11 号左右由 "吉祥" 轮运出。

From: niul_export@dongyu.tea.com
To: rexparleymail@universal.industrial.com
Date: Friday, November 16, 20__, 11: 26 am
Subject: Re: Insurance on Our Order No. 101

Dear Mr. Parley,

We have received your email dated November 15, requesting us to effect insurance on 200 cases of Green Tea Extract Powder and 300 cases of Zisha Tea Set for your account.

We are pleased to confirm having covered the above shipment with the People's Insurance Company of China against All Risks for 110% of the invoice value. The policy is being prepared accordingly and will be forwarded to you by the end of the week together with our debit note for the premium. Please remit the premium to us by T/T upon receipt of our debit note.

We wish to draw your attention to the fact that generally for commodities like ours, claims are payable for that part of the loss, that is over 4%.

For your information, this consignment will be shipped on s/s "Ji Xiang", sailing for your port as scheduled on or about the 11th next month. We will send you a shipping advice very soon.

We trust the above information will serve your purpose and await your further news.
Yours sincerely,
L. Niu
Export Sales Manager

Notes

1. effect insurance on the captioned shipment for your account   对标题项下的货物投保，费用由贵方承担

for one's account   由某人付费，类似的表达有 at one's cost/expense

2. having covered the above shipment with the People's Insurance Company of China against All Risks for 110% of the invoice value   已向中国人民保险公司按发票金额的 110%对上述船货投保了一切险

3. The policy is being prepared accordingly.   该保单正相应地办理中。

保险单（insurance policy），简称为保单，又称为大保单。它是保险人与被保险人订立保险合同的正式书面证明，是主要的出口单据之一。

保险凭证（insurance certificate），简称为小保单，又称为保险条。保险凭证是保险人签发给投保人的，表明已接受其投保的证明文件，是一种简化的保险单。保险凭证上不载明保单背面保险条款，其余内容与大保单完全相同，且法律效力与大保单相同，但不能作为对保险人提出诉讼的依据。在实务中，小保单一般由保险人签发，也可由保险经纪人作为预约保险单代为签发。

4. claims are payable for that part of the loss, that is over 4%   损失索赔只支付超过 4% 的部分

5. serve purpose   满足需要，符合目的，起作用

2. An Email from Buyer Asking for Quotation on CFR Basis

Background: 新加坡 Lion 工艺品进出口公司要求中国厦门星光家居工艺品公司报一千个金属烛台的成本加运费报价而非成本加保费价，因为 Lion 公司可从一向有商务关系的伦敦的劳埃德保险公司获得较低的保险费。

From: richardlee@lionarts.com.sg

To: rosaligood@hotmail.com

Date: Tuesday, December 7, 20_ _, 13: 16 pm

Subject: Quotation for 1,000 Pieces of Metal Candle Holders

Dear Ms. Li,

We have received with thanks your quotation for 1,000 pieces of Metal Candle Holders on CIF terms. As our usual practice we prefer to receive quotations or offers on CFR terms.

Our position is that we have taken out an open policy with the Lloyd Insurance Company, London. Under the policy, all we have to do when a shipment is sent is to advise them of the particulars. Furthermore, we are on very good terms with them. We usually receive from our insurers quite a handsome premium rebate at regular intervals.

We await with interest your early reply.

Yours sincerely,

Richard Lee

Purchasing Manager

Notes

1. as our usual practice 按照我方惯例
2. taken out an open policy with the Lloyd Insurance Company, London 向伦敦的劳埃德保险公司办理了预约保单

   预约保险单（open policy），是指保险人或保险经纪人以承保条形式签发的承保被保险人在一定时期内发运的以 C 组术语出口的或以 F 组术语进口的货物运输保险单。它载明保险货物的范围、承保险别、保险费率、每批运输货物的最高保险金额以及保险费的计算办法。凡属预约保险单规定范围内的货物，一经起运保险合同即自动按预约保险单上的承保条件生效，但要求投保人必须向保险人对每批货物运输发出起运通知书，也就是将每批货物的名称、数量、保险金额、运输工具的种类和名称、航程起讫点、开航或起运日期等通知保险人，保险人据此签发正式的保险单证。这种保险单据目前在我国一般适用于以 FOB 或 CIF 价格条件成交的进口货物以及出口展览品和小卖品。

3. be on very good terms with sb 和某人关系良好
4. insurer n. 保险人，保险商，保险公司，也可以说 insurance company
5. quite a handsome premium rebate 很多的保险费折扣

   quite a handsome 大量的，许多的
6. at regular intervals 定期地，按期地
7. the scope of cover 保险范围，险别，也就是 coverage

   cover 与 coverage 的区别：

   cover n. 保险，也常说 insurance cover

   According to the contract, you should arrange all necessary insurance cover. 根据合同，你方得安排所有必要的保险。

   Our policy has provided adequate cover against breakage. 我方的保险单已经提供了适当的破碎险。

   coverage n. 保险范围

   Broader coverage is necessary to this kind of goods. 对这种货物来说，更广泛的保险是有必要的。

3. An Email from Buyer Requesting to Cover Insurance against All Risks

Background: 中国天津丽晶工艺品公司与澳大利亚 Rema 水晶玻璃制品公司就 100 箱水晶奖座达成交易。销售合同中的保险条款是按一般产品投保 WPA。丽晶公司认为水晶工艺品价值高而且易碎，因此要求 Rema 公司将保险范围改成包含碰损破碎险的一切险。

From: xuphoebe@lijing.crystal.com

To: rosspritt@remacrystal.com.au

Sent: Wednesday, July 23, 20＿＿, 15: 22 pm

Subject: Insurance in S/C No. DY2308

Dear Ms. Pritt,

I am pleased to receive your S/C No. DY2308 for 100 cases of "Spirit" Crystal Awards. On perusal, both the manager and I find the terms and conditions in accordance with our negotiated contents in the previous emails except that one thing should be mentioned and altered. I notice that the insurance terms in the Sales Contract stipulate that insurance is to be effected against WPA as usual terms but the goods traded this time are of high value and fragile. Such being the case, I think the insurance should be covered against All Risks since it includes Clash and Breakage Risk.

I wish you could agree with the above amendment and send your new contract in order for us to countersign it.

I will be very happy to receive your early reply.

Yours sincerely,

Phoebe Xu

General Manager

Notes

1. crystal award   水晶奖座
2. Clash and Breakage Risk   碰损破碎险

Reply

Background: 澳大利亚 Rema 水晶玻璃制品公司表示同意投保一切险，但告知天津丽晶工艺品公司对于碰损破碎险，保险公司通常都规定 5%的免赔率。

From: rosspritt@ remacrystal.com.au

To: xuphoebe@ lijing.crystal.com

Sent: Thursday, July 24, 20＿＿, 8: 12 am

Subject: Re: Insurance in S/C No. DY2308

Dear Ms. Xu,

Thank you for your email of July 23, in which you kindly remind us of the insurance coverage.

I'd like to tell you that we agree to alter the insurance to cover All Risks instead of WPA as the goods are valuable and fragile.

In addition, I wish to mention that Clash and Breakage Risk normally is subject to a 5% franchise according to business practice of the insurance company. That is to say no claims for damage can be entertained, if the breakage is examined to be less than 5%.

I will send you the new contract with our signature as soon as possible and after your countersignature we will carry out the contract accordingly.

Best regards.

Sincerely yours,
Ross Pritt
Business Manager

Notes

1. franchise   n. 免赔率，是指不赔金额与损失金额的比率。保险公司认为某些易碎、易短量的商品在运输途中遭受一定比例的损失是不可避免的，故投保这类商品规定在某百分比范围的破碎或短量可以免赔，该百分比就是免赔率。免赔率分为相对免赔率与绝对免赔率两种。相对免赔率（Non-deductable Franchise）是指保险人对免赔率以内的损失不赔，如损失超过免赔率时，则对全部损失都赔。绝对免赔率（Deductable Franchise）是指保险人只赔偿超过免赔率的部分，对免赔率以内的损失绝对不赔。

   The class of goods is sold with a franchise of 3%.   此类商品按免赔率 3%出售。

2. no claims for damage can be entertained   对此损失所提出的索赔不予受理

   insurance claim   保险索赔，指当被保险人的货物遭受承保责任范围内的风险损失时，被保险人向保险人提出的索赔要求。在国际贸易中，如由卖方办理投保，卖方在交货后即将保险单背书转让给买方或其收货代理人，当货物抵达目的港（地），发现残损时，买方或其收货代理人作为保险单的合法受让人，应就地向保险人或其代理人要求赔偿。

4. An Email from Buyer Asking for Additional Risks

Background: 买方想为货物投保两种附加险，向卖方解释原因，并表示一收到卖方投保成功后的消息就立即用电汇方式将保险费打入卖方账户。

From: rohitshanker@navadaimports.com
To: tavonspirit@essentialoil.com
Sent: Friday, August 4, 20＿＿, 13: 14pm
Subject: Asking for Additional Risks

Dear Tavon,

Apart from the coverage mentioned in our email of August 3, we want to make an emphasis that the consignment must be covered against "Fresh Water and Rain Damage" and "On Deck Risk", because both the loading port and the unloading port are now confronted with a rainy season. We suffered great damage last summer because of the rainy weather, and we do not want to experience another loss for the same reason.

We shall refund the premium to you by T/T upon receipt of your notification.

We shall appreciate your cooperation.

Regards,

Rohit Shanker
General Manager

Notes

1. apart from   除此之外

   Apart from that, everything goes well.   除了那个，一切都还顺利。

   Multicolor options are also available apart from single color designing and printing.   除了单色的设计和印刷，还有多种颜色供您选择。

2. Fresh Water and Rain Damage   淡水雨淋险，也可缩写为 F.W.R.D.

3. On Deck Risk   舱面险

Reply

From: tavonspirit@essentialoil.com
To: rohitshanker@navadaimports.com
Sent: Saturday, August 5, 20_ _, 15: 24pm
Subject: Re: Asking for Additional Risks

Dear Rohit,

We have received your email of August 4, asking us to add the additional risk "Fresh Water and Rain Damage" and "On Deck Risk" for your consignment, besides the All Risks you mentioned in your earlier letter of August 3.

We are pleased to inform you that we have covered the shipment with The People's Insurance Company of China against All Risks for USD12,000.

It was found that your request was acceptable and we have covered against "Fresh Water and Rain Damage" and "On Deck Risk" for your consignment. Please make payment by T/T for the extra premium of USD1,000 to our account for this policy.

Best regards,

Tavon Lewis
Export Executive

Notes

1. additional risk   附加险
2. earlier   adj.   早期的，初期的
   earlier this year   今年年初

Sample: Insurance Policy

PICC

中国人民保险公司
The People's Insurance Company of China
总公司设于北京 一九四九年创立
Head Office Beijing   Established in 1949

货物运输保险单
CARGO TRANSPORTATION INSURANCE POLICY

发票号(INVOICE NO.) SD537	保单号次	
合同号(CONTRACT NO.)	POLICY NO.	
信用证号(L/C NO.) 25DF/05		
被保险人(INSURED) TO ORDER		

中国人民保险公司(以下简称本公司)根据被保险人的要求，由被保险人向本公司缴付约定的保险费，按照本保险单承保险别和背面所载条款与下列特款承保下述货物运输保险，特立本保险单。

THIS POLICY OF INSURANCE WITNESSES THAT THE PEOPLE'S INSURANCE COMPANY OF CHINA (HEREINAFTER CALLED "THE COMPANY") AT THE REQUEST OF THE INSURED AND IN CONSIDERATION OF THE AGREED PREMIUM PAID TO THE COMPANY BY THE INSURED, UNDERTAKES TO INSURE THE UNDERMENTIONED GOODS IN TRANSPORTATION SUBJECT TO THE CONDITIONS OF THIS POLICY AS PER THE CLAUSES PRINTED OVERLEAF AND OTHER SPECIAL CLAUSES ATTACHED HEREON.

标 记 MARKS&NOS	包装及数量 QUANTITY	保险货物项目 DESCRIPTION OF GOODS	保险金额 AMOUNT INSURED
AS per Invoice NO. SD537	100CTNS	Sport Shoes	GBP15,120

总保险金额
TOTAL AMOUNT INSURED: GREAT BRITAIN POUNDS FIFTEEN THOUSAND ONE HUNDRED & TWENTY

	启运日期		装载运输工具：
保费 As	DATE OF		PER
PREMIUM: arranged	COMMENCEMENT: 15th. Sept. 2005		CONVEYANCE: _____
自	经		至
FROM: Qingdao	VIA		TO London

承保险别
CONDITIONS

所保货物，如发生保险单项下可能引起索赔的损失或损坏，应立即通知本公司下述代理人查勘。如有索赔，应向本公司提交保单正本(本保险单共有　份正本)及有关文件。如一份正本已用于索赔，其余正本自动失效。

IN THE EVENT OF LOSS OR DAMAGE WITCH MAY RESULT IN A CLAIM UNDER THIS POLICY, IMMEDIATE NOTICE MUST BE GIVEN TO THE COMPANY'S AGENT AS MENTIONED HEREUNDER. CLAIMS, IF ANY, ONE OF THE ORIGINAL POLICY WHICH HAS BEEN ISSUED IN ( ) ORIGINAL(S) TOGETHER WITH THE RELEVANT DOCUMENTS SHALL BE SURRENDERED TO THE COMPANY. IF ONE OF THE ORIGINAL POLICY HAS BEEN ACCOMPLISHED, THE OTHERS TO BE VOID.

赔款偿付地点
CLAIM PAYABLE AT　　London In GBP
出单日期
ISSUING DATE　　　10th. Sept. 2005

中国人民保险公司
The People's Insurance Company of China

Authorized Signature

Unit 12　Shipment
装　运

背景知识

1. Means of Transportation

In international trade, there are many means of transportation. Goods can be transported by train, truck, plane, ship, through pipelines and, if the product is software, by Internet. Of the various means of transportation available, ocean freight is by far the most important one. Commodities such as coal, grain, chemicals and iron ore are often shipped by this means. Slower as it is, transportation by ship is less expensive. In most of the movements of goods, three parties are normally involved: the consignor, the consignee and the carrier.

2. Process of Shipment

As an exporter (usually the consignor), he must always be kept informed of the names of steamers and their sailing dates from his port. On receipt of the relative L/C, he should contact the ship's agents or the shipping company for the booking of shipping space and prepare for the shipment in accordance with the importer's shipping instructions. As soon as the goods are on board, the master of the steamer or the ship's agents will give him a receipt of the goods shipped. That receipt is called the Bill of Lading. The exporter sends the Bill of Lading together with the invoice and other shipping documents to his bank for the negotiation of his draft on the opening bank of the L/C. At the same time, he sends a shipping advice, usually by fax or email, informing the importer of the name of steamer, the sailing date and other details.

催装运写作步骤

1. Reference to the Details of the Goods
2. Reasons for Urging Shipment
3. Hoping the Close Cooperation

催装运常用语句

1. Reference to the Details of the Goods

● We are very anxious to know about the shipment of our Order No. 123 for 1,000 cases of Tin Plates.

我方急欲了解第 123 号订单项下 1000 箱锡板的装运情况。

● We refer you to the S/C No. 1456, which stipulates shipment to be made is no later than December 10. We regret that up till now we have heard nothing from you.

请参阅第 1456 号销售确认书，该确认书规定发货不迟于 12 月 10 日。很遗憾到目前为止，我方尚未收到贵方的任何消息。

● We refer to the captioned contract signed between us on July 1, 2009 for 6,000 long tons of wheat, which is stipulated for shipment in October, 2009. However, up till now we have not received from you any information concerning this lot.

兹关于双方于 2009 年 7 月 1 日签署的合同项下 6000 长吨小麦。合同规定 200 年 10 月装运。但迄今为止我方未得到关于此批货物的任何讯息。

● We would like to call your attention to the fact that no news come from you about the shipment, although the time of shipment is now weeks overdue.

我方希望贵方能注意到这个事实：装运日期已逾期几周之久，但我方却没有收到来自贵方的任何消息。

● Please let us know when we may expect delivery of "Butterfly" Brand Sewing Machines ordered some four weeks ago. Our letter of credit opened with our bank in your favor must have reached you for quite some time.

请告知我方于四周前订购的蝴蝶牌缝纫机何时能交货。我方通过银行开立的以你方为受益人的信用证应该抵达你处一段时间了。

● As stipulated, the above goods should have been shipped in three equal lots in October, November and December. But until now the first lot has not yet been delivered.

按照规定，以上货物应当平均分三等份，分别于 10 月、11 月和 12 月装运。但是至今第一批货物仍未运送。

● Concerning our Order No. 123 for 1,000 pieces of the captioned goods, up till now we only received half of the goods which you delivered on December 3 last year.

关于我方第 123 号订单项下的 1000 件标题项下的产品，至今我方仅收到去年 12 月 3 日发来的一半货物。

2. Reasons for Urging Shipment

● As the contracted time of delivery is rapidly falling due, it is imperative that you inform us of the delivery time without any further delay.

由于合同规定的交货期临近，贵方必须尽早告知我方具体的交货期。

● As our end users are in urgent need of this material, we intend to send our vessel S. S. "Feng Qing" to pick up the goods, which is expected to arrive at Vancouver around the end of November.

由于我方客户急需该原料，所以我方打算派"丰庆"轮中途带货，该轮预计在 11 月底左右抵达温哥华。

● It is our hope that you could ship the goods, by the next steamer "Feng Qing", which is due to sail from your city on or about the 15th May to our port, as our clients are anxious to have these machines within the next month.

由于我方客户下个月急需这些机器，所以希望贵方将货物装上下一艘"丰庆"轮，该轮预计于 5 月 15 日左右从你市启航驶往我港。

3. Hoping the Close Cooperation

● You are requested to let us have your immediate reply by fax whether you are agreeable to this proposal. If not, please let us know exactly the earliest time when the goods will be ready.

请尽快传真回复是否同意此建议。如不同意，请告知货物备妥的最早的确切时间。

● Please do your very best to hasten shipment. We hope that by the time you receive the letter, you will have the goods ready for shipment.

请尽快装运。希望收到此函时，货物已备妥待运。

● As the date of shipment is further extended, we believe there will be no difficulty in having the goods shipped in time.

由于装运期再次推迟，我方相信货物应能及时装运。

● We trust you will see to it that the order is shipped within the stipulated time, as any delay would cause us no little inconvenience and financial loss.

我方相信贵方定会在规定时间内装运，因为任何延误都会给我方带来极大的不便和经济损失。

● Your failure to deliver the goods within stipulated time has greatly inconvenienced us. It has to be stressed that shipment must be made within the prescribed time limit, as a further extension will not be considered.

你方未能在规定时间内交货给我方带来了极大的不便。我方强调必须在规定的时间期限内装运，我方不会再次推迟。

● It is important that the goods be completed for delivery as stipulated in the L/C, say by October 20. If not, you should be responsible for any loss that might be caused by the delay of shipment.

按照信用证规定于 10 月 20 日完成装运是十分重要的。如不能装运，贵方应对延迟装运所造成的损失负责。

- Your delay caused us considerable difficulties and we must ask you to do your utmost to dispatch the overdue goods as soon as possible, otherwise we shall be compelled to cancel the orders in accordance with the stipulations of the contract.

  贵方的延误给我方带来很大的困难。我方必须要求你方尽力将逾期的货物尽早装运，否则我方将被迫根据合同条款取消订单。

- We have been put to great inconvenience by the delay in delivery. In case you should fail to effect shipment in November, we will have to lodge a claim against you for the loss and reserve the right to cancel the contract.

  由于延迟交货使我方处境不利。如果贵方不能在 11 月装运，我方不得不因损失向你方提出索赔，并保留撤销合同的权利。

装运延误常用语句

- We have to advise you that we are unable to dispatch your order in time due to a great shortage of shipping space.

  由于船舱的大量短缺，我们不得不告知贵方我方无法及时运送贵方的订单。

- We are, for sure, aware that your goods are long overdue, but work at the plant was suspended for three weeks owing to the earthquake.

  我们固然知道已远超过交货时间，但工厂作业因地震中断了三周。

- The remaining 60% may be subject to a delay in delivery until the end of July.

  余下的 60% 的货物可能得推迟到 7 月底发货。

- Owing to the manufacturer's production delay, we have missed the May shipment and loaded your order on the first available June vessel for your destination.

  由于厂家生产上的延误，我方错过了 5 月的船期，因此将贵方订货装上 6 月驶往贵地的第一艘货轮。

- We regret very much to inform you that despite strenuous efforts having been made by us, we are still unable to book a space of vessel on May 20.

  我方万分遗憾地告知贵方，尽管我方已经尽了最大的努力，我方仍旧无法预订到 5 月 20 日的舱位。

- We assure you that we are doing everything we can to ship the electronic calculators ASAP and will email you immediately when we have arranged shipment.

  我方向贵方保证尽我们所能尽快装运这些电子计算器，并且在出货安排完毕后立即给贵方发电子邮件。

- We apologize for the inconvenience the delay has caused to you.

  因延误而给贵方造成不便，我们非常抱歉。

装船指示常用语句

- Our customer requests the shipment should be made in three equal lots, each every two months.
  我方客户要求货物分三批等量运来，每两个月一批。

- As stipulated in the contract, shipment is to be made during June, July and August in three equal lots of 1,000 tons each.
  按合约规定，货物将在 6、7、8 月份分三批平均装运，每批 1000 吨。

- We shall appreciate your arranging to ship the first four items by the first available steamer sailing to New York direct right after receipt of our L/C.
  若贵方能于收到我方信用证后马上将前四项货品交由驶往纽约的第一班直达货轮承运，我方将不胜感激。

- Please ship the first lot under Contract No. 122 by S. S. "China Prince" scheduled to sail on or about May 2.
  请将第 122 号合同项下的第一批货物由预计 5 月 2 日左右启航的"中国王子"轮运来。

- Since the purchase is made on FOB terms, you are to ship the goods from Liverpool on a steamer to be designated by us.
  由于交易是按 FOB 价达成，贵方必须将货物装上我方指定的货轮由利物浦运来。

- It is of great importance to our buyers that the arrival date of this order should be arranged as early as possible to meet their requirements. So you are supposed to ship the goods by a steamer s/s "Princess", the main reason is that their steamers offer the shortest time for the journey between China and Germany.
  为了满足我方客户的要求，货物尽早抵达十分重要。因此，请贵方将货物装上"王子"轮，因为该轮提供的中国与德国间的航程最短。

- In reply to your letter of April 3, please send 50 dozen of our goods, marked A 1-50, per s/s "May" as soon as possible to our port, and the other 50 dozen afterwards by next steamer.
  兹答复贵方 4 月 3 日来函，请尽快将 50 打货物，标记为 A 1-50，由"五月"轮发运到我港，其余 50 打用下一艘货轮运来。

- For the goods under our Contract No. SC456 we have booked space on S. S. "East Wind" due to arrive in London around May 15. Please communicate with B & W Bros. Co., Singapore, our shipping agents, for loading arrangements.
  我们已在"东风"轮订妥舱位，以便装第 SC456 号合同货，该轮约在 5 月 15 日左右抵达伦敦。有关装船事宜，请与我方运输代理新加坡 B & W 兄弟公司接洽。

- It is stipulated that shipment should be effected in October. However, we shall appreciate it if you will arrange to advance the shipment to September to enable us to catch the busy season.
  按照规定，货物应在 10 月装运。但是若能将装运提前到 9 月以便我方赶上销售季节，将十分感激。

- As the market is sluggish, please postpone the shipment of our ordered goods to March.

由于市场萧条，请将我方订购货物推迟至 3 月装运。

- In order to cut down handling and shipping expenses as much as possible, we suggest that you ship the above large order in containers.

为了尽量减少装卸和运输费用，我方建议贵方采用集装箱装运上述大宗订货。

- Please take necessary precautions that the packing can protect the goods from dampness or rain, since these goods are liable to being spoiled by damp or water in transit.

由于货物在途中非常易于受潮或受雨淋而变质，因此务必采取必要的防护措施使得包装能够防潮和免遭雨水侵蚀。

装船通知写作步骤

1. Informing the Buyer of the Completion of the Shipment
2. Enclosing the Relevant Shipping Documents
3. Hoping the Punctual Arrival of the Goods

装船通知常用语句

1. Informing the Buyer of the Completion of the Shipment

- We are pleased to inform you that Contract No. 231 for 3,000 Zhonghua Brand Bicycles has been dispatched by S. S. "Mayflower" which sailed from Shenzhen yesterday and is due to arrive at London on August 9.

现欣然奉告第 231 号合同项下的 3000 辆中华牌自行车已装入"五月花"轮，该轮昨日从深圳启航，预计于 8 月 9 日抵达伦敦。

- We have pleasure in notifying you that we have shipped you today S. S. "Peace" 200 cartons of Alarm Clocks. They are to be transshipped at Hong Kong and are expected to reach your port early next month.

很高兴地告知贵方 200 箱闹钟已于今日装入"和平"轮。在香港转船后预计下月初抵达你港。

- Immediately upon receipt of your instructions, we approached the shipping company here. We are pleased to write to inform you that we have completed shipment today of 5,000 Men's Shirts in accordance with the stipulations of the said L/C, on board S. S. "Qingdao" which is due to sail from Shanghai and arrive at London on July 15.

一俟收到贵方的装船须知，我方与此地的船运公司联系。现告知我方已按照上述信用证的规定于今日将 5000 件男式衬衫装上从上海启航的"青岛"轮，预计 7 月 15 日抵达伦敦。

- We have pleasure to inform you that shipment per s/s "Light" has gone forward and hope that it will arrive at the destination in perfect condition.

现欣然奉告货物已由"光"号轮装走，希望能完好无损地抵达目的地。

- The goods have been packed and marked exactly as directed so that they may be shipped by the first ship available toward the end of this month.

  货物已严格按照要求包装妥当，刷好唛头，以便交第一艘可装货的船只于本月底运出。

2. Enclosing the Relevant Shipping Documents

- Enclosed please find one set of the shipping documents covering this consignment, which comprises:

  随函附寄该批货物的装船单据一套，包括：

- In compliance with the terms of the contract, we forwarded you by airmail a full set of duplicate shipping documents to you immediately after the goods were shipped, thus you may find no trouble in taking delivery of the goods when they arrive.

  按照合同条款，在货物装船后我方立即向贵方航寄全套装运单据副本，以便贵方到货后顺利提货。

- The original of the shipping documents are being sent to you through the Bank of China.

  装船单据的正本由中国银行寄送给贵方。

- The commercial invoice, together with clean on board ocean Bills of Lading, have been sent through the Bank of London, with our sight draft under your L/C.

  商业发票随同清洁海洋已装船提单，已经通过伦敦银行与本公司凭贵方信用证所开立的即期汇票一并寄出。

- Further details, including packing and marks, are contained in our invoice No. 487 enclosed in duplicate.

  随函附寄我方第 487 号发票一式两份，里面包括包装及唛头等详情。

3. Hoping the Punctual Arrival of the Goods

- We are glad to have been able to execute your order as contracted and we believe that the goods will reach you in good condition on time and prove to be fully satisfactory.

  能够按合约订明的要求为贵公司效劳，我方深感荣幸。相信该货物将会完好无损地及时运抵贵公司，并使贵方满意。

- We hope this shipment will reach you in time and turn out to be your entire satisfaction.

  希望货物能及时抵达，并能让贵方满意。

- We are looking forward to hearing from you that the goods have arrived safely and in good order and that you are pleased with them.

  期盼得到货物安全无损抵达以及贵方满意的消息。

货物抵达常用语句

- We regret to inform you that the goods have arrived in a damaged condition that some of them are out of action.

我们很遗憾地告知贵方，货物抵达时已有破损，有一些已出现故障。

- We appreciate your responsible and professional shipment, which helps to dispatch the goods safely.

贵方负责任和专业的装运使得货物能够安全运达，对此我方深表谢意。

- We are glad to inform you the goods have arrived today, and thank you for the efforts you have made for the early shipment.

我们高兴地通知贵方货物已于今日抵达，感谢贵方为提早装运所做出的努力。

- We are delighted to inform you that the digital cameras you ordered are now in stock and available for picking up at the address in the enclosed sheet.

很高兴地通知您，贵方订购的数码相机现在已经到货，您可以按照随函附上的地址提货。

- We should be much grateful if you would unpack and examine them as soon as possible after delivery and in the event of any losses let us know at once.

提货后请立即开箱检查。如发现有损失，请及时予以告知，我方将不胜感激。

装船标识常用语句

- diamond　菱形
- triangle　三角形
- circle　圆形
- rectangle　长方形
- hexagon　正六角形
- cross　十字形
- downward triangle　倒三角形
- star　星形
- square　正方形
- heart　心形
- oval　椭圆形
- three diamond　三菱形
- 识别标志：
    箱（包）号：CASE＃
    重量（毛）：WEIGHT（GROSS）
    重量（皮）：WEIGHT（TARE）
    重量（净）：WEIGHT（NET）
    体积标志：MEASUREMENT MARK 表示为：LONG×WIDE×HIGH 或 L×W×H
    批号：LOT NO.或 BATCH NO.
    尺寸 cm：DIMENSIONS IN CM
    数量：QUANTITY 或 Q'TY

规格：SPECIFICATION 或 SPEC

原产国标志：COUNTRY OF ORIGIN

收货人：CONSIGNEE

发货人：CONSIGNOR

发运人：SHIPPER

由……到……：FROM…TO…

经由：VIA

港：PORT

货号：ARTICLE NO.

● **装箱标志（操作位置）**

由此起吊（此处悬索或挂绳位置）：SLING HERE；LIFT HERE；HEAVE HERE

从此开启（此处打开）：OPEN HERE

暗室开启：OPEN IN DARK ROOM

用滚子搬运：USE ROLLERS

装箱标志（操作动作）

小心轻放：HANDLE WITH CARE

小心搬运；小心装卸：CARE；WITH CARE；CARE HANDLE

易碎物品：FRAGILE

玻璃器皿，小心轻放：GLASS WARE，HANDLE WITH CARE

切勿投掷：NO DUMPLING；NOT SHOOT

切勿坠落（小心掉落）：DO NOT DROP；NO DROPPING

请勿用钩（勿用手钩）：USE NO HOOK；NO HOOK

装箱标志（放置位置）

重心在此：CENTER OF GRAVITY

必须平放：KEEP FLAT；STOW LEVER

切勿平放：NOT TO BE LAID FLAT

竖直安放：TO BE KEEP UPRIGHT

此端向上：THIS END UP

切勿挤压：DO NOT CRUSH

请勿踩踏：DO NOT STEP ON

上部：TOP

下部（底部、下端）：BOTTOM

装箱标志（放置条件）

切勿受潮：KEEP AWAY FROM MOISTURE；CAUTION AGAINST WET

防潮（防湿）：CAUTION AGAINST WET

防冷（怕冷）：TO BE PROTECTED FROM COLD

防热（怕热）：TO BE PROTECTED FROM HEAT

请勿受热（远离热源）：KEEP AWAY FROM HEAT

勿近锅炉（远离锅炉）：STOW AWAY FROM BOILER（HEAT）

防火：INFLAMMABLE

放于凉处；放于冷处；保持冷藏；宜冷藏：KRRP COLD；STOW COOL

勿置于磁场中：DO NOT EXPOSE TO MAGNETIC FIELDS

装箱标志（商品性质）

液体货物：LIQUID

易腐物质：PERISHABLE

易燃物品：FLAMMABLE

易碎物品：FRAGILE

酸性物品，小心：ACID WITH CARE

小心有毒：POISON，WITH CARE（POISONOUS）

有效期：TERM OF VALIDITY BEST BEFORE

保质期：PRESERVATIVE PERIOD

怕光：KEEP IN DARK PLACE

怕压（不可装在重物之下）NOT TO BE STOWED BELOW OTHER CARGO

写 作 范 例

1. Urging Shipment

Background: 中国云南绿元实业有限公司与意大利德尔派橄榄油公司签署了第 478 号合同，从德尔派公司进口 280 公吨橄榄油。绿元公司于 6 月 5 日将信用证开抵德尔派公司，但直到 7 月 5 日绿元实业有限公司仍未收到货物装运的消息。于是采购经理孙女士发电子邮件给德尔派公司，表明运货延误，如不立即采取行动，会丧失此订单。

From: juliasun5465@ynlvyuan.com

To: salvatore@longo.chemicals.com

Date: Friday, July 5, 20＿＿, 9: 32 am

Subject: Contract No. 478 for 280 M/Ts of Olive Oil

Dear Mr. Longo,

We wish to invite your attention to our Order No. 5781 covering 280 metric tons of olive oil under Contract No. 478, for which we sent to you about 30 days ago an irrevocable L/C—expiration date July 20. Up to the present no news has come from you about the shipment under the subject contract.

As the season is rapidly approaching, our customers are badly in need of the goods contracted. We are grateful if you will effect shipment as soon as possible, thus enabling them to catch the brisk demand at the start of the season.

Under the circumstances, we would like to emphasize that any delay in shipping our booked order will undoubtedly involve us in no small difficulty and we may be compelled to seek an alternative source of supply.

As your prompt attention to shipment is most desirable to all parties concerned, we hope you will fax us your shipping advice without further delay.

Sincerely yours,
Julia Sun
Purchasing Manager

Notes

1. urge shipment   催装运
2. expiration date   到期日
3. up to the present, up till now, up to now, so far   到目前为止，句中用现在完成时
4. As the season is rapidly approaching…   由于销售季节很快来临……
5. contracted   adj. 合同项下的，订妥的
6. catch the brisk demand   赶上市场的大量需求
7. booked order   被确认的订单
8. seek an alternative source of supply   寻求其他货源
9. shipping advice   装船通知

   装船通知也叫装运通知，是出口商在货物装船后发给进口商的包括货物详细装运情况的通知，其目的在于让进口商做好筹措资金、付款和接货的准备。货物装船后，卖方应及时向买方发出装船通知，尤其是在 FOB 或 CFR 条件成交的情况下，因为买方接到通知后，要即刻办理保险手续。如果卖方没有及时通知买方，使买方没能办理投保或延误了办理投保的时间，那么由此而产生的经济损失将由卖方承担。如果是按照 CIF 条件成交的，虽说是由卖方办理保险，但货物装船后，也要及时向买方发出装船通知，因为买方需要做好接货、卸货准备，以办理进口报关手续等。

   装船通知主要包括所发运货物的合同号或信用证号、品名、数量、金额、运输工具名称、启航日期、启运地和目的地、提单号码、运输标志等。此外通知中还可能出现包装说明、ETD（船舶预计离港时间）、ETA（船舶预计进港时间）、ETC（预计开始装船时间）等内容。

Reply

Background: 意大利德尔派橄榄油公司进口部经理 Salvatore Longo 为延误装运致歉，并解释原因，说明已采取实际行动做出补救，将货物分两批出运，并希望延展信用证的装运期和有效期。

From: salvatore@longo.chemicals.com
To: juliasun5465@ynlvyuan.com

Date: Friday, July 5, 20_ _, 16: 28 pm
Subject: Re: Contract No. 478 for 280 M/Ts of Olive Oil

Dear Ms. Sun,

We have received your email this morning, requesting us to expedite the shipment of your Order No. 5781 for the subject goods.

Upon receipt of the email, we immediately contacted the shipping company, but we are sorry to tell you that as the result of the storming weather these days, the ship carrying our goods will be postponed for sailing and the only direct steamer which calls at your port once a month has been fully booked. In order to ship within the contract time, we booked m.v. "EMMA" which is due to sail on July 13, with transshipment at Singapore. But its shipping space has been almost fully booked. We have no choice but to ship 50 metric tons of olive oil by this steamer and the remaining 230 metric tons by the next available steamer "ANNA", which is due to sail two days later.

Such being the case, it is impossible for us to ship as the contract required. Please extend the shipment date of L/C to July 20 and validity to August 5 accordingly.

We hope the goods will reach you in sound condition and that you will be satisfied with the quality of our products.

We appreciate your kind understanding and great support.

Yours sincerely,
Salvatore Longo
Import Manager

Notes

1. expedite the shipment   加速装运
2. postpone   vt. 推迟
    They decided to postpone signing the contract owing to the difficulty beyond their control.   由于出现难以控制的困难，他们决定推迟合同的签署。
3. call at your port   停靠你港
4. with transshipment at...   在……转船
5. shipping space   舱位

2. Shipping Instructions (1)

Background: 英国 KT 高级服装贸易公司向中国天津宏达制衣有限公司订购了 4000 打真丝

裙，并于 8 月 10 日通过曼彻斯特第一国家银行开立了用以支付第 CK215 号订单的信用证。在电子邮件中，KT 公司区域经理 Eric Evans 告知宏达公司关于货物装运的各项事宜。

From: ericevans@ktfashion.com
To: jiangmb2003@tjhongda.com
Date: Tuesday, August 10, 20＿＿, 10: 25 am
Subject: Shipping Instructions for Our Order No. CK215

Dear Mr. Jiang,

The irrevocable letter of credit No. 7634, amounting to USD168,000, for payment of our Order No. CK215 for 4,000 dozen silk dresses has been opened this morning through the First National Bank of Manchester. Please arrange shipment of the goods immediately. We are informed by the local shipping company that S. S. "Victory" is due to sail from your city to our port about the 10th September and please ship by that steamer.

We have instructed our forwarder to contact you and you shall hear from them in a day or two.

Please mark the cartons with our initials, the destination and order number as follows:
　KT
　LONDON
　CK215
　CTN No. 1 up

This will apply to all shipments unless otherwise instructed.

Please make sure there are no Chinese characters on any print material. Please make sure there will be no grammatical mistakes with English words on print material.

Please make sure all payment and shipping documents, such as contract, bill of lading, commercial invoice, packing list, certificate of origin, certificate of quality and quantity, will be made correctly as indicated:

　The brand name is "CENTURY GOLDEN"
　Model: KI229LP

We'd like to draw your attention to the fact that all the above notes are very important for our customs clearance.

If this trial order proves satisfactory to our customers, we can assure you that repeat orders in increased quantities will follow shortly.

Thank you very much for your close cooperation. In the meantime we await your shipping advice.

Yours sincerely,

Eric Evans

Area Manager

Notes

1.　shipping instructions　装船须知，装船指示（是买方发给卖方的，说明其对货物装运的要求，卖方按照买方的指示来办理货物装运事宜）

2.　amount to　总计

3.　due　adj. 预计的，预期的

　　When are the goods due at Xingang?　货物预计什么时候到达新港？

　　The ship is due to leave/arrive on or about May 10.　该轮预计 5 月 10 日左右离港/抵港。

4.　forwarder　n. 货代，运输代理人

5.　mark the cartons with　在纸箱上标记

6.　CTN No. 1 up　在没有确定具体箱数之前，用 up 表示该批货共有 N 箱。确定了箱数后，如在卖方发货的时候，就不能用 up 了。在唛头中直接写出 N 到底是几。如，NO.1-10，就表示这批货共有 10 箱。

7.　unless otherwise instructed　除非另有说明

8.　customs clearance　清关

　　customs　n. 海关

　　清关（Customs Clearance），即结关，习惯上又称通关，是指进口货物、出口货物和转运货物进入或出口一国海关关境或国境必须向海关申报，办理海关规定的各项手续，履行各项法规规定的义务；只有在履行各项义务，办理海关申报、查验、征税、放行等手续后，货物才能放行，货主或申报人才能提货。货物在结关期间，不论是进口、出口或转运，都是处在海关监管之下，不准自由流通。

　　报关（Customs Declaration），又称申报，是指在货物进出境时，进出口商或其代理人向海关申报，请求办理货物进出口手续的行为。在报关时，要填写报关单，并交验海关所规定的各项单证。实际业务中，一般都说出口报关，进口清关。

3.　Shipping Instructions (2)

Background: 中国上海星光电脑公司从美国戴尔公司处按照 CIF 条件订购了电脑及显示器、主板、驱动器若干，订单号为 FR-009。星光公司对所购产品的装运提出了各项要求。

From: mona_asiaarea@starcomputers.com

To: nsioreed@dell.com

Date: Thursday, June 28, 20＿＿, 13: 42 pm

Subject: Shipping Instructions for Our Order No. FR-009

Dear Mr. Reed,

We have received with thanks your fax of June 27, from which we understand that you have booked our Order No. FR-009 for 2,000 sets of DELL E5400 computers and respective 300 pieces of color monitors, main boards and drivers. Our confirmation of order will be forwarded to you in a few days.

Since the purchase is made on CIF basis, you are to send the goods to Shanghai by the end of August.

As these goods are susceptible to shock, they must be packed in seaworthy cases capable of withstanding rough handling. The bright metal parts should be protected from water and dampness in transit by a coating of lubricant that will keep out dampness, but will not liquefy and run off under changing weather conditions.

Please mark the case with our initials in a diamond, under which comes the destination with contract number and stencil conspicuously the words "FRAGILE, HANDLE WITH CARE" on both sides of the case.

We trust that the above instructions are clear to you and that the shipment will give the users entire satisfaction.

Yours sincerely,
Mona Hu
Area Manager

Notes
1. book order   接受订单
2. respective 300 pieces of color monitors, main boards and drivers   彩色显示器、主板、驱动器各 300 件
3. confirmation of order   订单的确认函
4. forward   vt. 发送，寄送，运输，类似的说法有 send, deliver, dispatch
   forwarder, forwarding agent, shipping agent 运输代理人，是根据委托人的要求，代办货物运输业务的机构。它既可以向货主承揽货物，也可以代理货主向承运人办理托运，且可以兼营两方面的代理业务，在承运人和托运人之间起着桥梁作用。
5. be susceptible to sth   易受……的影响，类似的说法有 be liable to, be subject to
6. capable of withstanding rough handling   能够经受得起野蛮装卸
7. be protected from water and dampness   防水防潮
8. a coating of lubricant   一层润滑油
9. liquefy and run off   液化并流失
10. stencil conspicuously the words   清晰地刷制上……的字样

4.   Shipping Advice (1)

Background: 中国天津伊诺户外休闲用品公司向荷兰 Sollar Collection 贸易公司出口 300 套户外藤编沙发，并按照第 7634 号信用证将货物装上 "Pandit" 轮。现通过电子邮件给对方发装船通知，同时航寄相关装船单据副本一套。

From: xujgbusiness@chinayino.com

To: muirmichael@slcollection.net

Date: Friday, September 13, 20＿＿, 15: 31 pm

Subject: Shipping Advice for Your Order No. C215

Dear Mr. Muir,

I am pleased to advise you that your Order No. C215 covering 300 sets of outdoor rattan sofa under L/C No. 7634 has been shipped via S. S. "Pandit" which is sailing directly to Rotterdam, estimated time of departure from Tianjin is September 15 and estimated time of arrival at Rotterdam, October 10.

I have airmailed one set of duplicate shipping documents so that you may make all the necessary preparations to take delivery of the goods when they arrive at your port.

Invoice No. 44156 in duplicate

Packing list No. 7895 in duplicate

One Non-negotiable Copy of the Bill of Lading No. AD785

One Copy of the Insurance Policy No. DB478

One Copy of the Survey Report No. TF1445

I am glad that we have been able to execute your order as contracted. I am sure you will find the shipment satisfactory and look forward to more opportunities of serving you.

Yours sincerely,

J. G. Xu

Export Coordinator

Notes

1.   rattan   n. 藤，藤条
2.   estimated time of departure   预计启航时间，简称 ETD
3.   estimated time of arrival   预计到达时间，简称 ETA
4.   duplicate   n. 副本
5.   take delivery of the goods   提货
6.   packing list   装箱单（说明箱内装了什么货物，如机器、轻工业品等。但是大批散装货物，

如肥料、大豆等，则用重量单或磅码单 weight memo）

7. non-negotiable copy of the bill of lading   提单副本（提单正本是 original bill of lading）

提单，简称 B/L，在对外贸易中，运输部门承运货物时签发给发货人的一种凭证，用以证明海上货物运输合同和货物已经由承运人接收或者装船，以及承运人保证据以交付货物。收货人凭提单向货运目的地的运输部门提货。提单须经承运人或船方签字后始能生效。提单是海运货物向海关报关的有效单证之一。

提单的主要关系人是签订运输合同的双方：托运人和承运人。托运人即货方，承运人即船方。其他关系人有收货人和被通知人等。收货人通常是货物买卖合同中的买方，提单由承运人经发货人转发给收货人，收货人持提单提货。被通知人是承运人为了方便货主提货的通知对象，可能不是与货权有关的当事人。

提单有正本和副本之分。正本提单一般签发一式两份或三份，这是为了防止提单流通过程中万一遗失时，可以应用另一份正本。各份正本具有同等效力，但其中一份提货后，其余各份均告失效。副本提单承运人不签署，份数根据托运人和船方的实际需要而定。副本提单只用于日常业务，不具备法律效力。

8. survey report   检验报告

5. Shipping Advice (2)

Background: 美国绿叶机电设备有限公司向中国上海欧捷五金样品公司出口 120 台 NIP23 型钻孔机。按照双方签署的第 3511 号销售确认书，货物已于 5 月 1 日顺利装上 "HANSA" 轮，预计 5 月中旬抵达。绿叶公司发来装船通知，希望货物能赶上销售旺季并欢迎欧捷公司验货。

From: henrypatel773@greenleaf.com

To: qianrt1998@oujie.hardwares.com

Sent: Monday, May 2, 20＿＿, 8: 10 am

Subject: Shipping Advice for Sales Confirmation No. 3511

Dear Mr. Qian,

This is to inform you that instructions filed under the subject number have now been carried out and that the 120 sets of Model No. NIP23 drilling machines were dispatched per S. S. "HANSA" yesterday.

All items were examined before being packed in special containers. You may rest assured that they should reach you in good condition by the middle of May. I should be glad if you would unpack and examine them immediately on arrival. Any complaints as to damage should be notified to us and to the shipping company within ten days.

I trust the goods will reach you in time for the summer selling season and prove to be entirely satisfactory to you. I will personally expect to receive your further orders before long and ensure that you receive our prompt and careful attention at all times.

Yours sincerely,

Henry Patel

Export Sales Manager

Notes

1. You may rest assured that...   请放心，我方向贵方保证……
2. drilling machine   钻孔机
3. in good condition   状况良好

   The machine is in good condition without deformation.   机器状况良好，没有变形。
4. complaint   n. 申诉

6. An Email from Importer about Change in the Means of Delivery

Background: 青海西宁的宏泰服饰贸易公司为了适应市场需求，抓住商机，临时更改运输方式，要求将部分货物尽快空运，并请 Pop Garment 公司航空邮寄单据，而剩余货物希望能在规定的日期前按照原先约定的运输方式装运完毕。

From: evahongtaidown@hongtaiyr.net.cn

To: solangefashion2000@popgarment.com

Sent: Thursday, October 28, 20＿, 8: 46 am

Subject: Requesting for the Change in the Delivery Means for Order No. 325

Dear Ms. Belluz,

We refer to the subject order dated October 1 for the eiderdown outwears. Please now dispatch the first 500 sets of this order by air and for the rest of the order we would like to dispatch them by sea as usual.

We are so sorry that we know it would be quite inconvenient for you since we change the way of delivery all of a sudden. But the temperature falls so unexpectedly that they are urgently demanded by our customers, and we hope that we can brisk demand at the beginning of this season.

As for the rest, we hope you will arrange the shipment before November 2 and we should be thankful if you would send us by airmail a copy of packing lists included in each case to be sent by sea, duplicates of the Insurance Certificate as well as the Commercial Invoice.

We appreciate your early reply.

Yours sincerely,

Eva Dai

General Manager

Notes

1. eiderdown outwear 羽绒服，可简称为 down coat，或 down jacket
2. brisk v. 使活跃起来，刺激

   Business always brisked up before Christmas.   圣诞节前生意总是十分兴隆。

   brisk   adj. 兴隆的，繁荣的

   Its sales have been brisk since July.   自 7 月以来销售一直很旺。

   Prices are stable and the market is brisk.   物价稳定，市场繁荣。
3. a copy of packing lists included in each case to be sent by sea   一份包括各箱海运货物装箱单的复件

7. An Email from Exporter about Delay in Shipment

Background: 由于天气原因，在进口商规定的时间内，没有货轮开往其港口。但出口商向进口商承诺会尽一切努力以保证在合同期限内完成装运，并告知进口商最快开出的货轮名和日期。

From: amanda_freezer0108@yehos.com

To: timsjf_shs@osssc.com

Sent: Wednesday, August 19, 20_ _, 10:51 am

Subject: Advice of Delay in Shipment

Dear Mr. Rapier,

Regarding your instruction of delivering the 1,000 refrigerators under S/C No. 364, we have consulted the shipping company and now regret to inform you that there is no vessel sailing to your port during the time you requested owing to the forecast of storm. So far as we know, the earliest vessel sailing to your port is M.V. "Sky", which is scheduled to leave at the beginning of September.

We will, however, do everything possible to ensure that the goods are shipped within contracted time. But we are so sorry that we cannot give you a definite date of shipment for the time being.

At any rate, please accept our apologies for the inconvenience you have been put into. But please try to understand that this is a case of force majeure. We hope you will extend the credit accordingly.

We are looking forward to your early reply.

Yours sincerely,

Amanda Lao

Sales Manager

Notes

1. forecast   n. 预报，预测

2. so far as we know   就我们所知

   so far as   只要

   so far as it goes   就其本身而言，就目前的情况而论

   so far as that is concerned   事实上

3. M.V.   货轮，motor vessel 的缩写

4. at any rate   无论如何，至少，相当于 however，in any case

5. force majeure   不可抗力

   不可抗力事件的范围主要由两部分构成：一是由自然原因引起的自然现象，如火灾、旱灾、地震、风灾、大雪、山崩等；二是由社会原因引起的社会现象，如战争、动乱、政府干预、罢工、禁运、市场行情等。不可抗力的后果一般有两种：一种是解除合同，一种是延期履行合同。

8. An Email from Importer about Notification of Product Arrival

Background: 货物在合同期限内安全抵达，尽管外包装有破损，但由于有内包装的保护，货物完好无缺。进口商对出口商完全按照要求包装和刷唛表示感谢，并希望继续与对方合作。

From: davidg_sjdf@hunnt.com

To: owenzhang_garmentjhg@haoyugarment.com

Sent: Thursday, August 11, 20＿＿, 9:23 am

Subject: Notification of Product Arrival

Dear Mr. Zhang,

We are glad to inform you that the goods under our Order No.109 covering 1,000 pieces of jeans have reached us on August 10, the exact date you instructed us. As payment for your Invoice No.156, we airmail our bank check for US$25,000.

Through careful inspection, we found that two cartons were damaged, but fortunately, since the jeans were packed by polybags firstly, they are still in good condition. Also, we are glad to see that the goods were packed and marked completely according to our instruction so that we could find them out easily.

We thank you for your speedy and careful service and expect a continued and close cooperation with you.

We are looking forward to hearing from you upon receipt of our check.

Yours sincerely,

David Gruber

CEO

Notes

1. bank check　银行支票

   银行支票是银行签发的，承诺自己在见票时无条件支付确定的金额给收款人或持票人的票据。

2. inspection　n. 检查，视察

   inspection certificate　检验证书

   customs inspection　海关检查，验关

   The goods were inspected by the Commodities Inspection Office before shipment.　这批货物在装船前是经过商品检验局检验的。

Unit 13　Claim and Settlement
索赔和理赔

1. Definition of Claim and Settlement

During the execution of a contract, if one party fails to perform the contract and thus bring economic loss to another party, the latter may ask the former for compensation according to the contract stipulations. This is called claim. To handle the claim lodged by the suffering party is what is called settlement on the part of the responsible party.

Claim must be made within the term of validity stipulated in the contract (generally within 30 days after the arrival of the goods at the destination).

Towards claim and settlement, all parties concerned should have amicable attitude and seek truth from facts. Serious investigation is needed to ascertain what the real cause is and which party is responsible for the loss. The amount of loss and the way of compensation are to be fixed. In some cases, adequate documents or certificate issued by the Commodity Inspection Bureau are to be provided. All the careful and skillful handling and reasonable settlement are to be desired so as to avoid resorting to arbitration.

2. Writing of Settlement

The concrete writing of letters in reply to complaint or claim should be in accordance with concrete case.

2.1 Agreeing to the Customer's Request (Complete Agreement)

Such letters are easy to write, since you are agreeing to the customer's request. You may begin with the following openings:

"We wish to express our deepest regret over the unfortunate incident."

"Enclosed please find our check for... This is the amount that you were overcharged on our recent invoice."

The body of such a letter should be written in details—how the merchandise should be returned or whether the overcharge is being credited to the customer's account or returned in a cash refund. Further measures are to be taken—how the firm is attempting to keep the problem from happening again. The body probably includes an apology and an assurance that future orders will be satisfactorily executed.

The closing should be courteous and preferably contain a request for future business.

2.2 Making Adjustments at the Customer's Request (Partial Agreement)

The letter of this type is not to meet the whole demand but to make some adjustments or concession. The letter may begin with a "Thank you" or an apology and a repetition of the particulars of the shipment in question. For example:

"We are sorry that our last shipment was found short weight upon its arrival."

"Thank you for telling us the problems you have encountered."

The body of the letter explains the reasons why the adjustment is being made, why it is fair, what the company's policies are, and how this is a reasonable settlement for both sides.

The closing should be courteous in that it expresses a hope that the customer be satisfied with the adjustment.

2.3 Rejecting the Customer's Request (Complete Disagreement)

It is difficult to write a letter that completely rejects the customer's request while you still want to keep in a good relationship with the customer.

For those claims that are not consistent with the fact, or not reasonable, or not within the responsibility at the exporter's side, state your case and reject it courteously and tactfully. To those that you cannot settle promptly, reply first, by letter or email, explaining that you are making investigation and will give a definite answer right after it. Sometimes along with the refusal you can suggest an alternative that the opposite side will find reasonable.

The closing is often a summary and request for the customer's understanding.

索赔写作步骤

1. Stating the Details of the Commodity
2. Stating the Case (the Problem and a Request for an Explanation)
3. Putting Forward the Solution

索赔常用语句

1. Stating the Details of the Commodity

- Please refer to our Order No. 303 and your Sales Confirmation No. 165 which have clearly stated that the time of shipment is no later than the end of March. This is the third time we write to invite your attention to the fact that up to date we have received no news from you about the shipment.

我方第 303 号订单及你方第 165 号销售确认书均清楚地表明装运期不能迟于三月底。这是我方第三次去函提醒你方注意迄今为止我方未收到这批货的任何消息。

- In accordance with your Sales Confirmation No. 1358, the universal lathe we bought from you last month is unconditionally guaranteed for a year.

  根据你方第 1358 号销售确认书，我方上月从你方购买的万能车床应无条件保质一年。

- This is to inform you that we have received 15 cases of medical and surgical instruments this morning, consigned by you on May 3.

  兹告知我方于今晨收到你方 5 月 3 日运来的 15 箱医疗和手术器械。

- We regret to inform you that the goods are not in accordance with our orders.

  很遗憾地告知货物与我方订单不一致。

2. Stating the Case (the Problem and a Request for an Explanation)

Late Delivery

- As the cycling season is approaching and our users are pressing us for assurance of effecting delivery in time, there isn't much time left before we give our clients a definite reply.

  由于销售周期即将到来，我方用户敦促我方及时交货，所以我方没有太多时间了，必须立即给予确切的回复。

- We have been urging you for an immediate dispatch of these foods, and unless this order is already on the way, it will arrive too late for the season, and so be of no use to us.

  我方曾敦促你方立即装运这些食品。除非货物已经在途中，否则到货太晚，以致错过销售季节，货物对我方就毫无用处了。

- The goods were promised to be delivered within a week, and we have been put to considerable inconvenience through the long delay.

  你方承诺一周内交货。现在延迟交货给我方带来很大的不便。

- If this were the first time you had failed to send us our orders on time, we should not complain, but we had the same experience last year.

  如果此次是你方第一次延迟交货，我方也不会申诉，但去年也发生过类似事件。

- Nearly 15 days has passed since then, yet we have heard nothing from you about the consignment.

  至今已过去了近 15 天，但我方未从你方处收到关于这批货的消息。

Wrong Delivery

- To our surprise, however, upon opening the same we found that none of the quantities or specifications corresponds with your invoice of the same date. Obviously, you have sent us the wrong goods.

  然而使我方惊讶的是，我方一打开这批货物，就发现其中的数量或规格与你方当日的发票不一致。显然，你方错发了货物。

- Evidently some mistake was made and the goods have been wrongly delivered.

  显然发生了差错，货物错发了。

Inferior Quality

- We find that the machine has broken down completely. We have had a mechanic look it over. He reports that the rotators appear to have been cracked before the machine was installed.

  我方发现机器已经完全损坏。经机械师仔细检查后发现机器在安装前旋转器就已破裂。

- The goods in question have not turned out to our satisfaction, the quality being so poor as to render them unsuitable for the requirements of this market.

  该货不能令我方满意，质量如此低劣，以致不合此地市场需要。

- We are sorry to have to complain of the quality of shipment of wheat, but it is inferior to the sample you sent us.

  很抱歉我方不得不对这批小麦的质量申诉，因为比你方提供的样品质量低劣。

- The goods delivered are not up to the standard of samples. The pattern is uneven in places and the color varies.

  所交货物未达到样品的质量标准，多处花样不匀，颜色各异。

- When unpacking the bale/case, we found that the color/weight/quality/finish is unsatisfactory.

  开包/箱之后，发现颜色/重量/质量/工艺不能令人满意。

- We feel sorry to inform you that the cargo we just received is not up to your usual standard. The products seem to be too roughly made and out of shape.

  歉告，我方刚收到的货物未达你方往常的标准，看得出这些产品制作草率，而且变形。

Short Weight

- The Survey Report has proved that the difference between the actual landed weight and the weight shown on your shipping advice is 5,500 kg.

  检验报告证明实际运抵重量比你方装船通知中的重量少 5500 千克。

- We thank you for the prompt dispatch of the goods, but regret to draw your attention to the fact that a shortage in weight of 1,760 kg was noticed when the consignment arrived.

  感谢贵方立即发货，但遗憾地提醒贵方注意的是到货时发现短重 1760 千克。

- There is a discrepancy between the packing list of Case No. 15 and your invoice: 3 dozen Tea Services are correctly entered on the invoice but there were only 2 dozen in the case.

  第 1 号箱的装箱单与发票不符，发票所列 3 打茶具是正确的，而箱内只装了 2 打。

- Carton 17 was found to be 5 packages short. As the carton was in good shape and does not appear to have been tampered with, we surmise that they must have been short-shipped.

  第 17 号箱短少 5 包。由于箱子完好，似未遭撬动，推测是短装。

Poor Packing

- We regret to find on opening up 10 cases of the toys delivered here yesterday that 10% of them are broken and nearly all are badly scratched.

  昨日运抵此处的 10 箱玩具打开后，我方遗憾地发现 10%损坏，几乎所有的玩具都被严重地刮破。

- On unwrapping the cases, we find the goods partly soaked by rain.

  开箱后，我方发现部分货物因雨淋受湿。

- We have examined them one by one, and found that each of them was leaking more or less.
  我方逐一检查了货物，发现每一个都或多或少有渗漏现象。

- The seams of the gunny bags do not appear to have been strong enough, with the result that they have given way, thus allowing the contents to run out.
  麻袋的缝口似乎不够牢固，结果缝口开裂，袋内物品外漏。

- We have had the case and contents examined by the insurance survey, but as you will see from the enclosed copy of his report, he maintains that the damage was due to insecure packing and not to any unduly rough handling of the case.
  我们已请保险公司检验人员检验了木箱和箱内货物。从随附的检验报告副本中，你方将注意到，他认为损坏是由于包装不牢固，并非搬运不当所致。

- It looks as if the case was not strong enough to stand the voyage. We have examined the contents and find that 15 pieces were missing and the rest unfit for use.
  看来箱子不够牢固，经不起海运。经检查，发现缺货 15 件，其余物品都已无法使用。

3. Putting Forward the Solution

Quality

- Such being the case, we could do nothing but to lodge a complaint with you. Please let us know what you will do as to this discrepancy on quality and color.
  既然如此，我方不得不向你方提出申诉。请告知你方如何处理质量和花色的不符。

- Would you please replace them by another 2,000 pieces, with their quality and color up to our requirements or compensate our economic losses?
  请发来 2000 件质量和花色符合我方要求的商品以做替代，否则赔偿我方的经济损失。

- Since you have service man in here, we are obliged to return the machine to you. We hope you can send us a new one within a few days.
  由于此地有你方的维修人员，所以如果能将机器退还你方，我方将很感激。希望不久能发来一台新机器。

- Since it is agreed that we have the right to reject the goods when they are unqualified upon examination by the China Commodity Inspection Bureau at the port of destination, we regret to inform you that we have to return the goods to you at your expense.
  由于双方同意货物在目的港经中国商品检验局检验如质量低劣，我方有权拒收货物，所以很遗憾我方将货物退还给你方，费用由你方负担。

- We cannot possibly deliver the merchandise in this condition to our customers, but might accept the lot at a reduction of 20% on the contract price.
  我方不可能将这种货物交给我方的顾客，但如按合同价减少 20%，也许可以接受。

- As the whole parcel is quite useless to us, we must ask you to refund us the invoice value and the inspection fee as per the statement of claim enclosed. We trust our claim will have your prompt attention, and as soon as settlement is made, we shall return the goods to you at your expense.
  由于全部货物对我方毫无用处，务请贵方退赔发票金额和检验费，详见所附的索赔清单。希望你方立即处理我方索赔，一旦解决，我们就退回货物，费用由你方负担。

- Please do not trouble to send a replacement, but adjust your invoice.
  请不用麻烦发来替代品，只需调整发票即可。

Delivery

- Please fax whether you can give delivery at the end of this month. If not, we shall have to cancel the order, as we can not wait any longer, and shall be compelled to place our orders with others who can and will give delivery at the stipulated time.
  请传真告知你方是否能在本月底前交货。如不能，我方将撤销此订单，因为我方不能再等待了，不得不向能在规定时间内交货的人订购。

- We have to hold the same at your disposal pending your reply. Please fax us when we may expect the correct goods as soon as you receive this letter.
  我方保留该货，等待你方回复告知如何处置。请收到我方信函后立即传真告知何时正确的货物能到。

- Please inform us by return mail what we are to do with the goods. Shall we return them to you or hold them at your disposal?
  请回复告知如何处置这批货物。我方退还给你方还是保留货物以等待你方处置？

- We feel that some advice of this delay should have been given, and we await your early explanation on these points.
  我方认为此次延迟应告知，我方等待你方对此事的解释。

Short Weight

- After inspection of the shipment, we found it 34 boxes short. In view of the small quantities involved, we hope you will promptly settle this matter and seeing the case to a satisfactory close.
  经检验，我方发现短少 34 盒。由于短少的数量不多，我方希望你方能立即圆满地解决此事。

- As the packing was intact, it is obvious that the cargo was short weight before shipment. Under the circumstances, we have to file a claim against you to the amount of US$435 plus inspection fee.
  由于包装完好，显然货物在装运前就短重。因此，我方不得不向你方提出金额为 435 美元加检验费的索赔。

理赔写作步骤

1. Expressing Regret
2. Giving a Proposal

理赔常用语句

1. Expressing Regret

- We much regret the delay and can assure you that we have done our utmost to expedite delivery, but the great pressure of orders for these goods has made it impossible for us to deliver as promptly as we could, in spite of the fact that our people are working overtime.

  我方对延迟很遗憾，请放心，我方会尽早交货。但由于我方所接订单很多，压力很大，即使工人加班生产，我方都无法立即交货。

- We exceedingly regret to find that, owing to a mistake in the packing department, the wrong goods have been sent to you. We assure you that such a thing has never happened to us before during the whole of our experience. It only occurred now by reason of a figure being misread by a new clerk.

  我方很抱歉地发现由于包装部门的一个失误将货物错发给了你方。请相信此类事件在我方整个业务过程中是第一次出现。这是由于我方一新职员将一数字读错所致。

- We have received with great regret your complaint of April 5, referring to your Order No. 2061 for Toys.

  我方很遗憾收到了你方 4 月 5 日第 2061 号关于玩具的订单的申诉。

- We are sorry to learn that you are not satisfied with the quality of the goods supplied to your order.

  我方很遗憾地获悉你方对我方提供的货物质量不满意。

- We very much regret to learn from your letter of July 5 that contents of five of the thirty crates of chinaware you received from us on that date were badly damaged.

  我方从你方 7 月 5 日的来函中很遗憾地获悉该日收到的 30 个板条箱中有 5 箱瓷器严重受损。

- We deeply regret to learn from your message of … that 2 cases of … per m.v. Red Flag arrived in a damaged condition.

  我方很遗憾地从贵方……的来函中获悉，由"红旗"轮运去的……，有 2 箱到货受损。

- We acknowledge receipt of your letter of March 5, in which a claim was lodged for a short delivery of 5,000 kg chemical fertilizer. We wish to express our much regret over the unfortunate incident.

  你方 3 月 5 日因短交 5000 千克化肥向我方索赔的来函收悉。我方对此不幸事件表示遗憾。

- We hope that you will not be put to any serious inconvenience through this unexpected accident.

  我方希望此次意外事件没有给你方带来太大的不便。

- We apologize sincerely for any inconvenience this may have caused you.

  我方对给贵方造成的不便致歉。

2. Giving a Proposal

Positive Reply

- We have instructed the shipping company to deliver your goods tomorrow without fail. Please hand the damaged goods over to the shipping company, whom we have instructed to recollect.

  我方指示船运公司务必于明日运出你方货物。我方指定的船运公司将至你处收取受损货物。

- We propose to have the goods inspected immediately. If the inspection confirms the accuracy of your estimate, compensation will be allowed at once.

  我方建议立即检验货物。如证明货物受损程度如你方估计，将立即赔偿。

- We have today sent a replacement of 12 sets. We hope you will be pleased with the new lot.

  我方于今日运出 12 台以替换。希望你方对这批货物满意。

- The wrong pieces can be returned per next available steamer for our account, but it is preferable if you can sell them out at our price in your market.

  错发的货物请由下一班轮运来，费用由我方负担。但最好能在你方市场按我方价格出售。

- We are sending the correct consignment to you by air freight. It should reach you within a week.

  我方现航寄正确的货物，应于一周内到货。

- We have taken necessary precautions to prevent a recurrence of similar mistake in future.

  我方已采取必要措施以防将来类似事件再次发生。

- We trust that the arrangement will satisfy you and look forward to receiving your further orders.

  相信我方的安排能使贵方满意，期盼再次收到订单。

Negative Reply

- We are prepared to make you a reasonable compensation but not the amount you claimed, because we cannot see why the loss should be 50% more than the actual value of the goods. Please reconsider the matter.

  我方打算给予你方合理的赔偿但不是你方要求的金额，因为损失不可能比货物实际总值还高 50%。请你方重新考虑。

- It would not be fair if the loss totally imposed on us as the liability rests with both parties. We are ready to pay 50% of the loss only.

  我方认为在双方都有责任的情况下由我方赔偿全部损失不公平。我方愿赔偿一半的损失。

- We may compromise, but the compensation should, in no case, exceed US$35,000, otherwise this case will be submitted to arbitration.

  我方让步，但赔偿金额绝不能超过 35000 美元，否则此事提交仲裁。

- The shortage you alleged might have occurred in the course of transit, and this is a matter over which we can exercise no control.

  你方所说的短少可能是在运输途中发生的，这是我方无法控制的。

- We have shipping documents to prove that the goods were received by the carrier in perfect condition; therefore, they must have been damaged in transit.

  我方的装运单据证明承运人接收货物时完好无损，因此货物一定是在运输途中受损的。

- As the shipping company is liable for the damage, your claim for compensation should, in our opinion, be referred to them for settlement.

由于船运公司负责此次损坏，我方认为你方关于赔偿的索赔应要求他们理赔。

● Such deviation between the products and samples is normal and permissible, therefore, the claim for compensation cannot be allowed.

此类产品和样品间的差异是正常且允许的，因此你方要求赔偿的索赔无法受理。

● Without sufficient evidence to support, your claim is untenable, and we can see no point in pursuing it further.

你方索赔没有充分的证据来证明，因而是不实的，所以我方无法理赔。

● The documents produced by you to support the claim for compensation are insufficient; therefore, we cannot take your claim into consideration.

你方出具的支持赔偿索赔的证明文件不充分，因此我方不能理赔。

● We hope with sincerity this matter will not affect our good relations in our future dealings. We await your kind confirmation.

我方真心希望此次事件不会影响双方未来的良好关系。期盼你方确认。

写 作 范 例

1. Complaint about Wrongly-delivered Goods

Background: 中国上海雅安化妆品进出口公司在收到美国 Binks 化妆品集团有限公司由 "EXPLORER" 轮运来的货物后，发现第 1-34 号箱内货物不符合第 145 号订单所列内容，于是发电子邮件给对方询问原因并希望告知如何处置第 1-34 号箱内货物。

From: dickjiang@yaancosmetics.com

To: dominicshute@usbinks.com

Date: Monday, July 2, 20＿＿, 15: 33 pm

Subject: Our Order No. 145 by S. S. "EXPLORER"

Dear Mr. Shute,

We duly received the documents and took delivery of the goods on arrival of the S. S. "EXPLORER" at Shanghai.

We are much grateful to you for the prompt execution of this order. Everything appears to be correct and in good condition except in Case No. 1-34.

Unfortunately when we opened this case we found it contained completely different articles, and we can only presume that a mistake was made and the contents of this case were for another order.

As we need the articles we ordered to complete deliveries to our customers, we must ask you to

---

arrange for the dispatch of replacements at once. We attach a list of the contents of Case No 1-34, and shall be glad if you will check this with our order and the copy of your invoice.

In the meantime, we are holding the above-mentioned case at your disposal. Please let us know what you wish us to do with it.

Yours sincerely,
Dick Jiang
Regional Manager

Notes

1. complaint   n. 申诉，投诉，抱怨
   make/lodge/lay/file a complaint against sb with a department about sth   因为某事向某部门投诉某人
   complain   vi. 申诉，投诉
   complain to sb of sth   向某人投诉某事
   complain about sth   投诉某事
   许多用户对你方空调噪音过大向我方售货服务部门投诉。
   Many end users make a complaint against you with our Service Dept. about the excessive noise of your air conditioners.
   Many end users complained to our Service Dept. of the excessive noise of your air-conditioners.
2. be obliged to sb for sth   因为某事感谢某人
3. in good condition   状况良好
   in perfect condition   完好无损
   in poor condition   状况不良
   in seriously damaged condition   严重受损
4. presume   vt. 推测
5. replacement   n. 替代品
6. at your disposal   由贵方处理
   put/leave sth at one's disposal   把某事交由某人自行处理

Positive Reply

Background:美国 Binks 化妆品集团有限公司对错发货物事件解释原因并致歉，告知雅安化妆品进出口公司会尽快将符合第 145 号订单的货物运出。同时希望对方先暂时保留第 1-34 号箱内货物，等待船运代理处理。

From: dominicshute@usbinks.com
To: dickjiang@yaancosmetics.com
Date: Tuesday, July 3, 20＿＿, 16: 46 pm
Subject: Re: Our Order No. 145 by S. S. "EXPLORER"

Dear Mr. Jiang,

Thank you for your email of July 2. We were glad to know that the consignment was delivered promptly, but it was with great regret that we heard Case No. 1-34 did not contain the goods you ordered.

On going into the matter we find that a mistake was indeed made in packing, through a confusion of number, and we have arranged for the right goods to be dispatched to you at once. Relative documents will be airmailed as soon as they are ready.

We will appreciate it if you will keep Case No.1-34 and contents until called for by the local agents of Jihang Shipping Co., Ltd., our forwarding agents, whom we have instructed accordingly.

Please accept our many apologies for the trouble caused to you by the error.

Yours sincerely,
Dominic Shute
Operational Manager

Notes

1. It was with great regret that... 非常抱歉……

    regret   vt. 抱歉，遗憾，后悔

    (1) 后接名词

    We regret this oversight on our part.   我们对我方的疏忽感到抱歉。

    We regret our inability to comply with your wishes.   很抱歉未能按你方意愿办理。

    (2) 后接动名词

    They very much regret having caused us so much trouble.   他们非常抱歉给我方造成了这么多麻烦。

    We regret being unable to offer you this article at present.   很抱歉现在无法给你方出售此商品。

    (3) 后接从句

    We regret that we cannot accept your price.   很抱歉不能接受你方报价。

    We regret that business has slowed down.   很遗憾业务的进展缓慢了下来。

    (4) 后接不定式，多用于 to say，to find，to learn，to note 等

    We regret to say that you delayed 30 days to open L/C.   很遗憾，你们的信用证迟开了 30 天。

    We regret to note that you cannot make any headway with our offer.   得悉你方对我方报盘未能取得任何进展，甚为遗憾。

    regret   n. 遗憾，抱歉，常用于 to one's regret，表示"令人遗憾的是"

    We note with regret that your price is on the high side.   我们遗憾地注意到你方价格偏高。

Much to our regret, no more orders can be accepted this year owing to our heavy commitment.

非常抱歉，由于订单过多我方今年不能再承接了。

regretful   adj. （指人）感到遗憾的

We are regretful that we didn't open L/C in time.   我们为未能及时开证而感到抱歉。

regrettable   adj. 令人遗憾的

This is a regrettable matter.   这是一桩憾事。

2.   on going into the matter   一经调查此事

3.   a confusion of number   号码的混淆

4.   call for   拜访，访问，要求

5.   forwarding agent   运输代理

2. Complaint about Goods of Poor Quality

Background: 美国 ITG 国际纺织集团在收到中国上海鼎丰工贸有限公司由"Christina"轮运来的呢绒后，声称货物的质量和颜色与样品不符而不得不以九五折销售。同时提醒对方注意 ITG 集团在 5 月 15 日的电子邮件里因为五月初由"Sword Fish"轮运来的藏青哔叽质量存在问题致使公司不得不打折销售的事件进行过投诉。ITG 集团希望类似事件不要再次发生并盼望早日得到解决。

From: dudleycroker@itggroup.com

To: elinorqiao@shdingfeng.com

Date: Tuesday, May 28, 20＿＿, 10:58 am

Subject: Consignment Shipped by S. S. "Christina"

Dear Ms. Qiao,

Since we last emailed to you on May 15, we have received your consignment of woolen piece goods shipped by S. S. "Christina" and regret to report that it is not of the quality and color of the sample we sent you. Not only is the cloth supplied of poorer quality, but it is also of a lighter shade. When we passed it to our customers they at first refused to accept it. It was only after repeated persuasion that they agreed to take with an allowance of 5% of the quoted price.

We are attaching our account sales for this consignment and also for the blue serge shipped by S. S. "Sword Fish" at the beginning of May, together with a draft for USD 3,872.00. As already explained in our email of May 15, this serge was also unsatisfactory and compelled us to sell at a 5% discount. There have also been complaints on a number of other occasions.

We hope to be able to send you further orders shortly, but must ask you to make sure that there is no repetition of the difficulties to which these two and some earlier consignments have given rise. We cannot always hope to be successful in selling goods that are not exactly as ordered.

Kindly resolve the matter. Please give us a feedback immediately by email or you can call me at 1-408-721-5000.

Yours sincerely,

Dudley Croker

Purchasing Agent

Notes

1. woolen piece goods   呢绒
2. color 与 shade 的区别：

    color 一般指红、黄、蓝等不同的颜色，而 shade 是色彩的浓淡，指同一种颜色的浓淡程度，引申为形形色色或细微的差别，如：

    various shades of red   各种深浅不同的红色

    There are solutions of all shades.   有不同浓度的溶液。

    These two words have delicate shades of meaning.   这两个字在意义上有细微的差别。
3. an allowance of 5% of the quoted price   报价 5%的折扣
4. account sales   销售清单，售货清单
5. blue serge   藏青哔叽
6. send you further orders   继续向贵方下订单
7. give rise to   引起，产生，句子的主语表示原因，宾语表示结果

    Late delivery has given rise to complaint.   迟交货引起了申诉。

    Quality discrepancy gives rise to difficulties in selling the goods here.   品质差异造成这些商品在此地销售的困难。

Negative Reply

Background: 中国上海鼎丰工贸有限公司以合理的理由向美国 ITG 国际纺织集团解释了货物不可能出现质量和颜色方面的问题，并指出 ITG 集团的客户有故意索要折扣之嫌。鼎丰公司表明货物的利润空间已经很小，希望 ITG 集团能充分理解。

From: elinorqiao@shdingfeng.com

To: dudleycroker@itggroup.com

Date: Wednesday, May 29, 20＿＿, 11: 54 am

Subject: Re: Consignment Shipped by S. S. "Christina"

Dear Mr. Croker,

Thank you for your letter of May 28 attaching account sales for the last two consignments and your draft for USD 3,872.00, the amount of which we have credited to your account.

We are very surprised that you complained about the quality of the woolen piece goods. Because of your earlier complaints we made it our business to inspect this cloth personally before it was packed and satisfied ourselves after so careful examination that it exactly matched your sample in quality. As for the differences in shade, the cloth is specially dyed to your sample and any difference there may be is so slight that no dyer would guarantee a closer match.

We have again compared your samples with reference sample of the blue serge supplied and find the qualities are identical. This has been confirmed by the manufacturer, who assures us that both were taken from his stock of the same grades.

We think it only fair to tell you that yours are the only complaints we have received, and as there have been a number of them recently we cannot help feeling that some of your customers are complaining with the sole aim of obtaining an allowance. From now on, we shall not accept any reduction in price invoiced to you and if you cannot dispose of our materials on the terms which our other agents in your country find satisfactory, we are afraid further business between us will no longer be financially worthwhile.

We very much regret having to email to you in this way, but hope you will understand when we explain that we conduct our business on very narrow profit margins, which we cannot reduce. Meanwhile, we are expecting your favorable reply.

Yours sincerely,
Elinor Qiao
Sales Coordinator

Notes

1. credited USD 3,872.00 to your account　把 3872 美元记入你方账户的贷方，存入你方账户，也可以说，credit your account with USD 3,872.00
   credit 的反义词是 debit（记入借方，由某人负担）
   Please debit our account with any expenses incurred on the cases sent in error.　错送货物的有关费用都由我方负担。

2. We made it our business to inspect this cloth personally.　我方把亲自检验商品看作是我方的职责。

3. any difference there may be is so slight that no dyer would guarantee a closer match　即使可能有差异，也是很微小的，没有一个染色技师能保证比我方染的更近似样品的颜色

4. reference sample　标准样品，基准样品

5. identical　adj. 一致的，一样的
   The consignment we provided is identical to your requirement.　我方提供的货物与贵方的要求一致。

6. we cannot help feeling that…　我方不得不认为……，也可以说 we cannot but feel that…
   We cannot help turning down your offer, as it is out of line with the market.
   We cannot but turn down your offer, as it is out of line with the market.
   我方不得不谢绝你方的报盘，因为它与当前的行市不符。

7. invoice　vt. 开发票
   You may invoice the goods at contract price less 3% commission.　你方可以按照合同价格除

去 3%的佣金开发票。

You may invoice the price as agreed upon.　你方可以按照双方同意了的价格开发票。

We shall invoice you on the basis of survey report made out at the port of loading.　我方将根据在装运港开具的检验报告向你方开发票（收款）。

8.　on very narrow profit margins　利润很少

3. Claim for Improper Packing

Background: 中国天津大朗地毯实业有限公司从迪拜 Faydh 地毯贸易公司进口了 20 箱羊毛地毯，到货后发现由于不当包装，有 13 箱地毯外露。大朗公司附寄保险公司检验员及船运代理的检验报告，建议 Faydh 公司削价 20%，否则将退货并要求换货。

From: lesleyliang@tjdalang.com

To: jemimafarr@dubaifaydh.com

Sent: Tuesday, September 8, 20＿＿, 15: 23 pm

Subject: Our Order No. C426

Dear Ms. Farr,

We received this morning the 20 cartons of Woolen Carpet under our Order No. C426 per S. S. "Chang Fu". The ship's agent noticed that Carton No. 23 was split. We immediately had the carton opened and the contents examined by a local insurance surveyor in the presence of the shipping company's agents. Besides Carton No. 23, one side of 8 cartons were worn and torn and 4 cartons were broken and the carpets were in the open. It was obviously attributed to improper packing.

Though the carpets can be used, we have to sell them at a price much lower than usual. In view of the above we suggest you give us 20% discount on the invoice value or we will return the goods to you and ask for replacements.

We faxed the surveyor's report and the shipping agents' statement. Please let us know your decision as soon as possible. Meanwhile, we should like to take this opportunity to suggest that special care be taken in your future deliveries as prospective customers intend to misjudge the quality of your goods by the faulty packing.

Yours sincerely,

Lesley Liang

Purchasing Manager

Notes

1.　claim　n. 索赔，赔偿

提出索赔：lodge/file/raise/lay/make/issue/register/render/enter/bring up/set up/put in a claim

表示索赔的原因，接介词 for，如：claim for damage

表示索赔的金额，接介词 for，如：claim for US$10,000.00

表示对某批货物索赔，接介词 on，如：claim on this consignment of goods

表示向某人索赔，接介词 against 或 with，如：claim against the insurer

We shall lodge a claim against the insurance company for the goods damaged during transit. 对于货物在运输途中损坏，我方将向保险公司提出索赔。

We file a claim against you for the short delivery of 145 lbs. 我方向你方提出短交 145 磅的索赔。

claim　vt. 索赔，要求赔偿，通常宾语为索赔的金额或 compensation, amount 等名词，如：claim US$10,000.00　索赔一万美元

claim a compensation of US$10,000.00 for damage　因损坏要求赔偿一万美元

We should claim US$1,500.00 from you for the loss caused by improper packing. 我方必须为由于不良包装所造成的损失向你方索赔 1500.00 美元。

因为某事对于某批货物向某人索赔若干金额

claim (n.): lodge a claim against sb for sth for (amount) on the goods

claim (v.): claim (a compensation of) (amount) from sb for sth on the goods

我方因为短装所造成的损失对第 67 号订单项下的货物向你方索赔 1000 美元。

claim (n.): We lodge a claim against you for the loss caused by short delivery for US$ 1,000 on the goods under Order No. 67.

claim (v.): We claim (a compensation of) US$ 1,000 from you for the loss caused by short delivery on the goods under Order No. 67.

2. improper/inferior/defective/faulty packing　不良包装

3. a local insurance surveyor　本地保险验货员

4. worn and torn　磨损

5. be in the open　暴露在外

6. return the goods　退货

7. ask for replacements　换货

replace　vt. 替换，代替

用 A 代替 B：replace A by/with B = send a replacement of B for A，如：

We agree to replace Model 501 by Model 601 of the photocopier at a difference (of) RMB ￥2,500 per set in our favor. 我们同意以 601 型来替换 501 型复印机，每台需补我们差价人民币 2500 元。

We agree to send a replacement of 800 sets of photocopiers Model 601 for Model 501. 我们同意发去 800 台 601 型复印机以替代 501 型。

Negative Settlement—Suggesting a Claim against the Shipping Company

Background: 迪拜 Faydh 地毯贸易公司对货物受损表示遗憾，但表明责任不在己方，并附寄了清洁的海运提单以兹证明，同时建议中国天津大朗地毯实业有限公司向达飞船运公司提出索赔。

From: jemimafarr@dubaifaydh.com
To: lesleyliang@tjdalang.com
Sent: Wednesday, September 9, 20＿＿, 14: 56 pm
Subject: Re: Our Order No. C426

Dear Ms. Liang,

We regret to learn from your email of September 8 that your Order No. C426 for 20 cartons of Woolen Carpet arrived in poor condition.

If we were at fault we would be responsible to agree to your proposal. But in view of the fact that our goods were carefully packed by experienced workmen and sent out in perfect condition as shown by a copy of the clean B/L which we attach herewith, we are certain they were damaged through careless handling while in transit.

We therefore suggest you had better enter a claim immediately against the shipping company, DAFEI Shipping Co. If you will send us the papers which show exactly the condition the goods reached you, we will take up the matter for you with a view to recovering damages from the shipping company.

We are awaiting your reply with keen interest.

Yours sincerely,
Jemima Farr
Sales Manager

Notes

1. settlement   n. 解决，偿付
   settlement of a claim   理赔
   settlement by amicable arrangement   以友好方式解决
   settlement by arbitration   以仲裁方式解决
   settlement of balance   结清余额
   to enclose a check in settlement of…   随函附上支票一张以……
   settle   vt. 解决，调停
   settle an argument/a dispute/an issue   解决或调停争论/争议/争端
   settle an account   清算账目
2. be at fault   犯错，失误
3. in view of the fact that…   鉴于，考虑到，由于（表示原因），也可以用 considering that…
4. papers   n. 单据，即 documents

5. take up the matter with sb　向某人提出某事要求处理或答复

6. with a view to　为了，以……为目的（表示目的）

7. recover　vt. （根据法律程序）取得，获得

They sought to recover damages from that firm.　他们设法向那家公司索取损害赔偿金。

4. Claim for Short Weight

Background: 中国上海华宏生态农业科技有限公司从美国施得力农业化肥集团公司购买了 10 公吨化肥，但到货后经上海商品检验检疫局检验发现短重 500 千克，华宏公司向施得力集团公司提出金额共计 310 美元的索赔，并随附第 607 号检验报告。

From: manueljiamail@huahong.tech.com

To: michaelhope@stollar.com

Date: Thursday, October 24, 20＿＿, 13: 12 pm

Subject: Our Order No. 234 for 10 M/Ts of Chemical Fertilizer

Dear Mr. Hope,

We have just received the Survey Report No. 607 from Shanghai Commodity Inspection and Quarantine Bureau evidencing that the subject goods unloaded here yesterday was short-weight 500 kg. A thorough examination showed that the short weight was due to the improper packing, for which the suppliers should be definitely responsible.

On the basis of the SCIQB's Survey Report, we hereby register a claim with you as follows:

　　Short-weight value:　$ 160.00

　　Survey charges:　$ 150.00

　　Total claimed:　$ 310.00

We are attaching the Survey Report No. 607 and look forward to your settlement at an early date.

Yours sincerely,

Manuel Jia

Import Sales Manager

Notes

1. short weight　短重

作名词时，可写作 shortweight, short-weight, short weight

作形容词时，可写作 shortweight, short-weight

The shipment of Tin Foil Sheet ex S. S. "Dong Feng" is shortweight 4.82 M/Ts.　由"东风"号轮运来的锡箔纸短重 4.82 公吨。

We lodge a claim against you for a short weight of 4.82 M/Ts.　我方为短重 4.82 公吨向你方提出索赔。

作"短少的，短缺的，不足的"之义的 short 可与许多名词和过去分词构成合成词，其写法与上面的 shortweight 类似，有写成一个词的，有用连字符的，也有分开写的。如：

Surely this shipment is **short-invoiced**.　这批货物的发票一定是少开了。

Your payment to cover the amount of claim is **short-calculated**.　你方支付索赔的金额少算了。

Enclosed please find a check for the **short-paid** amount of US $ 786.　随函附寄少付款金额 786 美元的支票一张。

The **short-shipped** Men's Shirts will be forwarded together with your next order.　短装的男式衬衫与你方下批订货一起运出。

That part of **short shipment** will be forwarded by the next steamer.　短装部分将由下一次货轮运出。

We will look into the matter why your Ginseng was **short-delivered**.　对你方的人参为什么短交一事我方将进行调查。

The shipping company informs us that the **short delivery** of your goods occurred in transit. 船运公司通知我方，你方的货物短交发生在运输途中。

We assure you that the **short-landed** goods will be made up by us immediately.　我方向你方保证，短卸的货物将由我们立即补偿。

We found your L/C is **short-established/short-opened** by HK$ 296.　我方发现贵方信用证少开了 296 港元。

2.　survey report　检验报告，检验证明
3.　Shanghai Commodity Inspection and Quarantine Bureau　上海商品检验检疫局
4.　evidencing/proving that…　证明……

Positive Settlement

Background: 美国施得力农业化肥集团公司对短重事件表示抱歉，并解释了事故的原因，表示同意向中国上海华宏生态农业科技有限公司理赔。

From: michaelhope@stollar.com
To: manueljiamail@huahong.tech.com
Date: Friday, October 25, 20＿＿, 16: 22 pm
Subject: Re: Our Order No. 234 for 10 M/Ts of Chemical Fertilizer

Dear Mr. Jia,

Regarding your claim for a short weight of 500 kg Chemical Fertilizer, we wish to express our much regret over the unfortunate incident.

After a check-up by our staff, it was found that some 28 bags had not been packed in 5-ply strong paper bags as stipulated in the contract, thus resulting in the breakage during transit, for which we tender our apologies.

In view of our longstanding business relations, we will make payment by check for ＄310.00, the amount of claim, into your account with the Bank of China, upon receipt of your agreement.

We trust that the arrangement we have made will satisfy you and look forward to receiving your further orders.

Yours sincerely,

Michael Hope

Export Coordinator

Notes

1. 5-ply　五层

   ply　n. 层，股，厚度

   three-ply wood　三合板

   a two-ply rope　一根双股的绳子

   The cartons should be strengthened by two-ply nylon straps.　纸箱必须用双股尼龙带加固。

2. tender an apology　致歉

   因为某事向某人致歉：apologize to sb for sth 或 make an apology to sb for sth

3. make payment by check for ＄310.00, the amount of claim, into your account with the Bank of China　通过中国银行以支票向贵方支付索赔金额 310 美元

5. Claim on Damaged Medical Instruments

Background: 中国天津博特医疗器械及保健品贸易有限公司从加拿大米勒医疗器械集团订购了 15 箱医疗器械。到货后所有的货物都严重受损。博特公司不得不凭借天津商品检验局出具的第(03)303 号检验报告向米勒公司提出总金额为 485000 美元的索赔。

From: lfwang_business@tjbote.com

To: andrewcotton@miller.medicals.com

Date: Tuesday, July 22, 20＿＿, 16:02 pm

Subject: Claim on 15 Cases of Medical Instruments

Dear Mr. Cotton,

The 15 cases of medical instruments ordered by us have been received. But to our great disappointment, all the cases without a single exception have been badly damaged.

In accordance with a thorough examination made by the Tianjin Commodity Inspection Bureau, the said cases of instruments had been violently shocked and crashed before they were unloaded here.

As this consignment proves entirely useless to us, we are compelled to place a claim with you for returning us the invoice value and the inspection charges for the total amount of US$ 485,000.00. As soon as the claim is settled, we will return the said consignment to you immediately.

We attach the Survey Report No. (03)303 issued by the Tianjin Commodity Inspection Bureau and look forward to hearing that this matter be settled soon.

Yours sincerely,
L. F. Wang
Sales Executive

Notes
1.   medical instrument   医疗器械
2.   inspection charges   检验费

Refusing a Claim
Background: 加拿大米勒医疗器械集团认为货物在出运前已经过了仔细的包装和严格的检查，并有检验员出具的检验证书证明，所以建议中国天津博特医疗器械及保健品贸易有限公司向保险公司或船运公司索赔。

From: andrewcotton@miller.medicals.com
To: lfwang_business@tjbote.com
Date: Wednesday, July 23, 20_ _, 10: 12 am
Subject: Re: Claim on 15 Cases of Medical Instruments

Dear Mr. Wang,

We are in receipt of your letter of July 22 lodging a claim with us on the 15 cases of damaged medical instruments.

While expressing our regret at this unfortunate incident, we have to emphasize that both the packing and the shipping of the instruments underwent careful checking and thorough examination by the independent surveyor here. And the surveyor's Certificate of Inspection attached can evidence this.

Such being the case, we have reason to believe that damage you mentioned in your letter is due to something happened during transit. This consignment has been insured against All Risks. With regard to the loss in damage, we would suggest that you make your claim with the insurance company's agent or the forwarding agent at your end; we really cannot accept any responsibility. And we hope the matter will receive immediate settlement.

Yours sincerely,
Andrew Cotton
Marketing Manager

Notes

1. undergo   vt. 经过，经历，也可用 go through
2. surveyor   n. 检验员
3. Certificate of Inspection   检验证书

Unit 14　Agency
代　理

1. Definition of Agency and Agent

Agency is a legal relationship between the principal and another party, named as agent, who is authorized to carry out the principal's instructions in transactions with a third party. Agent is often an individual or a firm who is employed to represent the company to deal with the business affairs in a certain area. Usually the agent is familiar with local conditions and the market, and can operate the business to mutual benefits. Agent buys and sells for the account of the principals, so he does not assume any financial risks in the transaction and the principals assume all risks instead.

An agent in export practice is one who acts for an exporter, the principal, and does not make a profit but earns a commission on all orders he has obtained, for which his principal will get eventual payment. Usually the agent does not go through the business procedures, though he may give help to the buyer in connection with shipping, discharge, cusoms clearance, transit, and so on.

Before signing an agency agreement, the principal should make an inquiry into the qualifications, experiences and personal qualities of the prospective agents, such as their reliability and financial soundness, their market connections and the effectiveness of their sales organization, their technical ability to handle the goods to be marketed. Once the agency agreement is signed between the principal and the agent, the agent must act in strict accordance with the provisions of the agreement.

2. Agent Agreement

The terms of agency are sometimes set out in correspondence between the parties, but where dealings are on a large scale, a formal agreement may be desirable; or the agreement may be drafted by one of the parties in consultation with the other.

The following is the main contents of an agent agreement:

(1) the nature and duration of the agency

(2) the territory to be covered

(3) the obligations of agent and principal

(4) the method of purchase and sales

(5) details of the commission and funds allowed

(6) law of the country related to agreement

(7) arbitration items while dispute is mediated

(8) other terms and conditions

常 用 语 句

Applying for an Agent

● We understand that you are looking for a reliable firm with good connections in medical equipment trade to represent you in North America.

我方获悉贵方正在寻找一家在医疗设备贸易方面值得信赖的且具有广泛联系的公司作为贵方在北美地区的代理。

● We are greatly interested to be your sole agent in Thailand for your automobiles.

我方对成为你方在泰国的汽车独家代理商很感兴趣。

● Since we have more than 25 years in selling netware and obtain a large market share, we hope we can have a cooperation with you.

我们经营网络设备已经超过 25 年了，并占据了大部分市场份额，因此我方非常希望与贵方合作。

● We should be pleased to learn that you are interested in our proposal and on what terms you are willing to conclude an agency agreement.

期望贵方对我方的建议感兴趣，并希望了解贵方按什么条件愿意达成代理协议。

● We should be glad if you would consider our application to act as your agency for the sales of your jewels.

如果贵方能考虑我们担任贵方珠宝销售代理的申请，我方将不胜感激。

● We are experienced in marketing products similar to yours, quite familiar with cusomers' need, and enjoying a business relationship with most leading wholesalers and retailers in this line, so we trust you will allow us to give you similar service.

我方在销售类似贵方产品方面很有经验，非常熟悉顾客的需求，与这一行业中的大多数主要的批发商和零售商有很好的业务联系，因此我方相信能得到贵方的同意，为贵方提供类似的服务。

● With wide and varied experience in this trade, we are convinced that we can handle as an agent the goods you are exporting in the most effective manner. We will do a lot of advertising in newspapers and on TV programs and we will send our salesmen around to promote the sales of your goods.

凭着我方在这一行业中的丰富经验，我方对自己能以最有效的方式代理贵方出口产品这一点非常自信。我方会在报纸和电视节目中刊登很多广告，并派出销售人员到各处促销贵方产品。

Accepting Application for an Agent

- We are pleased to confirm that we have appointed you as the agency of our products in the territory of North America. We are looking forward to a happy and successful working relation with you.

  我方很高兴确认任命贵方为我方在北美地区的代理，希望我们之间能建立友好成功的合作关系。

- We are quite happy to accept the agency agreement proposed by you. The commission of agency is 5%.

  我方很高兴地接受贵方提出的代理协议，代理佣金为 5%。

- We are glad to advise that we have decided to entrust you with the sole agency for our products in your country and we'd like to sign a sole agency agreement with you for a period of five years.

  我方很高兴通知贵方，我方已决定将我方产品在贵国的独家代理权委托给贵方并与贵方签订一项为期 5 年的独家代理协议。

- The appointment will be for a trial period of twelve months in the first instance. We shall pay you a commission of 5% on the net value of all sales against orders received through you.

  委托期先初步定为 12 个月。我方将根据从贵方处获得的订单的所有销售额的净值支付给你方 5%的佣金。

- If you confirm these terms, we will arrange for a formal agreement to be drawn up and when this is signed, prepare a circular for distribution to our customers in North America, announcing your appointment as our agents.

  如果你方确认上述条款，我方将安排拟制正式的协议。协议一经签署，我方将立即向北美地区的客户发出通函，宣布委托你方为我方的代理。

- With your excellent connections, we believe it will be possible to promote the sale of our products in your territory, and we hope your acting as our agent will be to our mutual benefit.

  凭着贵方众多的业务联系，我方相信在贵方区域内大力推销我方的产品是可行的，我方希望贵方担任我方代理将给我们双方带来收益。

Refusing Application for an Agent

- We think such an annual turnover for a sole agent is rather conservative. Unless you increase the turnover, we have to decline your proposal of acing as our sole agent.

  我方认为对独家代理来说，这样一个年销售量有些保守。除非贵方增加营业额，否则我方不得不谢绝贵方作为我方独家代理的建议。

- We don't think it proper to consider the matter of sole agency at present as the record of transactions shows only a moderate volume of business.

  我方认为目前不宜考虑独家代理问题，因为交易的记录表明现在的交易额尚不太可观。

- We regret having to inform you that since the Sole Agency Agreemet entered into between us ten months ago, you have not worked hard enough to exploit the potential of selling our products and your sales turnover is much below the minimum figure stipulated in the Agreement. Consequently, we consider it necessary to terminate this Agreement on August 8, 2012.

我方遗憾地告知，自十个月前我方签订独家代理协议以来，贵方并未尽力开发我方产品的销售市场，而且贵方的销售额也低于协议中所规定的最低水平。因此，我方认为有必要于2012 年 8 月 8 日终止此项协议。

代理协议范本

Example 1

Sales Agency Agreement

销售代理协议号：

NO:

日期：

Date:

为在平等互利的基础上发展贸易，有关方按下列条件签订本协议：

This Agreement is entered into between the parties concerned on the basis of equality and mutual benefit to develop business on terms and conditions mutually agreed upon as follows:

1. 订约人

Contracting Parties

供货人(以下称甲方)：

销售代理人(以下称乙方)：

甲方委托乙方为销售代理人，推销下列商品。

Supplier (hereinafter called "Party A"):

Agent (hereinafter called "Party B"):

Party A hereby appoints Party B to act as his selling agent to sell the commodity mentioned below.

2. 商品名称及数量或金额

Commodity and Quantity or Amount

双方约定，乙方在协议有效期内， 销售不少于……的商品。

It is mutually agreed that Party B shall undertake to sell not less than ... of the aforesaid commodity in the duration of this Agreement.

3. 经销地区

Territory

只限在……

In ... only.

4. 订单的确认

Confirmation of Orders

本协议所规定商品的数量、价格及装运条件等，应在每笔交易中确认，其细目应在双方签订的销售协议书中作出规定。

The quantities, prices and shipments of the commodities stated in this Agreement shall be confirmed in each transaction, the particulars of which are to be specified in the Sales Confirmation signed by the two parties hereto.

5. 付款

Payment

订单确认之后，乙方须按照有关确认书所规定的时间开立以甲方为受益人的、保兑的、不可撤销的即期信用证。乙方开出信用证后，应立即通知甲方，以便甲方准备交货。

After confirmation of the order, Party B shall arrange to open a confirmed, irrevocable L/C available by draft at sight in favour of Party A within the time stipulated in the relevant S/C. Party B shall also notify Party A immediately after L/C is opened so that Party A can get prepared for delivery.

6. 佣金

Commission

在本协议期满时，若乙方完成了第二款所规定的数额，甲方应按装运货物所收到的发票累计总金额付给乙方……%的佣金。

Upon the expiration of the Agreement and Party B's fullfilment of the total turnover mentioned in Article 2, Party A shall pay to Party B ... % commission on the basis of the aggregate amount of the invoice value against the shipments effected.

7. 市场情况报告

Reports on Market Conditions

乙方每 3 个月向甲方提供一次有关当时市场情况和用户意见的详细报告。同时，乙方应随时向甲方提供其他供应商的类似商品样品及其价格、销售情况和广告资料。

Party B shall forward once every three months to Party A detailed reports on current market conditions and of consumers' comments. Meanwhile, Party B shall, from time to time, send to Party A samples of similar commodities offered by other suppliers, together with their prices, sales information and advertising materials.

8. 宣传广告费用

Advertising & Publicity Expenses

在本协议有效期内，乙方在上述经销地区所做广告宣传的一切费用，由乙方自理。乙方须事先向甲方提供宣传广告的图案及文字说明，由甲方审阅同意。

Party B shall bear all expenses for advertising and publicity within the aforementioned territory in the duration of this Agreement and submit to Party A all patterns and/or drawings and description for prior approval.

9. 协议有效期

Validity of Agreement

本协议经双方签字后生效，有效期为……天，自……至……。若一方希望延长本协议，则须在本协议期满前 1 个月书面通知另一方，经双方协商决定。若协议一方未履行协议条款，另一方有权终止协议。

This Agreement, after its being signed by the parties concerned, shall remain in force for... days from ... to ... If either party wishes to extend this Agreement, he shall notice, in writing, the other party one month prior to its expiration. The matter shall be decided by the agreement and by consent of the parties hereto. Should either party fail to implement the terms and conditions herein, the other party is entitled to terminate this Agreement.

10. 仲裁

Arbitration

在履行协议过程中，如产生争议，双方应友好协商解决。若通过友好协商达不成协议，则提交中国国际贸易促进委员会对外贸易仲裁委员会，根据该会仲裁程序暂行规定进行仲裁。该委员会的决定是终局的，对双方均具有约束力。仲裁费用，除另有规定外，由败诉一方负担。

All disputes arising from the execution of this Agreement shall be settled through friendly consultations. In case no settlement can be reached, the case in dispute shall then be submitted to the Foreign Trade Arbitration Commission of the China Council for the Promotion of International Trade for arbitration in accordance with its provisional rules of procedure. The decision made by this Commission shall be regarded as final and binding upon both parties. Arbitration fees shall be borne by the losing party, unless otherwise awarded.

11. 其他条款

Other Terms & Conditions

(1)甲方不得向经销地区其他买主供应本协议所规定的商品。如有询价，当转达给乙方洽办。若有买主希望从甲方直接订购，甲方可以供货，但甲方须将有关销售确认书副本寄给乙方，并按所达成交易的发票金额给予乙方……%的佣金。

Party A shall not supply the contracted commodity to any other buyer(s) in the above mentioned territory. Direct enquiries, if any, will be referred to Party B. However, should any other buyers wish to deal with Party A directly, Party A may do so. But party A shall send to Party B a copy of Sales Confirmation and give Party B ...% commission on the basis of the net invoice value of the transaction(s) concluded.

(2)若乙方在……月内未能向甲方提供至少……订货，甲方不承担本协议的义务。

Should Party B fail to pass on his orders to Party A in a period of ... months for a minimum of ..., Party A shall not bind himself to this Agreement.

(3)对双方政府间的贸易，甲方有权按其政府的授权进行有关的直接贸易，而不受本协议约束。乙方不得干涉此种直接贸易，也无权向甲方提出任何补偿要求。

For any business transacted between governments of both parties, Party A may handle such direct dealings as authorized by Party A's government without binding himself to this Agreement. Party B shall not interfere in such direct dealings nor shall Party B bring forward any demand for compensation therefrom.

(4)本协议受签约双方所签订的销售确认条款的制约。

This Agreement shall be subject to the terms and conditions in the Sales Confirmation signed by both parties hereto.

本协议于……年……月……日在……签订，正本两份，甲乙双方各执一份。

This Agreement is signed on ... at ... and is in two originals; each party holds one.

甲方：

(签字)

Party A:

(Signature)

乙方：

(签字)

Party B:

(Signature)

Example 2

Exclusive Agency Agreement

本协议于 2012 年 9 月 20 日在中国青岛由有关双方在平等互利基础上达成，按双方同意的下列条件发展业务关系：

This agreement is made and entered into by and between the parties concerned on September 20, 2012 in Qingdao, China on the basis of equality and mutual benefit to develop business on terms and conditions mutually agreed upon as follows:

1. 协议双方

The Parties Concerned

甲方：青岛宏达实业有限公司

地址：中国青岛瞿塘峡路 25 号

电话：(0532)2877932

传真：(0532)2876415

Party A: Qingdao Hongda Industrial Co., Ltd.

Add: 25 Qutangxia Road, Qingdao, China

Tel: (0532)2877932   Fax: (0532)2876415

乙方：华兴贸易私人有限公司

地址：新加坡滑铁卢街 126 号(0718)

电话：3366436

传真：3397862

Party B: Huaxing Trading Company (Pte) Ltd.

Add: 126 Waterloo Street, Singapore 0718

Tel: 3366436   Fax: 3397862

2. 委任

Appointment

甲方指定乙方为其独家代理，为第三条所列商品从第四条所列区域的顾客中招揽订单，乙方接受上述委任。

Party A hereby appoints Party B as its Exclusive Agent to solicit orders for the commodity stipulated in Article 3 from customers in the territory stipulated in Article 4, and Party B accepts and assumes such appointment.

3. 代理商品

Commodity

"金鱼"牌洗衣机。

"Golden Fish" Brand Washing Machines

4. 代理区域

Territory

仅限于新加坡。

In Singapore only.

5. 最低业务量

Minimum turnover

乙方同意，在本协议有效期内从上述代理区域内的顾客处招揽的上述商品的订单价值不低于 10 万美元。

Party B shall undertake to solicit orders for the above commodity from customers in the above territory during the effective period of this agreement for not less than USD 100,000.

6. 价格与支付

Price and Payment

每一笔交易的货物价格应由乙方与买主通过谈判确定，并须经甲方最后确认。

付款使用保兑的、不可撤销的信用证，由买方开出，以甲方为受益人。信用证须在装运日期前 15 天到达甲方。

The price for each individual transaction shall be fixed through negotiations between Party B and the buyer, and subject to Party A's final confirmation.

Payment shall be made by confirmed, irrevocable L/C opened by the buyer in favor of Party A, which shall reach Party A 15 days before the date of shipment.

7. 独家代理权

Exclusive Right

基于本协议授予的独家代理权，甲方不得直接或间接地通过乙方以外的渠道向新加坡顾客销售或出口第三条所列商品，乙方不得在新加坡经销、分销或促销与上述商品相竞争或类似的产品，也不得招揽或接受以到新加坡以外地区销售为目的的订单，在本协议有效期内，甲方应将其收到的来自新加坡其他商家的有关代理产品的询价或订单转交给乙方。

In consideration of the exclusive rights granted herein, Party A shall not, directly or indirectly, sell or export the commodity stipulated in Article 3 to customers in Singapore through channels other than Party B; Party B shall not sell, distribute or promote the sales of any products competitive with or similar to the above commodity in Singapore and shall not solicit or accept orders for the purpose of selling them outside Singapore. Party A shall refer to Party B any enquiries or orders for the commodity in question received by Party A from other firms in Singapore during the validity of this agreement.

8. 商情报告

Market Report

为使甲方充分了解现行市场情况，乙方承担至少每季度一次或在必要时随时向甲方提供市场报告，内容包括与本协议代理商品的进口与销售有关的地方规章的变动、当地市场发展趋势以及买方对甲方按协议供应的货物的品质、包装、价格等方面的意见。乙方还承担向甲方提供其他供应商类似商品的报价和广告资料。

In order to keep Party A well informed of the prevailing market conditions, Party B should undertake to supply Party A, at least once a quarter or at any time when necessary, with market reports concerning changes of the local regulations in connection with the import and sales of the commodity covered by this agreement, local market tendency and the buyer's comments on quality, packing, price, etc. of the goods supplied by Party A under this agreement. Party B shall also supply Party A with quotations and advertising materials on similar products of other suppliers.

9. 广告及费用

Advertising and Expenses

乙方负担本协议有效期内在新加坡销售代理商品做广告宣传的一切费用，并向甲方提交所用于广告的声像资料，供甲方事先核准。

Party B shall bear all expenses for advertising and publicity in connection with the commodity in question in Singapore within the validity of this agreement, and shall submit to Party A all audio and video materials intended for advertising for prior approval.

10. 佣金

Commission

对乙方直接获取并经甲方确认接受的订单，甲方按净发票售价向乙方支付5%的佣金。佣金在甲方收到每笔订单的全部货款后才会支付。

Party A shall pay Party B a commission of 5% on the net invoiced selling price on all orders directly obtained by Party B and accepted by Party A. No commission shall be paid until Party A receives the full payment for each order.

11. 政府部门间的交易

Transactions Between Governmental Bodies

在甲、乙双方政府部门之间达成的交易不受本协议条款的限制，此类交易的金额也不应计入第五条规定的最低业务量。

Transactions concluded between govenmental bodies of Party A and Party B shall not be restricted by the terms and conditions of this agreement, nor shall the amount of such transactions be counted as part of the turnover stipulated in Article 5.

12. 工业产权

Industrial Property Rights

在本协议有效期内，为销售有关洗衣机，乙方可以使用甲方拥有的商标，并承认使用于或包含于洗衣机中的任何专利商标、版权或其他工业产权为甲方独家拥有。 一旦发现侵权，乙方应立即通知甲方并协助甲方采取措施保护甲方权益。

Party B may use the trade-marks owned by Party A for the sale of the Washing Machines covered herein within the validity of this agreement, and shall acknowledge that all patents, trademarks, copy rights or any other industrial property rights used or embodied in the Washing

Machines shall remain to be the sole properties of Party A. Should any infringement be found, Party B shall promptly notify and assist Party A to take steps to protect the latter's rights.

13. 协议有效期

Validity of Agreement

本协议经有关双方如期签署后生效，有效期为 1 年，从 2012 年 10 月 1 日至 2013 年 9 月 30 日。除非作出相反通知，本协议期满后将延长 12 个月。

This agreement, when duly signed by the both parties concerned, shall remain in force for 12 months from October 1, 2012 to September 30, 2013, and it shall be extended for another 12 months upon expiration unless notice in writing is given to the contrary.

14. 协议的终止

Termination

在本协议有效期内，如果一方被发现违背协议条款，另一方有权终止协议。

During the validity of this agreement, if either of the two parties is found to have violated the stipulations herein, the other party has the right to terminate this agreement.

15. 不可抗力

Force Majeure

由于水灾、火灾、地震、干旱、战争或协议一方无法预见、控制、避免和克服的其他事件导致不能或暂时不能全部或部分履行本协议，该方不负责任。但是，受不可抗力事件影响的一方须尽快将发生的事件通知另一方，并在不可抗力事件发生 15 天内将有关机构出具的不可抗力事件的证明寄交对方。

Either party shall not be held responsible for failure or delay to perform all or any part of this agreement due to flood, fire, earthquake, draught, war or any other events which could not be predicted, controlled, avoided or overcome by the relative party. However, the party affected by the event of Force Majeure shall inform the other party of its occurrence in writing as soon as possible and thereafter send a certificate of the event issued by the relevant authorities to the other party within 15 days after its occurrence.

16. 仲裁

Arbitration

因履行本协议所发生的一切争议应通过友好协商解决。如协商不能解决争议，则应将争议提交中国国际经济贸易仲裁委员会（北京），依据其仲裁规则进行仲裁。仲裁裁决是终局的，对双方都有约束力。

All disputes arising from the performance of this agreement shall be settled through friendly negotiation. Should no settlement be reached throught negotiation, the case shall then be submitted for arbitration to the China International Economic and Trade Arbitration Commission (Beijing) and the rules of this Commission shall be applied. The award of the arbitration shall be final and binding upon both parties.

甲方：青岛宏达实业限公司　　　　　　　乙方：华兴贸易私人有限公司

（签字）　　　　　　　　　　　　　　　（签字）

Party A: Qingdao Hongda Industrial Co., Ltd.   Party B: Huaxing Trading Company (Pte) Ltd.   (Signature)   (Signature)

写 作 范 例

1. An Email from a Dealer Applying for a Sole Agency

Background: 巴基斯坦的 Top Field 公司五年来一直在销售山东顺发打火机公司的电子打火机。由于产品在市场一直很畅销，Top Field 公司现欲申请做顺发公司电子打火机在巴基斯坦地区的独家代理，并就代理期限、年销售额、佣金提出了代理建议。

From: lilyho_industry@topfieldinc.com
To: katherinehappy2564@shunfa-lighter.com
Date: Tuesday, November 11, 20__, 3:44 pm
Subject: Application for Your Sole Agency for Electronic Lighters

Dear Ms. Zhen,

For the past five years we have been selling your Electronic Lighters to wholesalers and large dealers in all parts of Pakistan and our clients are very much satisfied with your products. The style and colors are very much to the taste of our market. We have built up a considerable number of well-established connections with excellent business partners.

As we understand that you have no agent in Pakistan, we would like to offer our services. For your reference, we would propose a sole agency agreement for duration of three years with annual turnover of 50,000, 60,000 and 70,000 pieces for the first, second and third years respectively.

On all sales, we are entitled to receive a commission of 9%. During the validity of the agency agreement, we shall not handle any other foreign products of the same line and competitive types. The area to be covered by the agency agreement is confined to Pakistan.
We believe there are good prospects of a very profitable market for your products here and large sales turnover can be achieved on the basis of sole agency. If you agree to grant us the sole agency we will devote full attention to the development of your products on the Pakistan market.

We look forward to receiving your favorable reply.

Sincerely yours,
Lily Ho
Marketing Director

Notes

1. well-established   adj. 历史悠久的，信誉卓著的，已确认的

    That well-established firm closed down with the loss of 6,000 jobs.   那家知名公司倒闭了，造成 6000 人失业。

    Payment by L/C is a well-established practice in our company.   用信用证支付是我方由来已久的做法。

2. duration   n. 期限

    The agreement is of two years' duration.   协议为期两年。

    The duration of the agreement is from July 1, 2012 to June 30, 2014.   本协议的期限从 2012 年 7 月 1 日到 2014 年 6 月 30 日。

3. be entitled to   使……有资格（做某事）；给予……权利（或资格）

    We are entitled to a repayment of the damaged goods.   我方有权利索取货物损坏赔偿金。

    Party B is not entitled to change the price quoted by Party A, but a proposal in connection with the price is acceptable.   乙方无权更改甲方所报价格，但是有关价格的建议是可以接受的。

4. validity   n. 有效期，效力；正确性

    extend the validity of your L/C   延长贵方信用证的有效期

    Article 12   The term of validity of an import licence shall be one year.   第十二条   进口货物许可证的有效期限为一年。

    They should have questioned the validity of those figures to avoid the loss.   为了避免损失，他们本来应该质疑那些数字的正确性。

Positive Reply

Background: 山东顺发打火机公司同意了巴基斯坦的 Top Field 公司提出的做电子打火机在巴基斯坦地区独家代理的申请，但只能给予 7% 的佣金。

From: katherinehappy2564@shunfa-lighter.com

To: lilyho_industry@topfieldinc.com

Date: Wednesday, November 12, 20＿＿, 10:21 am

Subject: Re: Application for Your Sole Agency for Electronic Lighters

Dear Ms. Ho,

We thank you for your email of November 11, in which you proposed to sell our electronic lighters on sole agency basis.

Based on your high portion in the local market and excellent service system, we are now glad to inform you that we have decided to appoint you as our sole agent. We believe both of us are expecting a win-win cooperation.

The commission of agency is, however, 7% simply because the profit margin on the lighters is not so large as you think. If we agree to your proposal about commission, it will leave us with very small margin.

The agreement is intended for the duration of three years and extendable. Attached is a draft of Sole Agency Agreement including detailed terms and conditions. We hope they will meet your approval.

Hope to receive your early reply.

Yours sincerely,
Katherine Zhen
General Manager

Notes

1. portion　n. 部分

   Self-employed workers also pay a portion of their earnings to the pension program.　个体经营者也把收入的一部分交给退休金计划。

2. appoint　v. 任命，委派，指定

   He was appointed president.　他被任命为总裁。

   We are glad to appoint you as our representative.　我方很高兴任命贵方为我方代表。

3. profit margin　利润

   A net profit margin of at least 10 percent is considered good.　纯利润率值至少在 10% 才被认为是好的。

   A 10% discount will reduce our profit margin.　10% 的折扣会压低我们的利润空间。

4. extendable　adj. 可延长的，可扩展的

Negative Reply

Background: 山东顺发打火机公司拒绝了巴基斯坦的 Top Field 公司提出的做电子打火机在巴基斯坦地区独家代理的申请，因为 Top Field 公司提出的年销售量过低。但顺发公司表示如果 Top Field 公司能够提高代理的销售量，顺发很愿意任命其为独家代理。

From: katherinehappy2564@shunfa-lighter.com

To: lilyho_industry@topfieldinc.com

Date: Wednesday, November 12, 20_ _, 10:21 am

Subject: Re: Application for Your Sole Agency for Electronic Lighters

Dear Ms. Ho,

Thank you for your email of November 11 regarding applying for our sole agency.

In reply, we wish to state that we appreciate your efforts in pushing the sales of our Electronic Lighters in Pakistan and we are satisfied with your work in the past. However, after serious consideration, we do not think conditions are ripe to entrust you with the agency at the present stage as the sales volume mentioned in your email is too small for us to grant you the sole agency.

To tell you frankly, the average annual quantity we sold to your country in the past few years is much larger than what you proposed.

In spite of this, please do not misinterpret our above remark, which in no way implies dissatisfaction. If bigger turnover can be realized to justify establishing the agency we would like you to represent us.

We hope you will agree with us on this point and continue placing orders with us as you have done so far.

Yours sincerely,
Katherine Zhen
General Manager

Notes
1. entrust sb with sth   委托某人做某事
   We will entrust you with exclusive agency if you undertake not to handle similar products of other origins.   如果贵方不经营其他来源的类似产品，我方将委托贵方担任独家代理。
   In view of the fact that the premium rate you quoted is reasonable, we have decided to entrust your company with the insurance of this shipment.   鉴于你方所报的保险费率合理，我方决定委托你方承保这批货物。
   entrust sth to sb   把某事委托某人
   We have entrusted the shipment of your order to our forwarding agent who will take care of the matter.   我方已将贵方货物的运输事宜委托给负责此事的运输商。
   We have entrusted the matter to our representative, who will have a discussion with you.   我们已将此事委托我们的代表和你方商谈。
2. justify   v. 证明……是合理的，认为……正当
   You should note that some price cut will justify itself by an increase in business.   请贵方注意的是商品的减价会带来销售的增长，因而减价是合理的。

2.   An Email from a Seller Seeking for Agency
Background: 珠海星港文具用品有限公司欲在马来西亚觅一名有经验的文具销售代理商。通过查询阿里巴巴网站，发现马来西亚的 Idea House 公司符合要求，因而发去电子邮件介绍星港公司并询问 Idea House 是否愿意做代理。

From: mellisaliu@yahoo.com
To: gilbersdnnhd_stationery@ideahousecorp.com
Date: Thursday, October 10, 20＿＿, 11:40 pm
Subject: Seeking for Agency for Our Stationery Products

Dear Mr. Liew,

With the steady increase in demand for our stationery products, we think we could sell far more of our products in your country and are therefore looking for an agent to represent us. We understand from www.alibaba.com that you have dealt in stationery and related products for many years and we are writing to ask if you would be interested in marketing our products in your country on a commission basis.

We are a large firm with a long history specializing in the manufacture of stationery of all kinds, and there is a steady sales for our products in many parts of the world. The attached catalog will give you a general idea of the wide range of our products, which need developing in your country. If you are interested in our proposal, please let us know which of our products are most likely to appeal to your customers, and also the terms for commission and other charges on which you would be willing to represent us.

We should be very grateful if, when replying, you could give us some idea of the market prospects for our products and suggest ways in which we could help you develop the market.

Sincerely yours,
Mellisa Liu
Market Development Director

Notes
1. steady increase in demand　需求的稳步增长
2. market prospects　市场前景

附录一: SWIFT 信用证

1. SWIFT L/C

1.1 SWIFT 介绍

SWIFT (Society for Worldwide Interbank Financial Telecommunication), 又称"环球同业银行金融电讯协会", 是国际银行同业间的国际合作组织, 成立于 1973 年。目前全球大多数国家大多数银行已使用 SWIFT 系统。SWIFT 的使用, 为银行的结算提供了安全、可靠、快捷、标准化、自动化的通讯业务, 从而大大提高了银行的结算速度。由于 SWIFT 的格式标准化, 目前信用证的格式主要都是用 SWIFT 电文。

SWIFT 信用证是指凡通过 SWIFT 系统开立或予以通知的信用证。在国际贸易结算中, SWIFT 信用证是正式的、合法的, 被信用证各当事人所接受的、国际通用的信用证。采用 SWIFT 信用证必须遵守 SWIFT 的规定, 也必须使用 SWIFT 手册规定的代号 (Tag), 而且信用证必须遵循国际商会 2007 年修订的《跟单信用证统一惯例》各项条款的规定。

1.2 SWIFT 特点

1. SWIFT 需要会员资格。我国的大多数专业银行都是其成员。
2. SWIFT 的费用较低。同样多的内容, SWIFT 的费用只有 TELEX (电传) 的 18%左右, 只有 CABLE (电报) 的 2.5%左右。
3. SWIFT 的安全性较高。SWIFT 的密押比电传的密押可靠性强、保密性高, 且具有较高的自动化。
4. SWIFT 的格式标准化。对于 SWIFT 电文, SWIFT 组织有着统一的要求和格式。

1.3 SWIFT 电文表示方式

1. 项目表示方式

SWIFT 由项目 (FIELD) 组成, 如: 59 BENEFICIARY (受益人), 就是一个项目, 59 是项目的代号, 可以是两位数字表示, 也可以两位数字加上字母来表示, 如 51a APPLICANT (申请人)。不同的代号表示不同的含义。项目还规定了一定的格式, 各种 SWIFT 电文都必须按照这种格式表示。

在 SWIFT 电文中, 一些项目是必选项目 (MANDATORY FIELD), 一些项目是可选项目 (OPTIONAL FIELD), 必选项目是必须要具备的, 如: 31D DATE AND PLACE OF EXPIRY (信用证有效期和有效地点), 可选项目是另外增加的项目, 并不一定每个信用证都有, 如: 39B MAXIMUM CREDIT AMOUNT (信用证最大限制金额)。

2. 日期表示方式

SWIFT 电文的日期表示为: YYMMDD (年月日), 如:

1999 年 5 月 12 日，表示为：990512；

2000 年 3 月 15 日，表示为：000315；

2001 年 12 月 9 日，表示为：011209。

3. 数字表示方式

在 SWIFT 电文中，数字不使用分格号，小数点用逗号"，"来表示，如：

5,152,286.36 表示为：5152286,36；

4/5 表示为：0,8；

5% 表示为：5 PERCENT。

4. 货币表示方式

澳大利亚元：AUD　　　港元：HKD　　　美元：USD

加拿大元：CAD　　　日元：JPY　　　英镑：GBP

人民币元：CNY

1.4 信用证中常见项目表示方式

1. 跟单信用证开证（MT700）

必选 20 DOCUMENTARY CREDIT NUMBER（信用证号码）

可选 23 REFERENCE TO PRE-ADVICE（预先通知号码），如果信用证是采取预先通知的方式，该项目内应该填入"PREADV/"，再加上预先通知的编号或日期。

必选 27 SEQUENCE OF TOTAL（电文页次）

可选 31C DATE OF ISSUE（开证日期），如果这项没有填，则开证日期为电文的发送日期。

必选 31D DATE AND PLACE OF EXPIRY（信用证有效期和有效地点），该日期为最后交单的日期。

必选 32B CURRENCY CODE, AMOUNT（信用证结算的货币和金额）

可选 39A PERCENTAGE CREDIT AMOUNT TOLERANCE（信用证金额上下浮动允许的最大范围），该项目的表示方法较为特殊，数值表示百分比的数值，如：5/5，表示上下浮动最大为 5%。39B 与 39A 不能同时出现。

可选 39B MAXIMUM CREDIT AMOUNT（信用证最大限制金额），39B 与 39A 不能同时出现。

可选 39C ADDITIONAL AMOUNTS COVERED（额外金额），表示信用证所涉及的保险费、利息、运费等金额。

必选 40A FORM OF DOCUMENTARY CREDIT（跟单信用证形式），跟单信用证有六种形式：

(1) IRREVOCABLE（不可撤销跟单信用证）

(2) REVOCABLE（可撤销跟单信用证）

(3) IRREVOCABLE TRANSFERABLE（不可撤销可转让跟单信用证）

(4) REVOCABLE TRANSFERABLE（可撤销可转让跟单信用证）

(5) IRREVOCABLE STANDBY（不可撤销备用信用证）

(6) REVOCABLE STANDBY（可撤销备用信用证）

必选 41a AVAILABLE WITH...BY...（指定的有关银行及信用证兑付的方式）：

（1）指定银行付款、承兑、议付

（2）兑付的方式有 5 种：

BY PAYMENT（即期付款）；

BY ACCEPTANCE（远期承兑）；

BY NEGOTIATION（议付）；

BY DEF PAYMENT（迟期付款）；

BY MIXED PAYMENT（混合付款）。

（3）如果是自由议付信用证，对该信用证的议付地点不做限制，该项目代号为：41D，内容为：ANY BANK IN。

可选 42a DRAWEE（汇票付款人），必须与 42C 同时出现。

可选 42C DRAFTS AT（汇票付款日期），必须与 42a 同时出现。

可选 42M MIXED PAYMENT DETAILS（混合付款条款）

可选 42P DEFERRED PAYMENT DETAILS（迟期付款条款）

可选 43P PARTIAL SHIPMENTS（分装条款），表示该信用证的货物是否可以分批装运。

可选 43T TRANSSHIPMENT（转运条款），表示该信用证是直接到达，还是通过转运到达。

可选 44A LOADING ON BOARD/DISPATCH/TAKING IN CHARGE AT/FROM（装船、发运和接收监管的地点）

可选 44B FOR TRANSPORTATION TO...（货物发运的最终地）

可选 44C LATEST DATE OF SHIPMENT（最后装船期），装船的最迟的日期。44C 与 44D 不能同时出现。

可选 44D SHIPMENT PERIOD（船期），44C 与 44D 不能同时出现。

可选 45A DESCRIPTION OF GOODS AND/OR SERVICES（货物描述），货物的情况、价格条款。

可选 46A DOCUMENTS REQUIRED（单据要求），各种单据的要求。

可选 47A ADDITIONAL CONDITIONS（特别条款）

可选 48 PERIOD FOR PRESENTATION（交单期限），表明开立运输单据后多少天内交单。

必选 49 CONFIRMATION INSTRUCTIONS（保兑指示），其中

CONFIRM：要求保兑行保兑该信用证

MAY ADD：收报行可以对该信用证加具保兑

WITHOUT：不要求收报行保兑该信用证

必选 50 APPLICANT（信用证开证申请人），一般为进口商。

可选 51a APPLICANT BANK（信用证开证的银行）

可选 53A REIMBURSEMENT BANK（偿付行）

可选 57a "ADVISE THROUGH" BANK（通知行）

必选 59 BENEFICIARY（信用证的受益人），一般为出口商。

可选 71B CHARGES（费用情况），表明费用是否由受益人（出口商）出，如果没有这一条，表示除了议付费、转让费以外，其他各种费用由开出信用证的申请人（进口商）出。

可选 72 SENDER TO RECEIVER INFORMATION（附言）

可选 78 INSTRUCTION TO THE PAYING/ACCEPTING/NEGOTIATING BANK（给付款行、承兑行、议付行的指示）

2. 信用证修改（MT707）

必选 20 SENDER'S REFERENCE（信用证号码）

必选 21 RECEIVER'S REFERENCE（收报行编号），如发电文的银行不知道收报行的编号，填写"NONREF"。

可选 23 ISSUING BANK'S REFERENCE（开证行的号码）

可选 26E NUMBER OF AMENDMENT（修改次数），该信用证修改的次数，要求按顺序排列。

可选 30 DATE OF AMENDMENT（修改日期），如果信用证修改没填这项，修改日期就是发报日期。

可选 31C DATE OF ISSUE（开证日期），如果这项没有填，则开证日期为电文的发送日期。

可选 31E NEW DATE OF EXPIRY（信用证新的有效期），信用证修改的有效期。

可选 32B INCREASE OF DOCUMENTARY CREDIT AMOUNT（信用证金额的增加）

可选 33B DECREASE OF DOCUMENTARY CREDIT AMOUNT（信用证金额的减少）

可选 34B NEW DOCUMENTARY CREDIT AMOUNT AFTER AMENDMENT（信用证修改后的金额）

可选 39A PERCENTAGE CREDIT AMOUNT TOLERANCE（信用证金额上下浮动允许的最大范围的修改），该项目的表示方法较为特殊，数值表示百分比的数值，如：5/5，表示上下浮动最大为 5%。39B 与 39A 不能同时出现。

可选 39B MAXIMUM CREDIT AMOUNT（信用证最大限制金额的修改），39B 与 39A 不能同时出现。

可选 39C ADDITIONAL AMOUNTS COVERED（额外金额的修改），表示信用证所涉及的保险费、利息、运费等金额的修改。

可选 44A LOADING ON BOARD/DISPATCH/TAKING IN CHARGE AT/FROM（装船、发运和接收监管的地点的修改）

可选 44B FOR TRANSPORTATION TO…（货物发运的最终地的修改）

可选 44C LATEST DATE OF SHIPMENT（最后装船期的修改），修改装船的最迟的日期。44C 与 44D 不能同时出现。

可选 44D SHIPMENT PERIOD（装船期的修改），44C 与 44D 不能同时出现。

可选 52a APPLICANT BANK（信用证开证的银行）

必选 59 BENEFICIARY (BEFORE THIS AMENDMENT)（信用证的受益人），该项目为原信用证的受益人，如果要修改信用证的受益人，则需要在 79 NARRATIVE（修改详述）中写明。

可选 72 SENDER TO RECEIVER INFORMATION（附言），其中：

/BENCON/：要求收报行通知发报行受益人是否接受该信用证的修改。

/PHONBEN/：请电话通知受益人（列出受益人的电话号码）。

/TELEBEN/：用快捷有效的电讯方式通知受益人。

可选 79 NARRATIVE（修改详述）

Sample 1: SWIFT L/C (with explanation):

Issue of a Documentary Credit   （开证行，一般为出口商的往来银行，须视开证行的信用程度决定是否需要其他银行保兑）

BKCHCNBJA08E   SESSION: 000   ISN: 000000   BANK OF CHINA   LIAONING   NO. 5 ZHONGSHAN SQUARE   ZHONGSHAN DISTRICT   DALIAN   CHINA

Destination Bank   （通知行 advising bank）

KOEXKRSEXXX MESSAGE TYPE: 700   KOREA EXCHANGE BANK   SEOUL   178.2 KA, ULCHI RO, CHUNG-KO   （一般由受益人指定往来银行为通知行，如愿意通知，其须谨慎鉴别信用证表面真实性；应注意信用证文本的生效形式和内容是否完整）

40A Type of Documentary Credit   （跟单信用证类型）

IRREVOCABLE   （信用证性质为不可撤销。在信用证中需明示其是可撤或不可撤，如无明示，信用证应视为不可撤；只有明确"可转让"信用证方可转让）

20 Letter of Credit Number   （信用证号码）

LC84E0081/99   （信用证号码，一般做单时都要求注此号）

31G Date of Issue   （开证日期）

990916

31D Date and Place of Expiry   （信用证到期时间地点。通常最后装船期的时间加上单据提示的时间就是信用证到期时间。通常要求在出口商国内到期。审证时也应注意信用证是否有条件生效条款，如"待获取进口许可证时才生效"）

991015 KOREA

51D Applicant Bank   （开证行）

BANK OF CHINA LIAONING BRANCH

50 Applicant（开证申请人）

DALIAN WEIDA TRADING CO., LTD.

59 Beneficiary （受益人）
SANGYONG CORPORATION　CPO BOX 110　SEOUL　KOREA （名称与地址与印就好的文件上的要一致，其他单据制作照抄此名址即可）

32B Currency Code, Amount （信用证结算货币和金额）
USD 1,146,725.04

41D Available with...by... （指定的有关银行和信用证兑付方式）
ANY BANK BY NEGOTIATION （意为任何银行议付，有的信用证为 ANY BANK BY PAYMENT，此为银行付款后无追索权；前则有追索权，就是有权限要回已付给你的钱，其实为贴现行、购票行，为善意第三人。通常要求在出口商国内交单，即交单行为国内银行）

42C Drafts at （汇票付款期限）
45 DAYS AFTER SIGHT （见证 45 天内付款）

42D Drawee （汇票付款人受票人）
BANK OF CHINA LIAONING BRANCH （亦称受票行 drawee bank，通常也是付款行 paying bank，付款人不能为信用证申请人）

43P Partial Shipments（分装条款）
NOT ALLOWED （此为分装不允许。UCP500 除非信用证明确不准分批装运，卖方即有权分批装运）

43T Transshipment （转运条款）
NOT ALLOWED （此为转船不允许。UCP500 如在信用证中没有是否允许转运的表述，则视为允许转运。对允许转运的货物，一般不宜接受"卖方指定中途港"或"卖方指定二程船公司或船名"等条件。如禁止转运，只要提单证明货物是装在集装箱、拖车或子母船上的，即使提单注明将有转船，也不做不符，但须由同一份提单包括整个航程）

44A Shipping on Board/Dispatch/Packing in Charge at/from（装船、发送和货物接收监管的地点）
RUSSIAN SEA （起运港）

44B Transportation to（货物发送的最终地）
DALIAN PORT, P.R.CHINA （目的港）

44C Latest Date of Shipment（最迟装运期）
990913 （44C 在 CIF 时使用，FOB 使用 44D SHIPMENT PERIOD。装期应便于合理备货及制作和申领相关单证，如生产包装、船期安排、内陆运输、制作商业发票和装箱单、报检取商检证、申领产地证、许可证、核销单及其他认证签证、投保取单、整理审理单证、报关查关及其他意外事故）

45A Description of Goods or Services（货物描述）
FROZEN YELLOWFIN SOLE WHOLE ROUND (WITH WHITE BELLY) USD770/MT CFR DALIAN QUANTITY: 200MT   ALASKA PLAICE (WITH YELLOW BELLY) USD600/MT CFR DALIAN QUANTITY: 300MT

46A Documents Required（单据要求） （单证及其他要求合理可行：备单不求人，应拒绝由客人或其授权人出具并证实的单证文件，如客检证，也要谨慎考虑由其他机构出具的单据文件证明认证能否办理或能否及时办理，所需份数尤其是正本份数能否如数提供，可参考 UCP500 第二十三条 b、c、d；单据填制是否合理，如要求出具记名提单等）（备单审单原则：单证相符）

1. SIGNED COMMERCIAL INVOICE IN 5 COPIES. （签字的商业发票五份）

2. FULL SET OF CLEAN ON BOARD OCEAN BILLS OF LADING MADE OUT TO ORDER AND BLANK ENDORSED, MARKED "FREIGHT PREPAID" NOTIFYING LIAONING OCEAN FISHING CO., LTD. TEL 86-411-3680288 （一整套清洁已装船提单，抬头为 TO ORDER 的空白背书，且注明运费已付，通知人为 LIAONING OCEAN FISHING CO., LTD.）（应谨慎处理正本提单直接寄送客人的条款）

3. PACKING LIST/WEIGHT MEMO IN 4 COPIES INDICATING QUANTITY/GROSS AND NET WEIGHTS OF EACH PACKAGE AND PACKING CONDITIONS AS CALLED FOR BY THE L/C.（装箱单/重量单四份，显示每个包装产品的数量/毛净重和信用证要求的包装情况）

4. CERTIFICATE OF QUALITY IN 3 COPIES ISSUED BY PUBLIC RECOGNIZED SURVEYOR.（由 PUBLIC RECOGNIZED SURVEYOR 签发的质量证明三份）

5. BENEFICIARY'S CERTIFIED COPY OF FAX DISPATCHED TO THE ACCOUNTEE WITH 3 DAYS AFTER SHIPMENT ADVISING NAME OF VESSEL, DATE, QUANTITY, WEIGHT, VALUE OF SHIPMENT, L/C NUMBER AND CONTRACT NUMBER.（受益人证明的传真件，

在船开后三天内将船名，日期，货物的数量、重量、价值，信用证号和合同号通知付款人）

6. CERTIFICATE OF ORIGIN IN 3 COPIES ISSUED BY AUTHORIZED INSTITUTION.（当局签发的原产地证明三份）

7. CERTIFICATE OF HEALTH IN 3 COPIES ISSUED BY AUTHORIZED INSTITUTION.（当局签发的健康/检疫证明三份）

47A ADDITIONAL INSTRUCTIONS　（附加指示）
1. CHARTER PARTY B/L AND THIRD PARTY DOCUMENTS ARE ACCEPTABLE. （租船提单和第三方单据可以接受）

2. SHIPMENT PRIOR TO L/C ISSUING DATE IS ACCEPTABLE.（装船期在信用证有效期内可接受）

3. BOTH QUANTITY AND AMOUNT 10 PERCENT MORE OR LESS ARE ALLOWED. （允许数量和金额公差在 10%左右）

71B Charges　（费用）
ALL BANKING CHARGES OUTSIDE THE OPENING BANK ARE FOR BENEFICIARY'S ACCOUNT.

48 Period for Presentation（单据提示日期）
DOCUMENTS MUST BE PRESENTED WITHIN 15 DAYS AFTER THE DATE OF ISSUANCE OF THE TRANSPORT DOCUMENTS BUT WITHIN THE VALIDITY OF THE CREDIT. （一般表明在提单出具后若干天，且在到期日内。通常最后装船期的时间加上单据提示的时间就是信用证到期时间，交单日必须便于合理制单结汇，一般如领取提单、签发汇票、制作受益人证明、整理审理单证、银行退回更正及其他意外事故等，且在有效期内。信用证有规定的，按规定交单，若信用证没有规定交单期，向银行交单的日期不得晚于提单日后 21 天，在有效期内）

49 Confirmation Instructions（保兑指示）
WITHOUT　（须视开证行的信用程度决定是否需要其他银行保兑）

78 Instructions to the Paying/Accepting/Negotiating Bank（对付款行、承兑行、议付行的指示）

1. ALL DOCUMENTS TO BE FORWARDED IN ONE COVER, UNLESS OTHERWISE STATED ABOVE.

2. DISCREPANT DOCUMENT FEE OF USD 50.00 OR EQUAL CURRENCY WILL BE DEDUCTED FROM DRAWING IF DOCUMENTS WITH DISCREPANCIES ARE ACCEPTED.

57A　"Advising Through" Bank（通知行）

KOEXKRSEXXX MESSAGE TYPE: 700 KOREA EXCHANGE BANK SOUTH KOREA 178.2 KA, ULCHI RO, CHUNG-KO

Sample 2: SWIFT L/C

2005JUL01　09:14:21		Logical Terminal Y005
MT S700	Issue of a Documentary Credit	Page 00001
		Func TJADPRQ2

MSGACK DWS7651 Auth OK, Key B10561937960C54, BKCHCNBJ BNPA**** record

Basic Header　　　　F　01 BKCHCNBJA200 1285 164024

Application Header　0 700 1913 050630 BNPATWTPAKAO 4733 017804 050630 1913 N

　　　　　　　　　　*BNP PARIBAS

　　　　　　　　　　*KAOHSIUNG

　　　　　　　　　　*(KAOHSIUNG BRANCH)

User Header	Service Code	103:	
	Bank. Priority	113:	
	Msg User Ref.	108:	
	Info. From CI	115:	
Sequence of Total	*27	: 1 / 1	
Form of Doc. Credit	*40 A	: IRREVOCABLE	
Doc. Credit Number	*20	: 00010LC40500287	
Date of Issue	31 C	: 050630	
Expiry	*31 D	: Date 050821 PLACE IN BENEFICIARY'S COUNTRY	
Applicant	*50	: CHINA METAL CORP.	
		885-10 CINAN ROAD, NANTZE	
		KAOHSIUNG	
Beneficiary	*59	: TIANJIN HUAXIA INDUSTRIAL AND	
		TRADING GROUP CO.	
		63 FUKANG ROAD, NANKAI DISTRICT	
		TIANJIN CHINA	
Amount	*32 B	: Currency USD Amount 69.875,	
Pos. / Neg. Tol. (%)	39 A	: 05 / 05	
Available with/by	*41 D	: L/C ADVISING BANK	

BY NEGOTIATION

Drafts at ...	42 C :	SIGHT FOR 100 PERCENT OF INVOICE VALUE
Drawee	42 D :	BNP PARIBAS
		KAOHSUING BRANCH
Partial Shipments	43 P :	ALLOWED
Transshipment	43 T :	NOT ALLOWED
Loading in Charge	44 A :	TIANJIN PORT
For Transport to ...	44 B :	KAOHSIUNG PORT
Latest Date of Ship.	44 C :	050731
Descript. of Goods	45 A :	

PRIME HOT ROLLED STEEL WIRE RODS IN COILS

QUALITY   : SWRCH8A (CHQ)/Q195L

PRICE TERMS   : (1) SWRCH8A (CHQ): USD481/MT CFR FO CQD
                    KAOHSIUNG PORT
                 (2) SWRCH22A (CHQ): USD481/MT CFR FO CQD
                    KAOHSIUNG PORT
                 (3) Q195L: USD390/MT CFR FO CQD KAOHSIUNG PORT

MILL   : TIANJIN STEEL STRUCTURE CO., LTD.

TOTAL QUANTITY : 150MT +/-5PCT

QUALITY/SIZE/QTY: (1) SWRCH8A (CHQ) : DIA. 5.5MM – 25MT
                                      DIA. 9.0MM – 38MT
                                      DIA. 12.0MM – 37MT
                 (2) SWRCH22A (CHQ) : DIA. 5.5MM – 25MT
                 (3) Q195L   : DIA. 5.5MM – 25MT

Documents required   46 A :

+COMMERICAL INVOICE IN SEXTUPLICATE MANUALLY SIGNED, INDICATING THIS L/C NO.

+2/3 ORIGINALS OF "CLEAN-ON-BOARD" OCEAN BILLS OF LADING MADE OUT TO THE ORDER OF BNP PARIBAS, KAOHSIUNG BRANCH MARKED "FREIGHT PREPAID" AND NOTIFY APPLICANT WITH NAME AND FULL

2005JUL01   09:14:22   Logical Terminal
Y005

MT S700   Issue of a Documentary Credit   Page 00002
                                                          Func TJADPRQ2

ADDRESS AND INDICATING THIS L/C NO.

+PACKING / WEIGHT LIST IN TWO FOLD.

+ONE ORIGINAL AND 1 COPY OF MILLS TEST CERTIFICATE ISSUED BY MILL.

+ONE ORIGINAL AND 1 COPY OF A NON-RADIOACTIVITY CERTIFICATE

ISSUED BY MILL.

+BENEFICIARY'S CERTIFICATE STATING THAT THEY HAVE FORWARDED ONE ORIGINAL B/L AND ONE COMPLETE SET OF NON-NEGOTIABLE DOCUMENTS DIRECT TO APPLICANT (ATTN: MR. XIAO-HUA XU) BY DHL WITHIN 2 DAYS AFTER THE DATE OF B/L IS EFFECTED.

+SHIPPING COMPANY OR THEIR AGENT MUST ISSUE A CERTIFICATE EVIDENCING THE AGE OF THE STEAMER

+CERTIFICATE OF ORIGIN IN ONE ORIGINAL AND 2 COPIES.

Additional Cond.   47 A：

+CHARTER PARTY BILLS OF LADING ALLOWED

+BILL OF LADING CLAUSED WITH "ATMOSPHERIC RUSTY" ARE ACCEPTABLE

+5 PCT MORE OR LESS ON EACH SIZE, TOTAL VALUE AND QUANTITY ARE ACCEPTABLE

+IF VESSEL'S AGE IS BETWEEN 16 AND 20 YEARS OLD, THE OVERAGE PERMIUM IS FOR SELLER'S ACCOUNT AT THE MAXIMUM RATE OF 0.375 PERCENT OF 110 PERCENT OF INVOICE VALUE. THIS AMOUNT TO BE DEDUCTED FROM INVOICE AMOUNT UPON NEGOTIATION OF L/C

+VESSEL'S AGE OVER 20 YEARS IS UNACCEPTABLE

+T/T REIMBURSEMENT ALLOWED

+"DOCUMENTS DISPOSAL CONDITIONS" – DISCREPANT DOCUMENTS PRESENTED WILL BE REJECTED AND HELD AT THE PRESENTER'S DISPOSAL. HOWEVER, IF OUR TRADE SERVICES DEPARTMENT DOES NOT ACTUALLY RECEIVE THE PRESENTER'S INSTRUCTION TO RETURN THE DOCUMENTS BY THE TIME THE APPLICANT HAS ACCEPTED AND/OR PAID FOR THE DOCUMENTS, WE, AT OUR SOLE DISCRETION, MAY RELEASE THE DOCUMENTS TO THE APPLICANT WITHOUT REFERENCE TO THE PRESENTER. IF THE DOCUMENTS ARE SO RELEASED, WE SHALL BE DEEMED TO HAVE ACCEPTED THE DOCUMENTS BUT SHALL NOT BE UNDER ANY OTHER LIABILITIES TO THE BENEFICIARY, NEGOTIATING BANK, PRESENTER OR ANY PARTIES.

+THE ADVISING BANK IS ALLOWED TO ADD THEIR CONFIRMATION TO THE L/C IF REQUESTED BY BENEFICIARY AT BENEFICIARY'S EXPENSES.

+YOU ARE NOT AUTHORIZED TO RELEASE THE L/C BEFORE COLLECTING YOUR ADVISING CHARGES OR GETTING BENEFICIARY'S CONFIRMATION TO PAY ALL CHARGES OUTSIDE TAIWAN EVEN IN CASE OF NON-UTILIZATION OF THIS L/C. UCP500 ARTICLE 18 C NOT APPLICABLE

+EXCEPT AS OTHERWISE STATED OR MODIFIED, THIS CREDIT IS SUBJECT TO THE UCP 500

Details of Charges   71 B：ALL BANKING CHARGES OUTSIDE TAIWAN AS WELL

AS OUR PAYMENT COMM. OF USD70.00 AND DISCREPANCY FEE OF USD60.00 OR ITS EQUIVALENT ARE FOR BENEFICIARY'S ACCOUNT AND WILL BE DEDUCTED FROM PAYMENT.

Presentation Period　　　48　: DOCUMENTS PRESENTED LATER THAN 21 DAYS AFTER THE DATE OF SHIPMENT BUT WITHIN THE VALIDITY OF THE CREDIT IS ACCEPTABLE.

Confirmation　　　　　*49　: MAY ADD

Instructions　　　　　78　:

+UPON RECEIPT OF YOUR TESTED TELEX/AUTHENTICATED SWIFT MESSAGE CONFIRMING THAT STRICTLY COMPLYING DOCUMENTS HAVE BEEN NEGOTIATED AND FORWARDED TO US AS INSTRUCTED ON THE SAME DAY THE SAID MESSAGE IS BEING SENT, WE SHALL REMIT COVER AS REQUIRED VALUE 3 WORKING DAYS AFTER RECEIPT OF SUCH TELEX/SWIFT

+THE NEGOTIATING BANK IS REQUIRED TO SEND ALL DOCS TO US IN ONE

2005JUL01　09:14:22　　　　　　　　　　　　　　　　Logical Terminal Y005

MT S700　　　　　　Issue of a Documentary Credit　　　　　Page 00003

Func TJADPRQ2

LOT BY COURIER (BNP PARIBAS, KAOHSIUNG BRANCH'S ADDRESS AS FOLLOWS: 10/F, NO.2 CHUNG CHENG 3RD ROAD, KAOSHIUNG, TELEX NO: 71161 BNPKB SWIFT CODE: BNPATWTPKAO)

Advising Through　　　57 D : FOR YOUR TIANJIN NANKAI SUB BRANCH TIANGUILI

　　　　　　　　　　　　　NO.2 BUILDING BAIDI STREET, NANKAI DISTRICT, TIANJIN

Send. To Rec. Info.　　72 D : THE L/C WILL BECOME AUTOMATICALLY OPERATIVE ONLY UPON ACCEPTING TO PAY FOR ALL CHARGES OUTSIDE TAIWAN AND ADVISING CHARGES BY BENEF.

Trailer　　　　　　　Order is <MAC: > <PAC: > <ENC: > <CHK: > <TNG: > <PDE: >

　　　　　　　　　　MAC: 7AA3A06A

　　　　　　　　　　CHK: 4C91E0AD387D

Sample 3: Application for an L/C

TO: NEW YORK BANK, OSAKA	
Beneficiary (full name and address): JIAHE INTER. TRADING CO., 60, NONGJU RD NANTONG JIANGSU CHINA	L/C NO. 5498 Ex-Card No. Contract No. GDS90882
	Date and place of expiry of the credit: MAR. 30, 2001 AT BNEFICIARY'S COUNTRY

Partial shipments	Transshipment	O Issue by airmail
⊗ allowed	O allowed	O With brief advice by teletransmission
O not allowed	⊗ not allowed	O Issue by express delivery
		⊗ Issue by teletransmission (which shall be the operative instrument)

Loading on board / dispatch / taking in charge at / from SHANGHAI PORT Not later than MAR.10, 2001 for transportation to OSAKA, JAPAN	Amount (both in figures and words) USD 26,520.00 SAY US DOLLARS TWENTY SIX THOUSAND FIVE HUNDRED AND TWENTY

Description of goods: 100PCT RAYON DISH CLOTH 30SX30S/56X54/45X45CM 2PLY CIF BUSAN CHINA ORIGIN	Credit available with O by sight payment O by acceptance O by negotiation O by deferred payment at against the documents detailed herein ⊗ and beneficiary's draft for 100 % of the invoice value at sight on NEW YORK BANK, OSAKA

	O FOB	O CFR	⊗ CIF
	O or other terms		

Documents required: (marked with x)

- (X) Signed Commercial Invoice in 5 copies indicating invoice no., contract no.
- (X) Full set of clean on board ocean Bills of Lading made out to order and blank endorsed, marked "freight ( ) to collect / (X) prepaid () showing freight amount" notifying ACCOUNT
- ( ) Air Waybills showing "freight ( ) to collect / ( ) prepaid ( ) indicating freight amount" and consigned to _____ .
- ( ) Memorandum issued by _____ consigned to _____ .
- (X) Insurance Policy / Certificate in 3 copies for 110 % of the invoice value showing claims payable in China in currency of the draft, bank endorsed, covering ( ) Ocean Marine Transportation / ( ) Air Transportation / ( ) Over Land Transportation ( ) All Risks, War Risks.
- (X) Packing List / Weight Memo in 3 copies indicating quantity / gross and net weights of each package and packing conditions as called for by the L/C.
- ( ) Certificate of Quantity / Weight in 2 copies issued by an independent surveyor at the loading port, indicating the actual surveyed quantity / weight of shipped goods as well as the packing condition.
- (X) Certificate of Quality in 3 copies issued by ( ) manufacturer / (X) public recognized surveyor.
- (X) Beneficiary's certified copy of FAX dispatched to the accountees within 3 days after shipment advising (X) name of vessel / (X) date, quantity, weight and value of shipment.
- ( ) Beneficiary's Certificate certifying that extra copies of the documents have been dispatched according to the contract terms.
- ( ) Shipping Co's Certificate attesting that the carrying vessel is chartered or booked by accountee or their shipping agents.
- (X) Other documents, if any:
  a) Certificate of Origin in 3 copies issued by authorized institution.
  b) Certificate of Health in 3 copies issued by authorized institution.

Additional instructions:

1. (X) All banking charges outside the opening bank are for beneficiary's account.
2. (X) Documents must be presented within 15 days after the date of issuance of the transport documents but within the validity of this credit.
3. ( ) Third party as shipper is not acceptable. Short Form / Blank Back B/L is not acceptable.
4. ( ) Both quantity and amount 10 % more or less are allowed.
5. ( ) Prepaid freight drawn in excess of L/C amount is acceptable against presentation of original charges voucher issued by Shipping Co. / Air line / or its agent.
6. ( ) All documents to be forwarded in one cover, unless otherwise stated above.
7. (X) Other terms, if any:

Advising bank: BANK OF CHINA, NANTONG BRANCH

Account No.:

Transacted by:

(Applicant: name, signature of authorized person)

Sample 4: Amendment to an L/C

INDUSTRIAL BANK OF KOREA

IRREVOCABLE LETTER OF CREDIT   REP-KJ87   KOREA May 8, 2009

THIS IS AN OPERATIVE AMENDMENT OF CREDIT INSTRUMENT

BENEFICIARY: **ADVISING BANK:**

TIANJIN HONGDA IMP. & EXP. CO., LTD.   BANK OF CHINA

578 ZIJINSHAN ROAD   TIANJIN BRANCH

TIANJIN CHINA   80 JIEFANG (N) ROAD

THIS AMENDMENT IS TO BE   **APPLICANT:**
CONSIDERED AS PART OF THE ABOVE
CREDIT AND MUST BE ATTACHED   SAMSUNG CORPORATION
THERETO

SAMSUNG-PLAZA BUILDING 263

SEOHYEON-DONG

DUNDANG-GU, SEONGNAM

GYEONGGI-DO, KOREA 463-721

DEAR SIR(S),

THE LETTER OF CREDIT REFERRED ABOVE IS AMENDED AS FOLLOWS:

* The place of expiry: In China, instead of in Seoul.

* The Number of the S/C: REP-FHS87, instead of REP-FSH87.

* Amend L/C at 30 days sight to be L/C at sight.

* The name of the goods is ANHUA BRAND SEWING MACHINE, instead of AIHUA BRAND SEWING MACHINE.

* The Art. No. should be 883YWI, instead of 886YWI

* The expiry date of the L/C should be May 25, 2009.

* Add the words "EXCEPT AS OTHERWISE STATED THIS CREDIT IS SUBJECT TO THE UNIFORM CUSTOMS AND PRACTICE FOR DOCUMENTARY CREDITS (1993 REVISION) INTERNATIONAL CHAMBER OF COMMERCE PUBLICATION NO. 500."

ALL OTHER TERMS AND CONDITIONS REMAIN UNCHANGED.

附录二：销售合同

SALES CONTRACT

合同编号：06KCSJ-109

Contract No.: 06KCSJ-109

签订地点：浙江温州

Signed at: Wenzhou, Zhejiang

签订日期：2006 年 9 月 25

Date: September 25, 2006

买方：纽约贸易总公司

The Buyer: GERENAL TRADING COMPANY, NEW YORK

Address: No. 133, TRADING MANSION, WASHINGTON STREET, NEW YORK, AMERICA

卖方：浙江宁夏自行车制造有限公司

The Seller: Ningxia Bicycle Making Co., Ltd., Zhejiang

Address: No. 6 SHUANGTA ROAD DONGFENG INDUSTRIAL ZONE OUBEI TOWN, WENZHOU, ZHEJIANG PROVINCE, PEOPLE'S REPUBLIC OF CHINA

双方同意按下列条款由卖方售出下列商品：

The Buyer agrees to buy and the Seller agrees to sell the following goods on terms and conditions as set forth below:

（1）商品名称、规格及包装 （1）Name of Commodity, Specifications and Packing	（2）数量 （2）Quantity	（3）单价 （3）Unit Price	（4）总值 （4）Total Value
自行车 BICYCLE BMX06-03 24×20M 红色 BMX06-03 24×20M RED	3000 辆 3,000 SETS	USD109/辆 CIF 纽约 USD109 PER SET CIF NEW YORK	USD 327,000.00 USD 327,000.00 (SAY US DOLLARS THREE HUNDRED AND TWENTY SEVEN THOUSAND ONLY)

每辆自行车装入一瓦楞纸箱，每 100 辆装入一集装箱 IN CONTAINERS OF 100 SETS EACH. INNER PACKING SHOULD BE CORRUGATED CARTON OF EACH SET.	（装运数量允许有 0%的增减） （Shipment Quantity 0 % more or less allowed）

（5）装运期限：2006 年 10 月 31 日前

（5）Time of Shipment：Before OCTOBER 31, 2006

（6）装运口岸：中国上海

（6）Port of Loading：Shanghai, China

（7）目的口岸：美国纽约

（7）Port of Destination：New York, USA

（8）保险：由卖方负责，按本合同总值 110%投保中国人民保险公司海洋货物运输保险条款一切险和战争险。

（8）Insurance：To be covered by the Seller for 110% of the invoice value against All Risks and War Risk as per ocean marine cargo clause of the People's Insurance Company of China.

（9）付款：凭不可撤销的即期付款信用证，信用证以浙江宁夏自行车制造有限公司为受益人并允许分批装运和转船。该信用证必须在 2006 年 10 月 5 日前开到卖方，信用证的有效期应为上述装船期后第 15 天，在中国温州到期，否则卖方有权取消本售货合约，不另行通知，并保留因此而发生的一切损失的索赔权。

（9）Terms of Payment: By irrevocable letter of credit in favor of Ningxia Bicycle Making Co., Ltd., Zhejiang payable at sight allowing partial shipment and transshipment. The covering Letter of Credit must reach the Seller before October 5, 2006 and is to remain valid in Wenzhou, China until the 15th day after the aforesaid time of shipment, failing which the Seller reserves the right to cancel this Sales Contract without further notice and to claim from the Buyer for losses resulting therefrom.

（10）商品检验：以中国商品检验检疫局所签发的品质/数量/重量/包装合格证书作为卖方的交货依据。

（10）Inspection: The Inspection Certificate of Quality / Quantity / Weight / Packing issued by the China Commodity Inspection and Quarantine Bureau shall be regarded as evidence of the Seller's delivery.

（11）装运唛头：N/M

（11）Shipping Marks：N/M

其他条款：

OTHER TERMS：

1. 异议：品质异议须于货到目的口岸之日起 30 天内提出，数量异议须于货到目的口岸之日起 15 天内提出，但均须提供经卖方同意的公证行的检验证明。如责任属于卖方者，卖方于收到异议 20 天内答复买方并提出处理意见。

1. Discrepancy: In case of quality discrepancy, claim should be lodged by the Buyer within 30 days after the arrival of the goods at the port of destination, while for quantity discrepancy, claim should be lodged by the Buyer within 15 days after the arrival of the goods at the port of destination. In all cases, claims must be accompanied by Survey Reports of Recognized Public Surveyors agreed to by the Seller. Should the responsibility of the subject under claim be found to rest on the part of the Seller, the Seller shall, within 20 days after receipt of the claim, send his reply to the Buyer together with suggestion for settlement.

2. 信用证内应明确规定卖方有权可多装或少装所注明的百分数，并按实际装运数量议付。(信用证之金额按本售货合约金额增加相应的百分数。)

2. The covering Letter of Credit shall stipulate the Seller's option of shipping the indicated percentage more or less than the quantity hereby contracted and be negotiated for the amount covering the value of quantity actually shipped. (The Buyer is requested to establish the L/C in amount with the indicated percentage over the total value of the order as per this Sales Contract.)

3. 信用证内容须严格符合本售货合约的规定，否则修改信用证的费用由买方负担，卖方并不负因修改信用证而延误装运的责任，并保留因此而发生的一切损失的索赔权。

3. The contents of the covering Letter of Credit shall be in strict conformity with the stipulations of the Sales Contract. In case of any variation there of necessitating amendment of the L/C, the Buyer shall bear the expenses for effecting the amendment. The Seller shall not be held responsible for possible delay of shipment resulting from awaiting the amendment of the L/C and reserves the right to claim from the Buyer for the losses resulting therefrom.

4. 除经约定保险归买方投保者外，由卖方向中国的保险公司投保。如买方需增加保险额及/或需加保其他险，可于装船前提出，经卖方同意后代为投保，其费用由买方负担。

4. Except in cases where the insurance is covered by the Buyer as arranged, insurance is to be covered by the Seller with a Chinese insurance company. If insurance for additional amount and/or for other insurance terms is required by the Buyer, prior notice to this effect must reach the Seller before shipment and is subject to the Seller's agreement, and the extra insurance premium shall be for the Buyer's account.

5. 因人力不可抗拒事故使卖方不能在本售货合约规定期限内交货或不能交货，卖方不负责任，但是卖方必须立即以电报通知买方。如果买方提出要求，卖方应以挂号函向买方提供由中国国际贸易促进委员会或有关机构出具的证明，证明事故的存在。买方不能领到进口许可证，不能被认为系属人力不可抗拒范围。

5. The Seller shall not be held responsible if he fails, owing to Force Majeure cause or causes, to make delivery within the time stipulated in this Sales Contract or cannot deliver the goods.

However, the Seller shall inform immediately the Buyer by cable. The Seller shall deliver to the Buyer by registered letter, if it is requested by the Buyer, a certificate issued by the China Council for the Promotion of International Trade or by any competent authorities, attesting the existence of the said cause or causes. The Buyer's failure to obtain the relative Import License is not to be treated as Force Majeure.

6. 仲裁：凡因执行本合约或有关本合约所发生的一切争执，双方应以友好方式协商解决；如果协商不能解决，应提交中国国际经济贸易仲裁委员会，根据该会的仲裁规则进行仲裁。仲裁裁决是终局的，对双方都有约束力。

6. Arbitration： All disputes arising in connection with this Sales Contract or the execution thereof shall be settled by way of amicable negotiation. In case no settlement can be reached, the case at issue shall then be submitted for arbitration to the China International Economic and Trade Arbitration Commission in accordance with the provisions of the said Commission. The award by the said Commission shall be deemed as final and binding upon both parties.

7. 附加条款（本合同其他条款如与本附加条款有抵触时，以本附加条款为准。）

7. Supplementary Condition(s) (Should the articles stipulated in this Contract be in conflict with the following supplementary condition(s)，the supplementary condition(s) should be taken as valid and binding.)

卖方（Seller）：　　　　　　　　　　　买方（Buyer）：

附录三：海运提单样本

Shipper JIANGXI CEREALS OILS & FOODSTUFFS IMPORT & EXPORT CORP. FOREIGN TRADE BUILDING, NANCHANG CHINA		B/L NO. COSU12160320 中远集装箱运输有限公司 **COSCO CONTAINER LINES** TELEX: 33057 COSCO CN FAX: +86(02) 6545 8984 **COPY** Port-to-Port of Combined Transport BILL OF LADING		
Consignee TO THE ORDER OF. UTTARA BANK LTD.				
Notify Party M/S GREENWAY BANGLADESH. MIJMIJI SIDDIRGONJ NARAYANGONJ AND UTTARA BANK LIMITED		RECEIVED in external apparent good order and condition except as otherwise noted. The total number of packages or units stuffed in the container, the description of the goods and the weights shown in this Bill of Lading are furnished by the Merchants, and which the carrier has no reasonable means of checking and is not a part of this Bill of Lading contract. The carrier has issued the number of Bills of Lading stated below, all of this tenor and date, one of the original Bills of Lading must be surrended and endorsed or signed against the delivery of the shipment and whereupon any other original Bills of Lading shall be void. The Merchants agree to be bound by the terms and conditions of this Bill of Lading as if each had personally signed this Bill of Lading. SEE clause 4 on the back of this Bill of Lading (Terms continued on the back thereof. Please read carefully.) * Applicable Only When Document Used as a Combined Transport Bill of Lading		
Combined Transport Pre-carriage by	**Combined Transport Place of Receipt**			
Ocean Vessel Voy. No. CHITAGONG SEA PORT IN BANGLADESH	**Port of Lading** QINGDAO, CHINA			
Port of Discharge CHITAGONG SEA PORT IN BANGLADESH	**Combined Transport Place of Delivery**			
Marks&Nos. Container/Seal No.	**No. of Containers or Packages**	**Description of Goods (If Dangerous Goods, See Clause 20)**	**Gross Weight (kgs)**	**Measurement (m³)**

GREEN/BTC/CTG CBHU0815900/3169298	42 BALES	TISSUE PAPER (M.G. TISSUE PAPER) SUB: 18GSM SIZE: 30"×40" QTY: 11.706M-TONS (1FCL×20') USD=630/MT.TOTAL USD=7374.671/-STRICTLY AS PER S/C NO.2002JXLCOF0015 DATED 21.04.2002 L/C NO.: 043502010162 FREIGHT PREPAID 1×20'	11,832.66 kg	25.305cbm ON BOARD Oct.15, 2001

Description of Contents for Shipper's Use Only (Not Part of This B/L Contract)

Total Number of Containers and/or Packages (in words)
Subject to Clause 7 Limitation　　　　　SAY: FORTY TWO BALES ONLY

Freight & Charges Declared Value Charge	Revenue Tons	Rate	Per	Prepaid	Collect
Ex. Rate:	Prepaid at QINGDAO	Payable at	Place and Date of Issue QINGDAO CHINA Oct.15, 2001		
	Total Prepaid	No. of Original B(s)/L THREE	Signed for the Carrier COSCO　　　　CONTAINER LINES		

附录四：外贸函电常用词汇缩写

A

@	at	每；以（价格）
&	and	和，与
AA	Automatic Approval	自动许可证
a.a.	after arrival	到达以后
AAR, aar	Against all risks	承保一切险
Acc.	Acceptance	承兑
	Accepted	接受
	account	账户
	Accident	意外事故（保险用语）
acpt.	Acceptance	承兑
ACN.	Air Consignment Note	空运托运单
A/D	after date	期后
A.D.	anno domini (L.)	公元（后）
Ad., advt.	advertisement	广告
Adval.	Advalorem (according to value)	从价计算
add.	Address	住址
adv.	advice	通知
A.F.	Advanced freights	预付运费
A.F.B.	Air freight bill	空运提单
Ag.	Agreement	同意
	Agent	代理人

A.l	first-class	一等，一流
amt.	amount	金额，总数，共计
anon.	anonymous	不记名
a/c, acc/o	account of	某人账户
a/or	and/or	与/或
A/P	Authority to Purchase	委托购买证
a.p.	additional premium	附加费
A/P, a.p.	Additional Premium	附加保险费；额外保险费
A.P.L., a.p.l.	As per list	按照表所列出的
app.	appendix	附录
Apr.	April	四月
approx.	approximately, approximate	大约
A.R.	All Risks	一切险
arr.	Arrival, arrived	抵达
a.s.	after sight	见票后
a/s	alongside	船边
assmt.	assortment	各种类，各色
asst.	assorted	分类，花式搭配
atten.	attention	注意
Aug	August	八月
A/V, A.V.	Advalorem (According to Value)	从价：按值
Av.	average	海损；平均
av., A/V, avg.	average	海损；平均
A/W	actual weight	实际重量，净重
A.W.B.	air way bill	空运运单

B

Bal.	balance	差额
bar., brl.	barrel	桶，琵琶桶
B.B. clause	Both to blame collision clause	船舶互撞条款
B/C	Bills for Collection	托收单据
B.C.	before Christ	公元前
b.d.	brought down	转下
B.D.	Bank draft	银行汇票
	Bill Discounted	贴现票据
b.d.i.	both dates inclusive	包括首尾两日
bdle., bdl.	bundle	把，捆
b.e., B/E, B.EX.	Bill of Exchange	汇票
B.f.	Brought	接下页
B/G	Bonded goods	保税货物
bg.	bag(s)	袋
bkg.	banking	银行业务
bkt.	basket	篮，筐
bl., bls.	bale(s)	包
Blading	Bill of Lading	提单
bot., bott., btl.	bottle	瓶
br.	brand	商标，牌
Brkge.	breakage	破碎
brls.	barrels	桶，琵琶桶
b/s	bags, bales	袋，包
Bs/L	Bills of Lading	提单（复数）

bu.	bushel	蒲式耳
bx.	box	箱，盒
bxs.	boxes	箱（复数），盒（复数）

C

c/-(or c/s)	cases	箱
ca., c/s, cs.	case or cases	箱
C.A.D., C/D	cash against documents	付款交单
canc.	cancelled	取消，注销
C.A.F.	Cost, Assurance, Freight (=C.I.F.)	成本加保费、运费价
canclg.	cancelling	取消；注销
cat.	catalogue	商品目录
C/B	clean bill	光票
C.B.D.	cash before delivery	付款后交单
c.c.	cubic centimeter	立方厘米；立方公分
c.c.	carbon copy	复写纸，副本
C.C.	Chamber of Commerce	商会
C.C.I.B.	China Commodity Inspection Bureau	中国商品检验局
C/d	carried down	转下
cent.	centum (L.)	一百
Cert., certif.	certificate, certified	证明书；证明
c.f.	Cubic feet	立方英尺
C/f	Carried Forward	接后，接转（下页）
cf.	confer	商议
	compare	比较

C.& F.	Cost and Freight	成本加运费价格
CFS, C.F.S.	Container Freight Station	集装箱中转站，货运站
Cg.	Centigram	公毫
C.G.A.	Cargo's proportion of General Average	共同海损分摊额
cgo.	cargo	货物
chges.	charges	费用
Chq	Cheque	支票
C.I.	Certificate of Insurance	保险凭证
	Consular Invoice	领事发票，领事签证
CIC	China Insurance Clause	中国保险条款
C.I.F.	Cost, Insurance, Freight	成本、保险费加运费价格
C.I.F.&C.	Cost, Insurance, Freight & Commission	成本、保险费、运费加佣金的价格
C.I.F.&E.	Cost, Insurance, Freight & Exchange	成本、保险费、运费加汇费的价格
C.I.F.&I.	Cost, Insurance, Freight & Interest	成本、保险费、运费加利息的价格
C.I.O.	Cash in Order, Cash with Order	订货时付款
cks.	casks	桶
cl.	class, clause	级，条款，项
CLP	Container Load Plan	集装箱装箱单
cm.	centimeter	厘米，公分
cm²	square centimeter	平方厘米，平方公分
cm³	cubic centimeter	立方厘米，立方公分
CMI	Comité Maritime International	国际海事委员会

CMR	Convention on the Contract for the International Carriage of Goods by Road	国际公路货物运输合同公约
c/n	cover note	暂保单，预保单
Co.	Company	公司
c/o	care of	转交
C/O, c.o.	Certificate of Origin	产地证明书
c.o.d., C.O.D.	Cash on delivery or Collection delivery	货到付款
COFC	Container on Flat Car	平板车装运集装箱
Com.	Commission	佣金
Con.inv.	Consular invoice	领事发票，领事签证
cont., contr.	contract	合同；合约
contd.	continued	继续，续（上页）
contg.	containing	内容
corp., corpn., cor.	corporation	公司
C/P, c. py.	charter party	租船契约
C.Q.D.	Customary Quick Dispatch	按习惯速度装卸
Cr.	Credit	贷方，信用证
	Creditor	债权人
Crt.	crate	板条箱
Ct.	Cent	分
	Current	当前，目前
	Credit	贷方，信用证
C.T.D.	Combined transport document	联合运输单据
CTB/L	Combined transport bill of lading	联合运输提单
C.T.O.	Combined transport operator	联合运输经营人

cu.cm, cb.cm	cubic centimeter	立方厘米；立方公分
cu.in., cb.in.	cubic inch	立方英寸
cu.m., cb.m.	cubic meter	立方米，立方公尺
cu.ft., cb.ft.	cubic foot	立方英尺
cur., curt.	current (this month)	本月
cur.	currency	币制
cu.yd., cb.yd.	cubic yard	立方码
C.W.O.	cash with order	订货时付款
c.w.t., cwt.	hundred weight	英担（122磅）
CY	Container Yard	集装箱堆场

D

d.	denarii's (L.), penny or pence	便士
D/A	Document against Acceptance	承兑交单
d/a	days after acceptance	承兑后若干天（交款）
D.D., D/D	Demand draft	即期汇票
	Delivered at docks	码头交货
D/d	documentary draft	跟单汇票
Dec.	December	十二月
deld.	delivered	交付
dept.	department	部，股，处
destn.	destination	目的港，目的地
D/f	dead freight	空舱费
drt.	draft	汇票
diam.	diameter	直径

diff.	difference	差额，差异
dis., disc't	discount	贴现，折扣，贴现息
Dmge.	Damage	损坏
D/N	debit note	欠款账单
doc.	document	单据
doc.att.	document attached	附单据，附证件
dols., dolls.	dollars	元
D/P	document against payment	付款交单
d.p.	direct port	直达港口
d/s, d.s., days.st.	days after sight	见票后若干天付款
ds., d's	days	日
dto., do	ditto	同上，同前
d.t.	delivery time	交货时间
dup., dupl., duplte.	duplicate	誊本，第二份，两份
D.W.T.	dead weight tonnage	载重吨
D/Y	delivery	交付，交货
dz.,doz.	dozen	打

E

ea.	each	每
E.C.	Exempli causa (for example)	例如
E/D	Export Declaration	出口申报单
E.E.	errors excepted	错误当查；错误当改
E.E.C.	European Economic Community	欧洲共同体
e.g.; ex.g.	Exempli gratia (L.)=for example	例如

end.	endorsed; endorsement	背书
encl.; enc.	enclosure	附件
E.&O.E.	errors and omissions excepted	错漏当查；错漏当改
E.O.M.	end of month	月末
E.O.S.	end of season	季末
eq.	equivalent	等值的，等量的
e.q.m.	equal quantity monthly	每月相等的数量
Et.seq.	Et sequential (and other things)	及以下所综述的
Et.al.	Et. alibi (and elsewhere)	等等
e.t.a.; eta; ETA	Estimated (expected) time of arrival	预计到时间
etc.	et cetera (L.)=and others	等等
ETCL; etcl	expected time of commencement of loading	预计开装时间
etd; ETD	estimated (expected) time of departure	预计离港时间
ETDEL	expected of time of delivery	预计交货时间
ETFD	expected time of finishing discharging	预计卸完时间
ETFL	expected time of finishing loading	预计装完时间
ex	per or out of	搭乘
ex.	excluding	除外
	example	例子；样本
Exch.	exchange	兑换；汇兑
Excl.	exclusive or excluding	除外
ex.int.	ex interest	无利息
exp.	export	出口
Exs.	expenses	费用
Ext.	extra	特别的；额外的

F

F	degree Fahrenheit	华氏度数
F.A.	free alongside (ship)	（船）边交货
f/a/a; F.A.A.	free from all average	分损不赔（保险用语）
f.a.c.	fast as soon as possible	尽快
f.a.q.; F.A.Q.	fair average quality	大路货；中等品质
f.a.s.; F.A.S.	free alongside ship	船边交货价
F.B.	freight bill	运费单
fc	franc	法郎
Fch.	frachise	免赔率（一般指相对的）
FCL	Full Container Load	整箱货
F.C.&.S.	free of capture and seizure clause	战争险不保条款
f.e.	for example	例如
Feb.	February	二月
f.f.a.	free from alongside	船边交货价
f.g.a.; F.G.A.	free from general average	共同海损不赔
f.i.	for instance	例如
	free in	船方不负担装船费
fig.	figure	数字
f.i.o.	free in and out	船方不负担装卸费
f.i.o.s.	free in, out and stowed	船方不负担装卸费及理舱费
f.i.o.s.t.	free in, out, stowed and trimmed	船方不负担装卸费、理舱费及平舱费
f.i.w.	free in wagon	承运人不负担装入货车费
F/O	in favor of	交付给……，以……为受益人
f.o.	free out	船方不负担卸货费

F.O.A.	free on aircraft	飞机上交货价
fo.vo.	filio verso=turn the page	转下页
f.o.r.; F.O.R.	free on rail	火车上交货价
f.o.s.; F.O.S.	free on steamer	船上交货价
f.o.b.; F.O.B.	free on board	船上交货价
F.O.B.S.	free on board stowed	包括理舱费在内的船上交货价
f.o.c.	free of charges	免费
f.ot.; fot	free on truck	卡车上交货价
F/P	fire policy	火灾保险单
F.P.	floating policy	总括保险单
F.P.A.	free from particular average	平安险
F.; Fr.	franc	法郎
frt.; frit.; fgt.	freight	运费
frt.ppd	freight prepaid	运费已预付
ft.	foot	英尺
ft.-lb.	foot-pound	英尺磅（功的单位）
f.w.d.	fresh water damage	淡水损失
fwd.	forward	前面；接下页
F.X.	foreign exchange	外汇

G

g.	gram	克；公分
G.A.; G/A	General Average	共同海损（保险用语）
gal.	gallon	加仑
gds.	goods	货物

gm	gram	克；公分
G.M.Q.	Good Merchantable Quality	上好可销品质
gr.	gross	总的；全体的；毛的（重量）
gr.; grm.	gram	克；公分
grs.wt.; G.w.; Gr.wt.	gross weight	毛重
g.s.w.	gross weight	装船毛重

H

h.; hr.	hour	一小时
H.D.	hook damage	钩损
H.O.	head office	总公司；总行
H.&O.	hook and oil damage	钩损和油损
Hund.	hundred	百
h.w.d.	heavy weather damage	恶劣气候损坏

I

I.C.C.	International Chamber of Commerce	国际商会
ICC	Institute Cargo Clauses	（伦敦保险）协会货物条款
Id.	idem (the same)	同样
i.e.	id est (that is)	即；就是
Imp.	import	进口
in.	inch	英寸
	interest	利息
In trans.	In transit (on the way)	在运输途中
Insp.	inspection	检验

Insur.; Ins.	Insurance	保险
inst.	instant	本月
Inst.cls.	Institute clauses	伦敦协会保险条款
Int.	Interest	利息
inv.	invoice	发票
I.O.P.	irrespective of percentage	不计免赔率（保险用语）
I/P	insurance policy	保险单
I.Q.	Idem quod (the same as)	同样
ISO	International Organization for Standardization	国际标准化组织
it.	item	项目；条款
ITV	Internal Transfer Vehicle	码头内运输车

J

J. and/or l.o.	Jettison and/or loss overboard	抛弃或落水损失
Jan.	January	一月
Jul.	July	七月
Jun.	June	六月

K

kilo; kg.	kilogramme	公斤；千克
kl.	kilolitre	公升；升
km.	kilometre	千米；公里
km²	square kilometre	平方千米；平方公里
km³	cubic kilometre	立方千米；立方公里

L

L/A	letter of authority	授权书
l.; lit.	litre	公升
Lb.	pound	磅
L/C	letter of credit	信用证
LCL	Less than a full Container Load Cargo	非整装箱货；拼箱货
ldg.	loading	装货；装载
L/G	letter of guarantee	保证书
lkge	leakage	渗漏
Lkge & bkge	leakage and breakage	渗漏及破碎
L.T.; L/T	long ton	长吨
Ltd.	Limited	有限

M

m.	metre	公尺
	mile	英里
m²	spuare metre	平方米；平方公尺
m³	cubic metre	立方米；立方公尺
max.	maximum	最高
Mar.	March	三月
M.B.D. or Mchy.dge	Machinery Breakdown Damage	机器损坏
mdse.	merchandise	货物；商品
Memo.	memorandum	备忘录
Messrs.	Messieurs	先生（复数）
M.Ex.C.	Marine Extension clause	海运扩展条款

mfd.	manufactured	制造的
mfr.	manufacturer	厂商；制造商
mg.	milligram	毫克
mi.	mile	英里
MI.	marine insurance	海险
M.I.C.C.	Marine Insrrance Cargo Clause	海上运输货物保险条款
mil.; ml.	millilitre	毫升
min.	minimum	最低；最小；起码
M.I.P.	Marine Insurance Policy	海险保险单
mk.	mark	唛头；商标
mm	millimetre	毫米；公厘
mm³	cubic millimetre	立方毫米
M/R	Mate's Receipt	收货单；大幅收据
Mr.	mister	先生
m.s.; m/s	motorship	轮船
M/S	months after sight	见票后 XX 月付款
M/T, m.t.	metric ton	公吨
M/T	mail transfer	信汇
M.Y.	marshalling yard	集装箱编号场

N

N/A	Non Acceptance	不承兑
Nav.	navigating or navigation	航行
N.B.	nota bene (take notice)	注意
N.C.V.	no commercial value	无商业价值

N.D.	not dated	不记载日期
N.d.	non delivery	提货不着
nil	nothing	无
N.M.	No Mark	无标志
Nom.	Nominal	名称
Nov.	November	十一月
N/P	No Payment	拒绝付款
N.W.; Nt.Wt.	Net weight	净重
N.Y.	New York	纽约

O

o/a	on account of	记……账
o/b	on or before	在或在……以前
O/B	on board	（装）在船上
O/C	open cover	预保合同
Oc.B/L	Ocean bill of lading	海运运输提单
OCP	Overland Common Point	内陆共同点
Oct.	October	十月
O.M.C.C.	Ocean Marine Cargo Clause	海洋运输货物条款
On a/c	on account	记账；挂账
O.P.	open policy	预保单
orig.	original	正本
oz.	ounce; ounces	盎司；英两
oz.apoth	ounce apothecary	药衡盎司
oz.av.	ounce avoirdupois	常衡盎司
oz.tr.	ounce troy (or fine ounce)	金衡盎司

P

P.	per	每
	page	页
P/a; P/AV.	particular average	单独海损
p.a.	per annum	每年
p.c.	per centum	百分比率
P.C.	Price Current	市价
pce.; pc	piece	件；个；只；块；匹
pch.	parcel	小包
P'd.; pd.	paid	已付
P.I.C.C.	The People's Insurance Company of China	中国人民保险公司
pkg.	package	包裹；件
P.O.B.	post office box	邮箱；信箱
P.P.	Parcel Post	邮包
ppd.	prepaid	预付
ppt.	prompt loading	即期装船
pr.	pair	双，对
	price	价格
prem.; pm	premium	保险费
pro raia.	proportionally	按比例
prox.	proximo	下月
P.T.O.	please turn over	请阅背面

Q

q.	quintal	百公斤；公担
Q.	quantity	数量
Qlty.	quality	品质
Qt.	quart	夸脱（=1/4 加仑）

R

R.; r.; Ry.	railway	铁路
re.	with reference to	关于
rect.; Recpt.	Receipt	收据
rd.	road	路
R.D.C.	Running down clause	碰撞条款
Ref.	reference	参考（号）
Reg.; Regd.	Registered	登记；挂号
r.i.	re-insurance	再保险
R.M.	remittance	汇款
R.O.D.	Rust Oxidation and Discolouration	锈损、氧化和变色

S

S/D	sight draft	即期汇票
s.b.s.	surveyed before shipment	装运前进行检验
Sept.	September	九月
SHEX.	Sundays and holidays excepted	星期天和假日除外
shipt.	shipment	装运；装载
S.I.	Sum insured	保险金额

sig	signature	署名；签字
S.G.		英国劳哈士保险单的一种格式名称
Sgd.	Signed	已签署；签字
Sld.	Sailed	已开航
Sling L.	Sling loss	吊钩损失
S/N	shipping note	装船通知
S.O.	shipping order	装货单；下货纸
S/O	shipowner	船东
sq.cm.	square centimetre	平方厘米
sq.ft.	square foot	平方英尺
sq.in.	square inch	平方英寸
sq.km.	square kilometre	平方千米；平方公里
sq.yd.	square yard	平方码
S.R.	Strike risks	罢工险
S.R.C.C.	Strike, Riots and Civil Commotions	罢工、暴动、内乱险
s.s.; ss.; s/s	steamship	轮船
s/t; s.t.; sh.t.	short ton (2,000lb.)	短吨
st.	street	街
std.	standard	标准
stg.	sterling	英币
S/W	Shipper's weight	发货人提出的重量
S.W.D.	Sea water damage	海水损失
str.	steamer	轮船
supp.	supplement	补遗；附录；补充

T

T.	ton	吨
tal.qual.	talis quality = just as they come; average quality	平均品质
teleg.	telegram, telegraph	电报
thro.	through	经由；联运
thru.	through	经由；联运
TOFC	Trailer on Flat Car	平板车装运载箱拖车
T.P.N.D.	theft, pilferage & non-delivery	盗窃及提货不着险
T/S	transshipment	转船
T.T.	Telegraphic Transfer	电汇
T/R	Trust Receipt	信托收据

U

U.C.P.	Uniform Customs and Practice for Documentary Credits	跟单信用证统一惯例
U/D	Under-deck	舱内
Ult.	ultino	上月
U/rs.	Underwriters	保险人
U.T.	Unlimited transshipment	无限制性的转船
U/W	Underwriter	保险人

V

ves.	vessel	船
via	by way of	经过，经由
Viz.	Videlicet (namely)	即；就是

voy	voyage	航海；航行；航次
v.s.	vide supra (see above)	参阅上文

W

W.A.	with Average	水渍险
W.B.	Way Bill	运单
Whse.	Warehouse	仓库
W.P.A.	With Particular Average	水渍险
Wgt.; Wt	Weight	重量
W.R.	war risk	战争险
w.r.o.	war risk only	仅保战争险
W/T	with transshipment	转船
wt.	weight	重量
w/w; w-w; whse-whse	warehouse warrent; warehouse to warehouse	仓库；从此仓库到另一个仓库

Y

Y.A.R.	York-Antwerp Rules	约克—安特卫普规则（即国际共同海损规则）
Y.B.	yearbook	年鉴
yd.	yard	码
yr.	year	年
	your	你们的

参考文献

1. Friffin, Jack. *The New Handbook of Business Letters*. Pinctice Hall, 1993
2. Harris, J. *Introducing Writing*. London: Penguin Book Ltd., 1993
3. *Incoterms 2000*, ICC Publication No. 560
4. *The Uniform Customs and Practice for Documentary Credits*, 1993 Revision, ICC Publication No. 500
5. 蔡惠伟编著. 外经贸函电教程. 上海: 华东理工大学出版社, 2007
6. 法小鹰、胡敏主编. 外贸英语单证与函电. 上海: 复旦大学出版社, 2008
7. 李国平、程艳红编著. 外贸英语函电. 北京: 北京大学出版社, 2008
8. 廖瑛编著. 实用外贸谈判英语. 北京: 中国对外经济贸易出版社, 2005
9. 陆墨珠编著. 国际商务函电(第四版). 北京: 中国对外经济贸易出版社, 2002
10. 罗恩·霍尔特、尼克·桑普森著. 国际商业书信. 北京: 外语教学与研究出版社, 1999
11. 吕红军编著. 国际货物贸易实务. 北京: 中国商务出版社, 2005
12. 孟庆升主编. 实用汉英外经贸翻译手册. 天津: 天津科技翻译出版公司, 1997
13. 聂相玲编著. 外贸单证与函电. 北京: 中国经济出版社, 2008
14. 隋思忠主编. 外贸英语函电. 大连: 东北财经大学出版社, 2007
15. 王慧敏编著. 外贸函电. 北京: 北京大学出版社, 2005
16. 王万义、李宁主编. 外贸英文函电实用教程. 北京: 中国商务出版社, 2008
17. 徐明莹、李强主编. 无敌商务英语信函. 大连: 大连理工大学出版社, 2009
18. 尹小莹、杨润辉编著. 外贸英语函电——商务英语应用文写作(第四版). 西安: 西安交通大学出版社, 2008
19. 张华慧. 英语商务书信实战写作案例110. 大连: 大连理工大学出版社, 2010
20. 赵银德编著. 外贸函电. 北京: 机械工业出版社, 2006
21. 诸葛霖、王燕希. 外贸英文书信. 北京: 对外经济贸易大学出版社, 2007

《实用进出口函电写作》
练习及参考答案

胡茵芃　　孟庆升　　编著

南开大学出版社

天　津

Contents

Contents

练习部分

Unit 1　Introduction to Letter and Email Writing

信函和电子邮件写作概述

练　习

I.　Translate the following job titles.

1. Accounting Manager
2. Assistant Manager
3. Business Controller
4. Receptionist
5. Deputy General Manager
6. Export Sales Manager
7. Financial Controller
8. General Manager/President
9. General Manager Assistant
10. Import Liaison Staff
11. Maintenance Engineer
12. Market Development Manager
13. Marketing Manager
14. Marketing Executive
15. Marketing/Sales Representative
16. Operational Manager
17. Plant/Factory Manager
18. Sales Coordinator
19. Sales Executive
20. Service Manager

II.　Make corrections in the format of the envelope.

Carbonite Corp.

Robert Kastens

Second Avenue 1333

Connecticut, Milford 06460

STAMP

Ms. Yvette Carlson

Haley-Richardson Company

14562 Detroit, MI

One Perry Park Plaza

III. Compare the following two sentences in the group and point out which sentence is more polite and considerate.

Group 1

1. We feel sure that you will be entirely satisfied.
2. We do not believe you will have cause for dissatisfaction.

Group 2

1. Perhaps next time we can send you what you require.
2. We regret our inability to serve you at this time.

Group 3

1. We won't be able to send you the brochure this month.
2. We will send you the brochure next month.

Group 4

1. This letter is to inform you of an important change in our policy concerning insurance.
2. Since you are our regular customer, we are writing to let you know about our important policy change in insurance.

Group 5

1. We offer the typewriter ribbons in three colors: black, blue, and green.
2. Take your pick of typewriter ribbons in three colors: black, blue, and green.

Group 6

1. We cannot offer you any refunds because the goods you returned are dirty and unusable.
2. You could obtain a refund if the goods you returned had remained clean and useable.

Group 7

1. The large scale of sales of our products will make your company more profitable.
2. You will find that our product will sell rapidly and afford you a profit margin.

Group 8

1. We are happy to tell you that we may ship the goods after September 8.
2. We are sorry that we cannot ship the goods until September 8.

Group 9

1. In the event that you speak to Mr. Wood in regard to production, ask him to give consideration to the delivery schedule.
2. If you speak to Mr. Wood about production, ask him to consider the delivery schedule.

Group 10

1. We are anxious to start business with you.
2. We are writing to you with a view to entering into business relations with you.

IV. Complete the following letter with its necessary elements on the lines provided.

此信是回复给 W. J. Parker 先生的，需通过 IHK 公司的 Judith Brown 小姐转交。Parker 先生来信的编号为 21/J，本信的编号为 06/AD。随信附上收据及样品介绍。此信是销售部 Mark Blumsky 写的，秘书 Amy Walters 打的。

_____

Your ref: _____

_____ : 06/AD

Mr. W. J. Parker

_____

IHK Company

28 Sunnyville Road

London N9 9ST

Dear Mr. Parker,

_____

We thank you for your Order NO. 589 of June 5 and have to inform you that we are expecting delivery of this kind of boots not later than the end of the next week…

We are glad to know that the two pairs previously supplied have given you satisfaction, as we recognize that a satisfied customer is our best advertisement.

We enclose the receipt of payment for your previous purchases, as requested.

Yours sincerely,

_____

Mark Blumsky

_____

V.　Arrange the following parts of a letter in the correct order and form, either in block style or modified block style. Address an envelope for the letter.

(1)　Sender's name: Tianjin Embroidery Export Corporation

(2)　Sender's address: 78 Hongxing Road, Hebei District, Tianjin 300543, China

(3)　Sender's telephone: +86-22-24561447

(4)　Sender's website: http://www.tjeec.com

(5)　Sender's fax: +86-22-24569865

(6)　Receiver's address: 58 Lancaster House, Manchester, M14 5RX, UK

(7)　Receiver's name: Manchester Trading Company

(8)　Salutation: Dear Sirs

(9)　Complimentary close: …

(10)　Body of the letter:

We have learned your name from the Chamber of Commerce of New York, and are writing to you with the hope of establishing business relations with you.

We specialize in the exportation of Chinese Embroideries which have enjoyed great popularity in world market. We enclose a copy of our latest price list for your reference and hope that you would let us know if any item is of interest to you.

(11)　Date: (today's date)

(12)　Enclosure: 1 price list

(13)　Signature: (your own name) (your position title: sales manager)

(14)　Carbon copy notation: Mr. James Brown

(15)　Attention line: Marketing Manager

(16)　Subject line: Embroideries

(17)　Reference number: Our ref.: HNE/325, Your ref: PLK/lsx

VI.　Translate the following words or phrases into Chinese.

1.　attachment

2.　computer virus

3.　junk mail

4.　recipient

5.　website link

6.　download

7.　netiquette

8.　incoming fax messages

9.　resolution

10.　scanner

11.　printer

12.　terminal

13.　transmit

14.　unattended

15.　autodialing

16.　fax cover

17.　signature block

18.　text

19.　digital photo

20.　salutation

21.　complimentary close

22.　emoticon

23.　default font

24.　messy code

25.　install

26.　click

27.　format

28.　folder

29.　homepage

30.　browser

VII. Translate the following email into Chinese.

From: Gale Xue <galexue@hotmail.com

Date: Thursday, August 27, 2009, 4:35 PM

To: David Smith <fetool@publicsz.net.com>

Subject: Specific Inquiry for Items No. 12 and 19

Dear Mr. Smith,

Today we have received 6 samples of your products Items No. 12 and 19 as requested in our email inquiry of August 20.

Please offer us your best export prices for these two items based on purchase in lots of 1,000 pcs of each item. We prefer that your quotations be CFR Vancouver.

We shall appreciate your prompt response to the above request.

Yours sincerely,

Gale Xue

Unit 2　Credit Inquiry

信用查询

练习

I.　Choose the best answer.

1.　For information ＿＿＿ our ＿＿＿ we refer you to the Bank of China, Shanghai Branch.

A. regards, credit standing
B. as to, standing credit
C. involving, credit stand
D. concerning, credit standing

2.　We understand that you will treat this information as ＿＿＿.

A. confidence
B. confident
C. confidential
D. confidently

3.　Any information you kindly give us ＿＿＿ in strict confidence and you are free from any responsibility.

A. will treat
B. will be treated
C. is treated
D. treats

4.　Will you please inform us, ＿＿＿, of the extent of their resources and their reputation as well?

A. with confidence
B. in confidence
C. as confidential
D. of confidentially

5.　We shall appreciate ＿＿＿ us ＿＿＿ an opinion as to the credit standing, respectability and responsibility of the following firm.

A. your providing, with
B. provided, by
C. to provide, with
D. your provision to, by

6.　＿＿＿ your decision to place regular orders with us, we respectfully request that you ＿＿＿ us with two references for the initial purchase.

A. As we thank, should give
B. When appreciating, will supply
C. Because we thank, provide
D. While appreciating, furnish

7.　Will you please let us know ＿＿＿ your experience ＿＿＿ in your dealing with him?

A. how, are
B. what, has been
C. which, is
D. that, have had

8.　This firm is a ＿＿＿ private company of import and export, ＿＿＿ in 1981.

A. high, registered
B. height of, to register
C. highly, registered
D. highest, to register

9.　We ＿＿＿ consider the said firm quite reliable for ＿＿＿ engagement as you mentioned.

A. should, such an
B. will, such as
C. shall, such a
D. would, such like

10.　Any information you kindly give us will be treated in strict confidence and ＿＿＿ on your part.

A. without any responsibility

B. hasn't any responsibility

C. is no responsibility

D. is not to have responsibility

II.   Fill in the blanks with proper words.

1. We believe that business transactions _____ this firm will prove satisfactory.

2. This company enjoys the fullest respect and unquestionable confidence _____ the business world.

3. We must advise you to regard their request for credit _____ caution.

4. Would you please let us have a report _____ the reputation and financial standing of the firm?

5. They have been a credit customer _____ ours.

6. It has always paid to its account _____ time.

7. We should be grateful if you would tell us _____ the above-mentioned company is reliable in their dealing with you.

8. We recommend Canadian Trading Co. Ltd. to you _____ no reservations.

9. We should like to know the financial and credit standing _____ the above-mentioned company.

10. We should also like your advice _____ the maximum amount for which it would be safe to grant credit on a quarterly account.

III.   Translate the following sentences into Chinese.

1. The above-mentioned information is given on the understanding that it is treated as strictly confidential.

2. The firm under inquiry enjoys a high reputation in the business circles for their punctuality in meeting obligation.

3. In answer to your inquiry of December 2, we should not hesitate to trust Mr. Jiang for any amount that he might order.

4. We feel free to say that you will find your dealings with him not only entirely satisfactory, but also agreeable personally.

5. We have done business with both of these firms for 5 years and I am sure that they will be willing to furnish you with any information you ask for.

6. Will you favor us two references as we have had no business transactions with you until now?

7. We should be grateful if you would let us know whether this credit is justified in view of their record in meeting payment dates.

8. The Victor Trading Corporation, with whom we have had considerable transactions for the past 10 years, would provide you with any information relative to our business standing.

9. The firm with whom we intend to deal has referred us to you for particulars respecting their business standing and trustworthiness.

10. Our records show that they have never failed to meet out bills since they opened an account with us. The monthly limit of credit that we feel we may safely grant them is approximately US$ 3,000. In addition, their sincere attitude toward trade and their extensive business activities merit high esteem.

IV.　Translate the following sentences into English.

1.　在贵市的 ABC 银行将提供贵方要求的有关我方资信状况的信息。

2.　如能对上述公司的财务状况和可靠性提出你方的意见，我方将十分感激。

3.　我们将很感激你们在这一方面提供给我方的任何信息。

4.　他们总是能够因准时交货、适中的价格和优异的质量而使客户彻底满意。

5.　他们在国内外的业务联系很广，其财务状况相当稳健。

6.　你方在 2 月 5 日来信中提到的那样一笔数额的信用贷款似乎是安全的。

7.　该公司的困境在于管理不善，尤其是超额贸易。

8.　由于他们准时履行义务，所以在贸易界享有很好的信誉。

9.　该公司信誉良好，资金储备雄厚。

10.　如果能让我们知道他们的财务状况是否相当好，那么我方将十分高兴。

V.　Translate the following letters.

(1)

敬启者：

　　ABC 公司现提出要做我公司的代理，销售我方的液晶显示器，并介绍我公司向贵行了解该公司的信用、业务能力和信誉的详细情况。

　　如贵行对该公司就上述几点提出坦率意见，我方将不胜感激。

　　贵行提供的任何资料，我方将严格保密。

　　感谢贵行的协助。

谨上

(2)

Dear Sirs,

We have received an order from Batik Corporation, Jakarta, with which you are now doing business and the firm gives us your name as a reference.

We shall be grateful if you will let us have the following information:

1.　How long have you been in business relations with the firm?

2.　What credit limit have you placed on their account?

3.　How promptly are terms met?

4.　Is there any account that is currently outstanding?

Any information you may give us will be treated as strictly confidential and expenses occurring from this inquiry will be gladly paid by us upon receipt of your bill.

Yours faithfully,

Unit 3　Establishing Business Relations

建立贸易关系

练 习

I. Find out the mistakes in the following sentences and make corrections. There is one mistake in each sentence.

1. We would appreciate if you could give us your quotation.
2. Some copies of our latest catalogs are being airmailed to you on separate cover.
3. Enclose please find a catalog which may be of some help to you in selecting items.
4. We informed that you are in the market for Men's Shirts.
5. If the products are of interesting to you, please let us know without any delay.
6. We approach with you for the delivery of the goods.
7. We are writing you at the hope of entering into business relations with you.
8. We have obtained your name and address to Singapore Chamber of Commerce.
9. We are a private enterprise trading with both the import and export of computer software.
10. We wish to enter business relations with your company for the supply of light industrial products.

II. Choose the correct word to complete each sentence.

quality	enter	opportunity	specialize in	expand	reasonable
requirements	market	information	leading	approach	

1. We have learned from the Commercial Counselor's Office of our Embassy in your country that you are in the _____ for Chinese electronic products.
2. We introduce ourselves as _____ exporters of all kinds of Chinese goods, especially of Silk Handkerchief.
3. We would like to _____ into business relations with you.
4. Our products are of high _____ and _____ price, and have long enjoyed a great fame at home and abroad.
5. We enclose a catalog for your _____ and trust some of the items will be of interest to you.
6. We wish to inform you that we _____ this line and hope to build up trade relations with you.
7. We recommend that you _____ our branch office for the matter directly.

8. By joint efforts we can _____ both friendship and business.

9. We would advise you to get in touch with them for your _____.

10. We take this _____ to recommend our new products.

III. Choose the best answer.

1. We would like to take this _____ to establish business relations with you.

A. opening   B. opportunity   C. step   D. advantage

2. We are sending you the samples _____ requested.

A. by   B. for   C. as   D. are

3. We are sure that both of our companies will _____ from the joint venture.

A. make benefit   B. benefit   C. be benefited   D. mutual benefit

4. We are _____ a copy of our catalog for your reference.

A. send   B. covering   C. closed   D. enclosing

5. We trust that you will find our goods _____.

A. attracting   B. to be attractive   C. attract your attention   D. attractive

6. Our products enjoy _____ in world market.

A. most popular   B. great popularity   C. good seller   D. selling fast

7. We are anxious to _____ the market for our products, which at present enjoy a limited sale in Europe.

A. increase   B. enlarge   C. expand   D. extend

8. If any of the items is _____ to you, please let us know.

A. interest   B. interesting   C. interested   D. interests

9. We would _____ very much if you send us some samples immediately.

A. thank you   B. appreciate it   C. appreciate   D. appreciate you

10. We should be grateful if you would send us your detailed list of all the items _____ for export.

A. providing   B. available   C. dealing   D. stock

11. Our products are of better quality than _____ from other countries.

A. this   B. that   C. those   D. it

12. We are very pleased _____ business relations with your firm.

A. to enter   B. to enter into   C. entering into   D. entering

13. Your letter _____ June 2 has been received by us.

A. in   B. at   C. from   D. of

14. We are a state-operated corporation _____ both the import and export of Medical Instruments.

A. handling   B. trading   C. dealing   D. making

15. We have pleasure in enclosing the samples _____ for in your letter dated December 12.

A. asking   B. asked   C. ask   D. asks

16. Your firm has been referred to us by the Fuji Co. of Japan, _____ we have done business for many years.

A. which   B. with that   C. whom   D. with whom

17. We will _____ you as soon as frozen foodstuffs come to the market.

A. contact with   B. contact   C. get in touch   D. get contact

18. For your selection, we are sending you a list of the items which might be suitable _____ your market requirements.

A. for   B. at   C. on   D. to

19. As we deal _____ refrigerators, we are glad to make you the following offer for your consideration.

A. for   B. at   C. with   D. in

20. We are willing to establish business relations with you on the _____ of equality and mutual benefit.

A. base   B. basis   C. bases   D. based

IV. Translate the following sentences into English.

1. 我公司是该地区电子产品的主要进口商之一。我方借此机会与贵方接洽，希望与贵方建立直接的贸易关系。
2. 我公司经营机械设备进出口业务已多年，我们的产品在许多国家享有盛誉。
3. 承蒙我国驻贵国大使馆商务参赞处介绍，我方得知了贵公司的名称和地址。
4. 我方了解到贵方是日用化学制品的制造商。我方有一客户欲购买贵国的化妆品。如能立即航寄目前可供货物的目录及价目表，我方将不胜感激。
5. 有关我方的资信状况，请向中国银行上海分行查询。
6. 兹具函自荐，我方是一家中国国营公司，专营电器产品。
7. 现另邮寄修订目录和价目表各一份。希望你方会对我方的瓷器感兴趣。
8. 所附说明书对每种型号的优点均有详细说明。
9. 现寄去我方全部瓷器的综合目录一份，希望贵方会对价格、质量和图案式样感到满意。
10. 我方备货充足，现寄上所需各花色款式图形。

V. Translate the following email and letter.

(1)

Dear Mr. Ma,

Thank you for your email dated 31 May, inquiring about our company and our products.

Attached are our latest brochures listing all the types of bicycles we manufacture as well as our financial statement for the year ending 31 last December.

We have not sold our products in the European market in the past, and we would be delighted to do business with your company.

Please go through the attachment. We would be happy to answer any questions that may arise.

We are looking forward to hearing from you.

Yours sincerely,

(2)

敬启者：

我们同 BPD 公司成功合作多年。从该公司得知贵公司经营各种纺织品材料的进出口。

我们是英格兰主要的羊毛毛衣经销商之一，并有意与贵方建立贸易关系，从贵公司进口羊毛毛衣。

如能提供各种毛衣的细节和价格，并附带照片和规格，我们将不胜感激。

期待贵公司早日且有利的回复。

谨上

Unit 4　Inquiry

询　盘

练习

I. Try to find out the mistakes and make corrections. There is one mistake in each sentence.

1. We welcome you for your inquiry of April 23 and the given catalog.
2. If your prices are competitive, we are prepared to order the sewing machines for large quantity.
3. We hope to include the business to our mutual benefit.
4. As regard walnut meat, we would inform you that the few parcels we have at present are under offer elsewhere.
5. If your price is on line, we will send you an order for 20,000 metric tons.
6. We shall place a large order for Women's Underwear from you, if the time of delivery is acceptable to us.
7. Being specialized in the import of garments, we express our desire to trade with you at this line.

II. Choose the best answer.

1. We thank you for your letter of May 17 and the _____ catalog.

A. sent　　　　　　　B. enclosed　　　　　　C. given　　　　　　D. presented

2. The letter we sent last week is an inquiry _____ color TV sets.

A. about　　　　　　B. for　　　　　　　　C. of　　　　　　　D. as

3. If you are interested, we will send you a sample lot _____ charge.

A. within　　　　　　B. with　　　　　　　C. for　　　　　　　D. free of

4. Your full cooperation _____.

A. will appreciate it very much　　　　　B. is to be appreciated

C. will be appreciated it　　　　　　　　D. will be appreciated greatly

5. This price is _____ of our 5% commission.

A. includes　　　　　B. covering　　　　　C. inclusive　　　　　D. including

6. We have received your inquiry of 15 October _____ you advise us of your interest in Cashmere.

A. in which　　　　　B. from which　　　　C. at which　　　　　D. which

7. We should be most obliged if you would send us your detailed list of all the items you _____ for export.

A. store   B. have   C. stock   D. deal

8. Our illustrated catalog _____ shows various types of bathroom fittings and their available sizes.

A. enclosed   B. that enclosed   C. is enclosed   D. which enclosed

9. I want to acquaint myself _____ the supply position of steel products.

A. of   B. with   C. for   D. about

10. Our new low-cost solutions may be _____ particular interest to you.

A. in   B. with   C. for   D. of

11. They found an opportunity to purchase six _____ leather shoes.

A. thousand pairs   B. thousand pair of C. thousands of pair D. thousand pairs of

12. What kind of products do you think _____ particularly interested _____?

A. are they, in   B. they are, in   C. are they, /   D. they are, /

13. It may interest you to know that there is a good demand here for Chinese Black Tea _____ prices.

A. at moderate   B. in cheap   C. for low   D. on dear

14. Please reply as soon as possible, _____ the earliest shipment date and terms of payment.

A. stated   B. as stated   C. stating   D. state

15. We inquire _____ glassware available _____ export.

A. for, to   B. for, for   C. to, for   D. of, about

16. We are pleased _____ your inquiry of July 12 for our children bedding.

A. to receiving   B. as received   C. receiving   D. to have

17. There is a ready demand in Europe _____ leather gloves _____ high quality

A. for, with   B. for, of   C. at, with   D. in, of

18. We assure you _____ our full cooperation.

A. for   B. at   C. with   D. of

19. We would allow you a discount _____ 2%.

A. with   B. for   C. on   D. of

20. We are happy to receive your letter _____ a catalog of our products.

A. asking   B. inquiring   C. requesting   D. request

21. From the enclosed price list you will see that we have a large _____ of ladies' hats.

A. assort   B. assortment   C. varieties   D. selection

22. The sale of our products has been _____ the decline these years.

A. at   B. down   C. under   D. on

23. We hope to receive your quotation with details _____ the possible time of shipment.

A. to include   B. to be included   C. including   D. being included

24. Will you please send us your prices for the items _____ below?

A. listing   B. being listed   C. to list   D. listed

25. We shall appreciate _____ us FOB Guangzhou.

A. you quote   B. your quoting   C. you to quote   D. your being quoted

26. If you can supply your goods immediately, we will _____ to place a prompt trial order.

A. be prepared   B. be preparing   C. prepare   D. preparing

27. We shall be pleased to receive from you all necessary information _____ these goods.

A. regarding   B. in regard   C. as regard   D. with regard

28. As we are one of the leading importers in this line, we are _____ to handle large quantities.

A. at a position   B. in a position   C. on a position   D. of a position

III. Choose the right answers.

(1)

A. production line   B. introduced   C. stand   D. displayed   E. Provided

Dear Mr. Simpson,

China Import and Export Fair will be held from April 15 to April 20. Some of our new products will be __1__ at the fair. You will find new products which should be of special interest to you. Furthermore, we have __2__ substantial improvements in our __3__ which would also be of interest to you.

We would be very happy if you could visit our __4__ number 398 in Exhibit Hall No. 2. After the visit to the fair, you are welcome to our factory.

__5__ you have decided on such a visit, we will forward you a formal invitation, with which you can apply for an entry visa.

We are looking forward to your favorable reply.

Yours sincerely,

(2)

A. describe   B. familiarize   C. regarding   D. toll-free   E. to my attention

Dear Mr. Lee,

Your email of inquiry __1__ our products line has been brought __2__ and I would like to thank you for your interest in our products.

I have attached a price list and data sheets which __3__ our full line of products that serve the automobile industry. This should help to __4__ you with our family of products and the high quality of our equipment.

If you have any further questions, please call us at our __5__ number, (800)867952555.

Thank you again for your interest.

Yours sincerely,

IV. Fill in the blanks with the words and phrases given below.

available	as per	enjoy great popularity	at your request
on the basis of	enclosed	for your reference	there is room for
free of charge	is inclusive of		

1. We want to find out if Article No. 23 is _____.
2. Please let us have your lowest quotation _____ CFR London.
3. _____ low-grade shoes in our market.
4. The quality must be exactly the same as that of the _____ samples.
5. Our products _____ in world market.
6. If you are interested, we will send you a sample _____.
7. _____ your Inquiry No. 456, we are sending you a catalog and a sample book for your reference.
8. This price _____ your 5% commission.
9. Catalogs and brochures of our products will be sent _____.
10. We are sending you under separate cover two catalogs and a price list _____.

V. Fill in the blanks with proper prepositions.

1. We are _____ the cotton goods business, especially _____ your line, and also handle other goods _____ the Pakistan market.
2. The British Embassy _____ Beijing has advised us to get _____ touch _____ you concerning the wholesale business _____ portable computers.
3. We understand _____ your advertisement _____ *Electric* that you are an exporter _____ silver spoons.
4. _____ regular purchase _____ quantities _____ not less than five gross of individual items we would allow you a discount of 10%.
5. We thank you for your inquiry _____ June 11.
6. We are much thankful _____ your inquiry.
7. Thank you for your inquiry _____ our vacuum cleaners.
8. We have the pleasure of sending you, _____ separate cover, a new catalog which lists the

complete line _____ our sporting goods.

9. _____ reply to your letter of July 23, we are enclosing the patterns of our goods _____ prices and date _____ delivery.

10. Would you please send us _____ airmail your trade particulars regarding the named goods in our inquiry note?

11. A full range _____ samples has been forwarded to you _____ separate post.

VI. Translate the following sentences into English.

1. 请报贵方最优惠的上海到岸价，包括我方 3%的佣金，并告知最早的装运期。

2. 如果贵方价格有竞争力的话，我方欲订购三百台液晶显示器。

3. 为了便于贵方了解我方产品，我们立即航寄我方最新的目录数份、样品簿 2 份以供贵方参考。

4. 随函附上我方第 235 号询价单，请贵方报离岸价。

5. 一俟收到贵方的具体询盘，我方将传真告知。

6. 如果贵方订货数量大，价格还可以进一步考虑。

7. 我方打算在温哥华试销该商品，因为我们了解到该商品在此地有长期需求。

8. 我方随函附寄每件货物的照片和规格，相信你方能按照我方要求生产，并报出最优惠的价格。

9. 如果贵方报价可以接受，并且机器令人满意，我方会向贵方定期下订单。

10. 按惯例，我方通常从欧洲供应商处得到 5%的佣金。

VII. Translate the following sentences into Chinese.

1. Please quote your lowest price CIF Shanghai for each of the following items.

2. We have pleasure in enclosing our Inquiry No. 732 against which you are requested to make us an offer on FOB basis.

3. If you can supply goods of the type and quality required, we may place regular orders for large quantities.

4. Please give this Inquiry your prompt attention.

5. Regarding your letter of March 4 inquiring for men's shirts, we wish to inform you that this article falls within the scope of business activities of China National Textiles Import and Export Corporation, to whom we have forwarded your inquiry for their attention.

6. We have seen your advertisement in the *Textile Journal* and should be glad if you would send us patterns and prices of quality cotton piece goods available from stock.

7. One of our clients has obtained an import license to import US$20,000 worth of various kinds of wires. Please quote us your lowest prices with the best discount and the earliest date of delivery.

8. When replying or quoting, please indicate the number of this inquiry for easy identification.

9. If you are unable to supply goods exactly as specified, would you please offer goods of the nearest specifications?

10. There is a great demand for microwave ovens in our country. We appreciate it very much if you

could give us your attractive quotation for models available at present.

VIII. Translate the following letter into English.

> 敬启者：
>
> 　　贵公司在大连国际贸易交易会展席上展示的 G3 笔记本电脑给我方留下了深刻的印象。我们预测贵公司的产品是满足我方市场需求的最佳之选。
>
> 　　请您就附寄问卷上所列的产品，报与我方至大连的运费、保险费在内价，并请告知我方您最早的交货期、付款条件以及订购超过 2000 台的折扣情况。
>
> 　　期盼早日回复，并希望此次交易能成为我们双方日后长期贸易关系和互惠互利的良好开端。
>
> 谨上

IX. Write an email according to the given situation.

　　伦敦雷文贸易有限公司（London Lanwen Trading Co., Ltd.）的 Linda White 对深圳成明公司经营的棉毛巾感兴趣。经研究，打算对以下货号的产品进行询盘。请以 Linda White 的名义用以下给定的格式向深圳成明公司发去一封电子邮件。

Article Nos.	Quantity
XF25-23	1,000 pieces
XF33-21	1,000 pieces

> From: lindawhite_trade@lanwen.com
>
> To: master@szhchengming.com
>
> Date: Friday, September 2, 20＿＿. 15:23 pm
>
> Subject:
>
> Dear Sirs,
>
> Best regards,
>
> Linda White

X. Write a specific inquiry according to the following requirements.

客户要求：

1) 报第 12 号和 81 号台灯的最优惠价格。
2) 请寄产品规格，最好带插图。
3) 报价为 FOB 中国港口价。
4) 标明最低出口起订量。
5) 请告知包装、重量、交货及其他必要详情。

Unit 5　Sales Promotion
推 销 信

练　习

I. Choose the best answer.

1.　The customers are _____ opportunities to alter the program.

A. offering　　　　　　B. given　　　　　　　C. to be given　　　　D. allowed

2.　We produce decorative fabrics _____ different kinds.

A. in　　　　　　　　　B. for　　　　　　　　C. of　　　　　　　　D. with

3.　We should be pleased to send you any of our typewriters on approval _____ our own expense.

A. at　　　　　　　　　B. for　　　　　　　　C. on　　　　　　　　D. in

4.　We are offering your goods _____ the very high quality.

A. of　　　　　　　　　B. at　　　　　　　　C. for　　　　　　　　D. with

5.　Our display is _____ Stand 23, where you will find our new range of furniture.

A. in　　　　　　　　　B. on　　　　　　　　C. at　　　　　　　　D. under

6.　We wish to offer you the new "Rose" paint we have _____ to the market.

A. given　　　　　　　B. introduced　　　　C. recommended　　D. reported

7.　As a special attraction to the customers, we are _____ a free gift of a new heater for every order exceeding US$1,000.

A. offering　　　　　　B. giving　　　　　　C. paying　　　　　　D. sending

8.　We look forward to _____ trial order.

A. receiving your　　　B. receive from you　　C. receipt your　　　D. receipt of

9.　In _____ of quality, our make is superior.

A. terms　　　　　　　B. term　　　　　　　C. connection　　　　D. connections

10. There is a steady demand here _____ leather gloves.

A. in　　　　　　　　　B. of　　　　　　　　C. for　　　　　　　　D. on

11. All the models you saw _____ the fashion show are obtainable.

A. in　　　　　　　　　B. at　　　　　　　　C. on　　　　　　　　D. from

12. Our stocks are _____ low.

A. falling　　　　　　　B. running　　　　　　C. becoming　　　　D. going

II. Rewrite to combine the following groups of short sentences into two sentences each.

1. Fill in the enclosed order form. It takes only a moment. There is no need for a postage stamp. Never mind if you are not satisfied when you receive the purchase. You can return it to us. If it is within 15 days we will refund your money. We will do so promptly.

2. We hope you will place an order with us. You should order on the above-mentioned terms. We feel sure you will be satisfied with this initial order. We ensure that you have full information on the wide range of fabrics we can offer. We will arrange for Mr. Cook to call on you. He will do so if you will complete and return the enclosed order card. You can note on the card when it would be convenient.

III. Fill in the blanks with proper prepositions.

1. These offering products are the result of months of careful research, and likely to revolutionize all the methods _____ use at present.

2. We expect you to try out our products and realize that they will meet _____ your full satisfaction.

3. We wish to assure you once more that we intend to adhere _____ our policy of providing products at a competitive price.

4. Our trade is so large that our stocks have to be constantly replaced, so you may rest assured that everything we offer you is new and _____ the latest style.

5. Not having heard from you, we should be glad to know if there is any disadvantage _____ our terms which we could remove.

6. We feel sure you will find a ready sale _____ this excellent material and that your customers will be well satisfied with it.

7. In order to popularize these products, all the catalog prices are subject _____ a special discount of 10 percent during the month of March only.

8. The selling prices run from US$ 2 to US$ 8 per pair. Your commission would be 25%, one quarter of the selling price. If you will give us two or three names _____ references, we shall be glad to send you samples.

IV. Translate the following sentences into English.

1. 该货独有的优点可使之成为畅销品。
2. 为推销这些产品，目录上所列价格在 2 月份内均打九折的特别折扣。
3. 如有订购，本公司能马上供应现货，敬请惠顾其他产品。
4. 从 9 月 2 日开始，我们对所有存货均按平常最低报价再减 2%～4%供应。
5. 我们提供的毛线衫保证穿着舒适美观。
6. 潜在顾客可来我们的展品室看展品或产品的实际操作表演，取得实际操作检验。
7. 我们的顾客可以拨打免费电话索取产品介绍书或询问具体信息。
8. 我们的玩具由于价格公道、包装别致，在美国很受顾客欢迎。

V. Translate the following sales letters.

(1)

Dear Office Manager,

Few business folks these days would deny that the fax machine has become an indispensable tool. Instead of waiting days for a letter to cross the country, you can push a button and fax it in seconds. Instead of paying the high price for global express service to deliver your document, you can fax it anywhere in the world for the price of a phone call. Moreover, fax is much safer than the e-mail, which is liable to computer virus.

Our on-staff experts will install and try the machine for you, and help you determine which features will best meet your needs.

There is a 5-year guarantee and life maintenance with your machine.

Just give me a call, and you will have the machine at your service.

Sincerely yours,

(2)

From: xiazs_solar@meida.com
To: dsdy2004@yahoo.com
Date: Tuesday, October 23, 20_ _, 16:12 pm
Subject: New Product to be Introduced in the Market

Dear Sirs,

We are sure that you would be interested in the new "Meida" Hair Dryer which is to be placed on the market soon. Most of the good points of the earlier types have been covered into this appliance which possesses, besides, several novel features having been perfected by years of scientific research.

You will find that a special contrivance enables it to run on more than half the current required by appliances of equal capability. Further, most of the working parts are readily interchangeable and, in the event of their being damaged, they are thus easy to be replaced.

The special advantages it offers will make it a quick-selling line, and we are ready also to cooperate with you by launching a national advertising campaign. Moreover, we are ready to assist to the extent of half the cost of any local advertising.

Bearing in mind the rapid turnover which is likely to result, you will agree that the five percent commission we are prepared to offer you is extremely generous.

You will find attached leaflets describing this Hair Dryer and we look forward to your agreement to handle our product as the sole agent in your district.

Yours faithfully,

Z. S. Xia

Sales Manager

(3)

敬启者：

　　您还在为如何装帧您的重要文档而烦恼吗？您也许和大多数生意人一样很难找时间来经济地美化您的文档，这就是为什么拥有一位专业人士来管理您最重要的文件是很必要的。

　　我们 Hope 文档公司拥有美化文档的经验和技术。我们可以为您提供一次免费的体验，让您切身感受到仅支付低廉的费用也可以让您的文档美轮美奂。

　　如您愿意，请致电我公司免费电话 800-884-445，与工作人员约定您的体验时间。

谨上

VI. As the sales manager for Boot Company, write a sales letter for your product based on the following points.

（1）高质量的皮靴

（2）公司重质量，每双皮靴均按一定规格加工

（3）选用高级皮革

（4）雇用经验丰富的工匠

（5）成品美观无皱，内衬牛皮

（6）有 22 种式样（见商品目录）

（7）价格：按照不同式样，每双由 95 美元至 300 美元不等

Unit 6　Offer

报　盘

I. Choose the best answer.

1.　A 3% discount was granted only _____ your order exceeds US$5,000.00.

A. depends on
B. for condition that
C. on condition that
D. on that

2.　Prices of raw materials _____ steeply since our offer of July 10.

A. rose
B. have risen
C. have rose
D. to have risen

3.　We are afraid that the recent exceptionally heavy demand for fur _____ impossible to promise delivery within one month after receipt of letter of credit.

A. is
B. has made
C. makes it
D. makes

4.　_____ the low stock of such goods, we would advise you to accept our offer immediately.

A. Owing to
B. Because
C. Since
D. As

5.　We are sending you by separate airmail a complete set of samples, _____ you will find them satisfactory.

A. to hope
B. hoping
C. hopefully
D. to hoping

6.　We confirm our email of yesterday, _____ as follows.

A. reads
B. read
C. which reads
D. which reading

7.　We confirm _____ you an offer for 50 tons of walnuts.

A. to have sent
B. having sent
C. sent
D. to send

8.　As _____ in your letter of May 2, we are sending you a catalog and our latest price list.

A. required
B. require
C. requested
D. request

9.　There is a steady demand in Europe for leather gloves _____ high quality.

A. at
B. to
C. of
D. for

10.　We would make you the following offer, subject to your fax acceptance _____ us not later than November 12, 2009.

A. reaches
B. being reached
C. reaching
D. reach

11.　Could you make us a firm offer _____ 3,000 metric tons _____ fertilizer?

A. for, of
B. on, in
C. of, for
D. for, for

12. _____ requested, we are enclosing a quotation sheet _____ our silk garments.

A. As, about   B. At, about   C. At, for   D. As, for

13. We would like to quote you our most favorable price _____ 800 pieces of Electric Blankets _____.

A. for, as follows   B. as, as following   C. with, as followed   D. of, as follows

14. We suggest your order _____ a minimum quantity of 10,000 tons.

A. calls for   B. call for   C. call on   D. call up

15. _____ developing the market in your area, we are airmailing you new models of our products.

A. Due to   B. Owing to   C. In order to   D. With a view to

16. We can not see our way to _____ this offer open for more than 5 days.

A. have   B. place   C. take   D. keep

17. Our offer _____ firm till May 3.

A. could be   B. is   C. for   D. /

18. The goods of your specifications are _____ short supply.

A. for   B. with   C. at   D. in

19. We will certainly accept your offer _____ you ship the goods during May.

A. except   B. provided   C. unless   D. but

20. In _____ of design, our products are perfect.

A. terms   B. term   C. connection   D. connections

II. Fill in the blanks with the words and phrases given below.

A. a good market   B. in a position to   C. advancing

D. heavy demand   E. free gift   ,   F. in bulk

G. charged   H. without engagement   I. subject to

J. refer to

1. Is it a firm offer or an offer _____?

2. Because of the _____ for our products, we recommend your early orders.

3. Our offer is _____ your reply reaching us before May 15.

4. There is _____ for our computers in Asia because of their high quality and favorable prices.

5. As the market is _____, we hope you will take advantage of our order.

6. To attract customers, we are offering a _____ of a Kangle Hair Drier for every order over US$ 60.00.

7. We are _____ offer you lawn mowers at particularly attractive prices.

8. The office buys paper _____ to keep down costs.

9. For detailed information, please _____ the attachment.

10. The communications group has _____ £500,000 for the service.

III. Fill in the blanks with proper prepositions.

1. We shall make a reduction _____ our price if you increase the quantity _____ 5,000 pcs.

2. I'd like to direct your attention _____ the quality _____ the goods which is superior _____ that

of other makes.

3. We are prepared to keep the offer open _____ 25 this month.

4. We refer _____ your offer _____ 14 March.

5. If you could make a reduction _____ 10% _____ quotation, we have confidence _____ securing large orders _____ you.

6. We will withdraw the offer if we would not hear _____ you _____ this period.

7. The middleman receives a commission _____ 5% _____ sales.

8. Thank you _____ your quotation _____ October 7 _____ 1,000 pieces _____ the captioned goods.

9. We offer you 200 cartons _____ Nylon Socks _____ US$260.00 _____ carton _____ the usual terms.

10. Provided we receive your order _____ 30 October, we make you a firm offer _____ delivery _____ the middle _____ November _____ the prices quoted.

11. We thank for your inquiry of December 14, and enclose our quotation _____ curtain material.

12. We require payment _____ confirmed irrevocable letter of credit payable by draft at sight.

13. We trust you will accept our offer without any delay as the demand _____ our cotton shirts is heavy.

14. Our quotation may change _____ notice.

IV. Fill in the blanks with suitable words.

1. Many of our clients requested us _____ approach you _____ offers.

2. We _____ you for 500 sets of suits _____ US$... _____ CIF London basis _____ June/July shipment.

3. This offer is firm, subject _____ your _____ _____ us before or _____ noon time June 16.

4. _____ orders _____ 500 pieces or more, we _____ a special discount _____ 4%.

5. It is regretful that we can not _____ your requirements.

6. As soon as the import license is approved, an L/C will be opened in your _____.

7. While we _____ your cooperation in giving us an offer, we regret to say that we are not in the market for this commodity now.

8. If your quality is good and the price is in line with the market at our _____, we would place a big order with you.

9. Our stock is running _____, so we suggest that you place your order without delay.

10. As our product has _____ a ready market _____ your end, we feel _____ that you can develop trade and _____ friendship between our two corporations.

11. Since we are _____ _____ with the department stores here, we are confident that we can _____ a number of orders _____ you.

12. We send under _____ _____ a catalog, in which you can find a _____ description of the goods you _____.

13. We shall _____ you our best prices and send you the _____ samples for your _____.

14. At present, we cannot see our _____ to entertain your order, as the market price has _____.

15. We are out of _____, therefore, we have to _____ your order.

16. We are not _____ to place our order _____ you, because your price is _____ of line _____ the prevailing market at our _____.

V. Complete the following sentences in English.

1. We shall book a trial order with you, provided _____
   a. 你们的价格有竞争性，货物品质优良
   b. 你们可以提前装运
   c. 你们愿给我们百分之五的佣金

2. If you find our terms and conditions agreeable, _____
   a. 请即来传真订货以便我们确认
   b. 请在本月底前将信用证开来以便我方安排运输事宜
   c. 请将你方订单寄来以便我们立刻组织货源

3. If the designs of your leather shoes agree with the taste of our market, _____
   a. 我们有信心向你们订购 5000 双作为试销
   b. 我们随即寄出订单，并开立以你方为抬头的信用证
   c. 我处的大百货公司会很快向你们订货，大力推销你公司的男式皮鞋
   d. 我们相信你们的皮靴能在这里畅销

VI. Translate the following sentences into Chinese.

1. We make you the following offer subject to your reply reaching us not later than noon time December 23.

2. We will be pleased to manufacture any article on the list according to your specification.

3. We confirm having sent you a fax this morning, offering firm 200 metric tons of Groundnuts, subject to your reply reaching us within one week.

4. We confirm having faxed you an offer for 100 metric tons of Walnut Meat at RMB￥10,000.00 per metric ton CIF European Main Ports for October shipment.

5. We are in a position to offer cotton piece goods at these low prices because we keep a large stock.

6. We have pleasure in attaching our current quotation for your reference and, as we are able to offer for prompt delivery, we look forward to receiving your order in the near future.

7. We faxed back this morning, offering you 250 metric tons of Shandong Groundnuts, Hand-picked, Shelled and Ungraded at RMB￥4,000.00 net per metric ton CFR Copenhagen or any other European Main Port for shipment during October/November, 2010.

8. As no doubt, you are aware that of late there has been a large demand for the above commodities and such a growing demand can only result in increased prices.

9. We are in receipt of your letter of March 21 and as requested, are airmailing you, under separate cover, one catalog and two sample books for our printed shirting, hoping they will help you make your selection.

10. Payment: By 100% confirmed, irrevocable letter of credit in our favor available by draft at

sight to reach the Sellers one month before shipment and remain valid for negotiation in China till the 15th day after shipment.

VII. Translate the following sentences into English.

1. 关于支付条件，我方通常要求保兑的、不可撤销的、凭即期汇票支付的信用证。

2. 如果 3 月 10 日之前收到你方订单，我方将报 5 月上旬船期的实盘。

3. 由于此货需求量很大，所以该盘有效期不能超过 5 天。

4. 兹报实盘，以我方时间 7 月 10 日星期二下午 5 时以前复到为有效。

5. 一俟收到贵方具体询价，我们将传真报价。

6. 如果你们答应提前交货，我们可以接受贵方报价。

7. 我方向贵方报盘 1500 辆永久牌自行车，CIF 拉各斯，每辆 32 美元，5 月份交货。

8. 我方高兴地向贵方发出 50 台 70 型咖啡机的报盘如下，以我方最后传真确认为准。

9. 我们现向你方报 500 辆好孩子牌自行车，每辆 35 美元 CIF 纽约价，包括 3%的佣金，7 月装运，以 5 月 5 日前收到贵方回复为有效。

10. 请以传真报最优惠盘，并注明原产地、包装、详细规格、可供数量及最早装运期。

VIII. Translate the following letters.

(1)

Dear Mr. Weber,

We are glad to receive your email dated May 12 and make you the following offer without engagement:

Brand Name: Annajia Fresh Mango
Origin: Philippine
Unit Price: USD 12.25 per box (changes weekly depending on the market)
Price Terms: FOB
Port: Manila
Payment Terms: L/C
Delivery Lead Time: 3-5 days from confirming order via air freight
Minimum Order: a 20-foot container
Supply Ability: readily available whole year around
Inner Packing: Average weight of 230-350 grams, 5 kg in a box

We are sure that you will find our price competitive and are awaiting your order.

Yours sincerely,

(2)

Dear Sirs,

We welcome your inquiry dated October 14. We are very grateful to you for your interest in our men's cotton shirts.

In reply to your inquiry in your last letter, we hereby send you our illustrated catalog and price list so as to provide you with details you would like to know. Apart from these, we enclose some samples by separate post. We are confident that the design, the quality and the competitive edge of our product will not let you down.

In reply to your inquiry, we would like to make you an offer as follows, provided your reply reaches us by October 24:

    Commodity: Men's Cotton Shirts

    Price: US$15 per piece CIF Dalian

    Payment: irrevocable L/C at sight

Considering this is our first transaction and you are a potential long-term business partner, we would allow you a discount of 5%, if the volume of your order is larger than 10,000 pieces.

We look forward to your order and long-term cooperation with you.

Yours faithfully,

(3)

尊敬的 Watwood 先生：

    我们收到了您 10 月 15 日对我公司海信牌 46 寸电视的询盘，对此我们深表谢意。

    我们的产品超薄、音质绝佳、图像比同类产品更清晰。

    我们很高兴地向贵方报价，此报价以我方最终确认为准。纽约成本加运保费价每台 800 美元。支付方式为不可撤销的即期信用证。

    请注意，我们的产品没有佣金。但是，如果贵公司的订单量超过 2000 台，我们可给予 5%的折扣。

    盼望收到贵公司的订单。

谨上

IX. Write an offer covering the following points.

    3 月 2 日关于 2 吨核桃仁的第 713 号询价单收到。

    按上月所寄样品报价如下：

    品名：核桃仁（见样品）

等级：二级

数量：2 公吨

包装：标准出口硬纸板箱

价格：上海离岸价每吨净价 860 美元

交货：2010 年 5 月或 6 月

付款：由装船前 30 天开立的保兑的、不可撤销的即期信用证支付

因货源短缺，订单须于三月底前寄到，逾期无法供应，请谅解。

X. Write a reply according to the incoming email. The following information is for your reference.

品名：第 145 号棉衬衫布

数量：一千码

单价：每码 150 美元，CIF 旧金山价，包括 4%的佣金

装运：2010 年 6 月或 7 月

付款方式：不可撤销的即期信用证

报盘有效期 5 天

The Incoming Email

From: davidbrown662@erwo.trading.com

To: jiangming@alibaba.com

Date: Thursday, May 23, 2010, 10: 45 am

Subject: Inquiry for Cotton Shirt Fabric Art. No. 145

Dear Mr. Jiang,

Thank you for your catalogs forwarded to us and we find some items are of interest to us.

We should appreciate it if you would give us the best offer for the 1,000 yards of your cotton shirt fabric, Art. No. 145.

If your prices are acceptable, we trust large business can be concluded.

We look forward to your early reply.

Yours sincerely,

David Brown

Purchasing Manager

Unit 7　Counter Offer

还　盘

练　习

I. Choose the best answer.

1. If you can reduce your price by, say 3%, we are ready to place with an order for _____ 600 sets of "Butterfly" brand sewing machines.

A. other　　　　　　B. the other　　　　　C. others　　　　　　D. another

2. We confirm _____ from you the following commodities.

A. to purchase　　　B. purchase　　　　　C. having purchased　　D. to have purchased

3. On October 5, our company entered _____ an agreement with your firm to purchase a total of 18,000 gallons of house paint.

A. to　　　　　　　B. on　　　　　　　　C. into　　　　　　　D. at

4. Please advise at what price your clients will place orders _____ us.

A. of　　　　　　　B. for　　　　　　　　C. by　　　　　　　　D. with

5. Please indicate on the enclosed copy of your order form _____ you want to place a cash order now.

A. when　　　　　　B. whether　　　　　　C. until　　　　　　D. unless

6. We offer firm as follows _____ the same terms and conditions as the previous contracts.

A. of　　　　　　　B. by　　　　　　　　C. on　　　　　　　　D. at

7. _____ an order for over 500 pieces we would allow a special discount.

A. In case　　　　　B. In case that　　　　C. In the case　　　　D. In case of

8. No discount will be granted _____ you place an order for more than 1,000 tons.

A. so that　　　　　B. till　　　　　　　　C. unless　　　　　　D. nevertheless

9. Since our prices are closely calculated, we regret _____ to grant the discount you asked for.

A. are unable　　　　B. being unable　　　　C. be unable　　　　D. being able

10. We are sorry we cannot _____ your counter offer, as your bid is too low.

A. agree　　　　　　B. agree with　　　　　C. entertain　　　　　D. decline

11. We cannot _____ our offer open for more than three days, so please fax us your acceptance immediately.

A. have　　　　　　B. leave　　　　　　　C. remain　　　　　　D. make

12. We are ＿＿＿ your letter of June 23 offering us 50 metric tons of groundnut kernels.

A. at receipt of   B. on receipt of   C. in receipt for   D. in receipt of

13. ＿＿＿ orders amounting to a certain value we allow a special discount of 6%.

A. On   B. With   C. At   D. Against

14. Information indicates that some similar goods of Japanese origin have been sold here ＿＿＿ about 25% lower than yours.

A. at a level   B. at something   C. at quotation   D. with a figure

15. We are of course ＿＿＿ that the time for completion of your project has already been exceeded.

A. know   B. to know   C. aware   D. sure

16. We feel ＿＿＿ that we must decline your counter offer.

A. regret   B. regretful   C. regrettable   D. regretfully

17. If you can reduce your price by 3%, we shall be prepared to ＿＿＿ for 5,000 pieces.

A. entertain your offer   B. decline your order

C. be in the market   D. make your order

18. We would suggest ＿＿＿ your own interest that you fax us your acceptance as soon as possible.

A. with   B. in   C. for   D. at

19. ＿＿＿ we appreciate your intention, we regret that we cannot entertain any fresh order.

A. As   B. While   C. Much   D. So

20. Great demand in the market resulted ＿＿＿ the increased prices of the digital cameras.

A. in   B. from   C. for   D. at

II. Fill in the blanks with suitable words.

1. We ＿＿＿ you 500 metric tons of sugar at GBP 100 per metric ton on CIF London ＿＿＿ for May shipment.

2. This offer is ＿＿＿ to your reply ＿＿＿ here before or at noon time October 23.

3. The best we can ＿＿＿ is to ＿＿＿ a reduction of 3% in our quotation.

4. We very much ＿＿＿ that we are unable to ＿＿＿ your counter offer.

5. As the market is ＿＿＿, we suggest you ＿＿＿ your price by 3%.

6. As soon as we are in a ＿＿＿ to make an ＿＿＿ for eyeglasses cases, we shall inform you by email.

7. As we are in the ＿＿＿ for table cloth, we should ＿＿＿ it if you would send us your best quotation.

8. We wish to draw your ＿＿＿ to the good quality of our products ＿＿＿ of price.

9. In ＿＿＿ to your letter, we enclose our latest illustrated catalog for your ＿＿＿.

10. Any order you ＿＿＿ with us will receive our prompt and careful ＿＿＿.

III. Choose the right answers.

(1)

A. in receipt of   B. out of line with   C. come to terms

D. make a little concession   E. in view of

Dear Mr. Hopley,

We are __1__ your letter dated April 12, offering us 200 Swiss Knives at USD 150.00

In reply, we have to point out that your price is __2__ the world market. If you can __3__, say a reduction of 10%, we may __4__. It is __5__ our long-standing business relations that we make a counter offer so favorable.

We hope you will accept our counter offer and await your favorable news.

Yours sincerely,

(2)

A. The best we can do   B. subject goods   C. make an exception
D. deprive us of   E. setting a precedent

Dear Ms. Zhao,

We acknowledge receipt of your email of July 15, counter offering us 1,000 sets of the __1__.

In reply, we regret to say that to reduce the price to the level you mentioned would __2__ all the profits. __3__ is 15% off the list price. However, in view of our long and mutually beneficial relationship, we are willing to __4__ to lower the price by 20%. I must stress that this departure from our usual practice relates to this transaction only. We cannot regard it as __5__ for future transactions.

We await your early reply.

Yours sincerely,

IV. Identify the error in each sentence.

1. <u>As requesting</u>, we <u>offer</u> you our new <u>pattern</u> of carpet as <u>follows</u>:
    A   B   C   D

2. We are <u>confident</u> that the machine we <u>offer</u> will <u>prove</u> <u>be satisfied</u> to you.
              A   B   C   D

3. We shall be <u>pleased</u> to offer you other items which <u>might</u> be <u>of interesting</u> to you
              A   B   C

<u>upon</u> receipt of your specific inquiries.
  D

4. <u>Regarding</u> the price, we'll <u>quote</u> you <u>at</u> CIF <u>basis</u>.
    A   B   C   D

5. Thank you <u>for</u> your letter of June 10, inquiring <u>for</u> our products and <u>to request</u>
            A   B   C

   terms <u>of</u> payment.
        D

6. Our calculation is so <u>close</u> that it is <u>simply impossible</u> for us to <u>make</u> any <u>farther</u>
                  A   B   C   D

   concession.

7. <u>Enclosed</u> please find one set of <u>shipping documents</u> <u>cover</u> this consignment, which
   A   B   C

   <u>comprises</u>:
    D

8. As you <u>perhaps</u> know, <u>demand of</u> the article you <u>enquire for</u> has ever been <u>heavy</u>
          A   B   C   D

   since last year.

9. We are <u>pleased</u> to confirm <u>to conclude</u> <u>with</u> you a transaction of 30 <u>metric tons</u> of
         A   B   C   D

   groundnuts.

10. <u>In reply</u>, we <u>regretful</u> to inform you that our buyers in Rotterdam <u>find</u> your price
    A   B   C

    <u>much too</u> high.
     D

V. Translate the following sentences into English.

1. 我方很遗憾你方的发盘比美国供应商的价格高出 5%。
2. 羊毛行市目前疲软，除非你方能降价 5%，否则无法成交。
3. 坦率地说，我们遗憾地发现你方的价格偏高，所以我们建议你们给我方一个折扣，如 6%。
4. 感谢你方 5 月 15 日的发盘，但我们必须指出你们地区的其他供应商给了我们更加有吸引力的报价，价格比你方低 10%到 15%。
5. 我们已经从你们的竞争者那里得到了一个更优惠的发盘，所以请给我们一个折扣，如在原价基础上减 10%，以便开始我们的合作。
6. 我们遗憾地说，你方报来的铁钉价格完全与我地市场行情不一致。
7. 眼前行市疲软，你方所报价格做不开。
8. 有迹象表明市场即将上涨，我们无法将货保留到 9 月底。
9. 近期原材料成本上涨，如按你公司所提降价 15%，将大大影响产品的质量标准。
10. 我们建议凡订单价值超过 5000 美元，降低 10%。

VI. Rewrite the following letter to make it more effective and then put it into Chinese.

Dear Sirs,

Subject: We regret that we cannot accept your counter-offer

In reference to your email of August 1, we cannot make a better offer than the one we suggested to you; we feel that offer itself is most generous under the circumstances.

In checking our books, we find that you have purchased from us twice as much in the first three months of this year as you did in the corresponding period last year. This indicates to us that you have been successful in distributing our merchandise.

We hope that upon reconsideration you will be able to accept our offer. We have been very pleased to have you on our list of accounts.

Best regards,

VII. Translate the following letters.

(1)

Dear Sirs,

Thank you for your letter concerning the offer for "Strong" Brand bicycles. Although we appreciate the quality of your bicycles, their price is too high for us to accept.

Referring to the Sales Confirmation No. 8965, you will find that we ordered 1,000 bicycles of the same brand at the terms and conditions stipulated in that Sales Confirmation, but the price was 10% lower than your present price.

Since we placed the last order, price for raw materials has been decreased considerably. Retailing price for your bicycles here has also been reduced by 5%. Accepting your present price will mean great loss to us, let alone make profits.

We would like to place repeat orders with you if you could reduce your price at least by 1.5%. Otherwise, we have to shift to the other suppliers for our similar request.

We hope you take our suggestion into serious consideration and give us your reply as soon as possible.

Yours faithfully,

(2)

敬启者：

贵方 10 月 18 日的电子邮件收到，不胜感谢。

得知贵方认为我方星牌 46 寸电视机的价格仍然过高，无利可图，我方深感遗憾。贵方也提到日本方面的产品报价大约比我方的低 10%。不可否认，我方产品的价格的确比同类产品要略高，但是我们的产品质量、设计、功能、售后服务都远胜于其他产品。

我们双方做贸易许多年了。我方一直很乐意提供给贵方合理的具有竞争力的价格。我方已经在之前报价的基础上降价 2%，但是贵方似乎对此还是不满意。虽然我方非常盼望能与贵方达成这笔交易，但是恕我方不能接受贵方的还盘甚至折中。

但考虑到双方长久的合作关系，仔细研究我们的价格后，我们决定将利润再次降低，给贵方价格再降 2%，希望这会促进双方的合作关系，拓展贵方市场。

我们相信这样的优惠会得到贵方的认同，并且我们强烈建议贵方利用这次难得机会尽快接受我方的报价。

谨上

VIII. Write a counter offer covering the following points.

A. 收到 6 月 26 日的电子邮件，关于第 2345 号印花细棉布。

B. 所报商品每码 95 便士价格不能接受，同行水平为 90 便士，所以请降至每码 90 便士。

C. 关于起订量，6 月 26 日的电子邮件中要求每花色一万码。但 5 月 20 日的电子邮件中要求每花色 7500 码。盼维持这一较低起订量。

D. 已定妥 6 个花色共四万五千码。

E. 请用传真确认。

IX. Write an email to decline a counter offer according to the following situation.

某海外贸易公司的 William Bright 对你们公司经营的童车质量很满意，但认为你方的报价偏高，要求你们降价 5%。收到该电子邮件后，经研究，你公司认为你方的报价与现行价格相符，因此拒绝他的还价。请你以 Amy Lee 的名义写一封电子邮件拒绝 William Bright 的还价，并在以下给定的格式中书写。

To: William@hotmail.com

Date: Friday, October 9, 20＿＿, 11:12 am

Subject: Re: 1,000 sets of Bee Brand Children's Bicycles

Dear Mr. Bright,

Best regards,

Amy Lee

Unit 8　Order

订　单

I. Find out the mistakes and make corrections. There is one mistake in each sentence.

1.　If your price compares favorably to those of other suppliers, we shall send you an order.

2.　The goods are urgently required, so promptly delivery will be necessary.

3.　Your terms are satisfied and we enclose an order.

4.　We are glad to inform you that your first shipment of shoes has received favorable reaction of our customers.

5.　If the first shipment is satisfactory, we can place for you many repeat orders.

6.　We will accept the order on your terms with a view to encourage business.

7.　Please be notified that the said contract as well as the enclosure have been received duly.

8.　We shall place repeat orders with you if the quality proves to be satisfaction.

9.　Please make sure that the terms in the L/C are in accordance with those in the S/C so as to avoid to amend the L/C.

10.　With an order sheet enclosed, we are pleased to have booked you an order for 6,000 M/Ts of oil seeds.

11.　Because we appreciate your order, we very much regret that we are unable to accept any fresh orders at present.

12.　We regret to inform you that we do not have in stock the goods in the desiring quantity.

II. Choose the best answer.

1.　We _____ your terms satisfactory and now send you our order for 2 sets of generators.

A. find　　　　　　　　B. believe　　　　　　　C. think　　　　　　　D. trust

2.　We place an order provided your goods can be supplied _____ stock.

A. out　　　　　　　　B. out of　　　　　　　　C. from　　　　　　　D. in

3.　In this case, the buyer _____ cancel the contract.

A. could　　　B. may have to　　　　C. has the right to　　　　D. reserve the right to

4.　As agreed upon in our negotiations, payment _____ L/C.

A. by　　　　　　　　B. will　　　　　　　C. is to be made by　　　D. is by

5. We regret to report that the second lot of silk piecegoods _____ Order No. 342 has not been delivered.

A. with   B. for   C. on   D. under

6. _____ the present market trend, we have to say that our price is really the best we can quote.

A. With   B. On   C. Because   D. For

7. We assure you of our full _____ in executing the contract.

A. corporation   B. attention   C. intention   D. appreciation

8. Within 48 hours of the telephone contact, we will issue, by fax, a purchase order document that will _____ the phone order.

A. confirm   B. conform   C. ensure   D. consolidate

9. As our factory is now fully occupied with orders, we regret having to _____ yours.

A. refuse   B. decline   C. reject   D. return

10. We are unable to _____ with your request in your letter dated January 31.

A. conform   B. compose   C. confirm   D. comply

11. Some customers requested us to _____ our price because they consider it too high.

A. bring down   B. get down   C. put down   D. take down

12. Thanks to a more _____ price contract we have signed with our supplier, we are now happy to be able to cut the prices of our pressure cookers by 8 percent.

A. favoring   B. favored   C. favorite   D. favorable

13. We shall make a reduction _____ our price by 5% if you increase the quantity to 5,000 M/Ts.

A. for   B. of   C. at   D. about

14. We find your quotation for _____ much too high.

A. woman blouses   B. woman's blouses   C. women's blouses   D. women blouses

15. I would appreciate _____ me an up-to-date price list for your supplies.

A. if you would send   B. you send   C. that you would send   D. your sending

16. Goods will be shipped _____ 30 days after receipt of the L/C.

A. to   B. on   C. for   D. within

17. We can supply this type of machine _____ very favorable terms.

A. for   B. to   C. against   D. on

18. Last year, this market was almost at its bottom, _____ which our trade is now only recovering.

A. from   B. for   C. on   D. against

19. _____ instructions from the importer, we have opened an irrevocable letter of credit for US$ 8,000 in your favor.

A. On   B. From   C. In accordance   D. According

20. Owing to heavy _____, we are not in a position to accept fresh orders.

A. commitments   B. work   C. order   D. amount

21. _____ to our regret, at present we cannot entertain any fresh orders.

A. Many   B. Much   C. More   D. Most

22. The business is _____ on CIF _____.

A. conclude, base   B. conclusion, basic

C. concluding, based   D. concluded, basis

23. The additional charge will be _____ your account.

A. with   B. of   C. for   D. in

24. We regret to say that the prices you have bid are too low to _____.

A. not accept   B. be acceptable   C. be accepting   D. be unacceptable

25. Quality of the present shipment is equal to _____ of last consignment.

A. this   B. these   C. that   D. those

26. We're pleased to confirm the emails _____ between us resulting in the conclusion of business of 50 M/Ts of fertilizer.

A. exchanged   B. exchanges   C. exchange   D. exchanging

27. Many of our clients are in the market for your _____.

A. demands   B. manufactures   C. orders   D. requirements

28. We think there is no room for further negotiation _____ you meet our requirement.

A. unless   B. except   C. if   D. though

29. An agreement is _____ as a result of the process of offer and acceptance.

A. included   B. reached   C. had   D. resulted

30. Please make out your Sales Contract in three _____.

A. triplicates   B. copy   C. pieces   D. originals

III. Fill in the blanks with proper prepositions.

1. We are pleased to confirm having concluded _____ you a deal of 30 metric tons _____ groundnut kernels.

2. We are pleased to have booked _____ you an order _____ 300 metric tons of Groundnut Oil.

3. Our buyers have agreed to allow partial shipments _____ this order, which will enable you to make shipment _____ the three months from April to June.

4. We have a stock _____ 300 dz. shirts, which we are selling off _____ USD 13.00 per dz.

5. We confirm coming _____ terms _____ you _____ the above goods and hope it will lead _____ more repeats.

6. We assure you that any further orders you many place _____ us will always be carefully attended _____.

7. Payment is to be made 100% _____ confirmed, irrevocable L/C _____ our favor to be available _____ sight draft, reaching us 45 days before the date of shipment.

8. We confirm your order _____ October 3 _____ 20,000 M/Ts _____ coal.

9. The shipping mark is _____ the seller's option.

10. We confirm the sale _____ you of 100 tons of groundnuts resulting _____ letters exchanged.

11. We hope we could come _____ business _____ you.

12. Please refer _____ the emails exchanged _____ us in April.

IV. Fill in the blanks with proper words.

1. We rely _____ you to _____ this order _____ the entire satisfaction _____ our customers and _____ the least possible delay.

2. We hope to come _____ terms _____ you _____ this trial order.

3. As a result _____ our recent exchange of faxes, we confirm having purchased _____ you 1,000 metric tons _____ the captioned goods _____ the following _____ and conditions.

4. We regret our inability to comply _____ your request _____ shipping the goods _____ early November, because the direct steamer sailing _____ your port calls at our port only _____ the 20th _____ November.

5. We take pleasure _____ sending you our Order No. 123 _____ 4,000 sets _____ Philips Color TV.

6. We are _____ our Sales Confirmation _____ duplicate. Please _____ and return one copy to us for our _____.

7. We are out of _____, therefore, we have to _____ your order.

8. We shall _____ an L/C _____ your favor _____ Barclays Bank here.

9. We are _____ to place our order _____ you, because your price is _____ of line _____ the prevailing market.

V. Match the following terms of payment frequently seen in the contracts with their names.

A. D/P at sight   B. sight L/C   C. remittance   D. D/A   E. D/P after sight

1. The buyer should pay 100% of the sales proceeds in advance by T/T to reach the seller not later than September 15, 2010.

2. Upon first presentation the Buyer shall pay against documentary draft drawn by the Seller at sight. The shipping documents are to be delivered against payment only.

3. The Buyer shall duly accept the documentary draft drawn by the Seller at 30 days upon first presentation and make payment on its maturity. The shipping documents are to be delivered against payment only.

4. The Buyer shall open through a bank acceptable to the Seller an irrevocable sight letter of credit to reach the Seller 30 days before the date of shipment valid for negotiation in China until the 15th day after the date of shipment.

5. The Buyer shall duly accept the documentary draft drawn by the Seller at 30 days upon first presentation and make payment on its maturity. The shipping documents are to be delivered against acceptance.

VI. Translate the following sentences into Chinese.

1. For a trial sale, we would like to order 200 sets of your products.

2. Within 30 minutes of placing your order on our website you will receive a confirmation email, which confirms we have received your order. This email also serves as your receipt. Once your order has been shipped you will receive a final shipping notification email.

3. We enclose our revised Order Sheet No. 231 for 150,000 yards of Printed Cotton. We are

looking forward to your confirmation of this order and also the sales contract.

4. We confirm having accepted your Order No. 85 for 100,000 yards of printed cotton, Art. No. 1002. Please let us know the color assortment and open the covering L/C in our favor in accordance with the contract stipulations.

5. Your order is receiving our immediate attention and you can depend on us to make delivery well within your time limit.

6. If you have no Sony Brand TV sets in stock, please make us an offer for Toshiba Brand ones or any other brands which can be immediately shipped from stock.

7. Your samples of Rubber Boots received favorable reaction from our customers, and we are pleased to enclose our order for 300 dozen pairs.

8. We are sending you our Sales Confirmation No. 904 with the request that you will countersign and return to us the duplicate as soon as possible.

VII. Translate the following sentences into English.

1. 如果贵方能给予我方 5%的佣金，我方将试购 500 台。

2. 我方正在执行贵方第 334 号订单。请相信我方一定将在贵方所规定的期限内安排装运。

3. 由于大量承约，许多订单都未完成，因此我方目前只能接受 10 月船期的订单。

4. 因为存货售罄，我们不能接受新订单。但是一俟新货源到来，我方即传真与贵方联系。

5. 贵方拟订购的产品已告售罄，故推荐 DPT-54 号货物作为理想的替代品。

6. 经双方的传真往来，现欲确认向贵公司订购虎头牌手电筒 6000 箱。

7. 由于国内市场的变化，我们想取消购买你方蓝牙的订单。

8. 所有这些商品都是我们客户急需的，因此我们希望你们尽早交货以便他们能够在圣诞节前售完。

9. 一俟收到你方的即期信用证，我们就安排由最早订到舱位的集装箱轮运出。

10. 我们很高兴收到你方的续订订单，我们保证，它将被及时履行。

VIII. Translate the following letters into Chinese.

(1)

Dear Mr. Smith,

Thanks for your continuous support. Your repeat order is a confirmation that you are doing well in your market.

As the Chinese sales season is drawing near, many of our domestic retailers are anticipating a big sale. Their orders have kept us quite busy for the last 3 weeks. Our manufacturers are doubling their efforts to keep up with the demand. We shall be able to accept new orders at the beginning of the next month. We will keep you updated of the supply position.

In the meantime, you may find some other items selling well in other markets. Enclosed are our latest catalog and an order form. Just fill in the form and return to us if you could find any items interesting.

Yours sincerely,

(2)

Dear Sirs,

We thank you very much for your letter of February 15 with patterns and price lists. We have chosen three qualities for which we enclose Order No. 777. The goods are urgently required, so we appreciate prompt delivery.

Yours faithfully,
Encl. Order No. 777

Order No. 777

ABC Co., Ltd.
London, England

Dear Sirs,

Please supply:

Quantity	Article No.	Price (USD, FOB Vancouver)	Delivery
250 doz.	3456	2 per doz.	August
160 doz.	7890	4 per doz.	August
90 doz.	2134	6 per doz.	August

Packing: Each dozen to be packed in a tin-lined carton, with 10 dozen cartons in a wooden case.
Insurance: W. P. A. for 10% over the invoice amount.
Shipping Marks: As usual with our previous orders.
Payment Terms: Draft at sight under an irrevocable letter of credit.

We have instructed our bank to open a letter of credit for the amount of this order. You will soon hear from your bank.

Yours faithfully,

IX. Translate the following into English.

(1)

敬启者：

　　7 月 10 日来函及价目单均收到，非常感谢。我方选购 Acer5022 型。现随函附寄第 988 号订单。货急用，请即装。

　　贵方对此订单的及时关注，我方将不胜感激。

谨上

附件：第 988 号订单

****

天津电子产品进出口公司

电话：022－85200829　　　传真：022－85200793

订　　单

2012 年 7 月 15 日

第 988 号订单
美国纽约
远东工业有限公司

请贵方提供：

数量	型号	单价	交货期
1000 台	Acer5022	每台 420 美元	八月份

包装：每台装一标准出口硬纸板箱，外用铁皮加固

唛头：如合同所示

价格：CFR 新港

付款：由中国银行开立的 100% 不可撤销跟单信用证，凭即期汇票付款

天津电子产品进出口公司

销售经理：张玉梅

(2)

孙先生：

　　非常感谢贵方 5 月 14 日给我公司发来的有关贵公司男士棉衬衫的报价及寄送的带有插图的产品目录和样品。

　　我方认为贵公司产品设计新颖、品质卓越，均符合我方的要求。贵公司的报价也比较有竞争力，比较合理。此外，我方还高兴地获悉在订购量不少于一万件的情况下，我方还可享受 5% 的折扣。据此，我方很高兴地向贵公司下如下订单：

　　数量：1 万件

　　规格：XL 号男士棉衬衫

　　目录号：M20

　　单价：大连成本加运保费价每件 15 美元

付款方式：不可撤销的即期信用证

因我方市场急需这批货物，如贵方能尽快发货，我方将不胜感激。

如首次交易成功，我方将非常乐意在不远的将来给贵方下更多的订单。

谨上

Unit 9   Packing
包　装

练　习

I. Choose the best answer.

1. We regret our inability to agree _____ your proposal to pack the goods _____ cardboard boxes, because transshipment has to be made at Hong Kong for the goods to be shipped to our port.

A. on, in   B. to, in   C. with, by   D. to, by

2. The buyer suggested that the packing of this article _____ improved.

A. was to be   B. had to be   C. would be   D. be

3. Packing lists help _____ contents of packages, either for Customs purposes or for the importers.

A. identify   B. be distinguished   C. recognizing   D. identification

4. Due to the fact _____ you urged quick delivery, we were not able to use our special packing.

A. which   B. that   C. when   D. to which

5. Outer packing _____ stenciled with shiping marks.

A. is not always   B. may be   C. must be   D. is usually not

6. Our ladies' pyjamas are packed in cartons, each _____ 12 doz.

A. to contain   B. contains   C. contained   D. containing

7. Please ship the goods in strong export packing to ensure good condition _____ arrival.

A. in   B. for   C. on   D. at

8. The loss was due to improper packing, _____ the suppliers should be responsible.

A. for which   B. to which   C. in which   D. which

9. It is important that the goods under Credit No. 878 _____ packed in double gunny bags.

A. will be   B. shall be   C. be   D. are

10. Seventy cases of Black Tea you sent us were found to be badly damaged. This was apparently attributable to _____ packing.

A. outer   B. domestic   C. neutral   D. faulty

11. We will not be held responsible for any damage which results _____ rough handling.

A. from   B. off   C. in   D. to

12. We give you on the attached sheet full details regarding packing and marking, which must be

strictly _____.

A. abide by   B. observed   C. submitted   D. seen

II. Fill in the blanks with the appropriate words given below.

customs duty	exporters	marked	quota	practice	commodity
neutral packing	importer	name	brand	package	trade mark

      As a rule, exports are also __1__ with countries of origin, such as "Made in China" or "Made in Swiss". But there are exceptions when __2__ is required. It is a general __3__ frequently used in international trade as a means to promote export sales. Neutral packing is the one that makes no mention at all of the __4__ of the country producing the goods and the name of the manufacturer on the __5__ and on the outer and inner __6__ .

      In some cases, though with no mention of the country of origin, to meet his requirement the __7__ may ask the exporter to use a special brand or __8__ for the goods, or in other cases, no __9__ or trade mark whatever appears. The purpose of using neutral packing is that the __10__ utilize it for breaking down the high __11__ or unreasonable import __12__ of the importing countries levied on their exports to the imports, thereby making it possible for the exporters to market profitably in the importing countries.

III. Translate the following sentences into Chinese.

1. To be packed in polypropylene woven bags, 50kg each, gross for net. The bags should be fairy good in quality and suitable for ocean transportation, on which the name of the goods, weight, country of origin and package date should be written / marked in English.

2. The goods are to be packed in tin-lined wooden cases, and the contents of each case clearly marked on the outside.

3. We prefer packing the goods in wooden cases of 100 kg net to double gunny sacks.

4. All the apricot kernels are wrapped in plastic bags and packed in cans, the lids of which are sealed with adhesive tape. Twelve cans are packed in a wooden case, which is nailed, and secured by overall metal straps.

5. As far as the outer packing is concerned, we will pack the goods 10 dozen to a carton, gross weight around 25 kilos a carton.

6. When you pack, please put 2 or 3 different designs and colors in each box.

7. Chemical foam represents a new method in the field of packing. Enclosed please find a brochure from which you will learn more about the possibilities of application.

8. The inside of the case may be lined with various materials to prevent damage by water, air or insects.

9. Our cotton prints are packed in cases lined with craft paper and waterproof paper, each consisting of 30 pieces in one design with 5 colors equally assorted.

10. In spite of every care in packing, it sometimes happens that a few barrels are broken in transit.

IV. Translate the following sentences into English.

1. 我们一纸箱装两打，每箱毛重 25 千克。
2. 10 支装入一小盒，100 盒装入一个纸箱。
3. 我们希望你们采取措施用尼龙条加固这种纸板箱。
4. 包装时请考虑到下面两种情形：这些盒子在我们这边很可能遭遇野蛮装卸；它们必须能承受在糟糕的路面上运输。
5. 我们将衬衫包装在塑料做内衬的防水的纸箱内，并且用金属条加固。
6. 这种又轻又结实的箱子能节约舱位，并且便于储存和分拨货物。
7. 根据贵方建议，我方已改进了内包装，以满足贵方市场消费者的需求。
8. 我方的男式衬衫的包装为每件装入一塑料袋内，5 打装入一内衬有防潮纸的纸箱内。箱外匣两道铁箍。

V. Translate the following letters into Chinese.

(1)

Dear Sirs,

We are pleased to place our order for your LT-93 machines and we should be very obliged if you would make shipment in May.

As these machines are precision instruments which cannot stand rough handling, proper packing and marking are quite necessary. For this reason, we insist that the machines be packed each in a sturdy wooden case supported with soft materials to prevent movement inside the case. Cases must be nailed, battened and secured by overall metal strapping with the wording "DO NOT DROP" marked in letters 3 inches high on every side.

Please see to it that these instructions should be strictly carried out.

We enclose our Order No. 7812 and hope to receive your confirmation as soon as possible.

Yours faithfully,

(2)

Dear Sirs,

Thank you for your inquiry of 20 March regarding our container service.

We provide both 10- and 20-foot containers. They open at both ends, thus facilitating loading and unloading.

For goods are liable to be spoiled by damp or water, our containers have the advantage of being watertight and airtight.

Containers are loaded and locked at the factory, rendering pilferage impossible.

For frozen or perishable goods, we offer special, temperature-controlled containers to ensure that such goods arrive at their destination in perfect condition.

There is also a saving on freight charges, since containerized goods carry lower insurance premiums than loose goods.

We enclose a copy of our list of charges and look forward to receiving your instructions.

Yours faithfully,

(3)

Dear Sirs,

We are writing to discuss the outer packing for our Order No. 897.

We would like you to pack our order by the standard packing. Make sure that each item is individually packed in polybag and every three dozen is packed in a carton. Each carton is lined with a polythene sheet and secured by overall strapping, thus preventing the contents from dampness and possible damage through rough handling. Before shipping, please pack these items in wooden cases, 10 cartons each.

In order to prevent the goods from dampness, please use moisture-proof packing and stamp a "KEEP DRY" sign in the outside of each wooden case.

We shall appreciate your early attention to our outer packing requirements.

Yours faithfully,

VI. Translate the following letters into English.

(1)

敬启者：
　　我们收到了贵方第 MG-230 号订单，谢谢。
　　按照贵方的要求，我们就包装情况通报如下：
　　货物将装入木箱，箱内衬防水锡纸，每一件货物均用油布包裹，15 件装一箱。

木箱将钉牢，外面用金属条箍紧。

相信贵方会接受我们的包装。我方保证会仔细处理贵方的到货。

谨上

(2)

敬启者：

兹来函商讨贵方第 825 号订货的包装方式。

在内包装方面，钢笔装在一个锦缎小盒内，再用一条蓝色的绸带系在盒子外面。

在外包装方面，我们可以用这种产品的出厂标准来包装。每个用塑料袋单独包装，每 4 打装一个纸箱。装运时，每 15 个纸箱装一个大木箱。

如果贵方在包装方面有任何特殊要求，请通知我方。

敬盼贵方的早日答复。

谨上

(3)

敬启者：

感谢贵方 11 月 20 日附寄的一式两份销售合同的电子邮件。

仔细检查合同后，我方发现包装条款不甚清晰。请注意，相关条款如下：

包装：适合海运的出口包装，适合于长途海洋运输。

为避免将来出现不必要的麻烦，我方特预先澄清我方的包装要求如下：

合同项下的茶叶应包装于国际标准茶叶箱，24 箱装一托盘，10 托盘装一整集装箱。请在外包装上标明本公司的英文名称缩写 SL、目的港上海及销售合同号 825。另外，警示性标志"请勿用吊钩"、"保持干燥"也应标明。

敬盼贵方的装船通知，并提前感谢贵方的合作。

谨上

Unit 10　Payment

付　款

I. Match the words and phrases with their Chinese meanings.

Group A

1. Import/Export License	A. 签名的商业发票
2. Documentary L/C	B. 清洁已装船提单
3. Signed Commercial Invoice	C. 重量单
4. Negotiable Insurance Policy	D. 进出口许可证
5. Clean on Board Bill of Lading	E. 正本保险单
6. Certificate of Origin	F. 跟单信用证
7. Air Waybills	G. 装箱单
8. Packing List	H. 原产地证明
9. Weight Memo	I. 数量/重量证明书
10. Certificate of Quantity/Weight	J. 空运单

Group B

1. payment by installment	A. 预先付款
2. collection	B. 破产
3. sight/time draft	C. 付款定金
4. payment in advance	D. 未偿还的
5. drawer/drawee	E. 结余，余额
6. down payment	F. 分期付款
7. bankruptcy	G. 出票人/受票人
8. balance	H. 托收
9. insolvency	I. 即期/远期汇票
10. outstanding	J. 无力偿还，破产

II. Choose the best answer.

1. After the contract is signed, we shall open _____ the Bank of China here an irrevocable L/C at sight in your favor.

A. with　　　　　　　B. at　　　　　　　C. by　　　　　　　D. in

2.　For exporters, we usually ask our buyers to open irrevocable letters of credit _____ sellers' documentary drafts at sight.

A. available by　　　B. available to　　　C. acceptable by　　　D. acceptable to

3.　If the amount exceeds that figure, payment _____ L/C will be required.

A. at　　　　　　　B. by　　　　　　　C. for　　　　　　　D. in

4.　Our contract stipulates that payment should be made by irrevocable L/C payable by sight draft, so you must act _____.

A. according　　　　B. honestly　　　　C. in advance　　　D. accordingly

5.　Please amend L/C NO. 283 to read "The L/C will _____ on February 22, 2009. In Singapore."

A. expire　　　　　B. valid　　　　　C. due to time　　　D. due

6.　We have enough stock _____ hand to fill your repeat order. If you would like us to do so, please call us at once.

A. on　　　　　　　B. in　　　　　　　C. off　　　　　　　D. by

7.　We are disappointed to note that so far we have not received your L/C which _____ us before April 2.

A. shall reach　　　B. must have reached　　　C. should have reached　　　D. is reaching

8.　We have instructed our bank to open a confirmed irrevocable letter of credit for US$10,560 _____ your favor.

A. in　　　　　　　B. at　　　　　　　C. for　　　　　　　D. by

9.　We will _____ that the L/C is opened within the stipulated time.

A. see to it　　　　B. seeing　　　　C. see it　　　　D. see to

10.　To our great surprise, nothing has been _____ you at all since we wrote you last time.

A. hear from　　　B. heard from　　　C. hear of　　　D. heard of

11.　We regret to find that your L/C has _____ arrive here within the time limit stipulated.

A. failed to　　　B. failed　　　C. to fail　　　D. failing

12.　We advised the bank to amend the clause _____ "Partial shipments are permitted."

A. to reading　　　B. to read　　　C. to be read　　　D. to be reading

13.　We thank you very much for your L/C and shipping instructions _____ your trial order.

A. being covered　　B. to be covered　　C. covering　　D. covers

14.　We thank you for the L/C No. 134, _____ we have been notified today by the Bank of China.

A. with which　　　B. for which　　　C. by which　　　D. of which

15.　You are requested to make amendment _____ L/C No. 789 without delay.

A. to　　　　　　　B. in　　　　　　　C. for　　　　　　　D. at

16.　The consignment will be dispatched as soon as possible, _____ to reach the final destination by mid-January.

A. so　　　　　　　B. as　　　　　　　C. so as　　　　　　　D. so that

17.　As stipulated in the contract, the bank _____ issue an L/C before the end of February.

A. will　　　　　　B. need　　　　　　C. shall　　　　　　D. ought

18.　The relative L/C should be issued through a third country bank in Italy _____ the sellers.

A. available by　　　B. available to　　　C. acceptable by　　　D. acceptable to

19. It needs _____ that the L/C should reach us 30 days before the month of shipment.

A. being mentioned　　B. to be mentioned　　C. mentioned　　D. mention

20. We find that there is no stipulation of transshipment _____ in the relative L/C.

A. which allowed　　B. being allowed　　C. allowing　　D. which allows

21. We invite your attention to the fact _____ the L/C covering your Order No. 907 has not reached us in spite of our repeated request.

A. what　　　B. that　　　C. where　　　D. there

22. Emphasis has to be laid to the point _____ shipment must be made within the validity of the L/C.

A. what　　　B. which　　　C. that　　　D. /

23. Considering the quality of the goods _____ we quoted, we do not feel that the prices are at all excessive.

A. which　　　B. that　　　C. for which　　　D. for that

24. We advised our bank to _____ L/C No. 889 to read "Partial shipments to be permitted."

A. change　　　B. amend　　　C. alter　　　D. add

25. As we are _____ of these goods, please expedite shipment after receiving our L/C.

A. in badly need　　B. in urgently need　　C. urgent in need　　D. badly in need

26. Any discrepancy _____ the quality of the delivered goods against the contractual stipulations is not allowed.

A. to　　　B. among　　　C. in　　　D. between

27. An L/C should be established _____ our favor available by documentary draft _____ sixty days' sight.

A. in, after　　　B. on, in　　　C. in, for　　　D. in, at

28. We regret _____ to accept your terms of payment and therefore have to return the order to you.

A. not be able　　B. cannot　　C. not able　　D. being unable

29. L/C at sight is _____ we request for all our customers.

A. where　　　B. when　　　C. what　　　D. why

30. The manager does not allow _____ the prices.

A. to cut down　　B. cut down　　C. us cut down　　D. cutting down

III. Fill in the blanks with the appropriate words given below.

provided that　　delivery　　called for　　extending　　in accordance with

has a right to　　in favor of　　amendment　　read　　be confirmed

1. In order to avoid subsequent amendments, please see to it that the L/C stipulations are _____ the terms of the contract.

2. The credit _____ by a prime bank which is acceptable.

3. If one side fails to fulfill the contract, the other side _____ cancel it.

4. The exporter should satisfy him that the terms, conditions and documents _____ in the documentary credit are in agreement with the sales contract.

5. The letter of credit not only provides a form of security for the parties involved but also ensures payment _____ the terms of the credit are fulfilled.

6. The buyer shall establish with the bank an irrevocable letter of credit in US dollars _____ the seller in the amount of the estimated total purchase price.

7. The Bank is not responsible for any _____ to the letter of credit.

8. It will be easier for us to make the necessary amendment if your letter of credit can reach us 15 or 30 days before _____.

9. Therefore please amend the L/C to _____: payment is to be made by L/C "at sight", instead of "at 60 days".

10. We would appreciate your _____ the shipment and validity of your L/C to June 15 and 30 respectively.

IV. Fill in the blanks with suitable prepositions.

1. As the said L/C calls for shipment on or before June 30, we regret being unable to make delivery _____ the time designated.

2. As the date _____ shipment stipulated in the mentioned L/C is July 15, which leaves us only 5 days _____ validity, which is too short _____ us to arrange shipment, we, therefore, request you to extend the shipment date _____ August 16.

3. As there isn't direct sailing _____ here to your port _____ this month, please extend the validity _____ the L/C _____ a further period _____ one month.

4. Please note that although the goods _____ our Sales Confirmation No. 654 are now ready _____ shipment, the relevant L/C has not yet reached us.

5. _____ the circumstances, we have to request you _____ an extension _____ the time of shipment _____ July 30.

6. _____ perusal _____ your L/C, we find that it calls _____ direct shipment which is not _____ conformity _____ the contract stipulations.

7. We wish to call your attention _____ the validity _____ the L/C, since there is no possibility _____ L/C extension.

8. After examination, we find the goods _____ high standard and are satisfied _____ the quality _____ the shipment.

9. We have only 300 kegs _____ iron nails _____ stock; therefore we request you to extend the shipment date _____ your L/C _____ the end _____ November.

10. If you could cut your price _____ the extent we have proposed, there is no question _____ our placing an order immediately _____ 100 metric tons.

V. Translate the following sentences into Chinese.

1. Payment is to be made against sight draft drawn under a confirmed, irrevocable, divisible and transferable letter of credit without recourse for the amount.

2. As the goods against your Order No. 2305 have been ready for quite some time, it's imperative that you take immediate action to have the covering L/C established as soon as possible.

3. Owing to the late arrival of the steamer on which we have booked space, we would appreciate your extending the shipment date and the validity of your L/C No. 3321 to April 20 and May 5 respectively.

4. We must insist on receiving payment by July 31, failing this we shall be compelled to take legal actions.

5. In order to avoid subsequent amendment, please see to it that the L/C stipulations are in exact accordance with the terms of the contract.

6. As there is no direct vessel sailing for your port this month, please amend your L/C No. 2345 to allow transshipment instead of "transshipment no allowed" as laid down in the L/C.

7. As there is no direct steamer from Tianjin to your port during April/May, it is imperative for you to delete the clause "by direct steamer", and insert the wording "partial shipments and transshipment are allowed".

8. On examination, we find that the amount of your L/C is insufficient. Please increase the unit price from RMB 0.55 to RMB 0.60 and total amount to RMB 37,000.

9. We wish to make it clear that in future transaction, direct payment will only be acceptable if the amount involved for each transaction is less than £1,000 or the equivalent in Renminbi. If the amount exceeds that figure, payment by letter of credit will be required.

10. It has been our usual practice to do business with payment by D/P at sight instead of by L/C. We should, therefore, like you to accept D/P terms of this transaction and future ones.

VI. Translate the following sentences into English.

1. 关于支付，我方要求按发票金额的 100%，凭保兑的不可撤销的信用证，允许分批装运和转船，凭即期汇票付款，并凭出示全套装运单据给我方议付行为有效。

2. 我方已通过中国银行向你方开出金额为 12000 美元的即期汇票，并指示该行在你方兑付汇票时交出单证。

3. 我们希望引起贵方注意，贵方第 1250 号订单的交货期已临近，但至今为止我方仍然未收到有关信用证。

4. 贵方第 1230 号信用证已收悉。经详阅后发现不准转船和分批装运，请即修改信用证。

5. 请将第 345 号信用证修改为：
   a. 长吨改为公吨
   b. 目的港伦敦改为汉堡
   c. 展装运期到 8 月底
   d. 允许分运转船

6. 当我方将贵方信用证与相关合同审核时，我方发现数量与合同不符，总金额相差 75.60 美元。请速改。

7. 兹关于贵方第 456 号信用证，请传真取消"银行费用由受益人负担"的条款。

8. 贵方第 457 号信用证已如期收到，但金额不足。请按合同增加 520 英镑（增至 3125.00 英镑）。

9. 请将贵方第 479 号信用证的船期和有效期分别展至 10 月 5 号及 10 月 20 号。

10. 鉴于我们之间的友好合作，我们准备接受 60 天远期付款交单的支付条件。

VII. Translate the following letters into Chinese.

(1)

Dear Sirs,

In the past, our purchases of steel pipes from you have normally been paid by confirmed, irrevocable letter of credit.

This arrangement has cost us a great deal of money. From the moment we open the credit until our buyers pay us, it normally ties up funds for about four months. This is currently a particularly serious problem for us in view of the difficult economic climate and the prevailing high interest rates.

If you could offer us easier payment terms, it would probably lead to an increase in business between our companies. We propose either cash against documents on arrival of goods, or drawing on us at three months' sight.

We hope our request will meet with your agreement and look forward to your early reply.

Yours faithfully,

(2)

Dear Mr. Lee,

Thank you for your letter of March 1, urging us to open an L/C. We feel regretful for the trouble you suffered by the late arrival of our L/C as we had to go through necessary formalities to apply for its establishment.

An irrevocable, confirmed L/C by draft at sight has been opened in your favor for a sum of RMB5,000,000 through ABC Commercial Bank, valid for negotiation until the 21st day after the shipment. We sent it to you this morning.

We shall greatly appreciate it if you ship the goods as soon as possible. We are awaiting your shipping advice.

Yours sincerely,

VIII. Translate the following letters into English.

(1)

敬启者：

我们已收到由中国银行长沙分行开立的关于 2000 台 IBM1201 型计算机的第 2345 号信用证，总金额为 2000000 美元。贵方信用证所列条款中，我方发现有下面三点与合同条款不符：

1）本合同号码为 010254，而不是 010154。

2）第 010254 号合同中规定贵方信用证允许分批装运，而我们手头的信用证上写着："不允许分批装运"。

3）目的港应该是"利物浦"，而不是"考文垂"。

请据此做出必要的修改。

谨上

(2)

敬启者：

事由：信用证展期

我们遗憾地告诉你方，直到今天我方才收到你方有关第 AFA45 号售货确认书的信用证。在该确认书上清楚地规定有关信用证应不迟于 8 月底到达我处。

虽然你方信用证到达的期限已过，但鉴于我们之间的长期友好关系，我们仍愿装运你方订货。然而，由于信用证迟到，我们不能按售货确认书所定时间装运货物。因此，需将信用证展期如下：

（1）将装运期延期至 10 月底。

（2）将信用证有效期展至 11 月 15 日。

请注意我们要求在 9 月 30 日之前收到信用证修改书。否则，我们无法如期装运货物。

期盼及早收到你方信用证修改通知书。

谨上

IX. Write letters in English asking for amendments to the following letters of credit by checking them with the given contract.

(1)

Commercial Bank

Melbourne, Australia

Irrevocable Documentary Credit No. F-12345

Date and place of issue: August 20, 2009, Melbourne

Date and place of expiry: November 15, 2009, Melbourne

Applicant: T. G. Salgo & Co., Melbourne, Australia

Beneficiary: Guangdong Yiyuan Trading Company Limited

Advising Bank: Bank of China, Guangzhou Branch

Amount: US$15,000.00 (Say US Dollars Fifteen Thousand Only)

Partial shipment and transshipment are prohibited.

Shipment from Guangzhou to Melbourne, latest October, 2009.

Credit available against presentation of the documents detailed herein and of your draft at sight for full invoice value.

Signed commercial invoice in quadruplicate.

Full set of clean on board ocean Bills of Lading made to order of Commercial Bank marked "Freight prepaid".

Insurance certificate or policy endorsed in blank for full invoice value plus 10%, covering All Risks and War Risk. Covering 50,000 tins of 500 grams of Snowflake Brand Canned Yellow Peaches at USD3.00 per tin CFRC 2% Melbourne.

As per Contract No. SP05-1234

附：合同主要条款

卖方：广东宜原贸易有限公司

买方：T. G. Salgo & Co., Melbourne, Australia

品名："雪花"（Snowflake）牌黄桃罐头

规格：450 克罐装

数量：50000 罐

单价：CFR 墨尔本每罐 3 美元，含佣 2%

总值：150000.00 美元

装运期：2009 年 10 月自广州至墨尔本，在香港转船

付款方式：凭不可撤销即期信用证付款

合同号码：SP05－1234

(2)

Copenhagen Bank

Date: 4 January, 2009

To: Bank of China, Beijing

We hereby open our Irrevocable Letter of Credit No. 112235 in favor of China Trading Corporation for account of Copenhagen Import Company up to an amount of GBP 1,455.00 (Say Pounds Sterling One Thousand Four Hundred And Fifty-Five Only) for 100% of the invoice value relative to the shipment of:

150 metric tons of Writing Paper Type 501 at GBP 97 per m/t CIF Copenhagen as per your S/C No. PO5476 from Copenhagen to China port.

Drafts to be drawn at sight on our bank and accompanied by the following documents marked "X":

(X) Commercial Invoice in triplicate

(X) Bill of Lading in triplicate made out to our order quoting L/C No. 112235, marked FREIGHT COLLECT

…

(X) One original Marine Insurance Policy or Certificate for All Risks and War Risk, covering 110% of the invoice value, with claims payable in Copenhagen in the currency of draft(s).

Partial shipments and transshipment are prohibited.

Shipment must be effected not later than 31 March, 2009.

This L/C is valid at our counter until 15 April, 2009.

附：PO5476 号合同主要条款

卖方：中国贸易公司

买方：哥本哈根进口公司

商品名称：写字纸

规格：501 型

数量：150 公吨

单价：CIF 哥本哈根每公吨 97 英镑

总值：14550 英镑

装运期：2009 年 3 月 31 日前自中国港口至哥本哈根

保险：由卖方按发票金额的 110%投保一切险和战争险

支付：不可撤销的即期信用证，于装运期前 1 个月开到卖方，并于上述装运期后 15 天内在中国议付有效。

Unit 11　Insurance

保　险

练　习

I. Choose the best answer.

1. Since three fifths of the voyage is in tropical weather and the goods are liable to go moldy, we think it advisable to have the shipment _____ the risk of mould.

A. covered insurance　　B. take out insured　　C. covered against　　D. insured for

2. As usual we are going to insure _____ for 110% of the invoice value.

A. order　　　　　　B. all risks and war risk　C. you　　　　　　D. shipment

3. Generally we cover insurance _____ definite instructions from our clients.

A. in absence of　　　B. in the absence of　　C. in no absence of　　D. in all absence of

4. Regarding insurance, the coverage is _____ 110% of the invoice value up to the port of destination.

A. for　　　　　　　B. at　　　　　　　　C. of　　　　　　　　D. on

5. The goods should also be insured against breakage _____ your cost.

A. in　　　　　　　　B. for　　　　　　　　C. on　　　　　　　　D. at

6. The insurance shall be _____ from the time of the engineer's departure from China up to the time of his arrival in China on return.

A. effective　　　　　B. effecting　　　　　C. effect　　　　　　D. effected

7. We note that you expect us to insure the shipments for you for the invoice value _____ 10%.

A. add　　　　　　　B. less　　　　　　　C. plus　　　　　　　D. minus

8. You may _____ assured that your wishes will be carried out.

A. resting　　　　　　B. be rest　　　　　　C. be　　　　　　　　D. rested

9. It is _____ that the extra premium should be _____ our account.

A. understanding, on　B. understood, for　　C. understood, borne　D. understanding, by

10. Please note that for the article of this nature we do not _____ Breakage.

A. include　　　　　　B. cover　　　　　　　C. coverage　　　　　D. accept

11. We have to ask for _____ coverage.

A. more　　　　　　　B. less　　　　　　　C. broader　　　　　D. wider

12. _____ the 500 TVs under Contract No. 212 we shall cover insurance ourselves.

A. On   B. With   C. By   D. In

13. We are pleased to confirm _____ the above goods against All Risks for USD 5,500.

A. have arranged   B. having assured   C. to have ensured   D. having insured

14. We thank you for your letter of March 13, requesting us to effect insurance on the captioned goods for your _____.

A. cost   B. amount   C. account   D. expense

15. Since the premium varies with the extent of insurance, extra premium is for buyer's account, _____ additional risks be covered.

A. if   B. as   C. must   D. should

16. Breakage is a special risk, for which an extra premium will have to be _____.

A. charged   B. covered   C. insured   D. arranged

17. Cargo insurance is a kind of insurance _____ cover for goods in transit.

A. providing   B. provided   C. provide   D. being provided

18. If an incident occurs _____ in damage or loss to the goods you could take action against the carrier.

A. results   B. resulted   C. result   D. resulting

19. _____ insurance on this shipment, please charge the cost on the account of our Dalian Branch.

A. As per   B. As to   C. According to   D. Due to

20. When the cargo _____ a loss, the insured should take the following steps.

A. suffers   B. takes   C. under   D. endures

II. Fill in the blanks with suitable prepositions.

1. Generally we cover insurance _____ War Risk and W.A. _____ the absence _____ definite instructions _____ our clients.

2. Insurance _____ the goods shall be covered _____ us _____ 110% _____ the CIF value, and any extra premium _____ additional coverage, if required, shall be borne _____ the buyers.

3. We are pleased to inform you that that we have booked shipping space _____ your Order No. 3322 _____ 30 cases _____ captioned goods _____ S. S. "Swan" which sails _____ your port _____ or _____ March 25.

4. Insurance is very closely related _____ foreign trade. People _____ international trade should have a thorough knowledge _____ it.

5. It is stipulated _____ the S/C that insurance is to be covered _____ Sellers _____ the amount of 30% _____ the invoice value _____ TPND, Fresh and/or Rain Water Damage _____ addition to WPA.

6. As the Gulf War broke out, the insurer had to charge all the insured _____ a higher rate.

7. As your Order No. 231 for our Pearl Necklaces, Bracelet and Earrings is placed on CFR basis, insurance will be arranged _____ your end.

8. The rate _____ premium for War Risk is 0.04%.

9. As your Order No. 458 _____ our Silk Handkerchiefs was booked _____ CIF basis, insurance

will be effected at this end.

10. We have forwarded the debit note _____ you _____ the premium.

III. Choose the right answers.

(1)

A. debit note

B. for your account

C. be forwarded to

D. serve your purpose

E. enjoying high prestige

Dear Mr. Nottingham,

Re: Order No. C422 for 1,000 sets of PCs

This is to acknowledge receipt of your letter dated July 3, requesting us to effect insurance on the captioned shipment __1__.

We are pleased to inform you that we have covered the above shipment against All Risks for USD 114,585.00 with the PICC which is a state-operated enterprise __2__ in settling claims promptly and equitably. The policy is being prepared accordingly and will __3__ you within a week together with our __4__ for the premium.

We trust the above information will __5__ and await your further news.

Yours sincerely,

---

(2)

A. extra premium is to be borne

B. effect insurance

C. 110% of the total invoice value

D. inquiring about the insurance

E. to your account

F. do accordingly

G. there is any difference in premium

H. concluded on CIF basis

I. premium receipt issued by

Dear Sirs,

In reply to your letter of November 13 __1__ on our CIF offer for "Teddy" Bear Toys made to you on October 20, we wish to give you the following information:

For transactions __2__, we usually __3__ with PICC against All Risks, as per Ocean Marine Cargo Clauses of PICC dated 1 January, 1981. If you require the insurance to be covered as per Institute Cargo Clauses (ICC), we would be glad to comply but if __4__ between the two it will be charged __5__.

We are also in a position to insure the shipment against any additional risks if you do desire, and the __6__ by you. In this case, we shall send you the __7__ the relative underwriter.

Usually, the amount insured is __8__. However, if a higher percentage is required, we may __9__ but you have to bear the extra premium as well.

We are looking forward to your order.

Yours faithfully,

IV. Translate the following sentences into Chinese.
1. Buyer's request for insurance to be covered up to the inland city can be accepted on condition that such extra premium is for buyer's account.
2. Insurance validity expires on the 60th day after the insured goods are unloaded at the final port of discharge.
3. The underwriters are responsible for the claim as far as it is within the scope of cover.
4. Insurance policy or certificate in triplicate covering all risks and war risk including breakage in excess of 5% on the whole consignment and including W/W up to buyer's go-down in Hong Kong.
5. Our quotation is on CIF basis. If you prefer to have the insurance to be covered at your end, please let us know so that we may quote you CFR prices.
6. Should the damage be incurred, you may, within 60 days after the arrival of the consignment, file a claim with the insurance company.
7. For transactions concluded on CIF basis, we usually effect insurance with PICC against All Risks, as per Ocean Marine Cargo Clauses of PICC dated 1 January, 1981.
8. Should any damage be incurred, you may, within 30 days after the arrival of the consignment, approach the insurance agent at your end and raise a claim with him to be supported by a survey report.
9. We are responsible for the claim as far as it is within the scope of cover, but the loss in question

was beyond the coverage granted by us.

10. The premium will cost USD140.00 and we could deduct it from the 2% commission payable to you. The balance of the commission will be remitted to you as soon as the proceeds from the letter of credit have been collected.

V. Translate the following sentences into English.

1. 请为我方所订的 1000 台录音机投保平安险。
2. 我们的惯例是对货物按发票金额 110%投保。
3. 卖方代买方按发票金额的 110%投保水渍险，保险费由买方负责。
4. 请向中国人民保险公司按发票金额的 110%对 50 公吨化肥投保一切险和战争险。
5. 一般情况下，在未收到我方客户的明确指示时，我们则投保水渍险和战争险。
6. 因为保险费率随着保险的险别险种变化，如果要加保附加险，增加的保险费由买方承担。
7. 该项保险仅保水渍险和战争险。如果投保一般附加险，则由买方负担额外的保险费用。
8. 如果贵方愿意，我们也可受理更广的保险范围，条件是额外的保险费由买方负担。
9. 由于我们的订单是按 CIF 条件达成，保险由你方办理，所以若你方为我方向保险公司接洽此事，我方十分感激。
10. 破碎险的保险费率是 0.08%。如你方愿意投保破碎险，我方可以代为办理。

VI. Translate the following letters into Chinese.

(1)

Dear Sirs,

Referring to your fax enquiry of June 10 for insurance issue, we have pleasure in informing you as follows:

First, we generally cover WPA and war risk in the absence of definite instructions from our clients. If you desire to cover all risks, we can provide such coverage at a slightly higher premium rate. Second, the goods are insured for 110% of the invoice value. If additional risks are covered, extra premium will be for buyer's account.

We trust the above information will turn out to your entire satisfaction and your early reply will be awaited.

Yours faithfully,

(2)

Dear Sirs,

We are in receipt of your letter dated June 15 and are pleased to note that you would like to insure with us a shipment of Chinese Porcelain from Tianjin to Genoa by sea.

We would advise that the rate now being charged by us for the proposed shipment against All Risks including War Risk is 0.5% subject to our own Ocean Marine Cargo Clauses and Ocean Marine War Risks Clauses, copies of which are enclosed herewith for your reference.

If you find our rate acceptable, please let us know, preferably by fax, the details of your shipment so that we may issue our policy accordingly.

We are looking forward to your early reply.

Yours faithfully,

VII. Translate the following letters into English.

(1)

敬启者：

　　我方非常遗憾地通知你方，不能对你方所订购的 1000 台计算机按发票金额 150%投保，因为我们的惯例是按发票金额 110%投保。另外，合同中规定保险由卖方按高出发票金额 10%向中国人民保险公司投保一切险和战争险。但是如果你们坚持你们的意见，我们可以办理，但额外保费应由你方承担。

　　请早日告知你方的决定。

谨上

(2)

敬启者：

　　关于我方第 345 号购货确认书项下的 5000 条白兔牌毛毯，现通知你方，我方已由中国银行开立了第 789 号保兑的、不可撤销的、凭即期汇票支付的信用证，总金额计 45000 美元，有效期至 8 月 31 日为止。

　　请注意上述货物必须在 8 月底前装运，保险须按发票金额的 130%投保一切险。我方知道，按照你方的一般惯例，你方只按发票金额另加 10%投保，因此额外的保险费由我方负担。

　　请按我方要求洽办保险，我方等候你方的装船通知。

谨上

VIII. Fill out the insurance policy according to the following terms.

保险人：中国人民保险公司

被保险人：天津飞达进出口公司

保单编号：JH-KL001

保单日期：20＿＿年 8 月 8 日

标记：参见第 JH-KL001 号发票

包装及数量：676 个纸箱

保险货物项目："长江"牌钟表

保险金额：24985 美元

总保险金额："保险金额"一栏的大写

运输工具（船名及航次）："金星"轮，V. 19

装运港：天津新港

目的港：科威特

投保险别：根据 1981 年 1 月 1 日公布的一切险和战争险

保险代理：J. G. SAFE & Co. A/S

        631 MAPLE ALLE, DK-254 VALBY

        KUWAIT

        TEL: (01) 413287   FAX: (01) 423384

偿付地点：KUWAIT

应缴保费：249.85 美元

投保日期：20＿＿年 8 月 8 日

Insurance Policy

1. Insurer		2. Insured	
3. Policy No.		**4. Policy Date**	
5. Marks & Nos.	**6. Quantity**	**7. Description of Goods**	**8. Amount Insured**
9. Total Amount Insured			
10. Per Conveyance S. S. Voyage No.		**11. Port of Shipment**	**12. Destination**

13. Conditions	14. Insurance Agent	
15. Claim Payable Address	**16. Name or Seal of Proposer**	
17. Premium		**18. Insurance Date**	

Unit 12   Shipment
装 运

练 习

I. Choose the best answer.

1.   The shipment date is October or November _____ your option.

A. to   B. in   C. at   D. on

2.   _____ the unforeseen difficulties on the part of the suppliers we regret being unable to ship the goods within the time limit of your L/C.

A. Owing to   B. As   C. Because   D. Since

3.   A container holds 240 bicycles; the whole cargo would therefore comprise 50 containers, _____ 8 tons.

A. and each weighing   B. each to weigh   C. each weighing   D. each weighs

4.   After going into the matter carefully we estimate that the damage might be due to _____ handling in transit or during unloading.

A. rough   B. tough   C. hard   D. heavy

5.   As the shipment was delayed, the buyers pressed the sellers _____ an explanation.

A. of   B. for   C. under   D. at

6.   Attached to this letter _____ a copy of B/L, along with copies of invoice and weight memo.

A. are   B. is   C. have been   D. has been

7.   We will inform our customers _____ the arrival of the shipment ourselves.

A. by   B. for   C. of   D. in

8.   We wish to _____ your attention to the shipment of our Order No. 301.

A. bring   B. pay   C. ask   D. call

9.   You must be aware that any further delay _____ shipment will bring about adverse effect on our future business.

A. on   B. for   C. with   D. in

10. Your order will be delivered on October 15 _____ you requested.

A. like   B. since   C. as   D. when

11. Our advice of dispatch was faxed to you three days ago and you _____ it by now.

A. will receive   B. received   C. must have received   D. have been received

12. As soon as the goods are dispatched, please send us full details of the shipment _____ us to arrange for the insurance here.

A. that enabled   B. so as to enable   C. thus enable   D. thus enabled

13. _____ your charges for air freight are concerned, we agreed to pay the extra costs you invoiced.

A. As well as   B. As much as   C. As good as   D. As far as

14. Every shipment of our exports is strictly inspected by our shipping department before loading, and each package is subject _____ a careful examination.

A. for   B. under   C. with   D. to

15. Unless otherwise _____, we wish to arrange to take out a TPND insurance policy for you on the shipment.

A. instructed   B. instructions   C. instructs   D. instructing

16. Please try your best to ship our order _____ that steamer.

A. by   B. for   C. in   D. with

17. For the goods under S/C No. 234, we _____ space on S. S. "East Wind" due to arrive in London around May 4.

A. have booked   B. have bought   C. have hired   D. have retained

18. In our letter of December 1, we make _____ clear that shipment be effected in March.

A. them   B. you   C. us   D. it

19. We _____ the shipment to be made in time.

A. assure you   B. assure you of   C. ensure you of   D. insure you of

20. _____ any change in the date of delivery, please let us know in advance.

A. There should be   B. Should there be   C. There would be   D. Would there be

21. All the losses _____ from your delay in shipping our goods will be for your account.

A. rising   B. arising   C. raising   D. arousing

22. _____ would the deadline for shipment be exceeded by one week.

A. In any case   B. By all means   C. In no case   D. Under all circumstance

23. All flights _____ because of the snowstorm, we decided to go by sea.

A. were canceled

C. having been canceled

B. having canceled

D. had been canceled

24. We look forward to _____ the goods in the fourth quarter.

A. your deliver   B. delivery   C. deliver   D. delivery of

25. Emphasis has to be laid on the point _____ shipment must be made within the validity of the L/C.

A. what   B. which   C. that   D. /

26. Our ladies' pyjamas are packed in cartons, each _____ 12 doz./sets.

A. to contain   B. contains   C. contained   D. containing

27. We give you on the attached sheet full details regarding packing and marking, which must be strictly _____.

A. abide by   B. observed   C. submitted   D. seen

28. The loss was due to improper packing, _____ the suppliers should be responsible.

A. for which   B. to which   C. in which   D. which

29. Kindly advise us of the steamer that call _____ your port every month.

A. for   B. in   C. on   D. at

30. Our containers are conformable to the specifications _____ by the International Standardization Organization.

A. lie down   B. lied down   C. lay down   D. laid down

II. Identify the error in each sentence.

1. The goods under Contract No. 1454 arrived here in fairly condition.
          A   B   C   D

2. We regret to inform you that upon examination, we discovered a short delivery of
          A   B   C

   210 lbs in weigh.
          D

3. As the Contract No. 2456 for the goods is now ready for shipment, please rush
                          A   B   C

   your L/C without the least possible delay.
          D

4. The cargo ex S. S. "Merry Captain" have been inspected and found satisfaction.
       A   B   C   D

5. Each pair of Nylon Socks is packed with a polybag and 12 pairs to a box.
       A   B   C   D

III. Fill in the blanks with the appropriate words given below.

| prompt delivery | find | shipment | direct steamer | effect |
| advice of shipment | packed | proved | allow partial shipment | transshipment |

1. Our Trip Scissors are _____ in boxes of 1 dozen, 100 boxes to a carton lined with waterproof paper.

2. We will do our best to _____ shipment to meet your requirements in time.

3. The cargo has been shipped on s/s Dong Feng for _____ at Hong Kong onto s/s Flying Cloud.

4. Because there is no _____ from here to your port, we suggest that you accept transshipment at Hong Kong.

5. The _____ time is June or July at our option and the goods will be shipped in one lot.

6. We would like to know whether the shipment that arrived has _____ to your satisfaction.

7. We shall be grateful for _____ as the goods are needed urgently.

8. We look forward to receiving your _____ at an early date.

9. Enclosed please _____ a set of duplicate copies of shipping documents.

10. As the manufacturers cannot get the entire quantity ready at the same time, it is necessary for the contract stipulations to be as worded as to _____.

IV. Fill in the blanks with suitable prepositions.

Dear Mr. Warner,

Referring 1._____ our Order No. 213 2._____ 1,000 sets of MD Brand Microwave Stove, we wish to draw your attention 3._____ the fact that up to the present moment, we have not received any information from you 4._____ the shipment.

When we place the order, we explicitly point out that punctual shipment was 5._____ special importance because our customers were badly 6._____ need of the goods ordered and we had given them a definite assurance 7._____ early shipment.

8._____ the circumstances, it is obviously impossible for us to extend L/C No. 89 again, which expires 9._____ December 2, and we feel it our duty to remind you of this matter again.

We hope you will make every effort to effect shipment 10._____ the stipulated time as any delay would cause us much trouble and financial loss.

Yours sincerely,

V. Fill in the blanks with the proper word, of which the initial is given.

Dear Sirs,

Re: Your S_____ Confirmation No. C215 C_____ 4,000 D_____ Shirts

We have for a_____ your letter d_____ August 19 in connection w_____ the above subject.

In r_____, we have the p_____ of informing you that the confirmed, i_____ Letter of Credit No. 7634, a_____ to ￡3,500 has been opened this morning t_____ the District Bank, Ltd., Manchester. Upon r_____ of the same, please arrange s_____ of the goods booked by us without d_____. We are i_____ by the local shipping c_____ that s/s "Browick" is d_____ to s_____ from your city to our p_____ on or a_____ September 10 and, if p_____, please do your u_____ to ship by that steamer.

Should this t_____ order prove s_____ to our customers, we can a_____ you that r_____ orders in increased q_____ will be placed.

Your close cooperation in this r_____ will be highly a_____. In the m_____ we a_____ your shipping a_____ by fax.

Yours f_____,

VI. Translate the following sentences into Chinese.

1. We are anticipating a prompt shipment. If this first consignment conforms to the sample supplied, we wish to establish a regular connection for the future.

2. We are pleased to inform you that 4,000 dozen shirts under Sales Confirmation No. C215, L/C No. 7634 have gone off on S.S. "Feng Qing", which sailed on the 23rd of November for New York.

3. We are pleased to inform you that all the goods ordered on the indent enclosed with your letter dated August 23 have now been ready for shipment. We have booked shipping space on S. S. "Haihe". The voyage normally takes three weeks.

4. You may recall that we have emphasized the vital importance of punctual shipment because these items are for display at an international exhibition to be held in Kunming on September 14.

5. We have examined our production schedule for the next three months and find we are fully committed. This makes it impossible to advance the delivery date we agreed on in our contract.

6. Please send us by return full instructions for the five cases for London, as to contents, value, consignee and the payer of all the charges.

7. The lead time for delivery to us is normally 13 weeks. We will, however, place our order for delivery by air freight. We should then be able to ship the goods before the end of this month.

8. Much to our regret a strike of transport workers in Liverpool is causing some delay in the dispatch of a number of our consignments. I am sorry to say that the goods you ordered on 25th June are among those held up.

VII. Translate the following sentences into English.

1. 长时间的延误交货已给我方带来很大不便。我们坚决要求立即发货，否则，将不得不取消原订合同的订货。

2. 我们所租的船只按期到达装运口岸后，如果你方不能按时备货装船，就应负担我方所遭受的损失。

3. 十月份以前货物必须装上船，否则我们就赶不上销售季节了。

4. 贵方订购的货物我方均有现货，可保证在 11 月份第一条便船上装出。

5. 很抱歉告知不能满足贵方 12 月份初装船的要求，因为直达轮在每月 20 号左右驶往你港。

6. 我方第 0618 号销售确认书项下第一批货物将由"大庆"号轮装运，预计在 12 月 5 号左右启航。

7. 提单上应该注明"运费预付"。

8. 假如贵方能把原来 6、7 月各装运一半改为 6 月装运 40%，其余的 7 月装运，即期发货有望。

VIII. Translate the following letters into Chinese.

(1)

Dear Mr. Perkins,

As requested in your letter of October 3, we have shipped, in partial fulfillment of your Order No. 889, 10 metric tons of walnuts per s/s "China Prince" which sailed yesterday. The consignment will have to be transshipped at Copenhagen.

Regarding the remaining 10 metric tons, we will try to hurry shipment and will advise you as soon as it is effected.

We trust the above shipment will reach you in sound condition and expect to receive your further orders before long.

Yours sincerely,

(2)

Dear Sirs,

We are glad to learn from your fax of May 15 that you have booked our order for two Model 121 Machines. Our Order Confirmation will be forwarded to you in a few days.

Since the purchase is made on FOB basis, you are to ship the goods from Liverpool on a steamer to be designated by us. As soon as the shipping space is booked, we shall advise you of the name of the steamer, on which the goods are to go forward. For further instructions, please contact our forwarding agents, ABC Company, Liverpool, who have continuously taken care of shipments from you.

We trust that the above instructions are clear to you and that shipment will give the users entire satisfaction.

Yours faithfully,

IX. Translate the following letters into English.

(1)

敬启者：
　　多谢贵方 4 月 5 日就第 984 号订单订购 10 台 MC646 磨粉机一事来函。
　　我方未能满足贵方要求提前装运全部货物，致歉。

我们双方签订销售协议时，清楚地知道装运期为 7 月。我方现在只能于 6 月提前装运 5 台磨粉机，再于 7 月装运其余 5 台。希望贵方能接受此建议。

如同意，请修改相关信用证，允许分批装运，并传真告知。

盼早复，以便通知厂商提前交货。

谨上

(2)

敬启者：

我们已收到贵公司的信用证，并很高兴地发现其内容非常令我方满意。

很高兴地通知贵公司，运输事宜已安排妥当，细节如下：

广州黄埔装运日期：2012 年 11 月 26 日

货轮："华山"号轮

预计抵达卡拉奇时间：2012 年 12 月 20 日

如果贵公司有问题或需要其他资料，请随时与我方联系。

谨上

Unit 13　Claim and Settlement
索赔和理赔

练习

I. Choose the best answer.

1. We are sorry to learn in your letter that 200 pairs of leather shoes _____ to your order are damaged when they reach you.

A. offered   B. demanded   C. supplied   D. requirement

2. We believe this is a matter for you to _____ with the shipping company or the insurers. The responsibility rests with either of the parties concerned.

A. take in   B. take on   C. take over   D. take up

3. We have lodged a claim _____ ABC & Co. _____ the quality of the goods shipped _____ m.v. "Peace".

A. against, for, by   B. with, for, under   C. on, against, as per   D. to, for, per

4. We shall lodge a claim for all the losses _____ as a result of your failure to ship our order in time.

A. to occur   B. occurred   C. to incur   D. incurred

5. Enclosed are sample parts _____ some of the problems we encountered.

A. show you   B. showing   C. will show   D. shown

6. The 50 cases of computer accessories you sent us were found to be faulty. This was apparently _____ to improper packing.

A. led   B. resulted   C. applied   D. attributed

7. _____ the goods, we discovered that they were inferior in quality to the sample.

A. After examination   B. On examination   C. Examination of   D. Upon examining

8. Consequently we find no _____ to compensate for the loss you claimed for.

A. land   B. ground   C. place   D. position

9. The goods under Contract No. 3617 left here _____.

A. in a good condition   B. in good conditions

C. in good condition   D. in the good condition

10. We are sorry for the trouble the printer has caused you, but we are confident that it can be fixed _____ your complete satisfaction.

A. with   B. to   C. at   D. in

11. Please _____ the matter and make sure the same thing will not happen in the second and third lots.

A. look to   B. look through   C. look into   D. see into

12. We regret _____ to accept your claim under such circumstances.

A. being unable   B. be unable   C. to be unable   D. not

13. As it is a matter concerning insurance, we hope you will refer it to the insurance company or their agents _____.

A. at your end   B. for you end   C. to your end   D. in your end

14. There is a _____ of 420 tons between the actual weight and the invoiced weight of this consignment.

A. short   B. difference   C. comparison   D. different

15. It is only appropriate for you to file your claim with the insurance company _____.

A. being concerned   B. concerning   C. concerned   D. be concerned

16. After check-up, it was found that _____ 36 bags had not been packed as stipulated in the contract.

A. some   B. any   C. many   D. more

17. Faulty packing cannot _____ rough handling in transit.

A. stand to   B. suffer   C. endure   D. stand

18. Kindly give the above your consideration and let us know if our proposal is _____ you.

A. agreeable to   B. agree by   C. agreed to   D. agreeably to

19. The second point concerns the currency to _____ in pricing and making payment.

A. base   B. be based on   C. basis   D. base on

20. We would appreciate your _____ attention to the question.

A. prompt   B. instant   C. first   D. immediately

II. Identify the error in each sentence.

1. We filed a claim to you on steels last June.
       A   B   C   D

2. We regret our unable to accept your claim because it is obvious that the shipping
                  A   B   C

company should be responsible for this.
                              D

3. The evidence you have provided is inadequate, therefore, we cannot consider your
                          A   B   C

claim as request.
          D

4. Claims beyond the responsibilities of the supply can not be entertained.
    A   B   C   D

5.   Please let us <u>know</u> how you <u>are going to</u> <u>dispose</u> this <u>shipment</u>.
                        A   B   C   D

6.   We <u>do</u> hope the <u>settlement</u> of this case could <u>reach</u> in <u>most friendly</u>
        A   B   C   D
     atmosphere.

7.   Your <u>claims</u> on <u>pilferage</u> have been <u>accepted</u> and will be <u>solved</u> soon.
              A   B   C   D

8.   Our <u>clear</u> views <u>in</u> this case have been <u>established</u> by our <u>representative</u>.
            A   B   C   D

9.   The damage is caused by <u>rough handling</u>. So the shipping <u>agency</u> should be
                                          A   B
     <u>blamed</u> for it. Neither I nor <u>you am</u> to blame.
        C   D

10. The container was <u>loaded</u> in the <u>warehouse</u>, so short <u>weight</u> must <u>happen</u> at that time.
                              A   B   C   D

III. Correct the mistakes in the following letter.

Dear Sirs,

We are sorry to learn in your letter the 10th May that 1,000 pairs of leather shoes supply under the above order are damaged when they reach you. We certainly replace them and already do so, replacements sent by parcel post this morning.

Despite the care we take to packing shoes sent by post, there are recently several reports of damage. To avoid further inconvenience for customers and expense for ourselves, we now seek advice of a packaging consultant and hope we are able to make improvements.

We regret the need for you to write to us and hope the steps we are taking ensure the safe arrival of all your orders in future.

Yours faithfully,

IV. Fill in the blanks with suitable prepositions.

1.   _____ arrival of the first consignment, it was found that about 30% of the goods were damaged.

2.   _____ examination, we find whole of the contents stained.

3.   As the shipping company is liable _____ the damage, your claim, in our opinion, should be referred to them for settlement.

4.   The clean B/L certifies that the goods under Order No. 12 left here _____ good condition, so we regret being unable to accept your claim.

5. We leave it to you to suggest a solution as we have full confidence _____ your fairness.

6. We trust that the arrangements we have made will satisfy you and look forward _____ receiving your further orders.

7. Your claims _____ this cargo have been settled.

8. _____ case no settlement could be reached, arbitration terms are necessary.

9. The Customs imposed a fine of two thousand dollars _____ him.

10. It is stipulated _____ the contract that arbitration shall take place in China.

V. Fill in the blanks with phrases given below.

It is estimated that	shortage and damage	is attributed to
be held responsible for	On the strength of	commodity inspection
in settlement of	in compliance with	make the compensation for
Upon perusal of		

1. _____ the document, it is found that the loss took place at the time of loading at Rotterdam.

2. The carrier should _____ the loss.

3. The survey report indicates that the damage _____ rough handling when unloading.

4. _____ the survey report issued by the said Bureau, we have the right to reject the goods.

5. _____ there are 500 kg short-delivered.

6. I enclose a check _____ your claim.

7. The above mentioned shipment was delivered to our premised warehouse on January 14 with _____.

8. Our company will take the responsibility of the damage and _____ it.

9. The goods in Carton No. 2 are not _____ the invoice. Please replace them at an early date.

10. The _____ should be completed within a month after the arrival of the goods.

VI. Choose the right answers.

(1)

A. in addition to

B. under such circumstances

C. was attributable to

D. in the course of

E. according to

Dear Miss Marple,

We note from the Survey Report that the damage __1__ improper packing, and was further aggravated by handling operations __2__ transit.

As you are well aware, __3__ Art. 2 in our Ocean Marine Cargo Clauses, damage caused by packing defects is not within the scope of our coverage. To be fair to the parties concerned, however, we agree to pay 50% of repairing fees __4__ your survey charges, totaling USD 205.00.

Please explain to the consignees that this is the best we can do __5__. We appreciate your bringing this to our attention and giving us the opportunity to resolve it to your satisfaction.

Yours sincerely,

(2)

A. investigated

B. in due course

C. complaining

D. arranged for

E. called for

Dear Mr. Laycock,

We are in receipt of your letter, __1__ about the wrongly delivered goods.

We regret that two of the five cases did not contain the goods you ordered. We have __2__ the matter and find that we did make a mistake in putting the order together.

We have __3__ the correct goods to be dispatched to you at once. The relevant documents will be mailed to you __4__.

Please keep those two cases and their contents until __5__ by our agents who have been informed of the situation.

We apologize for the inconvenience caused by our error. We appreciate your taking the time to make us aware of this situation. Your concerns and opinions are essential to our goal of producing the highest quality products and providing the best service.

Yours sincerely,

VII. Translate the following sentences into Chinese.

1. We regret these faulty sets of equipment were sent to you, and today have sent a replacement of 12 sets. We hope you will be pleased with the new lot.

2. You have confirmed our order, but much to our surprise, we haven't yet received the goods up till now or any advice from you when we may expect delivery.

3. You wrote that the goods under our Order No. 156 were almost ready for shipment and that your shipping advice would soon be enclosed. But nearly a month has passed since then, yet we have heard nothing from you about this consignment.

4. Carton No. 17 was found to be 5 packages short. As the carton was in good shape and does not appear to have been tampered with, we surmise that they must have been short shipped. Please

do not trouble to send a replacement, but adjust your invoice.

5. The wrong pieces may be returned by next available steamer for our account. But it is preferable if you can sell them out at our price in your market.

6. We have examined them one by one, and found that each of them was leaking more or less.

7. We deeply regret to learn from your letter of June 15 that 2 cases of Tea Sets per S.S. "Red Flag" arrived in a damaged condition.

8. We found the goods partly soaked by rain/broken/smashed/worn and torn/torn/beyond repair/unusable/unsalabe/damaged.

9. We have to ask for a compensation to cover the loss incurred as a result of the inferior quality of the goods concerned.

10. In our opinion, the damage was caused by improper packing. A machine of this size and weight should be blocked in position inside the export case.

VIII. Translate the following sentences into English.

1. 兹遗憾地通知贵方，9 月 10 日抵达我方的来货中箱号为 78、内装零件的箱子损坏严重。

2. 显然木箱不够结实，经不起长途海运。

3. 10 月 2 日来函收悉。得知由"红旗"号轮装运的货物，其中两箱瓷器抵达时已损坏，深表歉意。

4. 兹关于你方 8 月 19 日电传，我方很惊讶地获悉你方订购的茶具到货受损，因为发货前与通常一样由有经验的工人仔细包装且托运时完好无损，随函附寄的清洁提单副本即可证明。我方相信破损是由于运输过程中粗鲁搬运所致。

5. 由于全部货物对我方毫无用处，务请你方退还发票金额和检验费，详见所附的索赔单。

6. 希望你方立即处理我方索赔。一旦解决，我们就退货并要求你方运来 12 台替换设备，费用由你方负担。

7. 我方遗憾地指出，第 15 号箱的装箱单与贵方发票不符，货物到达时发现短重 210 磅。

8. 第 17 号箱短少 5 包，由于箱子完好，推测是短装。

9. 我们希望此次不幸的事件不会影响你我之间长期的业务关系。

10. 我们及时收到了你方为我方第 133 号订单所寄来的相关装运单据并于"总统"号轮抵达青岛时提取了货物。

IX. Translate the following letters into Chinese.

(1)

Dear Sirs,

We have recently received a number of complaints from customers about your clocks. The clocks are clearly not giving satisfaction and in some cases we have had to refund the purchase price.

The clocks complained about are part of the batch of five hundred supplied for our order No. 908 of 2nd April. This order was placed on the basis of a sample clock left by your representative. We have ourselves compared the performance of this sample with that of a number of the clocks complained about and there is little doubt that many of them do not tell the right time.

The complaints received relate only to clocks from the batch referred to. Clocks supplied before these have always been satisfactory. We are therefore writing to ask you to accept return of the unsold balance, amounting to 403 clocks in all, and to replace them by clocks of the quality our earlier dealings with you have led us to expect.

Faithfully yours,

(2)

Dear Sirs,

Our order No. 098 of 9 March for plastics has now been delivered. We have examined the shipment carefully and, to our great disappointment, find that they are not of the quality we ordered.

The materials do not match the samples you sent us. The quality of some of them is so poor that we feel that a mistake has been made in making up the order. The goods do not match the requirements of our company. We have, therefore, no choice but to ask you to take the materials back and replace them with materials of the quality we ordered.

We are very keen to resolve this matter amicably. If you can replace the materials, we are prepared to allow the agreed delivery time to run from the date you confirm that you can supply the correct materials.

We look forward to your early reply.

Yours faithfully,

X. Translate the following letters into English.

(1)

敬启者：

你方 7 月 12 号的来信收到。很遗憾地得知你方在彩电方面遇到了问题。

虽然我们有严格的检查标准，但是错误也时有发生，正如你方彩色电视机中不幸遇到的一样。

我们立即安排了装运换货。你们的满意对我们极其重要，我们对给你方造成的不便表示歉意。

感谢你们购买我们的产品。

谨上

(2)

敬启者：

有关上周发运的第 343 号定单的来信收悉。

对于货物在运送途中破损的事宜，本公司感到遗憾。本公司一向特别小心包装货物，然而不当的运输方法亦会引致损坏。

本公司将按照贵公司开列的破损货物清单更换新货，不日将运抵贵处。

本公司已就有关损失向保险公司索偿，烦请保留破损货物供保险公司检查。

不便之处，敬希见谅。

谨上

Unit 14 Agency

代 理

练 习

I. Fill in the blanks in the following sentences.

1. We are now _____ to develop our marketing and buying _____ for 2001.
2. With this in _____, we shall redouble our _____ to make this business a _____ even if there is _____ or no profit for us.
3. We are already represented by our _____ agents in your city for the _____ of our Enamelware.
4. As we have to compete _____ a number of major producers here and it is therefore _____ that we have a marketing _____ which can keep us _____ of developments and _____ the seller's "eyes and _____" in the _____.
5. We would like to open discussions _____ you before the Spring Fair to discuss a closer _____ in _____ of selling Chinese Antimony Trioxide in the USA.
6. We believe that through _____ efforts business can be _____ to our mutual _____.

II. Choose the best answer.

1. As explained in our recent letters, the market is presently in a difficult _____.

A. surrounding   B. place   C. situation   D. position

2. We are anxious to _____ the market for our Antimoney Trioxide, which at present enjoys a limited sale in Europe.

A. increase   B. enlarge   C. expand   D. extend

3. We look forward to _____ your favorable reply.

A. have   B. receive   C. receiving   D. be informed of

4. With this _____ mind, we are writing to inquire if we could now begin discussing the question of sole agency.

A. in   B. on   C. at   D. inside

5. The catalog you sent us last week _____ an extensive range of interesting items, which appear to be reasonably priced.

A. has   B. includes   C. gives   D. covers

6. We need an agent in that district to help us to _____ our products.

A. market   B. send   C. sell   D. buy

7. It is our hope that, after proving our ability to dispost of large quantities, you will appoint us as a(n) _____.

A. sell agent   B. selling agent   C. sale agent   D. exclusive agent

8. We are not _____ in your country now and would very much like to work an arrangement with you. We can provide our references from the leading banks.

A. buying   B. represented   C. selling   D. exporting

9. After careful consideration, we have decided to entrust you _____ the sole agency for our products in the territory of South Asia.

A. of   B. for   C. with   D. about

10. Please send us an indication of the conditions under which we can _____ your company in Brazil.

A. represent   B. work as an agent   C. handle   D. be on behalf of

11. The general agent has _____ to take care of the advertising and publicity.

A. entitled   B. authorized   C. been entitled   D. entrusted

12. We would like to know on what terms you are willing to _____ an agency agreement.

A. come   B. conclude   C. agree   D. arrange

III. Translate the following sentences into Chinese.

1. In accordance with increased volume of our trade in India, we have decided to appoint an experienced and reliable dealer as our agent.

2. We are now enjoying the exclusive privilege of exporting all products of General Electric Company, the biggest manufacturing company of Electric Machines and Appliances in our area.

3. Transactions with Government Bodies: Transactions concluded between government bodies of Party A and Party B are not restricted by the terms and conditions of this agency agreement, nor shall they be considered as the target fulfilled by Party B under this agreement.

4. Party B shall undertake to supply Party A once every three months with a market report in writing on prevailing market conditions as well as customers' comments on quality, packing, and price, etc. of the bicycles under this agreement. If there is any particular change of local import regulations, Party B shall notify Party A at once.

5. In case of a breach of any of the provisions of this agency agreement by one party, the other party shall have the right to terminate this agreement forthwith by giving notice in writing to its opposite party.

6. Commission: Party A agrees to pay Party B a commission of 5% (five percent) on FOB value of orders. The commission is to be paid only after full payment for each order is received by Party A. No commission shall be paid on orders secured and executed by Party A itself.

7. This Agreement, when duly signed by the parties concerned, shall remain in force for one year to be effective as from January 1, 2012 to December 31, 2012. If a renewal of this Agreement is desired, notice in writing should be given by either party within one month prior to its expiry.

8. Should one of the parties fail to comply with the terms and conditions of this Agreement, the

other party is entitled to terminate this Agreement.

9. Party A shall not supply the contracted commodity to other buyers in the above-mentioned territory. Direct inquires, if any, will be referred to Party B. However, should any other buyers insist on dealing direct with Party A, Party A shall have the right to do so. In the latter case, Party A shall send to Party B a copy of relevant S/C and reserve one percent commission for Party B on the net invoice value of the transactions concluded.

10. This agreement is made out in quadruplicate, each party holding two copies.

IV. Translate the following sentences into English.

1. 我们热切地盼望促进我方产品在贵地的销售。
2. 我方已委托琼斯公司销售我方的产品。
3. 作为我方的进口商和本地经销商，此公司与我方进行业务合作已有五年。
4. 我们已保持了十年密切的商业联系。
5. 作为我方在你区域的代理，你方必须熟悉我们的产品和经营方针。
6. 我们的客户一向对我们代理商完全可靠的服务感到满意。
7. 至于本公司的产品质量你们可以完全放心。
8. 我们的经销商就在你们附近，可随时为你们提供周到的服务。
9. 我们在等待你们尽早与我们取得联系。

V. Translate the following letters into Chinese.

(1)

Dear Sirs,

We hope very much to be the sole agent for your "Flyin" Brand Motor in our country.

As you may know, we have 25 years' experience in selling and repairing motors. We are quite familiar with customers' purchase habit. With high quality of your products and our well-developed after-sales service, we have full confidence in assuring you of an annual turnover of US$900,000.

We believe our cooperation may get a great success. A copy of detailed plan regarding handling your products, our sales channels and after-sales service is enclosed for your reference.

We hope to hear favorably from you.

Yours faithfully,

(2)

Dear Sirs,

Having carefully considered your letter of September 10, we should like to go further into your proposal for an agency in Scotland. Your work with Messrs. James Neil & Co. is not known to us and in view of your connections throughout the trade in Scotland we feel there is much you could do to extend our business there.

Our final decision would depend upon the terms and condition and as your Mr. Smith will be visiting our town next month, we think it would be better to discuss these with him rather than to enter upon what may develop into a lenthy correspondence. We therefore ask you to let us know when we may expect Mr. Smith to call.

Yours faithfully,

VI. Translate the following letters into English.

(1)

敬启者：

我公司获悉贵方希望寻找一个可靠且具有良好市场基础的公司作为贵方的代理商，在欧洲销售成衣。

我方在德国拥有 15 年以上的成衣销售经验，占据很大的市场份额，我方很希望与贵方达成合作协议。

如果可以，我方建议贵方同 Peet 先生会面，商讨双方代理协议的细节问题。

谨上

(2)

敬启者：

谢谢贵方 2 月 26 日来函提议做我方在贵方的代理。

我方对贵方的提议很感兴趣。我方正在仔细考虑贵方的申请。

如果贵方有意 3 月初访问武汉，我方将十分高兴和贵方进一步讨论代理协议的可能性。

我方希望尽早收到贵方的回复并静候 Peet 先生的电话。

谨上

答案部分

Unit 1　Introduction to Letter and Email Writing
信函和电子邮件写作概述

练 习 答 案

I.　Translate the following job titles.

1. 会计部经理
2. 副经理
3. 业务主任
4. 接待人员
5. 副总经理
6. 外销部经理
7. 财务主任
8. 总经理
9. 总经理助理
10. 进口联络员
11. 维修工程师
12. 市场开发部经理
13. 市场销售部经理
14. 销售主管
15. 销售代表
16. 业务经理
17. 厂长
18. 销售协调人
19. 销售主管
20. 服务部经理

II. Make corrections in the format of the envelope.

Robert Kastens Carbonite Corp. 1333 Second Avenue Milford, Connecticut 06460	**STAMP**
	Ms. Yvette Carlson Haley-Richardson Company One Perry Park Plaza Detroit, MI 14562

III. Compare the following two sentences in the group and point out which sentence is more polite and considerate.

Group 1: We feel sure that you will be entirely satisfied.

Group 2: Perhaps next time we can send you what you require.

Group 3: We will send you the brochure next month.

Group 4: Since you are our regular customer, we are writing to let you know about our important policy change in insurance.

Group 5: Take your pick of typewriter ribbons in three colors: black, blue, and green.

Group 6: You could obtain a refund if the goods you returned had remained clean and useable.

Group 7: The large scale of sales of our products will make your company more profitable.

Group 8: We are happy to tell you that we may ship the goods after September 8.

Group 9: If you speak to Mr. Wood about production, ask him to consider the delivery schedule.

Group 10: We are anxious to start business with you.

VI. Complete the following letter with its necessary elements on the lines provided.

Date:

Your ref: 21/J
Our ref: 06/AD

Mr. W. J. Parker
C/O Ms. Judith Brown
IHK Company
28 Sunnyville Road
London N9 9ST

Dear Mr. Parker,

Delivery of Boots

We thank you for your Order NO. 589 of June 5 and have to inform you that we are expecting delivery of this kind of boots not later than the end of the next week…

We are glad to know that the two pairs previously supplied have given you satisfaction, as we recognize that a satisfied customer is our best advertisement.

We enclose the receipt of payment for your previous purchases, as requested.

Yours sincerely,

Mark Blumsky

Mark Blumsky

Encls (2)

V. Arrange the following parts of a letter in the correct order and form, either in block style or modified block style. Address an envelope for the letter.

Block style

Tianjin Embroidery Export Corporation

78 Hongxing Road, Hebei Disctrict, Tianjin 300543, China

Tel: +86-22-24561447   Fax: +86-22-24569865

Website: http://www.tjeec.com

Your ref: PLK/lsx

Our ref.: HNE/325

September 2, 2009

Manchester Trading Company

58 Lancaster House, Manchester

M14 5RX

UK

Attention: Marketing Manager

Dear Sirs,

Re: Embroideries

We have learned your name from the Chamber of Commerce of New York, and are writing to you with the hope of establishing business relations with you.

We specialize in the exportation of Chinese Embroideries which have enjoyed great popularity in world market. We enclose a copy of our latest price list for your reference and hope that you would let us know if any item is of interest to you.

Yours faithfully,

Tianjin Embroidery Export Corporation

Jamie Xia

Jamie Xia

Sales Manager

Enclosure: 1 price list

C. C. Mr. James Brown

Modified block style

Tianjin Embroidery Export Corporation

78 Hongxing Road, Hebei Disctrict, Tianjin 300543, China

Tel: +86-22-24561447   Fax: +86-22-24569865

Website: http://www.tjeec.com

Your ref: PLK/lsx

Our ref.: HNE/325

September 2, 2009

Manchester Trading Company

58 Lancaster House, Manchester

M14 5RX

UK

Attention: Marketing Manager

Dear Sirs,

Re: Embroideries

We have learned your name from the Chamber of Commerce of New York, and are writing to you with the hope of establishing business relations with you.

We specialize in the exportation of Chinese Embroideries which have enjoyed great popularity in world market. We enclose a copy of our latest price list for your reference and hope that you would let us know if any item is of interest to you.

Yours faithfully,

Tianjin Embroidery Export Corporation

Jamie Xia

Jamie Xia

Sales Manager

Enclosure: 1 price list

C. C. Mr. James Brown

Envelope

Tianjin Embroidery Export Corporation   **STAMP**
78 Hongxing Road, Hebei Disctrict
Tianjin 300543
China

Marketing Manager
Manchester Trading Company
58 Lancaster House, Manchester
M14 5RX
UK

VI. Translate the following words or phrases into Chinese.

1. 附件	11. 打印机	21. 结尾敬语
2. 电脑病毒	12. 终端	22. 表情符号
3. 垃圾邮件	13. 传送，传递	23. 缺省字体
4. 收件人，收信人	14. 无人看管，无人值班	24. 乱码
5. 网站链接	15. 自动拨号	25. 安装
6. 下载	16. 传真封面	26. 点击
7. 网络礼仪	17. 签名档	27. 格式
8. 收到的传真	18. 文本	28. 文件夹
9. 分辨率	19. 数码照片	29. 主页
10. 扫描仪	20. 称呼语	30. 浏览器

VII. Translate the following email into Chinese.

发信人：Gale Xue <galexue@hotmail.com>
发送日期：2009 年 8 月 27 日星期四下午 4:35
收信人：David Smith <fetool@publicsz.net.com>
主题：对第 12 和 19 号产品的具体询盘

亲爱的史密斯先生：

今收到贵方按照我方 8 月 20 日电子邮件询价中的要求寄来第 12 和 19 号产品的 6 个样品。请按各项产品订购 1000 件的订货向我方报贵方最低价，我方希望能按 CFR 温哥华报价。如蒙尽快回复，我方将不胜感激。

谨上
Gale Xue

Unit 2　Credit Inquiry
信用查询

练习答案

I.　Choose the best answer.

1－5　DCBBA　　　6－10　DBCAA

II.　Fill in the blanks with proper words.

1.　with	2.　in	3.　with	4.　on	5.　of
6.　on	7.　whether	8.　with	9.　of	10. on

III.　Translate the following sentences into Chinese.

1. 上述资料应严格保密。
2. 该公司因按时履约而在商业界享有很高的声誉。
3. 兹答复贵方 12 月 2 日的查询，我方认为江先生的任何订购都是可信赖的。
4. 我方认为贵方与该公司的任何交易都将会感到满意且愉快。
5. 我方与这两家公司有 5 年的贸易往来，并且相信他们会乐意向贵方提供贵方询问的任何信息。
6. 由于这是我们双方第一次进行交易，请贵方提供两名证明人。
7. 根据此公司的还款记录，是否可以允许赊款？如果贵方可以告知，我们将不胜感激。
8. 维克多贸易公司在过去十年间曾与我们做过大量交易，他们会向你们提供有关我们业务信誉的任何资料。
9. 我们打算与之往来的商行要我们与你们联系，了解他们的业务能力和资信情况。
10. 查该公司自与本行往来，从未发生不能支付的情况。我们认为每月信用贷款 3000 美元是安全的。此外，他们对贸易的诚挚态度和广泛扩大业务活动能力博得好评。

IV.　Translate the following sentences into English.

1. The ABC Bank of your city will give information you required about our financial position and credit standing.
2. We should be obliged if you could furnish us with your opinion on the financial position and reliability of the above company.

3. We shall appreciate any information with which you may furnish us in this respect.

4. They have always provided complete satisfaction with punctual delivery, moderate prices, and superior quality.

5. They have wide connections both at home and abroad and their financial standing is quite stable.

6. A credit in the sum you mentioned in your letter of February 5 would seem to be safe.

7. The firm's difficulties were due to bad management and in particular to overtrading.

8. They are enjoying a good reputation in the business circles for their punctuality in meeting obligations.

9. The firm is of good reputation and has large financial reserves.

10. We should be glad to know if their financial position is considered strong.

V.　Translate the following letters.

(1)

Dear Sirs,

ABC Company is now offering to represent us in the sale of our LCDs, and has referred us to you for detailed information about its credit standing, business capacity and character. We shall appreciate it if you will give us your frank opinion on these points regarding the company.

Any information you may give us will be treated strictly in confidence.

Thank you for the help in this matter.

Yours faithfully,

(2)

敬启者：

我方收到雅加达 Batik 公司的订单。该公司现与贵公司有业务往来，并把贵公司作为证明人告诉了我公司。

如蒙提供下列资料，我方将不胜感激：

1、贵公司与该公司业务往来已有多久？

2、贵公司给该公司的信贷额有多大？

3、该公司还账是否及时？

4、目前该公司欠账多少？

贵公司提供的所有资料，我方将严格保密，所有的费用在接到贵公司账单后立即由我公司支付。

谨上

Unit 3　Establishing Business Relations

建立贸易关系

练习答案

I. Find out the mistakes in the following sentences and make corrections. There is one mistake in each sentence.

1. We would appreciate it if you could give us your quotation.
2. Some copies of our latest catalogs are being airmailed to you under separate cover.
3. Enclosed please find a catalog which may be of some help to you in selecting items.
4. We are informed that you are in the market for Men's Shirts.
5. If the products are of interest to you, please let us know without any delay.
6. We approach you for the delivery of the goods.
7. We are writing you in the hope of entering into business relations with you.
8. We have obtained your name and address from Singapore Chamber of Commerce.
9. We are a private enterprise trading in both the import and export of computer software.
10. We wish to enter into business relations with your company for the supply of light industrial products.

II. Choose the correct word to complete each sentence.

1. market　　　2. leading　　　3. enter　　　4. quality, reasonable　　　5. information
6. specialize in　　7. approach　　8. expand　　9. requirements　　　10. opportunity

III. Choose the best answer.

1. B　　2. C　　3. B　　4. D　　5. D　　6. B　　7. C　　8. B　　9. B　　10. B
11. C　　12. B　　13. D　　14. A　　15. B　　16. D　　17. B　　18. A　　19. D　　20. B

IV. Translate the following sentences into English.

1. We are one of the major importers of electronic products in this region. We would like to take this opportunity to approach you in the hope of establishing direct business relations with you.
2. We are dealing with the import and export of Machinery and Equipment for many years, which have enjoyed great popularity in many countries.

3. Through the courtesy of the Commercial Counselor's Office of your Embassy in our country, we come to know your name and address.

4. We are given to understand that you are the manufacturer of daily chemicals. One of our clients is in the market for cosmetics in your country. We shall be appreciated if you could send us immediately by airmail your catalog and price list covering the items available at present.

5. As to our finances and credit standing, please refer to the Bank of China, Shanghai Branch.

6. We are writing to you to introduce ourselves as a Chinese state-owned company specializing in electrical products.

7. We are pleased to send you by separate post our revised catalog and a price list. We hope you will be interested in our chinaware.

8. The enclosed literature describes the many superior features of each model.

9. We are pleased to send you a general catalog. It lists our complete line of chinaware. We hope you will find price, quality and design satisfactory.

10. We have a large stock and are pleased to send you patterns in various colors as requested.

V. Translate the following email and letter.

(1)

尊敬的马先生：

谢谢您 5 月 31 日询问我公司及其产品情况的电子邮件。

附件中一个是最新的产品手册，内列有我公司生产的所有型号的自行车。另一个附件是我公司截止到去年 12 月 31 日的财务报表。

我公司过去从未在欧洲市场销售过产品，因此我们非常高兴与贵方合作。

请仔细阅读附件。我们很愿意回答任何问题。

期盼早复。

谨上

(2)

Dear Sirs,

We have learned from BPD Company, with which we have been in good business relations for many years, that you are handling the import and export of various textile materials.

We are one of the leading dealers of wool sweater in England, and are interested in entering into business relations with you and importing wool sweaters from you.

We shall appreciate receiving the details and prices of various sweaters together with photos and specifications from you.

We are looking forward to your early and favorable reply.

Yours faithfully,

Unit 4　Inquiry

询　盘

练习答案

I. Try to find out the mistakes and make corrections. There is one mistake in each sentence.

1. We welcome you for your inquiry of April 23 and the enclosed catalog.
2. If your prices are competitive, we are prepared to order the sewing machines in large quantity.
3. We hope to conclude the business to our mutual benefit.
4. As regards walnut meat, we would inform you that the few parcels we have at present are under offer elsewhere.
5. If your price is in line, we will send you an order for 20,000 metric tons.
6. We shall place a large order for Women's Underwear with you, if the time of delivery is acceptable to us.
7. Being specialized in the import of garments, we express our desire to trade with you in this line.

II. Choose the best answer.

1—5 BBDDC　　6—10 ABABD　　11—15 DBACB　　16—20 DBDDC　　21—25 DDCDB
26—28 AAB

III. Choose the right answers.

(1) 1—5　DBACE　　　(2) 1—5　CEABD

IV. Fill in the blanks with the words and phrases given below.

1. available
2. on the basis of
3. There is room for
4. enclosed
5. enjoy great popularity
6. free of charge
7. As per
8. is inclusive of
9. at your request
10. for your reference

V. Fill in the blanks with proper prepositions.

1. in, in, in   2. in, in, with, of   3. from, in, of   4. On, for, of
5. of   6. for   7. for   8. under, of
9. In, with, of   10. by   11. of, by

VI. Translate the following sentences into English.

1. Please quote us your most favorable price, CIF Shanghai, inclusive of our 3% commission, stating the earliest shipment time.

2. If your price is found competitive, we intend to place an order for 300 sets of LCDs.

3. To enable you to have a better understanding of our products, we immediately airmail you several copies of our latest catalogs and 2 copies of sample books for your reference.

4. We are enclosing our Inquiry Note No. 235. Please quote us on FOB basis.

5. Upon receipt of your specific inquiry we will fax you.

6. On orders in large quantities, price reduction can be considered.

7. We are trying Vancouver market, where we are given to understand that the goods in question are in regular demand in this region.

8. We are enclosing the pictures and specifications for each item and trust you can manufacture them according to our requirements. Please quote us your best prices.

9. If your quotation is acceptable and the machine proves to be satisfactory, we shall place regular orders with you.

10. As a rule, we usually get 5% commission from the European suppliers.

VII. Translate the following sentences into Chinese.

1. 请向我方报以下每种产品的上海到岸最低价。

2. 现十分高兴附寄我方第 732 号询价。请贵方在离岸价基础上报盘。

3. 若贵方能供应我方需要的类型及质量，我方将向贵方长期大量订购。

4. 请对该询价给予及时的关注。

5. 兹关于贵方 3 月 4 日对男式衬衫的询价函，该产品属于中国纺织品进出口公司的经营范围，我方已将贵函转给他们办理。

6. 我方在《纺织品期刊》上拜读了贵方的广告。若蒙贵方向我方寄来可供现货的优质棉纺织品的图样及价格，我方将十分高兴。

7. 我方一客户得到一份允许进口 20000 美元各类电线的进口许可证。请报最低价及最大折扣和最早的交货期。

8. 回复或报价时，请注明询盘号，以便查对。

9. 若无法供应指定商品，请贵方提供最近似规格的产品。

10. 我国对微波炉的需求很大。请贵方对目前能供应的型号向我方报有吸引力的价格，不胜感激。

VIII. Translate the following letter into English.

Dear Sirs,

We were deeply impressed by your G3 laptop exhibited in your stand of the Dalian International Trade Fair. We assume your products would be most suitable for our market.

Would you please quote us the item listed on the enclosed inquiry form? And could you quote us your prices CIF Dalian, informing us of your earliest delivery date, your terms of payment, and discount for purchase of no less than 2,000 items.

We look forward to your early reply and hope this will be a good start for a long-term business relationship and mutual benefits.

Yours faithfully,

IX. Write an email according to the given situation.

From: lindawhite_trade@lanwen.com
To: master@szhchengming.com
Date: Friday, September 2, 20_ _. 15:23 pm
Subject: Inquiry Note No. 233

Dear Sirs,

Thank you for your catalogs forwarded to us and we are now specially interested in your Cotton Towels, and glad if you would give us the best quotation for the following items:

Article Nos.	Quantity
XF25-23	1,000 pieces
XF33-21	1,000 pieces

Would you please also let us have your detailed trade information concerning the listed goods, including the packing, terms of payment, the earliest delivery time and discount?

If your prices are in line and quality satisfactory, we trust large orders will follow.

We look forward to your early reply.

Best regards,
Linda White

X. Write a specific inquiry according to the following requirements.

Dear Sirs,

We learn from ABC & Co. Ltd. that you are a major exporter of desk lamps in your country. We used to purchase these products from other sources. And we are, at present, very much interested in buying from you large quantities of desk lamps, especially Art. 12 and Art. 81, because we understand that you are able to supply from stock at more attractive prices. In addition, we have confidence in the quality of your products.

We would be grateful if you would give us your most favorable price concerning the two articles mentioned on the basis of FOB China port and state the minimum export quantity and necessary details about packing, weight as well as delivery. Meanwhile, would you please let us know if you could forward illustrated specifications to us?

We look forward to hearing from you soon.

Kindest regards.

Yours faithfully,

Unit 5   Sales Promotion

推销信

练 习 答 案

I. Choose the best answer.

1－5   BCAAC   6－10   BAAAC   11－12   BB

II. Rewrite to combine the following groups of short sentences into two sentences each.

1.   Just fill in the enclosed post-free order form and mail it to us. If you are not satisfied when you receive the purchase, you can return it to us within 15 days and be refunded promptly.

2.   If you will place an order with us on the above-mentioned terms by completing and returning the enclosed order card, we are sure you will be satisfied with this initial order. To ensure that you have full information on the wide range of fabrics we can offer, we will arrange for our Mr. Cook to call on you, if you will note on the order card when it would be convenient.

III. Fill in the blanks with proper prepositions.

1. in   2. with   3. to   4. of   5. in   6. for   7. to   8. as

IV. Translate the following sentences into English.

1.   The special advantages it has to offer will make it a quick-selling line.

2.   In order to popularize these products, all the catalog prices are subject to a special discount of 10% during the month of February only.

3.   We can fill your orders at once from stock, and hope to invite your attention to our other products.

4.   From September 2, we began to offer the whole of our stocks at 2% to 4% less than our lowest quotations.

5.   Those sweaters we have offered you are guaranteed to wear well and look well all the time.

6.   Potential customers can come to our showrooms and see a display or a demonstration of our products and get hands-on experience.

7.   Our customers can call a toll-free number to request a sales literature or ask for specific information.

8. Being moderate in price and attractive in packing, our toys are very popular with customers in the U.S.

V. Translate the following sales letters.

(1)

尊敬的办公室主任:

　　商务人士一致认为传真机已成为必备的办公设备。只要轻松摁下按钮，你就可以在几秒内将传真发往国外，而无需等待若干天。你只需支付电话费而不是昂贵的全球快递费就可以将传真发往世界各地。此外，传真不会感染电脑病毒，因而比电子邮件更安全。

　　我们的专家可以为您安装、调试传真机，而且还可以帮助您挑选最适合您的功能。

　　我们的传真机 5 年内保修，终生保养维修。

　　欢迎致电，以便让我们为您服务。

谨上

(2)

发件人：xiazs_solar@meida.com
收件人：dsdy2004@yahoo.com
发送时间：20__年 10 月 23 日星期二下午 16:12
主题：新产品上市

敬启者:

　　贵公司一定会对即将投放市场的"美达"牌吹风机感兴趣。这款吹风机不但保留了原有型号的优点，而且多年的科研还赋予了其新的特点，使其更加完美。

　　贵公司会发现新产品上的一种机械装置能使该产品的耗电量约为相同功能吹风机的一半。而且，大部分零部件如有损坏，替换很方便。

　　这些特点使该产品十分畅销。因此，我公司愿与贵公司合作，在全国各地做广告，且我公司愿意负担当地一半的广告费用。

　　考虑到该产品可能会畅销，相信贵公司会认同付给贵方 5% 的佣金是十分优惠的。

　　电子邮件的附件是介绍该吹风机的产品手册。盼望贵公司能在贵处作为经销我公司产品的独家代理。

谨上
夏紫苏
销售经理

(3)

Dear Sir/Madam,

Are you having trouble getting your important documents bound beautifully? If you, like most business owners, have trouble finding the time to economically produce good-looking documents, this is why it is important to have a specialist take care of your most important documents.

At Hope Documents, we have the skills and experience to come in and help you make the best possible impression. May we stop by and offer you a FREE estimate of how much it would cost to get your documents looking great? If so, give us a toll-free call at 800-884-445 and set up an appointment with one of your friendly operators.

Yours faithfully,

VI. As the sales manager for Boot Company, write a sales letter for your product based on the following points.

Dear Sirs,

With the lifting of living standard of people in your city, you might be interested in high-quality boots. I'm writing to recommend to you our high-quality leather boots.

As we place stress on quality, we use fine leather and make every pair of boots to order by experienced workers. Our products, therefore, are fine looking, wrinkle-free and lined with cowhide.

We enclose our catalog for the 22 models, ranging from US$95.00 to US$300.00 per pair for your consideration and look forward to your specific enquiry.

Yours faithfully,

Unit 6　Offer
报　盘

I. Choose the best answer.

1—5　CBCAB　　6—10　CBCCC　　11—15　ADABD　　16—20　DBDBA

II. Fill in the blanks with the words and phrases given below.

1—5　HDIAC　　　6—10　EBFJG

III. Fill in the blanks with proper prepositions.

1. in/of, to	2. to, of, to	3. until/till	4. to, of
5. by/of, in, in, for	6. from, within/in/during	7. of, on	8. for, of, for, of
9. of, at, per, on/under	10. by/before, for, in, of, at	11. for	12. by
13. for	14. without		

IV. Fill in the blanks with suitable words.

1.　to, for

2.　quote, at, on, for

3.　to, reply, reaching, at

4.　On, for, allow/grant/give, of

5.　meet

6.　favor

7.　appreciate

8.　end

9.　low

10.　enjoyed/had, at, sure/confident, promote

11.　well connected, obtain, for

12.　separate cover, detailed, require

13.　quote, relevant, selection

14.　way, risen/advanced

15. stock, decline
16. prepared, with, out, with, end

V. Complete the following sentences in English.

1. a. your goods are competitive in price and of good quality

   b. you can advance delivery

   c. you would grant us 5% commission

2. a. please fax us your order for our confirmation

   b. please open your L/C which must reach us before the end of this month so as to enable us to make arrangements for shipment

   c. please send us your order so as to enable us to prepare the goods immediately

3. a. we are sure to place with you a trial order for 5,000 pairs

   b. we will immediately send you our order and open the relative L/C in your favor

   c. the large department stores here will soon place an order with you and energetically push the sale of your men's leather shoes

   d. we are sure that there is probably a ready market here for your leather boots

VI. Translate the following sentences into Chinese.

1. 现报盘如下，以你方 12 月 23 日中午前答复为有效。
2. 我们乐意按你们开列的规格安排生产货单上的商品。
3. 兹确认我们今天早晨给你方发传真，报 200 公吨花生的实盘，一周内复到为有效。
4. 兹证实我们已给你方发传真，报给你方核桃仁 100 公吨，每公吨欧洲主要口岸到岸价计人民币 10000 元，10 月船期。
5. 因棉布有大量备货，故能以此等低价向你方报盘。
6. 现附上时价表供你方参考，我方可立即发货，望早日订货。
7. 今晨我们已去传真报手拣去壳不分级山东花生 250 公吨，CFR 哥本哈根或其他欧洲主要口岸价每公吨人民币 4000 元，2010 年 10 月或 11 月装运。
8. 你方可能已经获悉近来对上述实盘的需求巨大，结果必将导致价格上涨。
9. 你公司 3 月 21 日来函收悉。兹按贵方要求另函航寄印花衬布目录一份和样本两份，希望有助于你方选购。
10. 付款方式：以我方为受益人的 100％保兑的、不可撤销的信用证凭即期汇票支付，信用证须在装运前一个月开到卖方，并在装船后 15 天内在中国议付有效。

VII. Translate the following sentences into English.

1. Regarding the terms of payment, we usually require an irrevocable, confirmed letter of credit payable by sight draft.
2. We will send you a firm offer for shipment in early May, provided we receive your order by March 10.
3. Because of great demand for these goods, the offer will remain valid only for 5 days.
4. We are making you a firm offer, subject to your reply reaching us by 5 pm, our time, Tuesday,

July 10.

5. As soon as we receive your specific inquiry, we will fax you our quotation.

6. If you promise an earlier delivery, we may accept your quotation.

7. We offer you 1,500 "Forever" Bicycles at USD 32 per piece CIF Lagos for delivery in May.

8. We take pleasure in sending you an offer for 50 sets of Coffee Makers Type 70 as follows subject to our fax confirmation.

9. We offer you 500 sets of Good Children Brand Bicycles at USD 35.00 per set CIFC3 New York for shipment in July, subject to your reply reaching here on or before May 5.

10. Please send us your best offer by fax indicating origin, packing, detailed specifications, quantity available and the earliest time of shipment.

VIII. Translate the following letters.

(1)

尊敬的韦伯先生：

很高兴收到您 5 月 12 日的电子邮件，现报虚盘如下：

品名：Annajia 鲜芒果

原产地：菲律宾

单价：每盒 12.25 美元（根据行情，价格每周有变）

价格术语：装运港船上交货价

装运港：马尼拉

付款方式：信用证

交货期：从确认订单起空运 3 到 5 天·

起订量：一个 20 英尺集装箱

供应能力：全年随时供应

内包装：每个芒果平均重 230 至 350 克，5 千克装一盒

相信贵方会认为我方报价具有竞争力，期待贵方的订单。

谨上

(2)

敬启者：

非常感谢贵方 10 月 14 日的询盘，感谢您对我公司男士棉衬衫的浓厚兴趣。

我方现给您寄送附图的产品目录和价格清单以回复您之前的询问函，以便给您提供您想获悉的细节。此外，我方还另函寄送了一些样品。我们相信我公司产品的设计、质量和竞争优势一定不会让您失望的。

对于贵公司的询盘，我公司愿意做出如下报价，条件是贵公司需要在 10 月 24 日前做出回复：

商品：男士棉衬衫

价格：大连成本运保费价每件 15 美元

支付方式：不可撤销的即期信用证

考虑到这是我们的首次交易，而且贵公司是一个潜在的长期商业伙伴，如果贵公司的订单超过 1 万件的话，我方愿意给出 5%的优惠。

期待您的订单，并希望能够与您长期合作。

谨上

(3)

Dear Mr. Watwood,

We received your letter of October 15 inquiring for our Hisense Brand TV sets inch 46, for which we thank you.

Our products are super-thin. The voice quality is perfect, and pictures are clearer than some sort of products.

We are pleased to inform you that we are now in a position to make you an offer, which is subject to our final confirmation. We offer you US$800 per set at CIF New York. Payment is to be made by irrevocable L/C at sight.

Please note that there is no commission on our products, but we may allow 5% discount if the quantity of your order is more than 2,000 sets.

We are expecting to receive your order.

Yours sincerely,

IX. Write an offer covering the following points.

Dear Sirs,

We thank you for your Inquiry List No. 713 of March 2 for 2 tons of walnut meat and are pleased to give you our offer as per the samples sent last month as follows:

Commodity: Walnut Meat (as per the sample)
Grade: Grade B
Quantity: 2 metric tons
Packing: In standard export cardboard cartons
Price: US$ 860.00 net per metric ton FOB Shanghai
Delivery: May/June, 2010
Payment: Confirmed, irrevocable L/C payable by sight draft to be opened 30 days before the time of shipment

As the goods are in short supply, please send your order by the end of March, otherwise the goods will not be available/the goods will be out of stock. We hope to have your understanding.

Yours faithfully,

X. Write a reply according to the incoming email. The following information is for your reference.

From: jiangming@alibaba.com
To: davidbrown662@erwo.trading.com
Date: Thursday, May 23, 2010, 15:12 pm
Subject: Firm Offer for Cotton Shirt Fabric Art. No. 145

Dear Mr. Brown,

Thank you for your inquiry for our Cotton Shirt Fabric. As requested, we are offering you 1,000 yards of Cotton Shirt Fabric, Art. No. 145 at USD 150.00 per yard CIFC4% San Francisco for shipment during June/July, 2010. We require payment by irrevocable L/C at sight and this offer keeps open for 5 days.

As you know, the item we offered is the most popular item of this year, we suggest you place an order with us quickly.

Yours sincerely,
M. Jiang
Export Manager

Unit 7 Counter Offer

还　盘

练习答案

I. Choose the best answer.

1－5　DCCDB　　6－10　CDCBC　　11－15　DDAAC　　16－20　BCBBA

II. Fill in the blanks with suitable words.

1. quote, basis
2. subject, reaching
3. do, make
4. regret, accept/entertain
5. declining, reduce
6. position, offer
7. market, appreciate
8. attention, instead
9. reply, information/reference
10. place, attention

III. Choose the right answers.

(1) 1－5　ABDCE　　　(2) 1－5　BDACE

IV. Identify the error in each sentence.

1－5　ADCCC　　　　6－10　DCBBB

V. Translate the following sentences into English.

1. We very much regret that your offer is 5% higher than those from the American suppliers.
2. As the market of wool is declining, there is no possibility of business unless you can reduce your price by 5%.
3. Frankly speaking, we regret that your price seems to be on the high side. So may we suggest you allow a discount on your price, say about 6%?

4. Thank you for your offer dated May 15, but we must point out that other suppliers in your area sent us more attractive quotations in which prices are 10%-15% below yours.

5. We have received a more favorable offer from your competitors, so please give us a discount, say 10%, on your price so as to start our cooperation.

6. We regret to say that your price for iron nails is out of line with the market here.

7. As the market is weak at present, your quotation is unworkable.

8. Indication shows that the market will advance soon. We are not in a position to reserve the goods for you up to the end of September.

9. The cost of raw material has risen rapidly recently, so to reduce the prices by 15% as you mention will considerably lower our standard of quality.

10. We suggest a reduction of 10% on all orders for USD 5,000 or more.

VI. Rewrite the following letter to make it more effective and then put it into Chinese.

Dear Sirs,

Thank you for your email of August 1. Your increased sale is a good indication that you are doing well in distributing our products.

We realize that price is a very important factor in maintaining and enlarging your market share. We have been doing our best to keep our price down without sacrificing quality. As a matter of fact, we have kept our margin to the minimum. That is why it is impossible for us to lower price any more given the present state of technology. However, we shall spare no efforts in further reducing our cost.

As an alternative, it might be viable to offer a lower grade with acceptable quality at a lower price. Attached is the data sheet of some of our varieties. Please let me know your interests.

Yours sincerely,

译文：

敬启者：

感谢 8 月 1 日的电邮。贵方增长的销售额是你方成功分销我方产品的有利证明。

我方认识到价格是维持、拓展市场的一个重要因素。在不降低质量的前提下，我方一直尽力降低成本。实际上，我方的利润率一直很低。这就是我方不能再降低价格的原因。但我方不会停止降低成本的努力。

作为一个选择方案，可行的方法也许是提供一个低档的但是质量仍可接受的低价产品。一些品种的说明书在附件中。请告知贵方对哪些产品感兴趣。

谨上

VII. Translate the following letters.

(1)

敬启者：

　　谢谢你们对"Strong"牌自行车报价的来信。我们虽然赞赏你们自行车的质量，但价格太高不能接受。

　　请参阅 8965 号销售确认书，按此销售确认书我方订购了相同牌号的自行车 1000 辆，但价格比你方现报价格低 10%。

　　自从上次订购以来，原材料价格跌落很多，这里你们自行车的零售价也下跌了 5%。接受你方现时的报价意味着我们将有巨大亏损，更不用谈利润了。

　　然而如果你们至少降价 1.5%，我们非常愿意向你方续订货。否则，我们只能转向其他供应商提出类似需求。

　　我们希望你们认真考虑我方建议，并及早答复我方。

　　　　　　　　　　　　　　　　　　　　　　　　　　　　　　　　　　　　　谨上

(2)

Dear Sirs,

Thank you for yor email of October 18.

We are very sorry to hear that our price for Star Brand TV sets inch 46 is still too high for you to work on. You also mention that Japanese goods are being offered to you at a price approximately 10% lower than quoted by us. It cannot be denied that our products are slightly more expensive than similar articles, but our quality, design, function and after-sales service are far superior to others.

We have done business for quite a long time. We are always ready to offer you a reasonable and competitive price. We have already reduced our previous quotation by 2%, but it still does not seem to satisfy you. Although we are really keen to do business with you this time, we regret that we cannot accept your counter offer or even meet you half way.

However, in view of longstanding business relations between us, after going carefully into the price again, we decide to cut our margin of profit to give you the benefit of a 2% reduction, in the hope that this would lead to an increase in business between us and help to extend sales and build up your market.

We trust that this will meet your approval and strongly recommend you to take advantage of this exceptional opportunity to accept our proposal as soon as possible.

Yours faithfully,

VIII. Write a counter offer covering the following points.

Dear Sirs,

We have received your email dated June 26 from which we note your offer for the Cotton Printed Shirting Art. No. 2345 at 95.00 pence per yard.

We like your products for their attractive designs and high quality, but we find that all our competitors are booking locally at 90 pence. In order to cope with the prevailing heavy competitions we have to book at 90 pence. We hope you can accept the above price.

As for the minimum quantity of 10,000 yards per design which you asked for in your email of June 26, we have to point out that in your previous email of May 20 the minimum was 7,500 yards. We ask you to maintain this lower minimum. We have booked a total of 45,000 yards in six designs.

Please let us have your fax confirmation at an early date.

Yours faithfully,

IX. Write an email to decline a counter offer according to the following situation.

To: William@hotmail.com
Date: Friday, October 9, 20＿, 11:12 am
Subject: Re: 1,000 sets of Bee Brand Children's Bicycles

Dear Mr. Bright,

We learn from your email that you find our price for the subject goods is on the high side.

Much as we would like to do business with you, we are regretful that we can't reduce our price by 5% as the price we quoted is in line with the prevailing market. In fact, we have already concluded considerable business with other customers at your end.

As our Children's Bicycles are strongly built and in good finish, they sell well in the overseas markets. If you see any chance to do better, please let us know.

Best regards,
Amy Lee

Unit 8　Order

订　　单

练　习　答　案

I. Find out the mistakes and make corrections. There is one mistake in each sentence.

1. If your price compares favorably to that of other suppliers, we shall send you an order.

2. The goods are urgently required, so prompt delivery will be necessary.

3. Your terms are satisfactory and we enclose an order.

4. We are glad to inform you that your first shipment of shoes has received favorable reaction from our customers.

5. If the first shipment is satisfactory, we can place with you many repeat orders.

6. We will accept the order on your terms with a view to encouraging business.

7. Please be notified that the said contract as well as the enclosure has been received duly.

8. We shall place repeat orders with you if the quality proves to be satisfactory.

9. Please make sure that the terms in the L/C are in accordance with those in the S/C so as to avoid amending the L/C.

10. With an order sheet enclosed, we are pleased to have booked with you an order for 6,000 M/Ts of oil seeds.

11. Though we appreciate your order, we very much regret that we are unable to accept any fresh orders at present.

12. We regret to inform you that we do not have in stock the goods in the desired quantity.

II. Choose the best answer.

| 1－5　ACCCD | 6－10　ABABD | 11－15　ADBCD |
| 16－20　DDABA | 21－25 BDCBC | 26－30　ABABD |

III. Fill in the blanks with proper prepositions.

1. with, of	2. with, for	3. for, within	4. of, at
5. to, with, for, to	6. with, to	7. by, in, by	8. of, for, of
9. at	10. to/with, from	11. to, with	12. to, between

IV. Fill in the blanks with proper words.

1. on, handle/execute, with, to, with
2. to, with, on
3. of, from, of, on/under, terms
4. with, for, in, to, on, of
5. of/in, for, of
6. enclosing, in, countersign, file/record
7. stock, decline
8. open/issue/establish, in, with/by/through
9. unable, with, out, with

V. Match the following terms of payment frequently seen in the contracts with their names.

1-5　CAEBD

VI. Translate the following sentences into Chinese.

1. 我方愿订购 200 台贵方产品来试销。
2. 在我们的网站上订购后半小时内，您将会在电子邮箱里收到一封确认函，表明我们已收到您的订单。这封确认函可作为您的购物的收据。您订购的商品一装运，我们将会给您的电子邮箱里发送最后的装运通知函。
3. 随函附寄第 231 号修正订单，订购 150000 码印花棉布。盼确认并寄售货合同。
4. 我们已接受贵方第 85 号购买编号为 1002 的印花布 10 万码的订单。请告知颜色搭配并按合同规定开立以我方为受益人的相关信用证。
5. 贵方的订单受到我方立即的关注。我方将在贵方规定的时间期限内交货。
6. 若你方没有现货索尼牌电视机，请报东芝牌或其他牌子的电视机的现货。
7. 我客户对你方橡胶靴子样品反映良好，现很高兴随函附寄三百打双的订单。
8. 随函附上我方第 904 号销售合同一式两份，请尽快签退一份供我方存档。

VII. Translate the following sentences into English.

1. If you are prepared to allow us 5% commission, we are pleased to place a trial order for 500 sets.
2. We are working on your Order No. 334. Please be assured that shipment will be effected within your stipulated time.
3. Owing to heavy commitments, many orders have not been handled. Therefore, we have to accept orders only for October shipment at present.
4. Owing to exhausted stock, we are not in a position to accept new orders. But as soon as fresh supplies become available, we will contact you by fax immediately.
5. The goods you intend to order are out of stock, but we recommend Art. DPT-54 as an ideal substitute.
6. As a result of our recent exchange of faxes, we wish to confirm our purchase from you of 6,000 cases of Tigerhead Flash Lights.

7. We'd like to cancel the order for your Bluetooth because of the change in the domestic market.

8. All these items are urgently required by our clients. Therefore, we hope you will make delivery at an early date so that they can sell them out before Christmas.

9. We shall arrange for dispatch by the first available container steamer upon receipt of your sight L/C.

10. We are very pleased to receive your repeat order, which, we assure you, shall be executed in due course.

VIII. Translate the following letters into Chinese.

(1)

尊敬的史密斯先生：

感谢贵方长期的支持。贵方发来的续订订单证实贵方在市场上表现良好。

由于产品在中国的销售旺季即将到来，所以我方许多国内的零售商期待产品能热销。他们的订单使我方连续三周以来都非常忙碌。我方制造商加倍努力以求满足需求。我方可以在下个月上旬接受新的订单。我方会随时通告供货情况。

同时，贵方也可找到一些在其他市场上畅销的产品。现随函附寄我方最新的产品目录和订单表格。若贵方对任何产品感兴趣，填写该表格并寄回我方即可。

谨上

(2)

敬启者：

2 月 15 日来函及所附花样和价目表均收到，非常感谢。我们选了三种，现随函附寄第 777 号订单。货急用，请即装。

谨上

附件：第 777 号订单

***第 777 号订单

英国伦敦

ABC 有限公司

敬启者：

请供：

数量	货号	单价（美元，FOB 温哥华）	交货期
250 打	3456	每打 2 美元	8 月份
160 打	7890	每打 4 美元	8 月份
90 打	2134	每打 6 美元	8 月份

包装：每打装一内衬锡纸纸盒，每 120 纸盒装一木箱

保险：按发票金额高百分之十投保水渍险

唛头：与我方以前订货相同

付款：不可撤销信用证凭即期汇票付款

我们已通知我方银行按本订单金额开立信用证，不久你方可收到你方银行的通知。

谨上

IX. Translate the following into English.

(1)

Dear Sirs,

We thank you for your letter of July 10 with a price list. We have chosen Acer5022 and shall be pleased to enclose our Order No. 988. As the goods are in urgent need, we highly appreciate your prompt delivery.

We hope your prompt attention to our order.

Yours faithfully,

Encl. Order No. 988

TIANJIN ELECTRONIC PRODUCTS IMPORT & EXPORT CORPORATION
Tel: 022－85200829   Fax: 022－85200793

Order Form

July 15, 2012

Order No. 988
Far East Industry Corporation
New York, U. S. A.

Please supply:

Quantity	*Model*	*Unit Price*	*Delivery*
1,000 sets	Acer5022	US$ 420.00 pet set	August

Packing: Each set is packed in a standard export cardboard carton, reinforced with iron straps outside

Shipping Marks: As per the Contract

Price: CFR Xingang

Payment: 100% by irrevocable, documentary L/C payable by sight draft opened through the Bank of China

For Tianjin Electronic Products Imp & Exp Corporation

Zhang Yumei

Sales Manager

(2)

Dear Mr. Sun,

Thank you very much for your quotation dated May 14, for your men's cotton shirts along with the illustrated catalog and samples.

We think both the design and quality of your products meet our requirement and the prices you quoted are competitive and reasonable. We are also delighted to know that you will allow us 5% discount on an order of no less than 10,000 pieces. Therefore, we take pleasure in placing an order with you as follows:

Quantity: 10,000 pieces
Specification: Men's cotton shirts XL
Catalog No.: M20
Price: US$15.00 per piece CIF Dalian
Payment: irrevocable L/C at sight

As these goods are urgently needed in our market, we should be obliged if you could dispatch the goods ASAP.

If this first order proves to be a success, we shall be happy to place further orders with you in the near future.

Yours sincerely,

Unit 9 Packing

包 装

练习答案

I. Choose the best answer.

1-5 BDABC   6-10 DCACD   11-12 AB

II. Fill in the blanks with the appropriate words given below.

1. marked   7. importer

2. neutral packing   8. trade mark

3. practice   9. brand

4. name   10. exporters

5. commodity   11. customs duty

6. package   12. quota

III. Translate the following sentences into Chinese.

1. 货物装入聚丙烯编制包装袋，每包重 50 千克，以毛重作净重。包装袋应该质量良好，适于海运。包装袋上用英语写上品名、重量、原产国别和包装日期。

2. 货物须用内衬锡纸的木箱包装，且外包装必须清楚地标明箱内所装货物。

3. 我们希望货物用净重 100 千克的木箱包装，而不是用双层麻袋包装。

4. 所有杏仁都用塑料袋包装，装入罐中，以胶带封住罐盖。每只木箱内装 12 罐，用钉子封箱，并用整条的金属条扎牢。

5. 就外包装而言，我方将把 10 打货物装入一纸箱内，每箱毛重大约 25 千克。

6. 包装时，请在每个盒内放入两至三种不同设计和颜色的产品。

7. 化学泡沫是新型包装材料的代表。随函附寄介绍该材料的手册，贵方可以从中了解关于这种包装材料的众多应用。

8. 箱内可内衬有不同材料以防止因漏水、空气或昆虫可能造成的损坏。

9. 我们的印花布是用木箱包装，内衬有牛皮纸和防潮纸。每箱 30 匹，一花 5 色，平均搭配。

10. 虽然尽力审慎地包装，但有时还是会发生运输途中有几桶破裂的情况。

IV. Translate the following sentences into English.

1. We'll pack them two dozen to one carton, gross weight around 25 kilos a carton.

2. Ten pieces are put into a box and 100 boxes into a carton.

3. We hope you will take measures to reinforce this sort of carton with nylon straps.

4. When packing, please take into account that the boxes are likely to receive rough handling at this end and must be able to withstand transportation over very bad roads.

5. We pack our shirts in plastic-lined, waterproof cartons, reinforced with metal straps.

6. Such light but strong cases can save shipping space and facilitate the storage and distribution of the goods.

7. As you suggested, we have improved our inner packing to meet the customers' demand in your market.

8. The packing of our Men's Shirts is each in a polybag, 5 dozen in a carton lined with waterproof paper and bound with two iron straps outside.

V. Translate the following letters into Chinese.

(1)

敬启者：

　　我们很高兴地向贵方订购 LT-93 型机器。如能在 5 月份装运，我方将非常感激。

　　由于这些机器是精密仪器，经不起野蛮搬运，因此适当的包装和唛头必不可少。为此，我们强调每只坚固的木箱装一台机器，内衬柔软衬垫以防机器在木箱内滑动。木箱必须用板条钉牢，外面用铁条箍紧。木箱的每一面用 3 英寸大的字母刷上"小心轻放"的字样。

　　请确保上述指示得到严格执行。

　　附件里是我方第 7812 号订单，希望尽快收到贵方的确认函。

谨上

(2)

敬启者：

　　多谢 3 月 20 日来函查询有关货柜服务事宜。

　　我方供应的集装箱有两种尺码，分别为 10 英尺和 20 英尺，能从两端开启，方便装卸。集装箱的防水和密封设计能避免货物受潮或沾水导致损坏。

　　所有集装箱都于工厂内装货和锁好，防止盗窃事件发生。

　　如需装运冷冻或易腐烂的食物，亦可使用能调控温度的特制集装箱，确保货物运抵目的地时完好无损。

　　此外，使用我公司集装箱装运货物所需保险费低于散装运送货物，能省回不少运费。

　　随函附寄收费表一张，期盼收到贵方的回复。

谨上

敬启者：

兹来函商讨我方第 897 号订货的外包装事宜。

我方希望贵公司能按照标准来包装我方的订货。请务必做到：每个用塑料袋单独包装，每三打装一个纸箱。每个纸箱内衬有塑料纸，全箱以铁箍加固，以防内装货物受潮或因粗暴搬运可能引起的损坏。装运前，每 10 个纸箱装一个大木箱。

为了防止货物受潮，请使用防潮包装，并在木箱外面加上"保持干燥"标志。

如果贵方及早关注我方的外包装要求，我方将不胜感激。

谨上

VI. Translate the following letters into English.

(1)

Dear Sirs,

We have received with thanks your Order No. MG-230.

As requested, we are pleased to inform you the packing conditions as follows:

The goods will be packed in tin-lined waterproof wooden cases, each piece wrapped in oilcloth, and 15 pieces packed in one case.

Cases will be nailed and secured by overall metal strapping.

We trust you will accept our packing and assure you of our careful attention when handling your order.

Yours faithfully,

(2)

Dear Sirs,

We are writing to discuss the way of packing concerning your Order No. 825.

As for inner packing, the fountain pen is placed in a satin-covered small box, lined with blue silk ribbon.

When it comes to the outer packing, we can pack your order with the standard packing. Each item is individually packed in polybag. Every four dozen is packed in a carton. Before shipment, we pack them in wooden cases, 15 cartons each.

Please inform us if there are any special requirements on the method of packing.

We look forward to your early reply.

Yours faithfully,

(3)

Dear Sirs,

We thank your for your email of November 20, attaching the sales contract in duplicate.

After going through the contract, we find that the packing clause in it is not clear enough. Please note that relative clause reads as follows:

Packing: seaworthy export packing, suitable for long-distance ocean transit.

In order to avoid possible further trouble, we wish to make clear beforehand our packing requirements as follows:

The tea under the contract should be packed in international standard tea boxes, two dozen boxes on a pallet, and 10 pallets in an FCL container. On the outer packing, please stencil our initials SL, with Shanghai as the destination port and our S/C No. 825. Besides, such warning marks as "USE NO HOOK", "KEEP DRY" should also be indicated.

We look forward to receiving your shipping advice and thank you for your cooperation in advance.

Yours faithfully,

Unit 10　Payment
付　款

练 习 答 案

I. Match the words and phrases with their Chinese meanings.
Group A: 1－5　DFAEB　　6－10　HJGCI
Group B: 1－5　FHIAG　　6－10　CBEJD

II. Choose the best answer.
1－5　AABDA　　6－10　ACAAB　　11－15　ABCDA
16－20　CCDBB　　21－25　BCCBD　　26－30　DDDCD

III. Fill in the blanks with the appropriate words given below.
1. in accordance with　　2. is confirmed　　3. has a right to　　4. called for
5. provided that　　6. in favor of　　7. amendment　　8. delivery
9. read　　10. extending

IV. Fill in the blanks with suitable prepositions.
1. within　　2. of, from, for, to　　3. from, in, of, for, of　　4. under, for
5. Under, for, of, to　　6. On, of, for, in, with　　7. to, of, of　　8. of, with, of
9. of, in, of, to, of　　10. to, about, of

V. Translate the following sentences into Chinese.
1. 付款需凭保兑的、不可撤销的、可分割的、可转让的、无追索权的信用证项下的即期汇票支付。
2. 由于贵方第 2305 号订单的货物已备妥相当长时间，故请务必立即采取行动，尽快开立相关信用证。
3. 因为我们预订舱位的船只到港延迟，请贵方将装运日期及第 3321 号信用证的有效期分别展至 4 月 20 号和 5 月 5 号。不胜感激。
4. 我方坚持在 7 月 31 日前结账，否则我方将被迫诉诸法律。
5. 为避免往后的修改，请务必做到信用证的规定与合同条款完全一致。

6. 因为本月没有驶往贵港的直达轮，请将贵方第 2345 号信用证改为准许转运，而非信用证中规定的"不准转运"。

7. 四月或五月没有从天津驶往贵港的直达轮，所以请贵方删去"用直达轮装运"，加上"允许分运及转船"。

8. 经审查，我们发现你方信用证金额不足。请将单价由人民币 0.55 元提高到人民币 0.60 元，总金额为人民币 37000 元。

9. 我方需要说明的是在将来，直接付款方式只适用于金额低于 1000 英镑或等值人民币的交易。否则，仍需以信用证付款。

10. 我方贸易惯例是用即期付款交单代替信用证，因此对于此次及将来的交易请贵方接受付款交单方式。

VI. Translate the following sentences into English.

1. For payment, we require confirmed and irrevocable L/C for 100% invoice value with partial shipment and transshipment allowed clause, available by draft at sight, against presentation of full set of shipping documents to the negotiating bank here.

2. We have drawn on you our sight draft for the amount of US$ 12,000 through the Bank of China, who has been instructed to hand over documents against your payment of the draft.

3. We wish to draw your attention to the fact that the date of delivery of your Order No. 1250 is approaching, but we still have not received the covering L/C up to date.

4. Your L/C No. 1230 has arrived, but on perusal, we find that transshipment and partial shipments are not allowed. Please amend your L/C immediately.

5. Please amend your L/C No. 345 as follows:
   a. Change "long ton" into "metric ton".
   b. The port of destination should be "Hamburg" instead of "London".
   c. Extend the date of shipment to the end of August.
   d. Partial shipments and transshipment are allowed.

6. When we checked your L/C with the covering contract, we found that the quantity in the L/C does not conform to that of the contract, the difference being US$75.60. Please amend it without delay.

7. With reference to your L/C No. 456, please delete by fax the clause "All the banking expenses/charges are for Beneficiary's account".

8. Your L/C No. 457 has duly arrived. But the amount is insufficient. Please increase by £520.00 (increase to £3,125.00) according to the contract.

9. Please extend the date of shipment and validity of your L/C No. 479 to October 5 and October 20 respectively.

10. In view of our friendly cooperation, we are prepared to accept payment by D/P at 60 days' sight.

VII. Translate the following letters into Chinese.

(1)

> 敬启者：
>
>   一直以来，本公司从贵公司订购钢管都是以保兑不可撤销的信用证付款。
>
>   这种付款方式花费我方大量资金。由开立信用证至收到客户付款，资金占用时间约为四个月。在现今经济气候不佳和利率高的环境下，这种付款方法给我方带来了极大的困难。
>
>   如蒙贵公司允许较宽松的付款方法，则可扩展双方业务。建议日后采用货到后凭单付款的方式或向本公司开立见票后三个月付款的汇票方式。
>
>   希望贵方能够同意我方的请求。专候佳音。
>
> 谨上

(2)

> 李先生：
>
>   我方已收到贵方 3 月 1 日的来函，催促我方开立信用证。由于我方需要办理必要的相关手续而导致了信用证开立的延迟。对此给贵方造成的不便，我方深表歉意。
>
>   我方已在 ABC 商业银行开立了一份以贵方为受益人的、保兑的、不可撤销的即期信用证，金额为人民币五百万元，信用证有效期为装运期后第 21 天止。该信用证已于今天上午寄往贵方。
>
>   敬请贵方早日装运。期待贵方的装船通知。
>
> 谨上

VIII. Translate the following letters into English.

(1)

> Dear Sirs,
>
> We have received your L/C No. 2345 issued by the Bank of China, Changsha Branch for the amount of US$ 2,000,000 covering 2,000 sets of IBM1201 computers. Among the clauses specified in your L/C, we find that the following two points do not agree with/conform to the contract:
>
> 1) The contract number is 010254 instead of 010154.
> 2) The Contract No. 010254 provides/stipulates that your L/C shall allow partial shipment, but the L/C in our hand reads/states: "PARTIAL SHIPMENT NOT ALLOWED".
> 3) The port of destination should read "Liverpool" instead of "Coventry".
>
> Please make the necessary amendments accordingly.
>
> Yours faithfully,

(2)

Dear Sirs,

RE: EXTENDING VALIDITY OF THE L/C

We regret to say that we have not received your L/C related to Sales Confirmation No. AFA45 until today. It is stipulated clearly in the Sales Confirmation that the relevant L/C must reach us not later than the end of August.

Although the reaching time of the L/C is overdue, we would like still to ship your ordered goods in view of long-standing friendly relationship between us. However, we can not make shipment of your goods within the time stipulated in the Sales Confirmation owing to the delay of the L/C. Therefore, the L/C needs to be extended as follows:

(1) The time of shipment will be extended to the end of October.
(2) The validity of the L/C will be extended to November 15.

Your kind attention is invited to the fact that we must receive your L/C amendment before September 30. Otherwise, we will not be able to effect the shipment in time.

Looking forward to receiving your L/C amendment at an early date.

Yours faithfully,

IX. Write letters in English asking for amendments to the following letters of credit by checking them with the given contract.

(1)

Dear Sirs,

Thank you very much for your L/C No. F-12345. However, on perusal, we have found some discrepancies and would request you to make the following amendments:

1) The place of expiry should be "in China" instead of "in Melbourne".
2) The amount both in figures and in words should respectively be "USD150,000.00" and "Say US Dollars One Hundred and Fifteen Thousand Only".
3) Transshipment should be allowed.
4) Delete insurance clause.
5) The specifications should be tins of "450 grams" instead of "500 grams".

Please make amendments as soon as possible so as to enable us to arrange shipment.

Yours faithfully,

Guangdong Yiyuan Trading Company Limited

(2)

Dear Sirs,

While we thank you for your L/C No. 112235, we regret to say that we have found some discrepancies. You are, therefore, requested to make the following amendments:

1. The amount both in figures and in words should respectively read "GBP 14,550.00 (Say Pounds Sterling Fourteen Thousand Five Hundred and Fifty Only)".
2. "From Copenhagen to China port" should read "from China port to Copenhagen".
3. The Bill of Lading should be marked "Freight Prepaid" instead of "Freight Collect".
4. Delete the clause "Partial shipments and transshipment are prohibited".
5. "This L/C is valid at our counter" should be amended to read "This L/C is valid at your counter".

Please confirm the amendments by fax as soon as possible.

Yours faithfully,

Unit 11　Insurance

保　险

练习答案

I. Choose the best answer.

1—5　CBBAD　　　6—10　ACCBB　　　11—15　CADCD　　　16—20　AADBA

II. Fill in the blanks with suitable prepositions.

1. against, in, of, from
2. on, by, for, of, for, by
3. for, for, of, by/per, for/to, on, about
4. to, in, of
5. in, by, for, above, against, in
6. at
7. at
8. of
9. for, on
10. to, for

III. Choose the right answers.

(1) 1—5　BECAD　　　　　(2) 1—5　DHBGE　　　6—9　AICF

IV. Translate the following sentences into Chinese.

1. 如果额外的保险费由买方承担，那么买方提出的货物保险到内地城市的要求可以接受。
2. 保险责任的期限到被保险货物在最后卸货港卸货后 60 天为止。
3. 只要是在保险责任范围内，保险公司就应负责赔偿。
4. 保单或保险凭证一式三份，投保一切险和战争险，包括破碎险，损失有 5% 的免赔率，按全部货物计算，仓至仓条款到买方在香港的仓库为止。
5. 我方报价是 CIF 价。如果你方想自己投保，请告知以便我方给你方报 CFR 报价。
6. 如果发生损失，你方可以在收到货物 60 天内向保险公司提出索赔。
7. 对于按 CIF 达成的交易，我们通常按 1981 年 1 月 1 日中国人民保险公司制订的海洋运输货物保险条款向中国人民保险公司投保一切险。

8. 如货物发生损坏，贵方可以在货物抵达后 30 天内凭检验报告与你处保险代理取得联系并提出索赔。

9. 只要是在保险责任范围内，我方就应负责赔偿，但这次损失不在我方承保的范围内。

10. 保险费为 140 美元，将在贵方 2％的佣金内扣除。佣金余额待信用证款项收到后，立即汇寄贵方。

V. Translate the following sentences into English.

1. Please cover FPA insurance on our order for 1,000 sets of Tape Recorders.

2. It is our usual practice to effect insurance on the goods for 110% of the invoice value.

3. Insurance is to be effected/covered by the Seller on behalf of the Buyer for 110% of the invoice value against WPA. The premium is to be for Buyer's account.

4. Please arrange insurance on 50 M/Ts of Chemical Fertilizer for 110% of the invoice value against all risks and war risk with PICC.

5. We generally cover WPA and war risk in the absence of definite instructions from our clients.

6. Since the premium rate varies with the scope of insurance, extra premium is for buyer's account, should additional risks be covered.

7. The insurance covers only WPA and War Risk. If additional insurance coverage is required, the buyer is to bear the extra premium.

8. Broader coverage, if desired, can also be arranged on condition that the extra premium involved is for buyer's account.

9. As our order was placed on CIF basis and you covered the insurance, we should be grateful if you would take the matter up for us with the insurers.

10. Premium for breakage is 0.08%. If you desire to cover breakage, we can arrange it for your account.

VI. Translate the following letters into Chinese.

(1)

敬启者：

　　兹回复你方 6 月 10 日传真询问保险问题的来函，现我方很高兴告知你方如下：

　　首先，如果没有接到我方客户的明确指示，我们一般只保水渍险和战争险。如果你方想投保一切险，我们可按稍高一点的保险费率承保该险别。其次，货物按发票金额的 110％投保。若投保附加险，额外的保险费由买方负担。

　　我们相信上述信息能使贵方完全满意并期盼贵方的回复。

谨上

(2)

敬启者：

　　6 月 15 日函收悉。欣悉你方愿将一批从天津装海轮运往热那亚的瓷器交给我们承保。

　　现奉告，根据我公司海洋运输货物保险条款和海洋运输货物战争险条款的规定，承保上述货物一切险包括战争险的现行费率是 0.5％。现随函附件上述条款供参阅。

　　如你方同意接受此费率，请最好来传真告知船货的详情，以便我公司据此出具保险单。盼早复。

谨上

VII. Translate the following letters into English.

(1)

Dear Sirs,

We are sorry to inform you that we cannot cover insurance on your order for 1,000 computers for 150% of the invoice value, as it is our usual practice to take out insurance for 110% of the invoice value.

In addition, it is stipulated in the Contract that insurance is to be covered by Sellers for 10% above the invoice value against All Risks and War Risk with PICC. However, if you stick to your arrangement, we may manage on your behalf, but the extra premium should be for your account.

We await your early reply.

Yours faithfully,

(2)

Dear Sirs,

We refer to our Purchase Confirmation No. 345 for 5,000 pieces of "White Rabbit" Brand Blankets. We are notifying you that we have opened through the Bank of China a confirmed, irrevocable L/C No. 789 payable by sight draft, for the amount of USD 45,000.00, valid until August 31.

Please see to it that the above mentioned articles should be shipped before the end of August and the goods should be covered insurance for 130% of the invoice value against all risks.

We are aware that according to your usual practice, you insure the goods only at invoice value plus 10%; therefore, the extra premium will be for our account.

Please arrange insurance as per our requirements and we await your shipping advice.

Yours faithfully,

VIII. Fill out the insurance policy according to the following terms.

Insurance Policy

1. Insurer			2. Insured	
THE PEOPLE'S INSURANCE COMPANY OF CHINA			TIANJIN FEIDA IMP. & EXP. CO., LTD.	
3. Policy No.　JH-KL001			**4. Policy Date**　AUGUST 8, 20＿＿	
5. Marks & Nos.	**6. Quantity**	**7. Description of Goods**		**8. Amount Insured**
AS PER INVOICE NO. JH-KL001	676 CARTONS	"CHANGJIANG" BRAND CLOCK		USD 24,985.00
9. Total Amount Insured		SAY US DOLLARS TWENTY-FOUR THOUSAND NINE HUNDRED AND EIGHTY-FIVE ONLY		
10. Per conveyance S. S.　Voyage No.			**11. Port of Shipment**	**12. Destination**
GOLDEN STAR　　V. 19			XINGANG, TIANJIN	KUWAIT
13. Conditions			**14. Insurance Agent**	
AGAINST ALL RISKS AND WAR RISK SUBJECT TO C. I. C. DATED 1 JANURARY, 1981			J. G. SAFE & Co. A/S 631 MAPLE ALLE, DK-254 VALBY KUWAIT TEL: (01) 413287　　FAX: (01) 423384	
15. Claim Payable Address			**16. Name or Seal of Proposer**	
KUWAIT			TIANJIN FEIDA IMP. & EXP. CO., LTD.	
17. Premium	USD 249.85		**18. Insurance Date**	AUGUST 8, 20＿＿

Unit 12 Shipment
装　运

练习答案

I. Choose the best answer.

1－5　CACAB　　　6－10　BCDDC　　　11－15　CBDDA

16－20　AADBB　　21－25　BCCDC　　26－30　DBADD

II. Identify the error in each sentence.

1－5　CDDDC

III. Fill in the blanks with the appropriate words given below.

1. packed　　　2. effect　　　　　3. transshipment　　4. direct shipment

5. shipment　　6. proved　　　　　7. prompt delivery　　8. advice of shipment

9. find　　　　10. allow partial shipment

IV. Fill in the blanks with suitable prepositions.

1. to　2. for　3. to　4. about　5. of　6. in　7. of　8. Under　9. on　10. within

V. Fill in the blanks with the proper word, of which the initial is given.

Sales, Covering, Dozen, acknowledgement, dated, with, reply, pleasure, irrevocable, amounting, through, receipt, shipment, delay, informed, company, due, sail, port, about, possible, utmost, trial, satisfactory, assure, repeat, quantity, respect, appreciated, meantime, advise, agent, faithfully

VI. Translate the following sentences into Chinese.

1. 我方盼望你方的及时装运。如果第一批货证实和提供的样品完全一致，希望建立长期的业务联系。

2. 我方很高兴地通知贵方，销售确认书第 C215 号、信用证第 7634 号项下的 4000 打衬衫已经由"丰庆"号轮运出，于 11 月 23 日启航开往纽约。

3. 我方高兴地告知贵方：随你方 8 月 23 日信函寄来的订单货物已备妥待运。我方已经预定"海河"号货轮的舱位，通常该轮航程为 3 周。

4. 你方可能还记得，我们强调准时装运的极端重要性，因为这些商品将在 9 月 14 日昆明举行的一个国际展览会上展出。

5. 我方核查了未来三个月的生产计划，发现计划编排紧密，所以我方无法将合同中协商好的交货日期提前。

6. 请回函寄给我方关于伦敦 5 箱货物内容、价值、收货人及付费人的详尽指示。

7. 从订货至货物运抵我方一般需 13 周。不过这次订货的交货方式改为空运，应能赶及在月底运出。

8. 很遗憾，利物浦运输工人罢工，我们托运的多批货物的发运延误了，你方 6 月 25 日所订货物也在其中。

VII. Translate the following sentences into English.

1. We have been put to considerable inconvenience by the long delay in delivery. We must insist on immediate delivery; otherwise, we shall be compelled to cancel the orders under the contract.

2. If you cannot get the goods ready by the time the ship chartered by us arrives at the port of loading, you will be responsible for the losses thus incurred.

3. Shipment has to be made before October; otherwise we are not able to catch the season.

4. The goods ordered are all in stock and we assure you that the shipment will be made by the first available steamer in November.

5. We regret our inability to meet your request for shipping the goods at the beginning of December, because the direct steamer sails for your port only around 20 every month.

6. The first lot under our Sales Confirmation No. 0618 will be shipped by/per S.S. "Da Qing" to be scheduled to/due to/to be expected to sail on or about December 5.

7. The bill of lading should be marked "freight prepaid".

8. The immediate shipment of your order can be expected if you modify your usual delivery arrangements by shipping 40% in June and the balance in July instead of two equal monthly shipments.

VIII. Translate the following letters into Chinese.

(1)

尊敬的 Perkins 先生：

按照贵方 10 月 3 日来函的要求，我方已部分履行了你方第 889 号订单，将 10 公吨的核桃仁装妥"中国王子"号轮，该轮已于昨日启航。这批货物将在哥本哈根转船。

关于剩余 10 公吨，我们将尽快装运，一俟装船当即奉告。

希望上述船货抵达贵方情况完好并期待日后更多的订单。

谨上

(2)

敬启者:

　　从你方 5 月 15 日传真获悉你方已接受我方定购两台 121 型机器的订单,不日将寄去我方订货确认书。

　　因这笔交易是按装运港船上交货价成交，你方必须在利物浦将货装上我方指定船只。一俟订舱完毕，我方将告知贵方即将装载该批货物的货轮名称。关于进一步的指示，请和利物浦我方运输代理行 ABC 公司联系，他们一直照管你方交运的货物事宜。

　　相信你方会完全明白上述要求，希望客户对所交货物完全满意。

谨上

IX. Translate the following letters into English.

(1)

Dear Sirs,

Thank you for your letter of 5 April regarding your Order No. 984 for 10 sets of MC646 milling machines.

In your letter, you ask for earlier shipment of the whole order. I regret to say that we are unable to comply with your request.

When the sale was agreed, we expressly stated that shipment would be made in July. The best we can do is to make a partial shipment of five machines in June and ship the remaining five in July. We hope this arrangement will meet with your approval.

If you agree to the new arrangement, please fax an amendment to the relevant letter of credit allowing us to effect partial shipment.

We expect your prompt reply so that we can ask the manufacturer to expedite delivery.

Yours faithfully,

(2)

Dear Sirs,

We have received your L/C and are delighted to find the contents in it are very satisfactory to us.

We are pleased to inform you that arrangements for shipment have already been made and the details are as follows:

Date of shipment from Huangpu, Guangzhou: November 26, 2012

Vessel: S.S. "Huashan"

ETA Karachi: December 20, 2012

If there are any questions you have or any additional information you need, please do not hesitate to contact us.

Yours faithfully,

Unit 13　Claim and Settlement

索赔和理赔

练习答案

I. Choose the best answer.

1—5　CDADB　　　6—10　DDBCB　　　11—15　CAABC　　　16—20　ADABA

II. Identify the error in each sentence.

1—5　BADCC　　　6—10　CDBDD

III. Correct the mistakes in the following letter.

Dear Sirs,

We are sorry to learn from your letter of the 10th May that 1,000 pairs of leather shoes supplied under the above order were damaged when they reached you. We will certainly replace them and have in effect already done so, replacements having been sent by parcel post this morning.

Despite the care we take in packing shoes sent by post, there have recently been several reports of damage. To avoid further inconvenience to customers and expense to ourselves, we are now seeking the advice of a packaging consultant and hope we will be able to make improvements.

We regret the need for you to write to us and hope the steps we are taking will ensure the safe arrival of all your orders in future.

Yours faithfully,

IV. Fill in the blanks with suitable prepositions.

1. Upon　　　2. On/Upon　　　3. for　　　4. in　　　5. in
6. to　　　　7. on　　　　　8. In　　　　9. on　　　10. in

V. Fill in the blanks with phrases given below.

1. Upon perusal of   2. be held responsible for   3. is attributed to

4. On the strength of   5. It is estimated that   6. in settlement of

7. shortage and damage   8. make the compensation for   9. in compliance with

10. commodity inspection

VI. Choose the right answers.

(1) 1－5　CDEAB   (2) 1－5　CADBE

VII. Translate the following sentences into Chinese.

1. 将有缺陷的设备运交给你方，致歉。今天另运出 12 台替换设备，希望你方能对这批新货感到满意。

2. 你方已确认我方的订货，但让我方十分诧异的是至今我方尚未收到该货，也未收到何时可以交货的消息。

3. 你方曾来信提及我方第 156 号订单项下的货物已基本备妥待运，装运通知不久随函附寄。但至今已近一个月，我方仍未收到有关这批货的消息。

4. 第 17 号箱短少 5 包。由于箱子完好，似未遭撬动，推测是短装。请不必另行补货，只修改发票即可。

5. 错发的货物请由下一班轮运来，费用由我方负担。但最好能在你方市场按我方价格出售。

6. 我们已逐件检查，每一件都或多或少有点渗漏。

7. 6 月 15 日的来函收悉，得知由"红旗"号轮所运的茶具中，有两箱抵达时已损坏，深表歉意。

8. 我们发现部分货物因雨淋受湿/破碎/粉碎/磨损/扯破/无法修理/无用/无法销售/受损。

9. 我方不得不向贵方提出索赔，以弥补由于相关货物质量低劣而招致的损失。

10. 在我方看来，这些损坏是由于包装不妥所致。一台这样大小和重量的机器应该是被密封在出口箱内的。

VIII. Translate the following sentences into English.

1. We regret to inform you that of your consignment, Case No. 78 containing spare parts reaching/arriving at us on September 10 is in a badly damaged condition.

2. It is obviously that the wooden case is not strong enough to withstand/stand the long-distance ocean/sea voyage.

3. We have received your letter of October 2 and deeply regret to hear/learn that 2 cases of chinawares per S.S. "Red Flag" arrived in a damaged condition.

4. With reference to your telex of August 19, we are surprised to learn that your ordered tea sets reached you in a damaged condition, for the goods were carefully packed as usual by experienced workmen before dispatch and shipped in perfect condition as shown by a copy of the clean B/L which we are enclosing herewith. Therefore we feel sure that the damage to the goods is attributed to rough handling while in transit.

5. As the entire/whole lot is of no use at all to us/As the whole lot is totally useless to us, we have

to ask you to refund us the invoice value and inspection fee detailed in/as per the enclosed claim statement.

6. We trust that you will settle the claim promptly. As soon as the settlement is accomplished, we will return the goods to you and ask you to send to us a replacement of 12 sets of equipment at your cost/for your account/at your expenses.

7. We regret to point out that there is a discrepancy between the packing list of Case No. 15 and your invoice and there is a shortweight of 210 lbs when the goods arrived.

    或 We regret to point out that the packing list of Case No. 15 is found not in conformity with your invoice and the goods are shortweight (210 lbs) when reaching us.

8. Case No. 17 is found 5 packages short and as the case is in good shape, we presume that they must have been short-delivered/short-shipped.

9. We hope this unfortunate incident will not have a negative impact on the longstanding business relations between us.

10. We duly received the relative documents for our Order No. 133 and took delivery of the goods on arrival of S.S. "President" at Qingdao.

IX. Translate the following letters into Chinese.

(1)

敬启者：

　　最近我们收到许多客户对你们钟表的投诉。这些钟表很显然令人不满意，有时我们不得不退款。

　　这些被投诉的钟表是四月二日我们第 908 号订单下一批五百件的一部分。我们订货是基于你方代表留下的样表。我们自己把样品和被投诉的钟表进行了对比，毫无疑问这些表中有许多都走时不准。

　　我方收到的投诉只与所说的这一批表有关。在此之前所提供的钟表一直令人满意。因此，我们要求你方接受未卖出部分的退货，共计 403 只，并换给我们之前交易品质的钟表。

谨上

(2)

敬启者：

　　三月九日订购的第 098 号定单项下的塑料现已运抵本公司。经查验后发现货物质量与商订的不相符合，本公司极感失望。

　　该批货物与样本相差甚远。部分质量极其低劣，令人怀疑订购过程可能出现了错误。由于货色与本公司要求不符，因此我们不得不要求退货，并换回定单要求之货物。

　　本公司诚意希望能友好地解决该问题。如贵公司接受上述安排，本公司准备待贵公司确定能供应合格货物起计算交货日期。

　　请早日回复。

谨上

X. Translate the following letters into English.

(1)

Dear Sirs,

Your letter of July 12 has been received, and we were very sorry to hear about the problem you experienced with our Color TV sets.

We maintain rigid inspection standards, but occasionally an imperfection does happen, as it unfortunately did in the case of your Color TV sets.

We have arranged a replacement order to be shipped to you at once. Your satisfaction is extremely important to us and we apologize for the inconvenience you have been caused.

Thank you for purchasing our products.

Yours faithfully,

(2)

Dear Sirs,

Thank you for your letter regarding your order No. 343 delivered last week.

We are sorry to hear of the breakages which occurred in transit. We always pack our shipments with great care but there are occasions when the merchandise is mishandled along the way.

We have had your inventory of the broken items and shall make up a consignment of replacements which should reach you shortly.

We have lodged a claim with our insurer for the loss. Please hold the broken items for possible insurance inspection.

Please accept our apologies for the inconvenience.

Yours faithfully,

Unit 14　Agency
代　理

练习答案

I. Fill in the blanks in the following sentences.

1. beginning, program
2. mind, efforts, success, little
3. exclusive (sole), sale
4. with, imperative, arm, abreast, be, ears, marketplace
5. with, relationship, terms
6. intensive, achieved, benefit

II. Choose the best answer.

1-5　CCCAD　　6-10　CDBCA　　11-12 CB

III. Translate the following sentences into Chinese.

1. 根据我方在印度贸易量的增加，我方决定在印度指定一名资深且可信赖的经销商作为我方的代理。
2. 我们现有通用电气公司全部产品的出口专有权，该公司是我们地区电气机械的最大制造商。
3. 政府机构之间的交易：由甲、乙双方政府机构之间所达成的交易不受本代理协议条款的约束，上述交易不被认为是由乙方在此协议下所达成的。
4. 乙方有责任每三个月向甲方提交一份有关本协议项下自行车的现行市场行情及客户对商品的质量、包装和价格等评论的书面报告。当地进口条例如有特殊变化，乙方应立即通知甲方。
5. 如果一方违反了本协议中的任何条款，一方有权以书面通知另一方的形式立即终止协议。
6. 佣金：甲方同意按订单的 FOB 价向乙方支付 5%（百分之五）的佣金。佣金须在甲方收到每份订单的全部货款后予以支付。由甲方自己所获得且执行的订单将不支付给乙方佣金。
7. 本协议一经双方签署，即开始生效，有效期为一年，即从 2012 年 1 月 1 日起至 2012 年 12 月 31 日止。如要延展本协议，任何一方都须于协议到期日前一个月内书面通知另一方。
8. 如果一方没有履行本协议条款，另一方有权终止本协议。

9. 甲方不得将合同所规定的商品提供给上述地区的其他买主。如有直接询价应介绍给乙方。然而，如果任何其他买主坚持要与甲方直接达成交易的话，甲方有权与其达成交易。在后者的情况下，甲方应向乙方发送一份相关合同的副本，并按照所达成交易的发票净值为乙方留出 1%的佣金。

10. 本协议一式四份，双方各持两份。

IV. Translate the following sentences into English.

1. We are look forward to promoting our sales in your area with a keen desire.

2. We have entrusted Messrs. Jones Co. with the sales of our products.

3. The company has cooperated with our company for five years as our importer and local distributor.

4. We have been in close business relations for ten years.

5. As our agent in your area, you shall be conversant with our products and our business policy.

6. Our customers are always satisfied with the perfect reliability of the service of our agent.

7. As for the quality of our produt, you shall be fully assured of it.

8. Our distributor is always at hand, ready to furnish you with attentive service.

9. We are looking forward to your approach at the earliest date.

V. Translate the following letters into Chinese.

(1)

敬启者：

　　我方非常希望成为贵方"飞翔"牌摩托车在我国的独家代理。

　　如您所知，我方在摩托车销售及维修方面有着 25 年的经验。我们熟知本地消费者的消费习惯。另外，贵方产品的质量上乘，加上我方完善的售后服务体系，我方完全有信心向您保证 900000 美元的年销售额。

　　我方相信，我们的合作会取得巨大的成功。随函附上贵方产品的详细推广计划、我方的销售渠道和售后服务，以供参考。

　　期盼收到贵方有利的回复。

谨上

(2)

敬启者：

　　我方仔细研究了你方 9 月 10 日的来函，现愿与你方进一步商谈你方要求在苏格兰建立代理的建议。你方为 James Neil 公司工作的情况，我们不了解，但鉴于你方在苏格兰的贸易关系，我们认为你方在该地发展我们的业务是可以大有作为的。

　　我们的最后决定取决于条款是否合适。因你公司 Smith 先生将于下月访问我地，我们愿与 Smith 先生面谈而不愿进行长时间的通讯往来。为此，请告诉我方 Smith 先生将于何时来我公司面谈。

谨上

VI. Translate the following letters into English.

(1)

Dear Sirs,

We understand that you hope to find a reliable company with good market basis to act as your agent for sales of your clothing in Europe.

We have more than 15 years' experience of selling clothing in Germany and obtain a large market portion. We hope greatly to cooperate with you.

If it permits, we would suggest you meet with Mr. Peet to discuss the details of an agreement to both of us.

Yours faithfully,

(2)

Dear Sirs,

We thank you for your letter of February 26, in which you proposed to act as our agent in your territory.

We are deeply interested in your application. Your application is now under our careful consideration.

If you can visit Wuhan at the beginning of March, we shall be pleased to further discuss the possibility of agency agreement in detail.

We are looking forward to your early reply and awaiting Mr. Peet's call.

Yours faithfully,